Southern England

Edited by Annabel Cook

YoungWriters

First published in Great Britain in 2007 by:
Young Writers
Remus House
Coltsfoot Drive
Peterborough
PE2 9JX
Telephone: 01733 890066
Website: www.youngwriters.co.uk

SB ISBN 978-1 84602 861 8

Foreword

This year, the Young Writers' *2007: A Poetry Odyssey* competition proudly presents a showcase of the best poetic talent selected from thousands of up-and-coming writers nationwide.

Young Writers was established in 1991 to promote the reading and writing of poetry within schools and to the young of today. Our books nurture and inspire confidence in the ability of young writers and provide a snapshot of poems written in schools and at home by budding poets of the future.

The thought, effort, imagination and hard work put into each poem impressed us all and the task of selecting poems was a difficult but nevertheless enjoyable experience.

We hope you are as pleased as we are with the final selection and that you and your family continue to be entertained with *2007: A Poetry Odyssey Southern England* for many years to come.

Contents

The Poems

Having Fun

Walking towards a park full of people,
Standing near a stage,
Turning to see a portable barbecue,
With meat straight on the flame,
Hearing people laughing and talking,
On a summer day,
Seeing people in the sun,
Buying different ice creams,
My sister and Ricardo having fun,
Hugging on the scene,
I took a picture on my camera,
My sister having fun.

Jaye Parker (13)
All Saints RC Comprehensive School, Dagenham

Stand To Attention

Thirty thousand faces stand to attention,
The colour of white faces,
All with the same uniform,
Standing still, no movement.

Thirty thousand voices saying,
Yes sir to the flight lieutenant,
Only one person listening,
Thirty thousand voices speaking.

Thirty thousand people marching,
One noise of feet hitting the ground,
One person commanding them,
Squad 'Halt!' one sound of feet stamp.

Thirty thousand people still,
Sergeant shouts out,
'Squad dismissed, all move to right,'
They march five paces, 'Everyone dismissed!'

Ross Francis (13)
All Saints RC Comprehensive School, Dagenham

Time Will Stand Still

Time will stand still,
When houses and planets all switch places,
With no mornings or afternoons
And we all live in parallel universes,
Then we all find out the world is one
Big joke.

Time will stand still,
When the world is one big balloon,
Which explodes like a bomb
And suck in everything,
Like one massive vacuum.

Time will stand still,
When vines dangle from the sky,
Then the world turns into a jungle
And humans and apes switch,
That is when time will stand still.

Maria Longe
All Saints RC Comprehensive School, Dagenham

I Love You

I want you, *I* need you,
I *L*ive you, I breathe you,
You're perfect, y*O*u're special,
I'll ne*V*er forget you,
Or hurt you or l*E*ave you,
I'll never deceive *Y*ou,
I pr*O*mise I'll stay tr*U*e
And most of all *I love you.*

Venessa Parker (16)
All Saints RC Comprehensive School, Dagenham

Time Will Stand Still . . .

Time will stand still,
When the clouds go dark,
The gloomy world comes to an end
And the Devil awakens,
In my endless dream.

Time will stand still,
When the planets awaken
Into our motionless Earth
And the world goes dark,
For evermore.

Time will stand still,
When a baby starts to cry,
In the middle of the night
And her endless tears,
Keep us doomed for hundreds of years.

Chantelle Williams
All Saints RC Comprehensive School, Dagenham

My First Day

My first day - wow this is great,
Feel so grown up as I enter the gate,
My new head's waiting at the door,
Can't wait to start and learn lots more,
My friends are here too,
We will have so much fun,
Just so long as we get our work done,
So thank you All Saints for accepting me,
As part of your educational family tree.

Michaela Robinson
All Saints RC Comprehensive School, Dagenham

A Face In The Sky

I see its beauty live and warm,
Her face is like a beam of light
And as the sun begins to dawn,
The sun gives us a brand new sight.

Her face is like a beam of light,
But wait what's that to her left and right,
The sun gives us a brand new sight,
Are they two horses in mid flight?

But wait what's that to her left and right,
A silhouette high in the sky,
Are they two horses in mid flight?
Does anything else catch your eye?

A silhouette high in the sky,
A giant face never to die,
Does anything else catch your eye?
What is that flying high?

A giant face never to die,
I am amazed at her beauty and grace,
What is that flying high?
They are starting to form a face.

I am amazed at her beauty and grace,
A face that will never be born,
They are starting to form a face,
I see its beauty live and warm.

Billy Michael (14)
All Saints RC Comprehensive School, Dagenham

It's Not The Lips Which Tell Love

It's not the lips, which tell love,
It's the eyes,
What the eyes speak are not words,
They speak poems,
Poems are not found in books,
They're found in women,
Not all women are poems either,
Just you,
Oh dear, does my heart,
Still not understand,
The lap of love?

What is this, my heart,
Is wandering elsewhere,
Is this love?

How will I say my love, so you will understand?
Oh leave me alone! Forgive me, I will love you,
As commanded,
My eyes will flutter,
You must follow their desires,
Is that right? If I ever do wrong, give me,
A kiss as punishment,
Is the punishment right?

When will you do your wrongs?
Tell me now,

I will tell you, but now,
Give me a kiss.

Kresan Panchardcharam (17)
All Saints RC Comprehensive School, Dagenham

Beginning Of The End

Time will stand still,
When the aliens stalk like merciless killers,
As quiet as tiny grey mice
And their eyes crimson blood-red,
With the unmistakable smirk of the angel of light.

Time will stand still,
When the human race, waits for their downfall,
Tears pour down their petrified soulless faces
And they look up at the sky, looking for a saviour or solution.

Time will stand still,
When the monstrous queen bears her snarling jaw,
Her petrifying talons wave like swords
And the blood from her jaw drips like treacle,
For her petrified meal almost ready for the feast.

Ayoola Adedeji (13)
All Saints RC Comprehensive School, Dagenham

My Sister

My sister pulls my hair,
She glares at me like a bear,
She never acts fair.

When I tell my parents she gives an innocent look
And starts reading a book.

She makes puppy eyes
And always lies,
So she can be treated with a delicious pie.

My parents think I'm the bad one,
When she's actually the one on the run.

She's always talking about perfection,
When she takes my possessions
And never does her corrections.

But no matter what she does,
I love her with all my heart.

Rajna Begum (12)
Clapton Girls' Technology College, London

Identity

Identity is a personal fact,
Wherever we go, it is our culture,
Be white or black,
Identity is being who and what you are,
The exact sameness of anyone.

I am African,
But live in England,
Christianity is my religion,
For now I do not know what I want to be,
I have got an identity.

Be not, ignorant of identity,
It is important, it has its own use,
Identity is a very heavy implement in our lives,
It is first in our lives,
Wherever we do it is our culture,
Identity, identity, identity.

Patience Eyare-Assinya Emarienah (12)
Clapton Girls' Technology College, London

Dreams

Dreams are not always what they seem to be,
They can turn out to be real,
Even though it may seem like a far journey up a hill,
Dreams are not always a fantasy,
If you truly believe it could happen,
Dreams are something that is a part of you,
They are like a little seed,
Just waiting to blossom into a beautiful flower,
Whatever your dream is you should embrace it,
Don't keep it locked away,
Shout it out if you must,
Don't feel embarrassed,
Just remember that dreams are like your inner passion
And that they show who you truly are!

Latrece Dunn (13)
Clapton Girls' Technology College, London

Identity!

What is identity?
It's my personality,
It's who I am.

My family is supportive,
My culture is very good,
I love to sing
And that's my thing.

I come from China,
But I live in London,
My location is Hackney.

I go to Clapton Girls' Techno College,
Which is my school
And it's very cool.

My friends think that I'm crazy,
But I think I'm lazy,
My favourite flower is a daisy.

I want to do well in life
And maybe be a good wife,
I'll never use a knife.

Jade Luong (13)
Clapton Girls' Technology College, London

What Matters?

Those idiots thought it was hilarious,
Shipping human beings from where they belong,
Selling them to others; like they are gods,
'They are not human beings,' they will say,
Not knowing it doesn't matter where you're from,
But what matters is who you are.

Sadness that cannot be cured has been formed,
By the loss of background and cultures,
Families, friends and neighbours,
'They haven't got feelings,' they will say,
Feelings? They have. It has now become sadness,
But do you have feelings?

Those idiots thought it was hilarious,
In pairs, groups, gangs they will be,
Saying mocking words just to build up sadness,
'You are different from us,' they will say,
Not knowing it doesn't matter whatever the differences,
But what matters is who you are.

'It is not hilarious, you fool,'
God has created us to be different,
Different colours, culture, background,
Difference. You should think about the word 'Different'.
Difference made this world a special place,
Do you now understand what matters the most? Now?

Folasade Amusa (15)
Clapton Girls' Technology College, London

The Inquisitive Poem

Why do the people we hate never seem to go away?
Why is it we realise the irrational things we do when it's too late?
Do our lives change because of random choices or is it set in a path?
You say a joke . . . do I have to laugh?
Why does everyone have to be labelled or be set in a group?
How can you tell a secret to the open-mouthed?
How can you trust the trustworthy?
How can you swim in someone else's glory?
How can you accept a long-lived lie?
How long does it take to realise that they do die?
How can you rely on statistics or think it's right?
Friends or enemies which is truly worse?
So many people surrounding us, but why do we still feel alone?
How can you commit to the already married?
Why do you desperately want to minimise the varied?
Why is the world seen as being small when everything costs so big?
What is good or bad? Is it all based on our morals?
Are your morals correct or just too formal?
Why do our dreams have to be so strange?
Why are the people we are close with change?
Nature or electricity, which is more important?
How can you tell if they are really confident or just brave?
How can one human being just murder another human being?
Is it because it's the suffering of those you're not seeing?
What is the real beliefs of a reverend?
How did you become so sly and malevolent?
How can anyone be sure when they are in love?
How do you know if the truth is a fact?
And . . . why are you all staring at me like that?

Chioma Abiaka (15)
Clapton Girls' Technology College, London

Imaginary Friend

My friend said
Flowers need sunshine,
Violets need dew,
All angels in Heaven,
Know I need you,
Years may fly,
Tears may dry,
But my friendship
With you,
Will never die,
She said,
A ring is round
And has no end,
That's how long,
I'll be your friend,
I was,
Motionless,
She was the
One there for me,
Always . . .
Her words,
'My friendship
With you
Will never die,'
But why is she
A pitch-black
Shadow?

Farhana Kazi (12)
Clapton Girls' Technology College, London

School

School is life,
School is education,
School is where you come every day,
School is your mind,
School is Monday, Tuesday, Wednesday, Thursday, Friday,
School is not Saturday and Sunday,
School is fun sometimes,
School is hard work,
School is learning,
School is books,
School is SATs,
School is GCSEs,
School is five years. Year 7, 8, 9, 10 and 11,
Sometimes when there's no school, I feel like going to school,
But when there is school, I want to go home,
School is the answer to everything,
School is school.

Zahira Yunus (13)
Clapton Girls' Technology College, London

My Imaginary World

My imaginary world is a place of peace,
My imaginary world is not a place of violence,
My imaginary world is like the ocean,
My imaginary world is a place of laughter and fun,
My imaginary world is a place that nobody has even imagined,
My imaginary world is like the sky so blue,
My imaginary world is a place of nature,
My imaginary world is like a tropical island
With rivers and plants,
My imaginary world is like the stars in the night,
My imaginary world is everything I've ever wanted,
My imaginary world is a place of my own.

Mika Codner (12)
Clapton Girls' Technology College, London

Memories And Relationships In Life

Looking through the mirror of time,
I see the once blossoming relationship,
Fully developed in the midst of summer,
The reflection of my smiles from within,
Are actually the smiles of loved ones,
Which makes life so fulfilling.

Friends and family are what makes life so precious,
Every moment you spend with them are those to be cherished,
What is that undeniable desire?
Money, fame or the unconditional love burning bright like fire.

Those that were once dreams are now reality,
Who knows what fate has in store for tomorrow,
As the future comes with no guarantee,
Morals and values are what makes you who you are,
That is why life should be embraced,
Because it only goes so far.

Mumina Begum (15)
Clapton Girls' Technology College, London

The Emptiness Inside Me

I lie on my bed and look at the ceiling,
I stare at the bold ceiling - mesmerised but look away,
As if there was nothing worth searching for.

I go to the kitchen and look in the fridge,
I stare into the overflowing fridge but suddenly hunger leaves me,
As if there was nothing worth eating.

I switch on the TV as I do every day,
I stare at the forever absorbing screen but lose interest,
As if there was nothing worth watching.

I enter my room and look in the mirror,
I stare at the forever truthful mirror and see nothing for a moment,
But then I look deeper, I look into my eyes
And that's when I realise why I see nothing,
What I see is emptiness.

Emptiness inside me has blinded what I see on the outside,
Emptiness inside me has blinded me for so long,
That it is only at this moment that I realise my loss.

There is no longer any gain, there is no longer any purpose,
Live for today and die tomorrow.

No. All wrong. This is what I think not feel,
Emptiness is inside me but not in my heart,
Your heart is what tells you the truth,
Your heart is what guides you.

My heart has guided me to love and appreciate,
My heart has guided me to see something worthwhile in everything
And do you know how I know?
My heart has told me so and so I believe it,
If I didn't I would feel emptiness.

But what I feel is my heart - full
Down to the very last part.

Catherine O Enilolobo (15)
Clapton Girls' Technology College, London

Dreams

What are dreams?
Ideas that consist of different themes?

It's the colours of our imagination,
That brings about a creation
And puts forward these ideas,
That could change into careers.

But how do we know how far
It is to reach this star,
That turns it into reality
And makes something of you in society?

It is only up to us,
Together with the trust,
Of what is inside,
The heart and mind.

No one can stop you from making decisions,
Whatever the superstitions,
They may have of your dream
And not be so keen
Because just remember,
There's no point to surrender,
As you might not be so far,
From stretching out and reaching your star!

Sobia Khan (15)
Clapton Girls' Technology College, London

Who Needs Dreams When We All Have Love?

Like people come and people go,
Like yesterday and the day before,
I'll throw my dreams all behind me
And you'll do it to just wait and see.
I know it is not a dream,
But it does not feel like reality,
It's like something falling from above,
Who needs dreams when we all have love?
Yet love is not always our dream come true,
I am sure you will find love can be quite cruel,
I am sure if love was a drink, we would all be sober,
Because most people in the world are love loners,
Because everyone goes for beauty and no respect,
I don't think the world is ready for true love not yet,
Love is the joker of the whole pack of life,
You may think you've found the one but love
happens more than twice,
Although most of the time love is a big fight,
Sometimes it will be a friend and give you love at first sight!
Love may take a period of time and you may try to make it perfect,
But I am sure at the end, it will all be worth it,
Love is a gift from God, use it
And don't abuse it!

Vicky-Rose Simon (13)
Clapton Girls' Technology College, London

My Dreams

My dream is to live in the big blue sky,
Up, up, up high,
It shines so well,
I love the colour baby-blue,
It makes me feel so cool,
To live in the beautiful sky,
I would die,
Just to live in the sky.

It's just like life and not like school,
But still it is so cool,
It feels so peaceful in the big blue,
Peace is what I'm here for!
Sometimes it makes me think of my grandma.

But not my grandpa,
But I still know that I have respect,
My dream is to live in the big blue sky,
Until I die,
Goodbye!
My dream is in the big blue sky with a kitten and not a tiger.

Tam Tran Thuthi (13)
Clapton Girls' Technology College, London

Just Ignore It

It's hard to say what's truly on my mind,
For I'm scared of what might come out,
I feel as though my teeth are glued shut,
So in truth, I'm just scared of what I'm thinking.

I've never felt this surge of energy before,
So it's hard to describe what it is,
Although feeling confused is not unusual to me,
So I guess I'll just ignore it.

Most of the time my mind notes down,
What happens throughout the day,
But as my dreams come to focus,
The day's events get switched around and
Played off against one another.

I'm tired of watching nothing become something,
So much that it pulls me further down,
All I want is to say what's on my mind,
But as usual I'll just ignore it.

Stephanie McKenna (15)
Clapton Girls' Technology College, London

She's The One

She's a little annoying cat,
She's as cute as a kitten,
She's as small as a mouse,
She's as smart as a teacher,
She's as helpful as a sister,
She shines like the stars in the night sky,
She makes me laugh and smile,
Her voice is sweet as an apple pie,
She cheers me up,
Out of all of us, she's the best,
She's the sun that shines all day,
She's loving and caring,
She's the sweet stuff that gets on your tongue,
That you can't remove,
She's the one who cares,
She's a little angel, guarding you at night,
She's like a fairy, granting your every wish,
She's always there for you,
She's a wonderful person to have in your family,
She's everyone's favourite,
She treats everyone the same,
She does not dislike anyone,
She loves everyone as her own,
She's the girl who waits for you,
She loves you to bits,
She'll love you till death,
She's the one who excepts you as part of her family,
She is the special one,
She's the one who listens to you,
She's a three-year-old kid,
She's my little baby sister Nadia Begum.

Rabia Begum (13)
Clapton Girls' Technology College, London

Who Is She?

This is a tale of a wonderful girl,
She is kind, loving and she always shares,
She always helps her mum but not at night,
When she's busy staring at the stars,
She loves ice cream and chocolate,
But hates Mars bars,
She goes to school,
Comes back with flu,
She blames the school,
For giving her the flu,
She wants to sue
She hates her dad, she thinks he's mad,
Because he's always sad,
She's kind but can't find her teddy, mind,
She likes to sing,
She always brings her teddy with her,
She loves sweets and also meat,
But she does not want to be covered with her sheet,
She has four sisters that she hates,
She prefers her mates,
Her sisters are fat and ugly, she says,
She thinks they're all so dumb,
She says they have very big bums,
She hates them,
She hates them,
But now she knows who she is,
She's a sister, friend, daughter and an auntie,
Also she is a loving caring girl,
That loves chocolate,
And loves looking at the stars, that's what she is.

Rushna Begum (13)
Clapton Girls' Technology College, London

Identity

She is annoying,
She is an immature brat,
She is a little fat,
She lives in the house next door,
She is a hairy ball,
She is so soft and fluffy,
She is a fearless beast,
She is a devil,
She is a repeated bug,
She is a teddy to cuddle,
She is a hungry lion,
She feeds on mice,
She's a phone bill package,
She's worth a lot,
She can be loving,
She can be caring,
She's a pretty face when you don't see her,
But a lion roaring when you can,
She is like a human being,
She has big brown eyes,
She has long brown whiskers,
Her name is Percy,
Do you know who she is?
If not, here is more of a description,
She has 4 legs,
She has a tail too,
Her fur is gingerish-brown,
She is breathing,
She is living,
She is my next-door neighbour's cat *Percy!*

Pooja Rani Kaur (13)
Clapton Girls' Technology College, London

Temi

As I walk into a class of girls,
Everyone looks the same,
As I look around the class,
My eye catches this one girl,
She looks so beautiful and yet so insane,
With all her features and design,
It's surprising, someone having this style,
With dark black extensions,
With highlights of red,
Light brown skin,
With all this colour,
Black eyeliner,
On top of green,
Brown eyes,
With red lips,
Wearing dark red lip-liner
And pale red lipstick,
All this and black painted nails,
Even wearing her uniform,
She has this own look,
Stripy black and white socks,
Not just plain black,
A skirt with black embroidered flowers,
Black shoes with patches of different material,
From a family of two different worlds,
Mum from America and Dad from Africa,
Coming from these worlds,
Doesn't stop her from looking like this,
By being insane,
She's intelligent too . . .

Suraiya Begum (13)
Clapton Girls' Technology College, London

Identity!

He is a loud monster,
He is an irritating little dog,
He is a repeating parrot,
He is a fat hippopotamus,
He is a fierce bull,
He is an ugly one,
He is a hungry tiger,
He is a jumping kangaroo,
He is a threatening rhino,
He is a miaowing cat,
He is a barking dog,
He is a beating stick,
He is an abusing pervert,
He is a lovely little badger,
He is a taming cat,
He is an eating crocodile,
He is a crying baby,
He is a roaring lion,
He is a whooshing sea,
He is a fast cheetah,
He is a tall giraffe,
He is a red devil,
'I don't know why she thinks of me like this,' I think
She is a pretty princess,
She is a quiet mouse,
She is a beautiful, gorgeous angel,
She is a skinny giraffe,
She is a friendly kitten,
She is a slow tortoise,
She is a funny clown,
She is a happy rabbit.

Maryum Ahmed (14)
Clapton Girls' Technology College, London

Her Identity

She is soft as a rabbit,
But big as a giant,
She has a beautiful heart,
But is ugly as a monster,
She has lovely eyes,
But is in the dark,
She had silky blonde hair,
But her violet stepmother cut it off,
She was like her mother,
But her mother died and made her life miserable,
She had a handsome father,
But inside he's not,
She had a beautiful half-sister,
Who never liked her at all,
She had a nice brother,
But her father killed him long ago,
She was lucky to escape,
But now she wishes she died as well,
She had a beautiful big room,
But now she had a small dark attic,
She had toys and games,
But her sister broke them and threw them away,
She had a few friends before,
But now they all hate her,
She loved school so much,
But now she cries to go,
Inside she is so beautiful,
But no one can see that,
She was so happy before,
But she's probably dead now,
And nobody cares.

Sophia Bodi (13)
Clapton Girls' Technology College, London

Who Is She?

Is she loud as a tiger,
    Or quiet as a mouse?
Does she have long dark hair,
    Or short blonde hair?
Does she have dark brown eyes,
    Or bright hazel eyes?
Is she as tall as a tree,
    Or short as a dwarf?
Is she as smart as Einstein,
    Or forgetful as a clown?
Can she speak fluent English,
    Or maybe fluent French?
Is she the Queen of England,
Or the Emperess of China?
Is she Asian or British,
    Or African or Irish?
Is she rich as the Sultan of Brunei,
    Or poor as a beggar?
Is she as old as a granny,
    Or as young as a child?
Can she ride a motorbike,
    Or maybe a car?
Is she as pretty as a daffodil,
    Or as ugly as a witch?
Is she as nice as a dolphin,
    Or as bad as a criminal?
Does she sing like a lark,
    Or is she really out of tune?
Can she dance like Michael Jackson,
    Or dance like a dad?
Who is she?

Dung Pham (13)
Clapton Girls' Technology College, London

Identity

Identity,
What is identity?
Religion, culture, family,
Somebody mentioned personality!
True, yet how can it be?
For in this world, people show and act differently,
Different from what is inside,
Yet I say have pride for you are what you are,
Identity is also your appearance,
But remember not for what others think,
Because God made you very unique,
Wear your clothes, shoes and accessories,
But say to yourself, *I like it not because of them but me!*
Identity could be DNA, the blood flowing through your veins,
The way your heart beats while somebody feels pain,
Parents say it's religion and culture!
It doesn't mean anything if it goes through one ear and out the other,
Respect! Respect each other, thank those whose prayer showers over,
Remember you are what you are, you are unique like no other,
When you forget that you're beautiful,
That is the end of my journey in
Identity!

Jannath Munira (12)
Clapton Girls' Technology College, London

My Poem

I am a nice loving girl like a little pony,
I have long hair like a giraffe only it is black,
I have dark brown eyes like melted chocolate,
I am sweet as candy but yet they take advantage of me,
I have a soft heart, soft as silk,
I have bushy eyebrows like a forest,
My skin is soft and gentle like the sea,
I have a nice sweet voice sweet like a bird singing,
I am quite funny, funny like a comedian,
I love to laugh loud like a hyena,
My life is open, my life is great,
My life is open like the wind,
I am a nice Jamaican girl with a Jamaican accent,
Who love going to the beach to feel the lovely warm water,
The sea beats down on my back like a stick beating a drum.

I'm standing here in the golden and warm gentle sand,
Running around on the sand and the sun beating
Down on my back.

I love my family, I wouldn't trade them for the world,
I love my mum and dad,
Without them I wouldn't be here experiencing the world,
Everybody likes being around me because
When I am around, they have fun.

Bianca Whittingham (13)
Clapton Girls' Technology College, London

What Is Identity?

They say to talk about identity,
But I don't know what to do,
What's so great about me?
I'm just an ordinary girl
Wearing a size 5 shoe,
I was born and raised in Britain,
But my culture is Dominican and
Jamaican, basically the Caribbean,
I live in east London, Hackney,
But some people call it Crackney,
People say it's a place for drugs and crime,
But I haven't got the time,
To just sit around and judge places,
Let alone people, religion or races,
I have *big* dreams you see,
I want to move out of Hackney,
Maybe even out of this country,
Buy a big house for each member of my family,
My family's always there to protect and defend me,
I'm a kind of girl whose family orientated,
I'm not the kind of girl that hates or is hated,
Yes, I enjoy being the centre of attention,
Oh! did I forget to mention,
My mother didn't raise no fool,
Every week day I go to school,
So I can fulfil my dreams to become an actress,
I know I can, I will, *I must!*
They say to talk about identity,
I now know what to do,
Write about yourself and what makes *you!*

Bria Dashan Francis (12)
Clapton Girls' Technology College, London

Emotions

Look around you, what do you see?
Loads of people looking shy, glad and unhappy,
When you look around, you don't know what to do,
But it's a question,
When they turn around and look at you.

When you're feeling down,
When you're feeling low,
When you feel you just want to get up and go,
Then someone comes up to you and asks if you're OK?
Then you simply reply, 'Today is not my day!'

Hold on a second, I just realised,
It takes a lot less muscles to smile,
When you take a stroll, the sky turns blue,
Everyone looks at your smile
And feels happy too!

So remember each and every word I said,
When you're trying something new!
Be it a feeling, an emotion or something else,
It's still a part of you!

Laura Rochelle Sutton (12)
Clapton Girls' Technology College, London

Forever Friends

Of all the friends I've ever met,
You're the one I won't forget
And if I die before you do,
I'll go to Heaven and wait for you,
I'll grant your wishes,
I'll play your games,
But please don't leave me,
It will cause me such great pain.

Blerta Hasbahta (13)
Clapton Girls' Technology College, London

My Friends

I've got a friend called Lauren, her surname is Jackson,
She is very pleasant and very fearsome,
I like the way she talks and makes me laugh,
She's a real good friend, she takes you to the right path,
She's talented, she's clever, she's also very intelligent,
She's pretty, she's cool and her clothes are very elegant,
She's number one in all her subjects,
If you ask her for help, she'll never give you a reject.

I've got a friend called Zahira, her surname is Yunus,
She's extremely small and never causes a fuss,
I like the way she walks in her heels and when she talks sweetly,
I also like the way she does her work very neatly,
She's polite, she's smart and she's exceedingly gifted,
She helps you around and her words are never twisted,
She leads you to the right trail and is my number one buddy,
She looks a bit like me, people get ever so muddily.

I've got a friend called Vicky Rose, her surname is Simon,
She offers me lots of sweets and treats,
I like the way she baby talks, it sounds very cute,
She is very healthy because she eats lots of fruits,
She's nice, she's kind, she's smart and she's artistic,
She'll help you sort out all your problems,
She is a good friend, trust me I know,
She'll never let you feel low.

My name is Sumaiyyah Kaji and this is what I think about friends,
Friends are wonderful and are always there for you,
They'll help you in your life and to get through,
I have friends, so should you, friends are loving, caring, friendly,
Wonderful and amusing.

Sumaiyyah Kaji (13)
Clapton Girls' Technology College, London

My Dream

One day I had a dream,
The dream was so sweet,
I had flown to the oceans of the sky,
I was catching the fishes of the sky.

I had rested on the moon,
I flew down to the clouds,
The clouds were so soft,
I saw the birds singing.

I was free,
No one to stop me,
I saw an orange coloured man up in the sky,
He smiled at me and said you are free.

I flew and flew up in the sky,
I grew too tired,
I went up to the moon,
A person was waiting for me,
She made me sleep,
She was an angel I thought.

I woke up to find myself,
Inside a room,
My room,
I was not free I thought.

I told myself it was a dream,
But my heart didn't believe.

Loga Loganathan (12)
Clapton Girls' Technology College, London

Friendship

I once had a friend,
Who always helped me with my work,
I liked caring for a friend,
Because they will like me more,
I love to be kind, considerate and caring towards others,
A friend is someone who you always have when you are alone,
Friends are always there for you whenever you want
them to be there,
Friends are always nice to you,
Friends always take your side,
They care for you,
They know everything about you,
They are the only ones who help you in school,
A friend is someone who understands you
And you who understands them,
Friends know what you want, always want
Friends know if you have a problem,
Friends are always nice to you,
Even if you don't talk to them,
You tell your secrets to a friend
And a friend tells you
Because they trust you,
They know you very well,
That's why I love friends.

Tasbiha Mustac-Amod (12)
Clapton Girls' Technology College, London

My Mysterious Pet

There it was swimming around,
But then I thought to myself *what if it drowns?*
My worries settled down in my head
And all I was thinking - was is it dead?

I cried until my eyes looked tired,
Then my mother said 'Why do you cry?'
Life has to end one day, she turned around,
To take a look and found out it was alive after all.

Immediately I jumped up to the sky
And didn't get sleep at all that night,
I got out of bed and walked on the creaky floor,
Then when I got to the living room, I opened up the door,
My dreams awaited to see it dipping in the shimmering water.

But then . . .
I screamed
I had totally lost my self-esteem.

My mother came running to me from her bed,
Then she saw my pet fish dead!
I had remembered my mother's words,
Why do you cry, life has to end one day?
There it lay flat floating at the top, my pet fish!

Lakhwinder Kaur (12)
Clapton Girls' Technology College, London

Changes

Who am I?
Where am I?
Is it true . . . that I am different?
'You have lost a lot of weight,'
That's what my friends say,
Telling me that I will change,
Taller, more confident and smarter,
They don't even like me,
So why do I call them my friends?
Pushing me around,
Talking about me behind my back,
It's as if they think of me as their slave.

But, being here, somewhere else,
At home in my bed, alone,
I feel *great*, as if I am on cloud nine,
Life is perfect; nothing can stop me from being unhappy,
Except when I am there, *wow!*

Soon, I wake up,
I get out of bed,
My room is looking gloomy,
More than it did before,
I opened the door,
Walking down the corridor,
Looking for my parents,
My brother and sister,
Hoping that they will find me,
I walked down the stairs,
I found them - hooray!
But now I see them crying,
And I see myself lying on the floor, *dead!*

Jasmine Rahman-Choudhury (12)
Clapton Girls' Technology College, London

I Once Had A Dream

I once had a dream,
That I was far away where nobody lives,
I was alone and by myself,
With no one else but myself,
I remember I had this dream more than once,
I did not like it,
But I was there for months,
The food was not nice, there was only rice,
I tried to get out,
But there was no way out,
Until I found a place where I then saw a face,
Finally I was not alone,
Not by myself,
But with someone else,
I asked for help,
But they did not understand,
I then asked again,
But still no answer,
This face must have thought I was gone in the head,
But I wasn't,
I knew I had been in this dream many times before,
So I would have thought,
I should have known my way around by now,
But didn't,
So again,
I was alone with no one else but myself!

Carla Emily Wallace (12)
Clapton Girls' Technology College, London

My Shining Star

Some people look up to celebrities,
Some people look up to their parents,
But I look up to . . . my shining star.

My shining star is tall and chubby,
My shining star is very, very cuddly,
My shining star is always there, no matter what,
He might be crazy but deep down inside,
I know he loves me.

My shining star helps me get out of trouble,
My shining star is there on the double,
My shining star can cook, clean and DJ,
My shining star is so talented he should be on TV,
But he's just as good the way he is.

My shining star goes to work
But always makes time for me,
My shining star never lets me get away with anything,
I have to pay a fee.

I love my shining star no matter what . . .

My shining star is my brother.

Rochelle Rosa Reid (13)
Clapton Girls' Technology College, London

My Dream

Life is hard,
Full of ups and downs,
My dream is being a lawyer,
But will it come true?
Only God knows,
I have to face my studies,
If I want to go somewhere,
Teachers try their best but
I have to try mine,
I can't sit down and watch life pass me by,
I have to stand up and don't let life pass me by,
I have learnt life is what you make it,
So I have decided to make my life softer,
I want to be a lawyer,
It might be hard but
Nothing is easy,
I have learnt if I want to go somewhere,
I have to buckle my shoes and
Start trying my best if I want to go somewhere,
High school, college, university degree,
Everyone has a dream but this is mine.

Victoria Oyebanjo (13)
Clapton Girls' Technology College, London

Who Am I?

Who am I?
I am a daughter,
I am a friend,
I am a sister,
I am a niece,
I am a student,
I am a dreamer,
But what do I dream of?
I dream of stars,
I dream of light,
I dream of things that shine so bright,
I dream of music, I dream of plays,
I dream to be a star one day,
But when will that day be?
It could be tomorrow,
It could be next week,
It could be next month,
Or even next year,
But what I do know is that one day,
My dream will come true,
But till then, I will be who I am.

Juwon Amisu (13)
Clapton Girls' Technology College, London

Qualities

People say I'm weird,
They say I'm like a clown from a funfair,
Is it so bad to have my hand stretch out all the way,
Back to my leg and reach my hands to my toes?
I have weird joints,
So what?
Well it matters to everyone else,
I can drink 8 glasses of water all in one go,
Is that weird?
Well it's a yes to everyone else,
I can move my hand all the way around,
Is that freaky?
Well it's a yes to everyone else,
I have no friends,
Because of my freaky bends,
Do you know what I think?
They are jealous,
I have so many qualities,
But, sometimes I just wish there was some equality,
I just never reach people's satisfaction,
I'm just too weird for them,
When I do my weird joints you should see their reactions,
With such qualities like this,
I will make sure I'm in the Guinness World Records,
I'm just too unique,
So that if I'm a freak,
By the way, I'm on TV in a week!

Shamima Khanom (13)
Clapton Girls' Technology College, London

Look Around You

When you look around you,
What do you see?
You don't really glance the sight of harmony,
But we have to put up,
Put up this fight,
Even though it's quite a plight.

This fight ain't easy,
It's hard, it's rough,
But we've got to stand up,
Act kinda tough.

The world around us,
So big and round,
So many people,
All sights and sounds.

People so different,
People so alike,
So many animals,
Many of them bite.

I'd like to end this
In a nice way,
So think how you act
Before you say.

Lauren Jackson (13)
Clapton Girls' Technology College, London

Imagine! Imagine!

Imagine if there was a magical world,
With all the things you have wished for,
Suddenly you get this feeling that you are in Heaven,
You are the queen of this magical world,
You are the richest woman in the world,
You are the queen of this magical world but,
The most atrocious devil that a human being has ever imagined,
Suddenly all her slaves make a wish
And it comes true,
Their wish was to make the queen
Of the magical world a pauper,
The queen went from a beauty queen,
To a pauper,
The pauper who wanted that wish to not come true,
Became a witch,
She cast a spell,
But that wish,
Was never to be broken again,
Never in the world,
So the disastrous pauper,
Was never to be a beauty queen again.

Beebee Boodoo (13)
Clapton Girls' Technology College, London

Best Friend

A best friend is someone,
Who's there for you,
A best friend is someone,
Who'll follow you,
If you feel left out or
Get into a fight,
A best friend is someone,
Who won't leave your sight,
A best friend is special,
Who'll stay with you,
A best friend is someone,
Who'll hang out with you,
If you want to share a secret,
Tell your best friend,
The relationship between friends,
Will never end,
A best friend is someone,
Who'll stick up for you,
A best friend is someone
Who's always true,
Remember that friends are forever,
So turn to your friend
And have fun together.

Mahfuza Rahman (13)
Clapton Girls' Technology College, London

My Move

My mother tells me,
I tell my friends,
We shed a few tears
And dread the days to come,
Life around me becomes ever so glum,
Friends support me,
Try to give me comfort,
The day's drawing near,
So much to fear,
Taken everything for granted,
This is not what I wanted,
The sadness has taken a high,
Too late to put up a fight,
Day has come,
Gladly walks out Mum,
Look behind,
Unlucky for some,
Sad tears,
Mum said, 'No fears,'
New life,
New beginning,
But not enough,
For the life I wanted
Was with old chums.

Hazera Begum (14)
Clapton Girls' Technology College, London

Destiny

Everyone wants their dreams to come true
And so do I,
Everyone has set themselves a target
And so have I,
When I am older, I want to do something major,
But will it be true?

I want to be a lawyer,
But I need to work day and night,
I want to be a model,
Because I want to prove to the world,
That I can be beautiful,
I want to be a fashion designer,
Because I know that I have the ability to.

In my dreams I want to do all,
But I know that I'll only have one or two chances,
I also dream about how I'll look,
Will I be slim? Will I be beautiful
Or will I be short or tall?

I also dream of whom will I marry?
Will he be tall, dark, and handsome?
Will he be short, ugly, smelly?
Will he be rich or poor?
Would I be with my family?

I need to wait!
Sometimes your dreams do come true, or not,
Marriage, career is all long away
And for now I'll look, I need to wait,
It's all not as long as you think,
Because, no sooner or later, you'll know or you won't,
That it all depends on destiny.

Ayesha Nayyer (13)
Clapton Girls' Technology College, London

Homelessness

At 19 I'm homeless, penniless too,
My life turned out so depressing it's true,
Life on the streets is hard and a struggle,
How did my life become such a muddle?
As a kid I dreamt of becoming something special,
A teacher, a doctor, maybe a general,
But then at 12, I found drugs, or they found me
And now my life is empty, meaningless and full of misery,
So a homeless person I've become,
I'd never have believed I'd be so dumb,
An addict, that's me,
No friends or family cause no one trusts me,
I steal, I lie, no one's friend, that's me,
Just another homeless person you see.

Darcy Collingwood (13)
Emerson Park School, Hornchurch

Homelessness Poem

She left home in her early teens,
In a torn shirt and her faded jeans,
Looking for the love she was never given,
Away from her family, she was driven.

She sits by the café every day,
Her lovely young face looking cold and grey,
Her sad blue eyes slowly searching around,
Looking for coins dropped on the ground.

With pleading eyes she holds out a hand,
In pouring rain for hours she will stand.

Marie Hillyard (14)
Emerson Park School, Hornchurch

Homelessness

Homelessness is bad,
It makes people sad,
They have to wear dirty rags
And all they have is bags,
Then can be urinated on
And all their friends can be gone,
Homeless people can't work,
They look at homeless people in evil ways
And they stay on the street for many days,
What can we do to stop homelessness?
It is an important discussion,
You could go to homeless people in need
And do a good deed,
People think they spent it on drugs
And people think they are liars,
They don't even have grains of food,
Is this really true?
Well you could judge people by the way they look,
But they don't have anywhere to cook,
They have to scavenge through bins,
Some people may be liars,
But the truth is some of them aren't.

Ahmad Lodhi (13)
Emerson Park School, Hornchurch

Homeless Poem

They sleep in your doorway,
All shapes and sizes
And try to stay put,
For as long as they can.

The police move them on,
Every hour or two,
Leaving them tired
And not knowing what to do.

The morning eventually comes,
In its own dismal way,
Meaning they have to beg,
For food to last the day.

Maybe they won't spend the money on drugs,
Passers-by will say,
Maybe the newspapers are wrong,
But I can't take that chance.

This leaves the homeless,
Tired and hungry,
For yet another day,
Things will never change.

Charles Lammin (13)
Emerson Park School, Hornchurch

Family Of Thieves

The mother is the oldest,
She hides all the loot,
I think that is hardest,
With the police round in a shoot.

The father goes out at night,
To see what he can find,
He goes to most houses,
The big sort of kind.

Then it's the daughter,
She goes with her dad,
She goes in the houses,
Guess what's really bad?

The son is the driver,
He drives them both away,
He drives them down the road,
To the parking bay.

This is the family of thieves
And it will always be,
So remember, be careful,
Where you put your house key!

Hannah Jacobs (12)
Emerson Park School, Hornchurch

A Poem About Homelessness

Why do people think all the homeless,
Are always such a mess?
Just cos they have nowhere to live,
Doesn't mean you can be a div
And mug the poor guy,
Who also might die.

Sometimes you may be drunk,
It's understandable,
But don't be a punk,
Leave the poor fellow alone,
After all,
What did he do to you?

Come on!
Just cos he has a watch,
Doesn't mean you have to nick it,
Leave it,
Leave him,
Leave here.

Andrew Murphy (13)
Emerson Park School, Hornchurch

On The Streets

On the streets,
Damp,
Cold,
Wet.

Tapping for money,
Luck,
Chance,
Nothing.

Hungry for food,
Empty
Bins
Scraps.

Down an alleyway tonight,
Dark,
Unsafe,
Scared.

Now you know what it's like to live like me.

Kelly Jarrold (14)
Emerson Park School, Hornchurch

A Poem About Homelessness

Living on the streets is a chore,
You think you have it bad? Listen more,
Psychos will kill you for your pack,
While drunks will pee on your back.

Think that's bad, that's just the beginning,
Wait until I tell you about the grinning,
The grinning of people when they beat you up,
Just because you have some pounds in your tapping cup.

What about sitting outside in the freezing cold,
In a cardboard box beside the road?
You used to have a job, a home, a family,
Before you were faced with the reality.

Getting up from the concrete ground,
You massage your bruises and ask around,
For coppers and money you haven't got,
The people you ask from would prefer you to rot.

Have I convinced you, yes or no
To not go onto the streets and leave your home?
Remember this; we all have a choice,
So if something bad has happened, use your voice.

Aimee Went (13)
Emerson Park School, Hornchurch

The House Of Terror

The door quickly swung open,
But there was no one there,
There was blood dripping from the ceiling,
I stopped and began to stare.

As I walked on the creaky floorboards,
I could hear a lady scream,
This house was not any normal house,
Things weren't quite as they seem.

If you have ever watched a scary film,
That has scared you off your seat,
That is nothing compared,
To what I was about to meet.

As I stepped into the back garden,
I could see a swing,
A ghostly figure was sitting on it,
She then began to sing.

'You have now disturbed,
The spirit of Jacqueline Mose,
I died in this house,
But how . . . nobody knows!'

What happened after that?
I can't remember,
But all I know is that, that girl,
That ghostly little girl haunts me every December.

Sam Hill (12)
Jo Richardson Community School, Dagenham

My Pets

Our cat is black and white,
Its name is Scooby,
Its hair is soft,
Its claws are sharp,
His tail is long,
It gives him balance,
For climbing trees,
Then back home,
To sleep all day
And sleep all night,
We play with Scooby,
He loves the string.

Outside we have some fish,
They are small but very fast,
For them we built a pond,
One foot up
And three feet down,
The pump and filter,
Keeps things clean,
So we can see
Our favourite fish,
A net protects them,
From their enemies,
From birds and other cats
And other dangerous things,
I love to feed,
Them every morning,
To swim all day
And swim all night,
I love my pets.

James Fairs (12)
Jo Richardson Community School, Dagenham

My Cat

I held him,
I kissed him,
I loved him,
He was fun,
He was strange,
But now he is gone,
I miss him so much.

I love him,
I wish he were still here,
Only if he was,
We would still be happy,
I now have stopped grieving,
Because I know he is still here,
He is up in Heaven looking down,
Looking after me,
Quietly, silently,
He sits on my windowsill,
Sleeping in his box,
Even though he is ashes,
He still has me locked in his heart,
My cat.

Ross Hardy-Bachan (12)
Jo Richardson Community School, Dagenham

Love

If I had one wish,
I would wake up to the feel of your breath on my cheeks,
Your heart beating in time with mine,
You are the one I will always love,
You are the apple to my tree,
The bubbles in my bath,
Most of all you are
The love of my life.

Victoria Heed (12)
Jo Richardson Community School, Dagenham

Haunted Mansion

No spiders crawling,
In or out,
No creaking floorboards,
Because no one's about,
In the haunted mansion.

But no more ghosts
And no more blood,
No more witches
And no more mud,
In the haunted mansion.

Dishes clean,
Cushions puffed,
Dormitories tidy,
Animals stuffed,
In the haunted mansion.

It's not scary,
Why is it not?
Food and drink,
Supplies the lot,
In the haunted house.

What's happened?
Where has it gone?
I'll tell you,
It's a big con!
Because when you go home tonight,
You'll find the haunted mansion,
Sleep tight and don't forget,
The gory ghosts you haven't yet met!
Where is the haunted mansion?

Yasemin Guven (12)
Jo Richardson Community School, Dagenham

I Am The Girl . . .

I am the girl you pushed around,
I am the girl who you made cry,
I am the girl who had no friends,
I am the girl who ate alone,
I am the girl who got good marks,
I am the girl who is top of the class,
I am the girl who did not speak a word,
I am the girl who you said was fat.

You are the girl who had all the friends,
You are the girl who made me cry,
You are the girl who pushed me around,
You are the girl who scared me,
You are the girl who made my life hell.

I am the girl who stood up to you,
I am the girl who had had enough,
I am the girl who told on you,
I am the girl who now has friends,
I am the girl who gained confidence,
To put this to an end!

Danielle Coulson-West (11)
Jo Richardson Community School, Dagenham

The Mouse Goes Tweet

The mouse comes out,
Creep, creep, creep,
The mouse comes out,
Peep, peep, peep,
The mouse says he would like to stay,
With me and my cat but hasn't got time today,
The mouse comes running back,
To his hole after stealing cheese!
Out of my roll!

Kayleigh Casey (11)
Jo Richardson Community School, Dagenham

My Mum's Little Helper

My mum's little helper puts frogs in my tea,
My mum's little helper makes fun of me,
My mum's little helper changes all the locks,
My mum's little helper changes my socks.

My mum's little helper rips all my books,
My mum's little helper gives me dirty looks,
My mum's little helper squirts soap in my eye,
My mum's little helper makes up very bad lies.

My mum's little helper puts snakes in my bed,
My mum's little helper digs up the dead,
My mum's little helper was once hired,
My mum's little helper is now *fired.*

James Collins (12)
Jo Richardson Community School, Dagenham

The Seaside

As I sit upon the sand,
With the sand between my toes,
I hear the waves crashing,
Against the rocks.

I sit there listening to,
The children making sandcastles
And splashing around in the sea.

How I wish I was
One of them.

Michaela Vickers (11)
Jo Richardson Community School, Dagenham

Who Can It Be?

Who can it be?
I don't know,
There's someone out there,
But it's definitely not me.

All I was doing was walking in the park,
The only thing is, it was very dark,
People say you shouldn't go out at night,
They say only to go out when it's very bright.

It's still very dangerous though,
'Cause they might jump out and pinch your toe,
Who knows what they could do,
I'm just like everyone else too.

I heard a footstep walk next to me,
But my friends just said who could it be?
There's someone out there and I don't know who,
Do you?

Donna Archer (12)
Jo Richardson Community School, Dagenham

Colours

A ring is gold,
Blue is cold,
Orange is old
And pink is *bold*.

Yellow's bright,
A feather is white,
Black's boring,
Purple is reassuring.

Eliza Parkin (11)
Jo Richardson Community School, Dagenham

What Is It?

What is it?
It is good,
Not bad,
Happy,
Not sad,
So what is it?

It is patient,
Not rushed,
It could be loud,
Or hushed,
So what is it?

It is kind and forgiving,
It is generous and giving,
It brings different emotions,
So what is it?

Cecilia Adjei-Sarpong (11)
Jo Richardson Community School, Dagenham

Just Me

I sit alone all by myself waiting for someone to talk to,
I start to cry as I clutch tight my teddy bear Lou Lou,
I hear footsteps coming toward me,
I jump with excitement,
Dad walked in and whispers those words . . .
'I'm sorry you're still on your own,
No brother, no sister, the baby wasn't too well,'
I cry, I cry, I run to him and say,
'Why, oh why, oh why?'

Lucy Evers (12)
Jo Richardson Community School, Dagenham

Woke Up

Woke up this morning,
Found my head,
Put it on my shoulders
And went back to bed.

Woke up this morning,
Found my feet,
Put them on my ankles
And went back to sleep.

Roxanne Butler (12)
Jo Richardson Community School, Dagenham

Christmas

Christmas is a day of celebration,
Jesus is on the way,
Lots and lots of presents
And much more to give away.

Just think of the Christmas dinner,
Hymns are sung as well,
All the Christmassy programmes
And warm-hearted stories to tell.

Christmas is full of love,
Jesus is here now so . . .
There is really a lot of presents,
But He took some though!

Christmas is almost over now,
Everyone put to bed,
So many sweet memories,
That will zoom into my head.

Jennifer Alegbeleye (11)
Park School for Girls, Ilford

The Birthday Countdown

Eight more days,
What did I hear you say?
That's right it will be my birthday,
Hip hip hooray, hip hip hooray.

Six more days,
So my calendar says,
Partying with my mates,
Who are just so great.

Two more days
And all my friends say,
What time shall we meet,
For your birthday treat?

Today's the day,
Happy birthday they all say,
Presents galore
And wow! So much more.

Liyah Satnarine (11)
Park School for Girls, Ilford

Love

Love is in the air,
Love is always there,
Love is like a dove,
Flying up above,
Love is holy,
Which we shall celebrate jolly,
Love goes through a path,
Which lovers have to catch,
Love goes on through life,
Which you'll choose to sacrifice,
Treat it with respect,
The easier it gets,
Love is like a bird,
It must never fly away.

Ibidayo Abudu (12)
Park School for Girls, Ilford

The Horrifying Dream

I had a dream about something so scary,
Nothing like an angel or fairy,
It had sharp claws and a hideous fang
And as it walked the floor went bang.

It swished its tail which was large and fat,
If it hit me, I'd probably be flat,
Its spiky horns and scaly skin,
Were as hard as the metal on a bin.

Its piercing eyes petrified me,
For a fraction of a second, I thought I might plea,
Then it said, 'You're such a delicious sight!'
I started shaking and everything went white.

Vision was coming back to me,
I woke up and I could finally see,
As I thought about the thing,
I realised that it was a mouse nibbling.

What could I do, I was only four,
I told my mum and she was laughing on the floor,
How could I be so dumb?
That was said by my mum.

Marwa Moughal (11)
Park School for Girls, Ilford

Autumn Time Is Here

Autumn time is finally here,
Leaves are falling everywhere,
The leaves fall every day but
The wind comes and blows them,
Away!

Autumn time is finally here,
The leaves are blowing everywhere,
Everybody gives a cheer,
Because autumn time is finally
Here!

The leaves are multicoloured,
Yellow, orange, green and red,
Yellow is bright, orange is cosy,
Green is beautiful but red is rosy.

Autumn time is finally here,
The leaves are falling everywhere,
Everybody give a cheer because
Autumn time is finally here!

Summertime has gone,
Autumn time has come,
Wintertime is nearly here,
So everybody beware!

Sara Sharif (11)
Park School for Girls, Ilford

Hallowe'en Ingredients

Open your cupboard,
Get out your list,
Because this is sure to send you round the twist,
Don't you worry,
Just crouch down low,
All we need is a vicious crow,
Bubbling and boiling in it goes,
This is sure to *make you grow!*
Next comes a foul smell,
Go on the sand, find a shell,
Next, we add a tree,
Some sea,
Maybe even a family,
Mix it all together,
Even add a mole,
I even sometimes add a troll,
Go on, have a taste,
Because this is sure to go to waste,
Now get some eggs,
A pair of legs and a couple of tatty pegs,
Take a swig, all I'll turn you in to is a pig!

Gabriella Marie Pollard (11)
Park School for Girls, Ilford

The Cat And The Rat

One day I bought a cat,
Who was really, really fat,
Later it sat on the mat,
Just when I gave it a pat.

But then he saw the rat,
Who looked juicy and fat,
But instead of my cat going to eat the rat,
My cat just gave it a pat.

Danielle Darcy (11)
Park School for Girls, Ilford

Magical Mermaid

I saw a magical mermaid,
While digging with my spade,
I saw a glimpse of her hair,
While sitting on my chair,
She waved at me with her hand,
Accidentally throwing sand,
She gave me a gift of a seashell,
Which glowed and had a lovely smell,
Then a beautiful ring,
With a pretty stone (bling, bling),
She swam away for a while,
But I still waited with a smile,
She came back in the evening,
To tell me something,
She took me far away,
To a magical place where I shall stay.

Harkiran Kaur (11)
Park School for Girls, Ilford

These Are The Sounds Of Silence

I hear the ocean's gentle voice,
I hear the Earth moving day and night,
I can hear the sun's fire from within,
No, these are the sounds of silence.

I can hear the birds flapping in the sky,
I can hear the sand in the sand timer,
I can hear my heart beating,
No, these are the sounds of silence.

I hear the plant growing steadily,
I hear the galaxies millions of miles away,
I hear the snowflakes falling,
No, these are the sounds of silence.

Chandni Nakum (11)
Park School for Girls, Ilford

Autumn

Leaves are falling everywhere,
Autumn is here!
Crunch, crunch, crunch,
Sticky leaves on my lunch!

Autumn brings festivals,
Divali, Eid
And don't forget Ramadan
Please!

Bonfire Night, the 5th of November,
A colourful evening, one to remember!
Chilly, crisp, clean air,
Bitter cold and quite bare.

My birthday's coming up!
A month filled with presents
Up to the top!

Anisah Rahman (11)
Park School for Girls, Ilford

Our Tree . . .

When spring comes round, our apple tree is very full of flowers
And when a bird sits on a branch, the petals fall in shadows,
When summer comes round, our apple tree is very full of green
And everywhere you look in it there is a leafy stream,
When autumn comes round,
Our apple tree is full of things to eat
And apples hang from every branch to tumble at our feet,
When winter comes around,
Our apple tree is full of snow and ice
And rabbits come to visit it . . .
We think our tree is nice.

Summaiya Shakir (14)
Park School for Girls, Ilford

Sunny Days

Sunny days are here again,
No more sadness and no more pain,
The pond is glistening in the blazing sun,
We are going to have so much fun!

Don't forget your sticky sun cream,
We're very lucky, we will have ice cream!
The older ones are swimming in the pool,
That water must be very cool.

The seat on the swing is very hot,
If you want to get your bottom burnt,
Sit on it (I'd rather you not!)
The luscious green grass,
I really hope this will last!

The day was good,
It was as it should be,
No more sadness and no more pain,
Sunny days are here again!

Rachel Dhliwayo (11)
Park School for Girls, Ilford

Christmas

Calling Dad to put up the Christmas tree,
I wonder what's in my present,
I wonder what it could be,
But I hope it's something pleasant.

25th December,
Only a few days away,
It will be something to remember,
If Santa Claus could come to stay.

It's Christmas tomorrow
And I've just realised,
I haven't bought a present for my sister,
I'll have to resort to lies.

My sister wants a bike from me
Otherwise she'll call me bad,
But I've spent all my money on our mum and dad,
My mum has bought her three,
I hope she doesn't forget me!

Rebecca Leal (11)
Park School for Girls, Ilford

Global Citizen

Citizens of the globe,
Can we honestly say,
We are not to blame for the treachery in the world?

Our world is changing,
The environment changes as we care less,
Listen to the songs of peace, harmony.

If we care for the world we live in,
Suffering and poverty will eventually stop,
Stop the poverty, stop the pollution,
Listen to sounds of peace, harmony.

Where is the rain,
For the flowers and plants?
They yearn for water,
In the heat of the sun.

Citizen of the globe,
Listen carefully,
Under the sky, sun and stars,
Listen to the sounds of peace and harmony.

Hansini Sivaguru (13)
Park School for Girls, Ilford

Disability

They think they know me,
But they don't, not really,
They look at me and suddenly,
Become omnipotent, they're not.

They think they understand me,
But they don't not really,
They don't know how,
I really work, they don't.

They act sympathetic,
But they're not, not really,
They don't give a damn for sure,
They don't.

They pretend to care,
But they don't not really,
They try to help,
To do their best, they don't.

They are always there,
They will never go away,
They have given up,
They are my family.

Zahra Hussain (13)
Park School for Girls, Ilford

Love

Captured, released,
Your guard is up, yet you're exposed,
Vulnerable, protected,
Once you have it, you can't let go,
It's powerful, has the strength,
To see through your soul,
Cut through your heart,
Tear you apart,
Then put you together again,
Makes you stronger, makes you weak,
Leaves you breathless, gives you life,
A beautiful prison, you're willingly trapped,
A safety net but can attack,
A fact of life, a mystery,
A gift from above . . .
Love.
A conversation lacking words,
A puzzle, merciless game,
Knows your secrets, knows your lies,
Sees behind your smile, behind your eyes,
Fills you with warmth, leaves in you in the cold,
You're flying, you're falling,
You're running away, you're calling,
Contradicting emotions,
Altogether different sensations,
Unite together to form,
A feeling of which you can't get enough,
Love.

Bolu Babalola (15)
Park School for Girls, Ilford

Global Warming

It rises in the air,
So silently it's unfair,
See it, we cannot,
The hole it makes proves it is a lot,
Cars and factories let out the trouble,
Nature plays its part as well,
The life will live, in our own little bubbles,
Will soon burst into hell,
We see the damage it makes,
But to stop it, money and time it takes,
It is the reason we go hot to cold,
Temperature changes cannot be told,
Our rivers become dirty and green,
But who will be the one to clean?
Who is the one to blame?
Let us begin this finger pointing game,
Both man and nature are the cause,
To stop it going further there must be new laws,
So let us start using our brains
And stop this vile pollution from causing earthly pains.

Janeet Jawanda (16)
Park School for Girls, Ilford

Hutchet

There was a man called Hutchet,
Hutchet Tucker was his name
And every letter in his name stood for something
Strange,
H means hideous I don't know why that was there,
Because Hutchet wasn't hideous, he was actually quite fair,
U stands for useless because he didn't do anything right,
Anything you ask him to do, he'll turn it into a fight,
T stands for tedious, he was a little bit like that,
All he does is go to the library,
With his bag on his back,
C stands for courage, he's got a lot of that,
If a lion stands up to him,
He will tell him to stand back,
H stands for hopeless, you can't rely on him,
If he was voted President,
The whole country would have to supervise,
E for enormous, Hutchet was really big,
Maybe that's why he's got a lot of courage,
Because compared to him, everyone is a little twig,
T stands for tiny,
I'm talking about his brain,
Now really apart from reading, everything swishes,
Passed him like a train.

Christena Thompson (12)
Park School for Girls, Ilford

The Seaside

The sun is orange and hot,
The sand is soft and warm,
The sky is blue without any clouds,
The sea is cold but strong.

I run about on the sand
And wash my feet in the sea,
I buy an ice cream to eat
And couldn't dream of anywhere else to be.

The ice cream is soft and sweet,
There are lots of waves to ride,
There are people swimming and sun bathing,
These are the parts of the seaside.

Shade Ogunyanwo (11)
Park School for Girls, Ilford

Winter

Outside is white,
So wrap up tight,
Or else you will get frostbite.

You are in here,
So do not fear,
By the fire for you a chair.

The trees are bare,
Frost is in the air,
So please take great care!

Kiran Virk (11)
Park School for Girls, Ilford

Night Love

I look outside the window every night,
To see the stars which shine so bright,
Thinking of you in my heart,
Wondering when this will start . . .

Knowing you're with someone else,
Makes me wanna hurt myself,
But the feeling of you with someone else,
Makes me wanna pray, that you will be with me some day.

It may happen now,
It may happen then,
But knowing one day,
We will share a true friendship that
No one will dare to stare.

When I look outside the window at the stars,
For some reason, it comes out with your name in hearts,
Waiting for my half and your half to be one part,
Wanting our names in some form of art.

Just drifting into bliss,
My eyes are about to shut,
Thinking of our future in my little heart . . .

Neha S Chandarana (14)
Park School for Girls, Ilford

A Teddy Bear's Dream . . .

I'm bought,
As a thought,
As I am rather short,
But I am never caught.

I gaze,
I laze,
I wonder,
I ponder,
I think,
I blink,
I daze,
I amaze,
I sense,
I'm tensed,
I play,
I lay,
But I never say!
I have fun,
In the sun,
I hear,
I care,
I share,
Just like a furry bear,
Which I already am!

Tasmeen Ahmed (13)
Park School for Girls, Ilford

What Am I?

I play through the day,
Or play through the night,
Loud or quiet I'm yours to decide,
My beat is perfection,
My rhythm in time,
So take a guess,
What am I?

Nicola Todd (12)
St Martin's School, Hutton

Ray

Ray walks on stage,
Ray has sunglasses on his face,
Ray moves to the piano,
Ray starts to sing,
Ray directs the band to swing,
Ray starts to move his body to the beat,
Ray moves his feet to the drums,
Ray does a piano solo,
Ray hears the crowd go wild,
Ray lets the saxophone do a solo,
Ray makes the band play again,
Ray finishes on a jazzy cool chord,
Ray hears the crowd cheer,
Ray is finished.

Perry Hughes (13)
St Martin's School, Hutton

Camp Green Lake

As you travel on the dry and bumpy road,
When you look out of the coach window,
You see hole after hole,
The dried up ground sweeps up the dust,
As you wander around, the sun hits you,
You feel dry and thirsty,
The shovel weighs you down,
As if you were carrying an elephant,
The cracked and jagged road around you has,
Lizards, snakes and scorpions hiding in the cracks,
You look around you and all you can see
Is miles and miles of nothing.

Emily Stanley (11)
St Martin's School, Hutton

My Horse

Gently, I pat him on his neck,
Slowly, I mount onto his beautiful silky back,
Bravely, I nudge him on,
Through the dark, wintry forest,
Wildly, he canters away,
Off into the distance,
Violently, I fall to the cold, hard floor,
Sadly, I will never see my horse again.

Emma Weaver (13)
St Martin's School, Hutton

What I Think About?

I have many different tastes
And some you may dislike,
You might buy me for a special reason
And I can be used for every season,
I can be moulded in lots of different shapes just for you
And part of me is made from the things that go moo!

Miss Fearn likes to tell us stories
And one of her stories, she spent her pounds
To go to the circus and be scared by clowns!

I grow blackberries,
They taste very nice,
But if you think about strawberries,
You better think twice.

Imagine,
The land was made of paper,
The sea was made of ink,
The trees were made of rubbers and rulers,
But what would be in a pencil case,
What do you think?

Robyn Slaughter (11)
St Martin's School, Hutton

RIP

Bang! Went the gun as the Germans open fire,
So the English hit back with a grenade and
The man that threw it went 'Got the blighter!'
Everyone cheered; the sergeant said 'Shut up,
We've still got more work to be done!'
So everyone kept going,
One man ran into no-man's-land,
He got shot down in his first couple of steps.

Overhead there were planes throwing bombs down
Like they ruled the skies,
The cannons on the fire step ruled the land
And the soldiers ruled themselves.

The soldiers felt like they needed a rest
And more importantly they felt the
War would just be over.

The war ends. Silence! Now the clouds rule the sky
And the poppies rule the land and
Most soldiers are dead and buried,
RIP, my friends who saved everyone's freedom,
Rest In Peace!

Douglas Bennett (13)
St Martin's School, Hutton

Football

Football, the greatest sport ever,
Once you start to get extremely addicted,
This is football fever,
Adrenaline pumping through your body at 1000mph,
Football is a game of rivals, passion and hate,
Football is a game of pure strength and power,
Football is a game you go to the wire to desire,
Once you pick a team, you're loyal all your life,
That's why you're always hearing about tragic fights,
Football, you support the game till you die.

Chris Chapman (13)
St Martin's School, Hutton

Roylott

A face seared with a thousand wrinkles,
A high, thin, fleshless nose,
A pair of deep set, bile shot eyes,
A long frock coat and a pair of high gaiters,
A black top hat and a hunting crop,
Swinging from his hand,
A particular mix of professional and the agricultural,
As tall as the doorway,
An aggressive, menacing murderer.

Max Rowley (12)
St Martin's School, Hutton

Friends

(For all my friends)

Friends are forever
And a day,
You'll be together,
All the way.

Sharing the laughter,
The tears too,
But no matter what,
They'll be there for you.

They'll take you shopping,
When you're down
And cheer you up,
By being a clown.

Friends are forever
And a day,
We will always be together,
In every way.

Sarah Golds (12)
St Martin's School, Hutton

Me!

Living in Brentwood is sometimes cool,
But however we have to go to school.

The weather is rainy and sometimes wet,
I have a little hamster, a really cool pet.

My house is in a little small street,
With many nice people that you can meet.

I enjoy playing sports in my local park,
Dogs chase the ball and sometimes bark.

All my mates live very near,
The pathway there is very clear.

This poem is all about me,
As you can probably see.

Now my poem's coming to an end,
I hope you'll be a nice new friend.

Here it comes the very last line,
I hope you thought my poem was fine.

Ryan Fletcher (12)
St Martin's School, Hutton

Proudly

Proudly you shake her hand,
Proudly you understand,
Proudly you stand up high,
Proudly you say goodbye,
Proudly you kiss goodnight,
Proudly you have no fright,
Proudly you take my hand,
Proudly you have no plan.

Nicole Gibbs (12)
St Martin's School, Hutton

Lovingly

Lovingly you hold my hand,
Lovingly you understand,
Lovingly you watch me grow,
Lovingly you let me go,
Lovingly you hold me near,
Lovingly you conquer my fear,
Lovingly you help me through,
Lovingly you always knew,
Lovingly you are my mother,
Lovingly you are there like no other,
Lovingly you said goodbye,
Lovingly you made me cry,
Lovingly you told me bad,
Lovingly you told me not to be sad,
You were going off to Heaven land,
Where there were blue seas and yellow sand,
You told me to be happy and smile,
How could I? I wasn't going to see you for a while,
Lovingly you held my hand,
Sadly I didn't understand,
I sat there and watched you die,
So I love you Mum and goodbye.

Jessie Gibson (12)
St Martin's School, Hutton

Hamsters

H amsters like to
A dventure around and
M unch their food and
S tore the food inside their cheeks and
T urn around in a wheel and
E at delicious nuts and fruits,
R un around their cage at night and
S leep all day till it's no longer light.

Eli Langley (12)
St Martin's School, Hutton

Cats

Cats, you hear them around at night,
Cats, you see their shadow, they give you a fright,
Cats, slowly padding along the wall,
Cats, if you tried you would probably fall!
Cats, you see the moon as you are passing by,
Cats, it is the reflection you see in their eye,
Cats, you see their eyes and button nose,
Cats, you see their paws and dainty toes,
Cats, you see them drinking in a puddle,
Cats, but to be honest, they are perfect for a cuddle.

Yasmin Ball (12)
St Martin's School, Hutton

Sunshine

The day is starting,
The sky is grey,
But suddenly the sun,
Comes out to play.

The sky is now bright
And the air is clear,
Now that the sun,
Again is here.

No rain, no dark,
Or stormy weather,
But sun and light,
To make it better.

Serena Reeves (13)
St Martin's School, Hutton

The Football Pitch

The smell of overcooked fumes filling the air,
The football pitch,
The smell of the cut grass wafting slowly towards me,
The football pitch,
The feeling of the greasy chips pressing on my fingers,
The football pitch,
The hooligans chanting as the home team win back the victory!
The football pitch,
The referee's whistle screaming in my ears,
The sound of the home team celebrating with just a few beers,
The football pitch!

Ellie Polston (12)
St Martin's School, Hutton

Wildly

Wildly, the lion roared,
The cheetah chased,
The leopard leapt,
The tiger targeted,
The jaguar jumped,
Wild the cat was.

Wildly, the shark snapped,
The crab clapped,
The jellyfish jerked,
The sea snake slithered,
The crocodile crushed,
Wild the sea was.

Wildly, the world goes on.

Bethany Horner (13)
St Martin's School, Hutton

Late Last Night

Late last night I lay in bed,
Thoughts were flashing through my head,
Of Sherlock Holmes and the Speckled Band,
Of raindrops falling on the sand,
Of holidays out in the sun,
Of greasy bacon in a bun,
Of roasts and chops all cooked to perfection,
Of what to wear and my reflection
And I was saying in my head,
Why can't I just go to bed?

James Allen (12)
St Martin's School, Hutton

Animals And Me

There's the lion,
There's the cat,
There's the disgraceful little rat,
There are voles,
There are moles,
There are really cute foals,
There are dogs,
There are frogs,
There are fat, ugly hogs,
There are bears, there are hares,
They all give me nightmares,
In the end you will see,
That I like the bee,
Thank you for listening to animals and me.

Ben Sach (12)
St Martin's School, Hutton

That Alley

It's down that distant alley, I always fear to go,
Dark, damp and smelly,
I never want to travel through,
Those eerie sounds
And darkened shadows that I don't know,
It comes today, I dread it now, it's something I must do.

One step, two step, three step, floor,
On my knees, I shake in fear,
That gloomy figure, I can't stop them, they're coming near,
It's the flicker of a shiny knife,
Oh no God! Don't end my life.

The Red River flows down the street,
The sirens on a car,
My life was not complete,
I'm not in my body, I must be very far.

Just a shadow now in the sky,
Now you know how I died.

Ronan Gallocker (12)
St Martin's School, Hutton

Passionately

Passionately, we move closer together,
Passionately, he holds my hand,
Passionately, he pulls me closer to his beating heart,
Passionately, I place my head on his soft torso,
Passionately, our eyes meet and fix,
Passionately, our lips touch in a moment of lust,
Sadly, it was all a dream.

Elise Whiteley (12)
St Martin's School, Hutton

Roylott

Roylott is a nasty man,
Roylott doesn't understand,
Roylott is mean to the girls,
Roylott the blacksmith he hurled,
Roylott has lots of pets,
Roylott doesn't know best,
Roylott did try and shake but
Roylott got bitten by a snake,
Roylott didn't understand so now,
Roylott is a dead man.

Rosanna Munday (12)
St Martin's School, Hutton

Seasons Change

The gigantic trees suddenly gave out an immense roar,
As their humongous arms swept down to the floor,
The leaves started to dance around the trees
And fly off into the sky whistling and whispering
And going round and round,
The mud was really muddy because it was autumn,
The trees were very unhappy because they were
Losing all their leaves,
But the leaves were happy because they were finally free,
The trees liked the summer best,
Because that was when they had their full grown haircut,
It was nice and green and bushy,
They liked spring as well,
Because all the new leaves were sprouting and blossoming,
The birds were singing and the lambs are running about,
They hate winter though because it is so cold
And all their leaves are all gone,
They're just standing there in the nude.

Sinead Bernard (12)
Sacred Heart of Mary Girls' School, Upminster

The Life Of Me

My life is who I am,
My life is mine to treasure,
Some days it brings the pain,
Other days it's the pleasure.

How can you sum up a life?
There are no words to describe:
But taking each day as it comes,
Without use of a personal bribe.

My life is one big routine,
But once you capture the core:
It is easy to see,
That to me, there is more.

My parents are not only my parents,
My sister's not only my sister:
These are the people who make me, mister,
Without them there is no me!

They are my everything,
Everything I could be:
My life is one long book,
With one too many scenes.

And hopefully if I'm lucky,
This is what my life means,
How lucky am I to have,
Something to special to me.

And although it's not always perfect,
It's exactly how I want it to be,
The life of me.

Amy Fish (13)
Sacred Heart of Mary Girls' School, Upminster

Living Lightning

He's coming so fast,
Fiercely firing a blast,
His deep loud voice,
Giving no one a choice,
But to keep on running ahead.

He cracks straight through the rock,
Everyone's in terrible shock,
They all run with fright,
He follows - he's so bright,
He now strikes the tree,
Showing how dangerous he can be.

Hannah Williamson (13)
Sacred Heart of Mary Girls' School, Upminster

Mr Snow

Tumbling, falling from the sky,
The snow is grated on a fly,
Cold and biting, sore and harsh,
Melting slowly on the marsh.

Whispering gently, crying for cold,
As it slips on the house just sold,
Plodding along the road so wide,
Making people slip and slide.

On the floor crunchy and crispy,
A tuft of white, a very small wisp,
Cold at heart not knowing nice,
Freezes in their steps the harmless mice.

Melting slowly off green leaves,
The mystery of water on peas,
Melted like water, runny and wet,
The snow is now dripping off my pet.

Serena Piras (12)
Sacred Heart of Mary Girls' School, Upminster

That Fateful Night

A dark and stormy night,
In the middle of the magnificent city of London,
Was suddenly illuminated,
By a yellow arm of light.

The lightning spread out its fingers,
Determined to reach its destination,
A house nearby was in its grasp,
It's time on Earth about to end.

There was the house,
Getting closer, closer,
The arm was inches away,
From doing its duty for another day.

In a flash the lightning struck,
A huge explosion shook the street,
Tongues of fire engulfed the house,
Clouds of smoke rose into the air.

But when the people looked for a meaning,
They found nothing nearby,
For where the lightning had once been,
Now stood an empty sky.

Annie McCarthy (13)
Sacred Heart of Mary Girls' School, Upminster

Goodbye To The Brook

As the big trees gossiped
And the leaves danced with no clue,
The moonlight was different,
That would become known with the morning dew.

The willow all curled up and dying,
The soil and the grass laughing at the mud,
As the big burrows curled up at sundown,
The destroyer leapt down with a thud.

Nosing around in the debris,
The leaf pile stood up to say 'No!'
But the evil was in no way dismissed
And slaughtered them before he could go.

The gathering trees with arms outstretched,
The news had reached the brook
And now the monster was coming,
To collect what had been took.

The forest reached out and pleaded,
But the killer refused to stop,
As he took out his saw and listened no more,
To the homeliness and welcoming arms of the brook.

Kate Oliver (13)
Sacred Heart of Mary Girls' School, Upminster

The Snow

The snow all bleak and white,
Falls from the dark in the night,
It is grated from an angel in the sky,
Sprinkling on the ground like sugar on pie.

Twirling and spinning, the snow lands,
Entwining itself and covering my hands,
The snow is like a magnificent magic,
Performing no heavy spells to tragic.

The snow's icy wand holds cold powers,
Soft to touch, but warm, melting the snow to showers,
My feet plod into marshmallow clouds,
As I dream of enchanted snowflake bands.

A dreamy song seeps through the blizzard,
Miming sweet music only written by a powerful wizard,
I listen so strong, to hear the beautiful song,
But as I lift my head up high, the music's gone.

Evergreen trees stand stately and proud in the breeze,
Rumbling their sketched out icicled leaves,
The snow gazes with one single small round eye,
As the sun comes out and wants the flakes to die.

I hold my breath, for one heartbeat,
Until there is anxiety in my feet,
I look up to see the snow has depressingly gone,
I sulk and walk away, till I hear that song . . .

The spellbound song seeped through the greyness of the sky,
Watching mesmerised me, myself and I,
I smile, my teeth snowy and white,
I sink entranced in a snow spell for the entire night.

In my dream I see only star-like shapes,
Snowflakes I notice as I shockingly gape,
My mind goes all fuzzy, like shizzely, fizshely . . . fizz,
I close my eyes and make a wish.

Rachael O'Flaherty (12)
Sacred Heart of Mary Girls' School, Upminster

Like A Child

The wind came running down the lane,
I saw it dance and prance and twirl,
Almost like a dancer or a singer,
Dancing or singing the sweetest thing,
Kicking up leaves and rustling my hair,
Holding my hand as I walked by
And whispering in my ears.

I left the wind and then I heard a howl,
Worse than a wolf or a baby crying,
It fell to the ground and kicked and thumped,
Blowing off rooftops with its racketing sobs
And sounding like it would prefer to die.

The wind blew towards me getting faster and faster,
Its eyes gleaming red and its hair wild
And it pierced through my heart,
Like a knife through a piece of steak.

The wind looked at me with shining eyes,
It blew and there were hurricanes,
It cried and there were tidal waves,
It kicked and there were sandstorms,
So sand grains and water droplets got in my eyes.

Suddenly I felt so sad,
Imagine not having anyone to love you or look after you,
I knew how that felt for I had no love as a child
And the wind was merely a baby,
Crying because it missed its mother.

I went to soothe it and it calmed down
And went on its way,
As if it had been dancing and prancing and twirling all day
And kicking up leaves and rustling my hair.

Amira McCarthy (12)
Sacred Heart of Mary Girls' School, Upminster

The Wind

The wind is like an enormous pair of arms swaying in and out,
Twisting in and out through the trees and buildings,
A whistling sound near enough to me,
A jolly big arm, hugging the tree,
Using its arms as a swaying machine,
Happy, nice and running past me,
The voice so high only there for a second,
As the wind is far gone in the town far ahead,
Laughing as it runs away from me,
The arms swaying in the air,
So delicate and friendly,
Shivering as it chatters its teeth,
The night comes as the day goes,
Leaving a happy wind, hugging a tree.

Aisling Brunskill (13)
Sacred Heart of Mary Girls' School, Upminster

The Sea Dance

The sea was dancing to the beat, twisting and turning about,
Enjoying warmth the sun gave out, it happily danced away.

The sea was glistening, its arms were waving and
Shouted out, 'How happy am I today?'
But sadly this wasn't all good right now, as the sun
started to go away.

The sea got calm, the winds went down, the clouds came out,
The sea tapped back, but was it ever to dance again?

It whispered, 'Take me back, take me back to the shore,
When it's happy and fun to be.
I can dance all day and wave my hands,
But here I have to sleep unhappily.'

Nadine Semaine (13)
Sacred Heart of Mary Girls' School, Upminster

The Derby Dancing Sea

The sea was humming her song,
But wait, what does she hear?
The sound of faded music,
She's off to see where it is,
When she gets there 'it's the dance of the ocean,'
She signs up,
Then she waits for her turn to dance,
Sitting, waiting, nervously
But a light shines on her and a nod from the lighthouse
Means go,
She whispers thanks and up she gets
And meets her partner rock,
The whistling starts and she goes,
Slowing tapping with her partner at first,
Then adding more movement and doing the jive,
She can't contain herself, she's being rough,
A boat draws near,
She goes towards it,
Bang!
It's silent again,
All you can hear is the sea humming her song.

Hollie Amanda Patricia Jiggins (12)
Sacred Heart of Mary Girls' School, Upminster

A Shattering Storm

The sun was out and the birds were singing,
But just wait till the storm comes with another mood swinging,
It's all going to happen at seven tonight,
With a big gust of wind, you could lose your kite,
You really, really can't miss this storm,
You should see the shape that the dust can form,
He's big, invisible and swirls things around,
He's so strong he can lift your feet off the ground,
All you can hear is his cry with rage,
If it was possible he'd be locked in a cage,
When the clock turns seven, he'll be out and about,
It'll be a miracle if you survive, which I really doubt,
Watch out, he could knock on any door,
Within seconds you could be on the floor,
I know you won't and can't believe me,
But just wait patiently and then you'll see,
Two grey clouds (these are his eyes)
Now you see how I am not telling lies,
Just watch out be careful and then you will see,
The shattering storm that's out to get you and me.

Danielle Brown (12)
Sacred Heart of Mary Girls' School, Upminster

Poor, Dear Winter

Winter shivered as it drifted to and fro,
Hailstones crashed and roared,
Smashing into the naked trees,
Temperature decreasing, now zero degrees,
Ice quivered as it painted the shimmering lake,
All of the leaves began to crackle and shake,
Winter nipped with her icicle fangs,
Moaning and groaning then a deafening bang,
Her extravagant snow cloak engulfed the green grass,
She sang sweetly to herself, with the sound of brass,
Sounding from the tempestuous wind,
She smiled coldly at the trees and plants,
They wouldn't accept her, so she did a dance,
She danced and pranced,
Would they ever give her a chance?
But no, they would not,
Everybody hated Winter a lot,
But why oh why,
Because she caused storms in the sky.

Catherine Shields (13)
Sacred Heart of Mary Girls' School, Upminster

Mr Winter

'Winter is on his way
In a frosty frozen sleigh.'
Hailstones thundering down,
Melting as soon as they touch the ground,
The sleigh floats over the treetops,
With Winter cackling non-stop,
His cloak stretches over the ground,
A soft white blanket, so silent, not a sound,
He takes his wand of ice and frost
And dips it in the lake,
The ice is smooth and intricate,
Like icing on a cake,
The bare trees tremble in the breeze,
Winter tore down all his leaves,
He paints the sky a cloudy grey,
All the raindrops come out to play,
His crisp sharp voice has scared the birds,
All the people and the farmer's herds,
But icicles have barred the way,
Cos Mr Winter's here to stay!

Olivia Odubanjo (12)
Sacred Heart of Mary Girls' School, Upminster

Windy The Wind

He loves to whistle, he loves to run,
Windy's the guy who'll have lots of fun!

He's hyperactive, crazy, jolly and huggable,
He's friendly, kind and really loveable.

He runs around your local park,
'I'm not that good!' an untrue remark.

He's as fast as an ostrich and he'll take you for a ride,
But stop to give every tree a hug arms open wide!

He zooms to the left and he zooms to the right,
If you think you're fast, you'll have a fright!

When Windy goes past, you'll fall on your bottom,
Just like poor Mrs Maglotton!

Then you have to say bye-bye to Windy,
But say hello to the sun, Cindy!

But don't be sad, he'll be back next time,
I guess that's the end because I forgot the next line!

Shannon Ryan (12)
Sacred Heart of Mary Girls' School, Upminster

The Wind

The flowing wind, a ballet dancer,
Flowing throughout the Earth,
The trees gently swaying, a tiny rustle in your hair,
It sings its gentle song, with choirs of angels in the background,
Happiness, peace and joy.

It hugs you, taking the pain away,
You inhale the fresh feeling of love
As it tiptoes away, blowing a kiss!

You hear its song, playing throughout your mind
And within your soul, ready to return to reality again.

Suddenly the evil twin arrives, playing its nasty game,
Its temperature piercing through your skin,
The wind, now a howling monster, prepared to attack,
The atmosphere a horror movie replaying in your mind,
The trees which once rustled, now lay dead upon the floor,
The wind a cackling witch, laughing at its success,
You may run and scream, but you will never escape.

Homes with no roofs, as the wind has its dinner,
Then a crack in the sky appears and the sun, father to the wind,
Shines over everyone,
The wind struggles and soon disappears,
As the sun smiles its bright smile,
People soon realise that they are safe!
The monster has gone.

Bianca Charles-Roper (12)
Sacred Heart of Mary Girls' School, Upminster

The Wind

The fierce Wind, he blew and blew,
He fiercely blew at passers-by,
He touched them with his tongue,
His howling groan,
His windy ways,
The fierce Wind, he blew and blew.

The fierce Wind, he blew and blew,
He made the weak trees shake,
Like a bully in the sky,
He had no fear,
Yet he put it in others,
The fierce Wind, he blew and blew.

The fierce Wind, he blew and blew,
He spread the cold and gust,
He blew every single speck, every speck of dust,
The fierce Wind, he blew and blew.

Amy Ransom (12)
Sacred Heart of Mary Girls' School, Upminster

The Storm

The storm was no longer imprisoned behind
The wings of his enemy, the sun,
He had broken free from his misery,
So confusion was unleashed, anger and fright,
As he spat over everything he envied and disliked,
Crying with anger while raindrops flew from his eyes,
He had such a sore throat, he sounded so screechy
As he let out a scream,
So he decided to whistle and whisper yet he sounded so violent,
He runs throughout the country to spread his rage,
By the end of the day, he became tired and bored,
He lay down for a while, big mistake!
Because the sun had burst loose, open to the world again.

Lois Hodder (12)
Sacred Heart of Mary Girls' School, Upminster

Monstrous Winds

Like a hand with a knife winds suddenly strike
And the plants and the trees are wildly blown,
Houses and rooftops are being uplifted,
In what was once a quiet peaceful town.

The cheeks of the source are doing their best,
To make sure they don't run out of breath,
Then with an angry face the wind loudly howls
And continues to demolish.

The foot of this monster kicks the leaves,
They fly up in the air like a gigantic tornado,
Scattering leaves on the roads and the gardens,
Showing no sign of defeat.

Then after a while the winds die down
And the horrified town is now at rest,
The wind flows gently like a fairy
And grasps your hand nicely.

It whispers in your ear with a quiet, soothing voice
And then you know it's all over,
No one knows when the winds will return,
To once again terrorise the town.

Rebecca Sadler (12)
Sacred Heart of Mary Girls' School, Upminster

Lector Lightning

The trees billowed in the darkness,
Louder and louder, deeper and deeper got the sound,
But the sound of what?
The sound of the electrifying lightning,
As petrifying as it was,
People were screaming,
Babies were crying,
But were they lying?
Could they really hear a sound?
Why were they running round and round?
The mood was alarming and terrifying,
Lector lightning was fast and ferocious,
Zapping every house in town,
His mood was scary and angry,
As angry as a charging bull,
His voice was like a drum booming every second,
Deep and crackling was the sound he made,
He came down at every minute like he was floating up above,
His face white and glowing,
Lector lightening flashed before your eyes and
In a matter of seconds he was gone,
The sky was dull and grey with only stars twinkling
In the moonlight,
No one would ever forget Lector the night he gave them a fright.

Courtney Samuels (12)
Sacred Heart of Mary Girls' School, Upminster

The Hero Of The Night

The trees reached out with their long scrawny fingers,
Ready to grab the little girl,
As the darkness swallowed her up,
The trees bellowed angrily at it,
The head of the moon shook peacefully
And he softly sighed,
He turned his beaming light on full power,
So the girl could choose her path,
The darkness choked
And darted away from the little girl,
The trees followed the darkness like a shadow
And the forest was untroubled again,
Its arms wide open,
Ready to welcome lots more victims!

Colleen Cox (12)
Sacred Heart of Mary Girls' School, Upminster

The Day That Winter Came

The naked trees shivered and shook their icy arms,
Everyone knew it was winter,
Crack! Crack! The ice swam across and masked the pond,
The icicles teeth hung from lamp posts
And the snowman's beady eyes,
He didn't want winter to expire but everyone else did,
The wind was icy and swirled, as it nipped and bit
Everything in its path,
'I take no prisoners,' the wind whispered sharply,
'After being hurt so badly, I am still suffering,
The pain gnaws at me until spring comes,
I will never give up,
I'll get you back, the summer has ruined my life,
I cannot beat the dire heat,
No one can, not even a human,
Nooooo!

Ceann Reid-Stiffell (12)
Sacred Heart of Mary Girls' School, Upminster

Windy

Windy was like a hyperactive child sweeping through the trees
And as he runs as fast as he can, he whistled to the bees.

His arms stretch further than the eye can see,
His legs run faster than you and me.

He zooms and he sweeps across the cities and towns,
All through the villages, he sees lots of frowns.

That is because they do not like him so,
They all wished he would just go.

Up to the hills and the land on thle moor,
They're trying to shut him out like a big wooden door.

But Windy will not have this, no, no way,
He just comes back and says, 'I'm here to stay.'

Even if I go in the night,
I'll still be back in the morning light.

Most people have not met Windy,
Because he is as fast as lightning and a blur to see.

But I can say in all honesty,
He is the friendliest, kindest, jolliest, craziest
Person there ever will be.

Suzanne Hughes (12)
Sacred Heart of Mary Girls' School, Upminster

I Wish

I wish I was at home but I'm at school,
I wish I could have the rabbit in my arms
That I had to give away,
I wish we would get less homework,
I wish I could have the sweets from America,
I wish I were in Dubai where I would swim
In the glittery clear water,
I wish I could lay on the grass at my house in America,
I wish I could go back to America to see my cousin,
I wish me and my mum and brother were in Pakistan
Visiting my cousins.

Danielle Zaidi (11)
Stratford School, Forest Gate

My Place Covered In Snow

I wish I lived in a bright blue place,
Where all people have a great big grin on their face,
I wish London were as immaculate as this place
And if it was, there would be more space,
For the sidewalk.

I wished I had a yap-yapping brown dog,
With his little face happy as can be,
I wish he had a lapping tongue,
He's having so much fun.

I wish there was no *bang, crash, help*,
In London, it's supposed to be nice,
I wish you knew the place,
So let me tell you, it's Canada.

Rianne Johnson (11)
Stratford School, Forest Gate

Wish List

I wish I could play football in France with the sky blue,
So it is matching the football kit.

I wish I could ride a bike in Italy with the sky green,
I wish I could go to space and see the pitch-black sky.

I wish the houses in the world were white
So they would stand out more.

I wish the grass in the world was blue
So then it would match the sky.

I wish the sun was red so then we would see
A red ball in the sky.

I wish the moon was yellow, so the sun
And moon would be in contrast.

I wish the clouds were orange so the sky would be colourful.

Pritesh Jadia (11)
Stratford School, Forest Gate

Dubai In My Dreams

I wish I lived in the Atlantic,
Glassed undersea hotel, Burujal Arab,
It's shaped like a sinking boat,
With a crystallised flashing blue light,
While the watery waves just crash upon the rocks.

The bright orange reflects on your face
And you feel the sandy, smooth safari sand,
While the prickly palm trees just sit there staring at you,
I wish I could just step inside that glamorous Burujal Arab Hotel
And feel relieved.

Tasnim Mala (12)
Stratford School, Forest Gate

My Pink Wonderland

I wish I could have my own pink wonderland,
So I can be myself,
I would be able to do whatever I want,
Like I was free for life.

The shimmering sun would gleam on me all day,
The fluffy white clouds would be like soft sheep,
The ground would be soft as fur,
My body would feel different like I was a different person.

I would feel happy and I will never want to leave,
Thinking of the wonderland makes me smile,
My life would be different!

Wouldn't you like to do that?

Najiya Anvar Musahaji (11)
Stratford School, Forest Gate

My Wish

I wish I were in America and eating a large
Bowl of vanilla coloured ice cream.

I wish I had an everlasting life,
It will be like a yellow sun shining upon me.

I wish my whole body were shining
And glittering with diamonds.

I wish I was very rich and
I have a house which is very big and
It has different colours everywhere.

I wish no one in my family died
And has an everlasting life like me.

Sean Cole (11)
Stratford School, Forest Gate

The Voice Of My Wishes

I wished I lived in Pakistan with all the colourful excitement,
Don't you wish you lived in a blithe and peaceful place
Like Saudi Arabia because I know I do.

I wish the entire world was made up of the
Illuminated joy I have and live,
I wish the whole world was as quiet as the blue Mediterranean.

I wish the gates of Pakistan were opened with a
White quiet voice, the voice of a god,
I wish all the countries were as friendly and kind
As the people and friends that I know.

I wish that the minds of people think like the
Blue peaceful minds of the religious ones.

I got a million and one wishes but all I wished for
Were the wishes above, *but* I got one final one!

I wish for freedom and justice, I wish for peace!

Aysha Karbhari (12)
Stratford School, Forest Gate

I Had A Wish

I had a wish,
I was rich.

I had a wish,
I was the ruler of the world.

I had a wish,
I was the owner of a Buggati.

I had a wish that,
No one else could fulfil but me.

I had a wish,
That I was the owner of the pyramids.

I had a wish,
That I was me.

Amritpal Singh (11)
Stratford School, Forest Gate

The Magic Box

(Based on 'Magic Box' by Kit Wright)

I will put in the box . . .
The buzz of a bee,
A gust of cold air as I opened the door in winter,
The first drop of rain at the start of a thunderstorm.

I will put in the box . . .
A ray of sunshine,
A sip of fresh water from the River Nile,
A fresh summer breeze.

I will put in the box three turquoise wishes spoken in Bengali,
The last bedtime story of an ancient auntie,
The first word of a baby.

I will put in the box . . .
Santa on a broomstick,
A witch riding on reindeers
And a strong whoosh of wind.

My box is fashioned from scarlet silk and silver, shiny steel
With golden sprinkles on the lid and stars full of gold
In the corners,
Its hinges are the toe joints of a rhinoceros.

I shall skate in my box,
On the great mountain of the wild Arctic,
Then ashore to the indigo sea.

Uzma Rehman (11)
Stratford School, Forest Gate

Around The World In Six Wishes

I wish I could drive a cream car to Cardiff,
I wish I could travel on a turquoise train to Thailand,
I wish I could drive a black bus to Blackpool,
I wish I could fly in an aqua aeroplane to the Amazon,
I wish I could ride a bright blue bike to Beijing,
I wish I could ride a golden coach home.

Daisy Cox (11)
Stratford School, Forest Gate

My Dreams And Wishes

I wish the world were silver and full of laughter,
I wish I bought a big blue mansion in Dubai,
I wish I visited a pink and beautiful place like Paris.

I wish the world were brown and full of chocolate,
I wish I visited a green and noisy place like India,
I wish I bought a yellow quiet place like Egypt.

I wish the sun were like a juicy orange,
I wish I lived in a white and beautiful place like Heaven,
I wish the stars were gold and shaped like diamonds.

I wish I bought a purple house in Jamaica,
I wish I visited a black and dark place like Saudi Arabia,
I wish the world were silver and full of laughter.

Ijaz Choudhury (12)
Stratford School, Forest Gate

My Dreamland

I wish I lived in Heaven,
Where the soft silky clouds fly all around you,
Where you get any wish you may wish,
Where the orange sun shines above you.

I wish I lived in Heaven,
Where there is a one hundred metre slide,
After hours of screaming you land in chocolate milkshake,
Where you eat . . . chocolate, ice cream, pizza,
burger and Coca-Cola.

I wish I lived in Heaven,
Where you drink and swim in honey and milk rivers,
Where the best rides in the world go,
But where is the sea?

Now that's where you have real freedom,
Joy and excitement!

Reem Othman (11)
Stratford School, Forest Gate

I Wish My Bedroom Was Heaven

I wish my bedroom was Heaven,
With pink fluffy pillows and a soft comfy bed,
I wish my bedroom was Heaven,
With blue walls you could bounce off and
Listen to relaxing, calm music.

I wish my bedroom was Heaven,
With purple springy beanbags and a cloud-like floor,
I wish my bedroom was Heaven,
With a vending machine and a balcony.

I wish my bedroom was Heaven,
With a clear view of an Arsenal football match,
I wish my bedroom was Heaven,
With a door open to all my friends to see.

Anisha Vadher (11)
Stratford School, Forest Gate

An Autumn's Day!

I could hear the wind blowing,
It's blowing harder again and again,
The conkers falling, the leaves dropping,
Oh what an autumn's day.

I could feel the breeze going past me,
The conkers are falling upon my knee,
The colourful leaves are glistening,
Oh listen to the birds singing,
Now it's finally here and now
It's the end of my fear.

Karishma Kaur (11)
Stratford School, Forest Gate

Video Games

My mum calls it a waste of time,
My dad says it should be made a crime,
But I still love playing video games
Black is its colour, PlayStation 2 is its name.

I'm trying my best to learn Fifa 2007,
If I want something easy, I play Kingdom of Heaven,
When I am feeling angry, I play Street Fighter,
But I go to play football outside when the weather is brighter.

If I don't like a game, I just play another
And keep on practising till I beat my older brother,
What I like the most is to see the look on his face,
When he loses to a kid, he thinks he is a disgrace.

Siraat Rangari
Stratford School, Forest Gate

My Place In The World

I wish my back garden were like America,
With the animals and tropical trees,
I'll be sure to warn you that the animals
Are not friendly!

I wish I were in France surrounded with skies,
But I'm afraid there are mostly lights
And the Eiffel Tower is standing tall,
Compare it to me, I look quite small.

I wish I lived in the Caribbean with the jungle,
But don't forget that the flowers are in bundles.

I wish my house was like India with the flying kites,
But all they do in the UK is fight
And I wish I were in New York City
And me standing next to the Statue of Liberty.

Vinay Patel (11)
Stratford School, Forest Gate

The Magic Box

(Based on 'Magic Box' by Kit Wright)

I will put in the box . . .
The crack of a firework going up on display,
The water from the river which flows all day,
The tip of the stars touching the sky,
I will put in the box . . .
The planets of the solar system,
A cloud from the sky so soft and smooth,
A drip of water from hailstones falling from the sky.
I will put in the box . . .
The tears of a baby crying all day,
The kindness of my mother
And the laughter of my sister.

Ruhina Begum (11)
Stratford School, Forest Gate

Dubai

I wish I lived in a beautiful and
Colourful place like Dubai,
Dubai, the colour of Dubai is white like bright,
Dubai is as lovely as a rose,
There is an acorn hotel called Burj Al Arab,
Burj Al Arab is a very festoon hotel,
Dubai is really warm as the sun is next to you,
You would love it in Dubai.

The beach is lovely and with wonderful surroundings,
The water has lovely waves to swim in,
The water nice colour blue,
It is hot as a cooking pot, very hot,
If you are wearing glasses,
It is so hot that the glasses steam up,
I want to live in a bright place like Dubai.

Fatima Bodiyat (11)
Stratford School, Forest Gate

Wonder And Dream . . .

I wish I lived under the sea,
With blue waving water
And seabeds like sand
And be just like a mermaid,
With shining green tail shining in the watery sun.

I wish I lived in a mansion,
With golden grapevines hanging from the rooftops
And be as big as it could be
And be as rich as the Queen
And as posh as I could be.

I wish I lived in the sky
And fly fluently through the sky,
With all the birds and animals
And be just like a butterfly,
Flying this way and that way
And twisting around and around.

I wish I lived all around the world,
With all my friends
Be around the world at once
And be just like a traveller
And travel all around the world,
To see all the sites and places.

I wish I lived in a dream world,
With wild and funky imagination
And wondering thoughts flowing through the air,
With unicorns and living objects and weird dreams
That you could dream
And be infinite like all your dreams.
And whatever you do, don't stop dreaming!

Jaini Mandoda (11)
Stratford School, Forest Gate

Magic Box

(Based on 'Magic Box' by Kit Wright)

I will put in the box . . .
A bomb with a thundering night,
An egg coming out of a seagull's head,
Make it like a whisper in your ear.

I will put in the box . . .
A particle of air,
Also a snowman
And a sip of turquoise water
And ice the colour of a golden car,

I will put in the box . . .
An egg coming out of a bird's head
And a golden piece of the sun in my hand,
A dark blue body in the sea,
A blank piece of face.

My box will be made of a star's sparkle
And the sun's hotness
And the best sense of humour and
Invincibility.

I will play football with my ox,
I will surf in my box,
I will go on the golden sun with my box.

Akeel Bashir
Stratford School, Forest Gate

My Dream

I wish my room would be bright blue like the sky,
I wish my room would be like a rainbow shining,
I wish my room would be full of happiness,
I wish my room would shine like the yellow sun,
I wish my room would be as quiet as a mouse,
I wish I could drive a silver Mercedes in my room.

Neelam Yaqub (11)
Stratford School, Forest Gate

The Magic Box

(Based on 'Magic Box' by Kit Wright)

I will put in the box . . .
The first ringing bells of Christmas,
Promising hope and joy,
The warm tingling glow of the first rays of sun,
Hard-worn feet, sifting through soft piles of sand.

I will put in the box . . .
A sip of fresh water in times of thirst,
A great gushing waterfall, triumphing over trembling barriers,
The electric blue sky on a tropical island.

I will put in the box . . .
The gentle touch of a mother's hand,
The magical charm of a tooth fairy's presence,
Innocence in the eyes of a child.

I will put in the box . . .
Icy tongues of ferocious fire,
The high-pitched cackle of a clumsy troll,
The sky beneath the Earth and the Earth above the sky,
A predator mouse stalking its lion prey.

My box is designed from all the gems of the natural world,
It is layered with whispers and secrets,
Interwoven with memories.

I will place my box,
In the rays of the sun,
To fulfil the magic,
That has already begun.

Zarmala Naeem (10)
Stratford School, Forest Gate

The Magic Box

(Based on 'Magic Box' by Kit Wright)

I will put in the box . . .
The sound of my favourite popstar singer,
A feather from a peacock's back,
A kiss from my mum on Valentine's Day.

I will put in the box . . .
The yellow sun at noon warming me up,
A shooting star flying in the air,
A slice of warm homemade bread.

I will put in the box . . .
The love from my parents' hearts,
A cuddle from my loved parents,
A goodbye from my mum.

I will put in the box . . .
The light shining in the sky,
A million stars racing on the clouds,
My best friend going away.

I will surf my box,
For my mum to say hi to me again,
I will take it to a land where no one will find it,
I will check it to make me feel better.

Zaklina Misurenkovaite (11)
Stratford School, Forest Gate

Unpleasant Memory

U npleasant memory stuck in my head,
N ow it doesn't budge, it's there when I go to bed,
P ain was there, in my body it buried,
L eft me there, and flipping worried,
E lation I can see in my eyes
A nd made me scared, not very wise,
S cared to death, as stiff as sticks,
A nxiously I lay, horrified out of my wits,
N othing like I ever felt before,
T eeth chatting more and more.

M emory lane - I can see,
E legantly, how I controlled me,
M oaning and shouting most of the time,
O h my gosh, I'm out of line!
R ight now I'm OK, but I still wonder,
Y is it that above my head is a rain cloud and thunder?

Rida Hisan (11)
Stratford School, Forest Gate

The One And Only

I wish I lived in a beautiful blue and cosy place,
Where it would be nice, colourful and tidy.

I wish it were colourful and cool,
Where the sun would shine as bright as gold.

I wish I were in a place where all the religions were respected
And I respected people living in my dream.

Saudi Arabia!

Zubair Kari (11)
Stratford School, Forest Gate

I Wish I Was There

I wish I was in Mauritius,
Swimming on the beach and having fun.

I wish I were in Saudi Arabia in Makkah praying Namaz
And doing Hajj and Umra under the golden dome.

I wish I could live in Dubai,
Eating laddoo and having a sunny day on the beach.

I wish I could live in Egypt
Visiting the pyramids on the desert.

Muntasir Mosafeer (12)
Stratford School, Forest Gate

Unpleasant Memory

U naware of what was going to happen,
N o worries at the beginning,
P atiently I waited,
L ulled into a false sense of security,
E xpecting a quick sharp pain,
A fter school was when it began,
S hocked about what happened,
A pprehensive for them to continue,
N ever before in my life had I been so afraid,
T rembling thoughts through my mind.

M emories of the day scare me to go back,
E nraged with fury,
M assive amounts of pain as they drilled through my tooth,
O ver at last,
R emembering that ghostly day,
Y ou were lucky you weren't there!

Sunil Varsani (11)
Stratford School, Forest Gate

Saudi Arabia

I wish I were going
To Saudi Arabia,
Because it is a
Beautiful place
And I wish I were there,
It is my dream,
I wanted to go there,
For a long time,
I love Saudi Arabia,
I wish I were there . . .

Sadain Ramjaun (11)
Stratford School, Forest Gate

Unpleasant Memory

U nfortunately I slipped, this was the start of a bad memory
N ever in my life had I felt so much pain . . .
P lunging into rock pools, I felt pain from my leg . . .
L azily limping towards me was a man, with a knife . . .
E motion was rushing through my head . . .
A bsorbing the pain I had to suffer . . .
S uddenly my leg was as stuck as the sword in the stone . . .
A fraid of the man coming towards me I started to cry,
N ot aware that my mum was coming towards me,
T errified I kept pulling at my leg but it didn't budge . . .

M iserably, I just gave up and stopped crying,
E xpecting them to put a knife in me, the man helped
me out of the rocks,
M y mum had finally come and was trying to calm me down,
O h my gosh, the nightmare was over,
R esting, I apologised to the man who helped me,
Y ear after year after year, I still have a scar!

Matthew Gwelo (11)
Stratford School, Forest Gate

The Magic Box

(Based on 'Magic Box' by Kit Wright)

I will put in my box . . .
The sound of the fans screaming their heads off,
The nervous players,
The two teams who are playing.

I will put in my box . . .
The football field,
Chelsea, the inferior team in the Premiership,
West Ham, the best team in the world.

I will put in my box . . .
The referee whistling to the players,
West Ham's players scoring the wonderful goals,
Chelsea missing the shots.

I will put in my box . . .
The whole football stadium,
The wonderful air,
The light of the stadium,
The kit of West Ham.

The box is made out of the smelly kit, grass,
The box is made out of everything about football.

I will put in my box . . .
Me (Hafeez).

Hafeez Khan (11)
Stratford School, Forest Gate

My Grandma

I dream of my grandma who is far, far away,
Standing by the dancing palms,
As she beckons me to lunch,
Of crispy pooris, spicy paneers and rice pudding.

I dream of my grandma who is far, far away,
Standing on warm golden sands,
As she caresses my hair and lulls me to sleep
And recounts stories of her childhood dreams.

I dream of my grandma who is far, far away,
Standing in the garden of flowers,
As the rain storms gather above,
As I hold her hand and look to the sky.

I dream of my grandma who is far, far away,
Now standing long, long away,
Whose pain is gone though mine remains,
As I stand alone on warm sands by the dancing palms.

I dream of my grandma who is far, far away,
Now looking down from a long, long away,
Like a bright, twinkling star in a boundless sky,
Radiantly beautiful and winking knowingly.

I dream of my grandma who is far, far away,
Who in my heart is not far, far away,
But sitting nearby and smiling at my pranks
And waiting over me by the dancing palms.

Vishnu Pillai (11)
Stratford School, Forest Gate

My Magic Box

(Based on 'Magic Box' by Kit Wright)

In my magic box you can hear Mick Foley fall
Off the ropes onto the table at Wrestlemania.
In my magic box you can see Jeff Hardy on the turnbuckle,
Getting ready for the Swanton Bomb.
In my magic box you can feel everyone chanting,
Your name while you get ready for the spiral tap.

In my magic box you can never hold the fans' love.
In my magic box you can never have friendships because
One day you will fight each other,
In my magic box you can never have dreams
Because you have fulfilled them.

In my magic box you can get the fans to like you,
By just performing for them.
In my magic box you have Eddie Guertero's last stint before he died,
In my magic box you can have Undertaker's armpit.

In my magic box you can Fu the Deadman,
In my magic box you can tag with A J Styles,
In my magic box you can become a member of D-Generation X,
In my magic box you can become Sting's Army.

The top part of my magic box is guarded by Great Khali,
Undertaker and Kane,
Around my box it is guarded by Batista, Bobby Lashley
And Rob Van Dam.

In my magic box you can fight at only pay-per-view,
In my magic box you can fight in any type of match,
In my magic box you can make your own wrestler.

Shahal Sardar Muhammad (11)
Stratford School, Forest Gate

The Light

I can see a light,
As stunning as can be,
As pretty as the moon
And all the stars in the midnight sky,
I can see a light,
As pretty as can be,
But what can it be?

I can still see a light,
But it's coming closer and closer,
I can see a light,
That I thought was so stunning,
But now I can see it up close and it's a black sphere,
With the sides glimmering,
But what can it be?

I can see a light,
As horrid as can be,
As horrid as a sea filled with gallons of blood
And I can feel a dreadful chill going down my spine
And I ask myself,
Is this the end?

Agim Zekaj (11)
Stratford School, Forest Gate

Me And My Bizarre Box

(Based on 'Magic Box' by Kit Wright)

In my box I will put 10 unknown languages,
The first and last word spoken in the world,
The 1000th joke from a wise man
And one billion new words.

In my box I will put a fragile elephant,
A hot and cold newspaper,
Someone crying from a broken heart on top of a crushed ant
And a microscopic meteor made of French cheese.

In my box I will put an orange floating hippopotamus in a beaming star,
Pictures showing dolphins invading Earth,
A lilac sky with dozens of moons
And a spectacular display of fireworks
With multicoloured dodos talking in the atmosphere.

My box is made out of 60 luminous bulbs in each corner,
1904 of the most rarest ruby diamonds,
Lime green coconut, rough, hairy skins
And 47 stains of reptiles DNA.

Extraordinary things I can do
And I guarantee it's true.

Vineeth Vijayakumar (11)
Stratford School, Forest Gate

The Box Of Life

(Based on 'Magic Box' by Kit Wright)

I will put in my box
The sound of breathing for people about to die,
The sensation of joy for whom has been saved from death,
The feeling that you get when you've done well for someone.

I will put in my box,
All the anti-venom in the world,
All the best doctors for people that need
Spare organs that I can use to save people.

I will put in the box,
Loads of last wishes,
The best joke in the world
And a touch that brings life.

I will put in the box
Long life for the elderly,
Strength and power
And I will put in my box money for operations.

My box is made of diamonds,
With rubies and a sapphire in the middle
And a lock that is voice activated.

I shall share my box,
Travel around the world on it,
Then pass it on to my son when
I run out of life.

Mark Akhtar Masih (12)
Stratford School, Forest Gate

Magic Box

(Based on 'Magic Box' by Kit Wright)

I will put in the box . . .

The hum of an engine in the old car,
Flaming hot fire from the exhaust of the dinosaur's tail,
The hand touching the silky grass.

I will put in the box . . .

An ancient erupting volcano with flaming red lava,
A sip of the milky clouds,
A kiss from the hot boiling sun.

I will put in the box . . .

Three miracle things about my friends.

I will put in the box . . .

A car top of a mini ant,
A turquoise moon,
The world.

My box is too good to look at and too powerful
To look at, it is made with real gold.

I will put everything in the world in my beautiful incredible box.

Jayed Ali (12)
Stratford School, Forest Gate

The Magic Box

(Based on 'Magic Box' by Kit Wright)

I will put in the box . . .

Sounds of Christmas bells that are shiny red
And silver in a cold winter night, I can feel the strong wind,
I can see the dragon's cold breath.

I will put in the box . . .
A snowman dancing in the winter, and a rush of ice water
Falling in my hands, ice-cold ice melting in my hands.

I will put in there, a picture of my big family,
My sister helping me with my homework
And my brother not annoying me.

I will put in the box . . .
My brother not annoying me, my friends being nice,
Always someone making breakfast for me,
Me having love and care.

My box is made from ice-white candyfloss,
The same as well for the blue and red shiny fake candyfloss
Hinges blue and red across.

I shall drive a flying car in my box
On a great flying Mercedes Benz on a big enormous
Huge, long roller coaster on a sunny shiny blue beach
Like the sky on a shiny yellow, sunny day.

Ahmed Jamea (12)
Stratford School, Forest Gate

The Magic Box

(Based on 'Magic Box' by Kit Wright)

I will put in my box . . .

The deafening roar of a lion in a safari jungle,
The laugh of a gentle monkey,
The touch of the elephant's trunk.

I will put in my box . . .

A dynamic human brain from the one above,
A warm fresh bright sun,
A soundwave from my teacher.

I will put in my box . . .
A kind lady helping others,
The respectful old man I see every day,
The honest child I play with.

I will put in my box . . .

My dad kissing a tree,
My mum licking a dog.

My box is designed from a silk burgundy dragon,
With chocolate on the lid and metallic books in the corners,
Its hinges are made from robots.

I shall ride in my box,
To the stars above in my everlasting rocket,
Then to the moon
And say hello to the magnificent aliens.

Saffron Browne (11)
Stratford School, Forest Gate

The Magic Box

(Based on 'Magic Box' by Kit Wright)

I will put in the box . . .

A bang of the most exotic colours exploding
In the pitch-black night,
The first pure snowflake of ice-white winter,
An emotional hug from a newborn baby.

I will put in the box . . .

Every colour of the world from top to bottom,
A high spark of lightning lighting the sky,
A ray of shine shining on the peaceful world.

I will put in the box . . .

The imagination of a young girl,
A whisper of a young boy,
A cry of a woman with great pain.

I will put in my box . . .

A huge white tooth of a Chinese dragon,
A flying boy who never grows up,
A magic train which goes to the past.

My box is fashioned from pure diamonds
With sapphires and rubies.

I shall fly with my box,
Where everything is made with dark smooth chocolate,
Then to the great blue seas,
The colour of the sky.

Sahar Pathan (12)
Stratford School, Forest Gate

Unpleasant Memory

U nder the van I hid,
N ervously shaking as I witnessed,
P ainful slaughter of people in my village,
L uckily the bad men did not find me,
E ven though my mum was not there,
A s she had left me and my
S ister and brother,
A lone in Rwanda,
N ever told anyone what I saw,
T errified and tired, I slept in the class

M y mum sent a letter to all of us from
E ngland,
M any tears I had cried,
O pening the door, I shook as I saw my mum,
R emembering my village,
Y ou will never know how I feel!

Afusa Makabarisa (11)
Stratford School, Forest Gate

Unpleasant Memory

U npleasant, scared, worried,
N ervous, what will they do?
P ain rushing to my head,
L oud, everyone worried,
E ager to get out of hospital,
A ccident very bad,
S hocked parents,
A ngry, why did I put my finger in the door?
N ervous, will they cut off my finger?
T errified will they cut off my finger?

M um scared
E motional, a very emotional moment,
M y finger got stuck in the door,
O bviously I am going to cry,
R unning out of time,
Y ou saw it didn't you?

Asiya Mallu (11)
Stratford School, Forest Gate

Unpleasant Memory

U ndisturbed in the park,
N ew experiences showered upon us,
P layfully frolicked in the haven of excitement,
L earning devastated us,
E cstatic experiences dominated us,
A whole park to explore,
S urprised at the size of it,
A tmosphere was intensely rewarding,
N ext thing I knew,
T rapped my foot on the roundabout!

M y precious foot got out in the end,
E xhilarated for me to be in one piece,
M emory will haunt me forever,
O ppression overcame me that day,
R roundabouts are quite good fun,
Y et my fate was different.

Sikandar Rana (11)
Stratford School, Forest Gate

Unpleasant Memory

U nreal speed,
N ew bike flying like a lunatic,
P eople dash out of the way,
L osing control,
E very time I rode faster,
A huge needle was in the way,
S mashing my head on the concrete in
A dramatic way,
N othing I felt, blocked out,
T otal silence.

M oving, twitching,
E mergency said the stranger,
M um did not know,
O h no! luckily the stranger saved me,
R ushed to hospital,
Y elping in pain they stitched me up.

Ishan Rajpal (12)
Stratford School, Forest Gate

My First Words Were Waves

My first few words came out in waves,
Slow, calm and uncertain,
Then evolved from words to sentences,
Like waves turning to tides,
Later they began crashing on rocks,
Fast, truthful and powerful,
These words came from my mother,
My first tongue and I found it was easy
To express myself,
Then I had to leave them behind with little knowledge,
Leave that ocean behind,
To arrive and discover a second tongue,
A new country, a new language, a new sea,
The unknown waters turn to tsunamis,
Deafening roar, gushing water,
Drowning my mother's tongue and I go with it,
Flowing new words, a new language,
A new communication, a new sea,
It took time to adapt to this cold bitter pool,
But then it warmed up considerably,
To shower me with new letters,
New words, new sentences
And now I can pour out my emotions,
The new sea engulfed my old one, enchanted,
Filled with knowledge so both languages are treated equally,
But I only belong to one so, this is now what now makes me up,
2 languages, 2 ways of communication,
One public, one private, passing me through life,
My new sea, my new tongue, my new world.

Atika Malik (14)
Stratford School, Forest Gate

My Fantastic Unnatural Box

(Based on 'Magic Box' by Kit Wright)

I will put in the box . . .

The swish and swoosh of the wind on a full moon,
The first fire from the sun in the desert,
The roughness of a hard sandpaper.

I will put in the box . . .

The coldness of winter,
A burning leaf,
The air in a tiger's mouth.

I will put in the box . . .

The cuteness of my cousin,
The love of my parents,
The smartness of my friend.

I will put in the box . . .

An alien from a leaf,
Food from the sky,
Bones that are burned,
The monsters from my game.

My box is formed from diamonds that are on the edges,
The texture is made from dinosaur's skin,
The lock is solid gold.

I shall find something which was never found in the world
At the tip of space.

Nathaniel Lukwago (11)
Stratford School, Forest Gate

Unpleasant Memory

U nexpectedly I went to India to get some medicine that was poxy,
N asty dry skin grew on my face,
P lethora of planes hoisted off from the airport,
L ots of shoes, when I got there I brought,
E ventually we arrived at the doctor's house,
A pprehensively I moved motionly as I saw a mouse,
S cared stiff as I sat on the chair,
A nxiously I let the doctor examine my face but he
messed up my hair,
N ow the doctor said it was going to go,
'T here' said my dad, 'I told you so.'

M edicine made me sick,
E xpected it to go in a tick,
M y mum said I had to put the cream on and sit in the sun,
O nly one thing can wind me up and that was the sun,
R age flew through my body and I had to do it every day,
Y elling out hip hip hooray as a few months later my
dry skin went away.

Dhara Patel (11)
Stratford School, Forest Gate

Unpleasant Memory

U nhappy, I got in the car and went to the hospital,
N ervously I walked into the hospital,
P ersonally petrified to have my 6 teeth taken out,
L ongingly I wished I could go back home,
E ver so quickly,
A ngrily in a sort of way, I lay on the hospital's creaky bed,
S hort silly nurses coming in and out,
A nother short nurse came to my bed,
N ow as the time to have my teeth taken out,
T errifying and terrible experience for me.

M etal instrument pulled my teeth out one by one, ouch,
E agerly I lay on the bed painfully,
M uch more blood was dripping from my mouth,
O pen mouthed like a fish I thought of my warm bed at home,
R eally relieved to have it all over,
Y et I still couldn't eat properly for another 3 weeks!

Abdullah Patel (11)
Stratford School, Forest Gate

Unpleasant Memory

U npleasant memory
N ervous as I walked to the hospital,
P etrified and in pain,
L azy doctors took so long,
E ye injury, that's what it was,
A ngry at what had happened,
S adly I had to have an operation on my eye,
A wful it was *awful!*
N ever thought this would happen,
T rapped in the room for what I thought was forever.

M ore pain started to come,
E xcited to return home and receive gifts,
M issing all my computer games already,
O ver now,
R unning towards my house,
Y es! At last I'm home!

Irfan Patel (11)
Stratford School, Forest Gate

Unpleasant Memory

U npleasant memory I have of when I was 11 years old,
N ervously waiting in the waiting room,
P eople walking in and out, making me feel dizzy,
L ost in scary thoughts of the razor-sharp needle
lowering into my arm,
E rupting in my brain,
A nxious and annoyed,
S weating with fear,
A t last I am called by the nurse,
N othing prepared me for this,
T railing down the corridor and into the room I went.

M urmuring internally as the nurse reaches for the
needle then starts to lower it into my arm,
E xcruciating pain made its way though my left arm,
M ore pain, awful pain, terrible pain but so relieved because it was
O ver
R emembering this unpleasant memory still brings me pain,
Y ou are very lucky, you did not suffer what I did that day, trust me!

Tessa Boakyewaa (12)
Stratford School, Forest Gate

Unpleasant Memory

U npleasant
N ever-ending
P ainfully I was
L ifted on the lime-green seat
E veryone looking towards me like I was about to die!
A metal instrument was entering my mouth.
S urprisingly, I wasn't nervous
A moment of shock scared me as I was
N early about to cry, when
T he water gushed into my mouth

M y memory jogged, I remembered all the bad things
that had happened
E motionally I cried
M y mum told me I would be all right
O h my God, the doctor pulled with force
R eady to experience pain
Y uk! There was blood in my mouth, the doctor had just forced
my molar out.

Zuber Patel (11)
Stratford School, Forest Gate

Unpleasant Memory

U nfortunately it was me,
N ot my two brothers, it was me,
P erhaps I should have moved cautiously,
L ullingly I was out,
E xhausted for the count,
A nxiously I waited,
S econds later I awoke,
A lthough I looked dead,
N obley I stood tall,
T auntingly, my brothers acted foolish.

M oments later my dad arrived,
E nduring the thought of my black out,
M y brothers fled,
O n time for bed,
R eassured I was back,
Y ours truly was back.

Ansarillah McHugh (12)
Stratford School, Forest Gate

Unpleasant Memory

U nder control,
N ow I had got my bike back, I was
P leased, very pleased that my bike was back,
L ee my next door neighbour,
E very time he wanted to have a bike race
A nd today was a day to race,
S unshine, beautiful day,
A lice his sister, had to go with Lee,
N ext, what happened is,
T hat I had my bike and he had to go.

M y god I said,
E very time this has to happen to
M e, I was so angry I didn't talk to him,
O n the other side, I had no sky I was
R eally angry you should have seen me,
Y eah he came back and we had a race, I won!

Izhan Malik (11)
Stratford School, Forest Gate

Morning Madness

The alarm's ringing,
I'm too sleepy,
I switch it on to snooze.

My mum is up,
My brother's snoring,
My dad's watching the news.

Five minutes later,
The alarm goes again,
I force myself to get up.

I go downstairs,
I make some toast,
Pour coffee in my cup.

I take a shower,
Put my uniform on,
Ladder three pairs of tights.

Turn on the telly,
There's a woman complaining,
Her and her husband have too many fights.

I pack my books,
Forget my lunch
And speed out of our front gate.

Run into school,
Race up to form,
Thank goodness I wasn't late!

Rachel Naylor (14)
The Chafford School, Rainham

My Life Of Fishing

When I am carping,
I feel the movement,
Of the carp tail patterns on the surface,
A carp is big and bold,
Dark and light,
With a big mouth,
Taking in the surface baits,
Like dog biscuits,
Or a piece of bread flake,
On the hook or spod,
Some bait into the lake,
Wait for a few minutes,
Bib, bib, bib,
My bait alarm strikes,
If one gets caught,
Running away from me,
Into a weed bed,
Turning around and splashing in the water,
An orange colour.

He's on the top flapping,
Splashing,
Slapping,
In goes my landing net
And he comes to me,
Swirling.

Luke Smart (13)
The Gateway Academy, Grays

Detention

Oh no not another one of those days,
Of sitting there after school,
Watching everyone leave but me,
I know what's to come,
It's my fourth one this week,
I tell you what I have to do,
Well it's not fun,
You sit there,
Writing a thousand words,
On how I got a detention.
The second day I had to pick off all the gum from under the table,
'Yuck,'
Then by the third day I was about to give up,
I trudged along to class 9D2,
Thinking of what I had to do,
I arrive and the teacher screams at me,
'What are you late?'
It cuts right through me like the cold wind's blow,
I sit down with sweat rolling off my face,
'Cracker,'
She said, 'Come up here and take the board erasers,
Bang them until every last bit of chalk dust has gone.'
I thought that the terror would never end,
But after an hour and a half,
It was all over,
The next day it was the last one to do,
I went to the class 9D2,
Where the teacher was ill,
The happiness ran,
Though my blood and in my head.

Connie Faraway (13)
The Gateway Academy, Grays

Teenage Love Poem

When you think you love someone,
Or have a crush on a friend,
It's only when you get to know them,
You let your heart bend.

You keep your feelings deep inside,
Until they feel the same,
These emotions confuse your mind,
But your love for them keeps you sane.

Love is difficult and confusing,
It can go either way,
When you love that person more than anyone,
It grows stronger day by day.

You realise the hardest thing is rejection,
That loving is the easy part,
Do they feel the same as you?
Will they accept the key to your heart?

When the day comes to face the music,
You start to doubt how you feel,
But the time has come to learn the truth,
Like cards you have to deal.

You made the first move, you went and dealt,
They turned you down; you now look to the sky,
Has this hard work and heartache been worth it
Because now all you want to do is curl up and die.

Peter Wright (13)
The Gateway Academy, Grays

Best Friends

Best friends are there for you when you are down,
Best friends will always be around,
In the rain and sun
And the blazing snow,
They will always be by your side.

They are someone you can tell your secrets to,
They are someone you can laugh and cry with,
They are someone you can trust.

You go through things together,
You will have your ups and downs,
What matters most through all of this,
To keep your friendship living,
Is being able to forgive and forget.

If you ever disrespect them,
Your friendship will be gone.

Amy Richards (12)
The Gateway Academy, Grays

Feeling Poem

At school or at home,
Or even when you're on your own,
You can feel happy or sad,
Or you can feel excited and glad,
You can feel upset and nervous,
Or you can feel worried and scared,
How do you feel?

You can feel sad and depressed,
Or you can feel bad and stressed,
You could feel joy or fear,
When that special someone is very near,
How do you feel?

Chantal Dilaimi (12)
The Gateway Academy, Grays

Midnight Blue

Midnight blue, midnight sky,
The stars are shining nice and bright,
For the whole world to see tonight,
The moon is also shining bright,
So don't be scared there's always a light,
That's always there for you to see all night,
Oh what a wonderful night it is,
Yes, it's wonderful indeed.

Angela Karuri (12)
The Gateway Academy, Grays

Winter

Winter is always dark and cold,
It always says as it's told,
Snow falls from the sky,
As days pass by,
Trees start to lose their leaves,
Like thieves have taken them.

The mornings are dark,
As the morning dogs bark,
The sun rarely shines,
As days go past in straight lines,
From morning to night,
The dark clouds come into sight.

People start to freeze,
From the cold breeze,
There is sleet on the ground,
Cars screech across the road with a sound,
Windows become cold and wet,
But not as cold as ice yet.

Winter is forever cold and there's no changing it.

Donaldson Daniel (13)
The Gateway Academy, Grays

School

School, school,
5 days a week,
15 different subjects,
All different teachers,
Some kind, some not so kind,
At lunch you can hear people shouting,
Running,
You feel like you are at a zoo with a herd of elephants,
My favourite subject is PE, lots of sport,
The changing rooms smell of sweaty bodies,
The only subject I don't enjoy is science,
There are people whose jobs are to annoy,
The best part of the day is home time and
That's where I am going now.

Phoebe Pearson (11)
The Gateway Academy, Grays

Real Friends

R eal friends are there for you when you need them,
E very day, every moment, every hour of the week,
A real friend will stick up for you,
L oving your friends is not wrong because the love
that you give to your friends is not the same love
that you give to your parents.

F riends are who you spend most of your time with,
R elationships with your friend is a part of life,
I n your school when you're not well, they will
always be beside you,
E very day, every moment, every hour of the week,
N ever feel lonely, never feel sad, never feel doubtful
and never feel bad,
D isappointed or in despair, your friends will always be there,
S omeone will always be there for you when you're
down and low, they'll always come and say hello.

Tajkiya Sultana (12)
The Gateway Academy, Grays

London City

Women's boutiques,
Graffiti smothered walls,
Flower filled gardens,
That is life in London City.

Fatty food restaurants,
Cars honking their horns,
Market sellers shouting in your ears,
That is life in London City.

Big Ben ringing,
Queues outside the museum,
Deafening music coming from all the clubs,
That is life in London City.

The changing of the guards,
The black cabs gliding along the road,
The homeless begging on the streets,
That is life in London City.

Sophie Austin (12)
The Gateway Academy, Grays

The Mystery Of My Sister's School Photo

I moved my sister's photo,
From on top of the TV,
The reason that I did this is,
Because she's uglier than me.

I have not decided,
Where I'm going to put it yet,
My dad's wardrobe is possible,
But so is the downstairs loo.

That will teach her not to
Borrow all my stuff and
She will stay off my case.

When you are eating your dinner,
You look up on the TV,
It puts you off your egg and chips,
Just looking at her face.

Lewis Brunger (11)
The Gateway Academy, Grays

Teenage Years!

Big dreams - stupid fights,
Sleep dreams - endless nights.

Broken hearts - mascara tears,
Cell phone bills - report card fears

Clothes too tight - shoes so high,
Out past curfew - another lie.

Eyeshadow colour - midnight blue,
Lipgloss flavour - cherry attack.

Belts with stars - boys with cars,
We're from Venus - they're from Mars.

That's not all, there's much more to hear,
Just a taste of
Teenage years.

Amber Scavolo (12)
The Gateway Academy, Grays

When I Came First

One day I got up on stage and danced the dance of Ireland,
Then after a minute I was finished,
I walked to the back and waited a few seconds
And then me and my friend bowed,
We walked off professionally.

After other dancers had danced,
It was then when everyone was scared,
It came down to the last three people,
Me and two other girls from other dancing schools,
One of the girl's names was called out,
I was getting more and more scared,
But in another way excited,
Then came the moment,
They announced second place
And it wasn't me,
I was so pleased I had won,
It was my very first time,
It was wonderful,
Everyone was pleased,
Especially my dancing teachers and my parents.

Cody Flynn (12)
The Gateway Academy, Grays

Buddy Poem

How does it feel to have your heart torn apart?
Your mum and your dad didn't get on from the start,
You cry yourself to sleep after hearing the fight,
You hope it was a dream that you had that night,
You wake up the next morning feeling so sad,
You go down the stairs and your dad's looking bad,
Your dad looks at you, you look back,
You just want to give him one almighty smack!

Gemma Ring (12)
The Gateway Academy, Grays

My Nan!

My nan is special, wonderful and kind,
She has a good spirit
And a lively mind,
She is always happy,
Which I love,
But now she is happier up above.

My nan was a cool nan,
She went to bingo a lot,
Once she actually won,
The first prize jackpot.

My nan used to go on a shopping spree,
It was only Friday that would make her pleased,
She used to go with my aunty,
When I was at school,
But when I haven't got to go to school,
It was also me.

I used to see her on Saturdays,
I used to do her make-up and
Massage her feet,
It was good when she was here,
But now her illness has appeared.

I miss her smile,
I miss her perfume,
I miss the way she laughs,
The only thing I am pleased,
For her is the pain has finally gone!

I get sad when I talk about her,
But know she is there watching me,
Making sure I am safe and happy,
Being good at school.

Alana Day (11)
The Gateway Academy, Grays

When The Baby Came

One day when I was watching the TV,
The phone rang,
Ring, ring,
I answered it, 'Hello,' I said,
'Is Mummy there Shannon? It's aunty Hazel,'
'Yes,' I said then, came my mum,
she started to smile,
'What's happened?' I said,
'It's here, the baby is here,'
'What has she been called?'
'Lyleigh,' my mum said.

Now 4 months later,
She's more beautiful than ever,
She has the sweetest smile,
You have ever seen,
She has the softest skin,
You could ever feel.

Shannon Girling (11)
The Gateway Academy, Grays

Secondary School

School is so difficult,
We have so many different subjects,
The hardest thing is having loads of homework,
Some of the teachers are absolutely crazy
And some of the teachers are caring.

It's hard remembering the way about
And it is a lot stricter,
When we are out in the playground,
It is like I am at a football match
And a team has just scored,
We have to bring loads of equipment and I normally forget it,
When we have PE, it smells of sweaty feet and different deodorants.

The dance in this school is very difficult,
It is fast, energetic and makes you sweat,
The drama club is after school and we are
Rehearsing for a Christmas show,
When we have to line up for lunch and break,
Sometimes you have to wait ages to get your dinner,
It drives me round the bend,
It is so manic.

Loren Stacey Dixon (11)
The Gateway Academy, Grays

The Mountain

The mountain is over 400 ft tall,
The mountain is frosty as a piece of meat in a fridge,
The mountain is beautiful,
The mountain has consumed lots of people
While trying to climb the rocky hill,
The mountain has a snowy peak,
The mountain has made loads of people famous,
The mountain is the tallest in the world,
The mountain lights up the dark sky,
The mountain has a dark and gloomy outline in the night sky,
I will go 500 miles just to see the mountain,
The mountain is Mount Everest.

Daryl Gill (11)
The Gateway Academy, Grays

My Cousin

My cousin, she is the funniest child,
I have ever met,
She comes out with nonsense,
She could make you laugh all day,
She comes out with stuff,
But it's like I understand her,
Her name is Siobhan,
She is Turkish,
She's only just turned 3,
She makes weird noises
And she dances around the room,
Once when we had slow music on,
She got up and said 'Ria'
And I looked at her and she said,
'Would you like to dance?'
That's why I love her to bits.

Ria Whiffen (12)
The Gateway Academy, Grays

The Last Time I Saw My Nan

The last time I saw my nan
Was when she kissed me on the cheek
And said, 'I love you,'
The last time I saw my nan
Was when she said, 'Goodbye'
And waved at me with joy,
The last time I saw my nan
Was when she said, 'See you tomorrow!'
She gave me a little sweet.

That's the last time I saw my nan.

The last time I saw my nan,
Was when she laughed with joy,
She said that I was funny,
The last time I saw my nan
Was when she came to my ninth birthday
And she gave me £10,
The last time I saw my nan,
Was when she ate my cake,
With chocolate all around her face.

That's the last time I saw my nan.

The last time I saw my nan,
Was when she was sitting on her chair,
Unable to move.

The last time I saw my nan,
Was when she was in the ambulance,
Suffering from a heart attack.

The last time I saw my nan,
Was when she was on the hospital bed,
Crying from disappointment.

That's the last I saw of my nan.

Sabian Godber (12)
The Gateway Academy, Grays

The Beach

As I go to the beach
The waves come crashing to the sand
Whirling higher and higher each time
The cold breeze goes right through my spine
Making me shiver every time
Making me go the colour of the sea
As I go to the beach
The waves come crashing to the sand
Whirling higher and higher each time
You look at the sea
It makes you feel calm
You feel the soft, silky sand going through your feet
As I go to the beach
The waves come crashing to the sand
Whirling higher each time
The smell oozes through my nose
The smell of salt
The sound of the waves
As I leave the beach
The sun begins to set
The day fades
I have loads of memories
Of what I just did
The day is over
But I am still going
We all get in the car
The engine starts
Brmm brmm
We're on our way home.

Nikki Turner (13)
The Gateway Academy, Grays

My Birthday

My birthday is always trouble,
It was three days after Christmas,
First present I ever had was
A spotty tricycle,
My second birthday,
I got a Ladybird baby
And a Ladybird buggy,
My third birthday,
I got a Barbie scooter
And a pair of slippers,
My fourth birthday,
I started to know a lot more,
So I got a 10-pound note,
My fifth birthday,
I got a party
And a box of Polly Pockets,
My sixth birthday,
Got a box of sweets
And a bike with extra wheels,
My seventh birthday,
I got a pair of skates
And a box of make-up,
My ninth birthday,
My mum got me,
A box of Barbies,
'Mum, too old,'
My tenth birthday,
I was given 20 pounds
And another box of make-up.

Kezlee Nairn (11)
The Gateway Academy, Grays

Young Writers Information

We hope you have enjoyed reading this book - and that you will continue to enjoy it in the coming years.

If you like reading and writing poetry drop us a line, or give us a call, and we'll send you a free information pack.

Alternatively if you would like to order further copies of this book or any of our other titles, then please give us a call or log onto our website at www.youngwriters.co.uk

Young Writers Information
Remus House
Coltsfoot Drive
Peterborough
PE2 9JX

(01733) 890066

When he shall die,
Take him and cut him out in little stars.
And he will make the face of heaven so fine.
That all the world will love with the night
And pay no worship to the garish sun

William Shakespeare

This book is dedicated to all the wonderful people
that touched and enriched Chris's life.
You know who you are.

Walk of Life

A Tribute to a " Remarkable" Son

by Mike Barratt

Special thanks to Rick Bower,
for his support of me over many years,
and for proof- reading this book
and providing many suggestions
for improvement.

Written by Mike Barratt © 2002
Edited by Karen J. Riffel
Published by Tree High Enterprises 2002
Castlebrook, Corndon Drive, Montgomery, Powys SY15 6RE
Printed by Y Lolfa, Talybont, Ceredigion SY24 5AP

ISBN 1-903937-02-7

If you wish to raise any issues or have any questions relating to this book, please contact the author, by e-mail, at **WalkContact@hotmail.com**

Preface

I was prompted to write this book after Chris's passing when I read the words that many people wrote to Annette and I which described him in terms that left us very much in awe of him. They described a side of Chris that we had not really seen. People kept asking us about Chris's various activities and it occurred to me that I wanted to capture all the tremendous and happy things we had done together and if possible some of his magic and humour. This was helped by the various stories and memories that his friends shared with us. One of those friends when trying to describe him was stuck for words and said simply, "Well ... he was just a star". In short he was wonderful, he was a *star*, and I hope that the following words go a little way to capturing at least some of that. I hope that I am up to the task of capturing some of the magic. At the very least they will provide Annette and I a book of memories.

This book is also a tribute to all the wonderful people that we came into contact with, those people that provided Chris, Annette and I with such marvellous and loving support - Chris's friends and now hopefully ours as well. This story is as much about those wonderful people as it is about Chris.

Producing lists is always fraught with danger, the danger of missing names and offending people, so if I have missed anyone I apologise. If Chris had written this list everyone who should be on it would have got a mention. So to Chris and Anne Bolton, Bob and Sandra Gerrard, Sharon and Billy Carrington, Norma and Dave Hellon, Josie Harpley, David Riffel, Pauline Evans and Jan Langley; Ian Shingler, Lorraine Churchman, Pauline Sallis, Di Brown, Chris Karling, Karen Flynn, Philip Kidman, Ceris Owen, Carol Watson, Frances Reeve, Pam Dowd, Andy Howie (at Dorin Park); Yvonne Bohdanowicz, Peter & Sue Herbert, Katie Gerrard, Melanie Carrington, Daniel Tyledsey Wain, Kirsty Bridge; Alex, Alyson, Anne, Annie, Kim, Lesley, Mary (all at Hope House); Kate Fox, Sarah Kelly, Jenny Whitall (at the NMC); Dr. John Gibbs, Dr. Ros Quinlivan, Sister Jenny Jones and Mrs Lorraine Mellor I thank you.

Finally, thanks to Joan Barratt (Nana), John and Julie Tilston, Paul Tilston, Clair Tilston and of course Annette's mum Dot, who we sadly miss.

When I hear his name again,
It makes me want to smile,
Remembering those moments,
When our paths crossed for a while.

Walk of life - CONTENTS

CHAPTER ONE (Beginnings)

Likely as not, the child you can do the least with will do the most to make you proud.

Mignon McLaughlin

Tuesday 9th January 1990 began differently to most mornings, for this was the day that Chris was to start 'proper' school, on a road that his Mum and I were sure would build on the very promising early signs and lead to a fulfilling education and life. The morning's preparations were well underway; up, washed and breakfasted, new school uniform on and shoes clean and shiny. Then the phone rang. "It'll be Nana to wish you luck," said my wife, Annette. I picked up the phone; sure enough it was Nana, but not with the message we expected. My Auntie Con had died.

The original plan was for me to go to work and for Annette to take Chris to school. We stuck to the second part of this, but I went off to express my condolences to Uncle Bert, an uncle who I had a great deal of time for, and who lived across the road from my mother and late father.

Annette duly delivered Chris to Dee Point School, into the class of Mrs Lorraine Mellor. Now Mrs. Mellor was a teacher of the 'old school', who on first sight was a formidable character, but who believed in good discipline, good time and an urgency for pupils to learn to read. Mrs Mellor's class was quite large and it was into this environment that Chris was launched. He'd never had any problems with going to Nursery School and likewise he had no problems with beginning school on that first day. He quickly established friends, many he kept over the forthcoming years; many, Melanie, Laura, Vicky, Helen being girls!

The day passed slowly for my wife, before she was able to go, with a degree of apprehension to see how things had gone, and collect Chris. Annette, like the other mothers, waited outside the school building before the doors were opened and they were invited in to collect their respective offspring. Annette searched the room for Chris, but before she could locate him Mrs. Mellor intercepted her.

"Is there anything wrong with your son?" Mrs Mellor enquired.

"No!" replied Annette, with a high degree of resentment.

"Well, he doesn't walk properly," persisted Mrs Mellor, adding, "He walks on his toes." Now Annette and I had not noticed this, indeed Chris had first walked just after his first birthday and used that ability a great deal.

"I've not noticed that," sighed my wife, upset that the teacher should be critical of our pride and joy.

"Has Christopher had his pre-school medical?" Mrs Mellor asked.

"Not yet," replied my wife, "he's not been called for one yet."

A month later we got an appointment through to see the School Doctor, Dr. Jayaram, a softly spoken lady who Chris liked immediately. She ran through a series of tests, covering amongst other things sight, hearing and dexterity. Having completed her tests Dr. Jayaram considered for a moment and then said that she thought Chris had a minor co-ordination problem and that she would like to refer Chris to her boss, Consultant Paediatrician Dr Bron Robinson, if we were happy to do so. Needless to say, we asked her to do so. A while later we received an appointment to attend Dr. Robinson's clinic, in early May, at the Countess of Chester Hospital. This appointment was to be the first of many that Chris, Annette and I would attend over the coming years. Dr. Robinson was a New Zealander by birth, a lady with grey hair and glasses, who you would easily mistake for your Grandmother or Great Aunt. She had a very gentle manner, but one which gave a great deal of confidence. Having introduced herself to Chris and then to us, she set about running through a similar set of tests to that which Chris had already undertaken. Patience was never one of Chris's virtues and he quickly became bored, wanting to get on to the next test and ideally get away altogether. Dr. Robinson persevered, gently cajoling Chris through the tests. Eventually, she announced that she was in agreement with Dr. Jayaram; Chris did have a slight co-ordination problem, that he should be referred to an Occupational Therapist, and "oh, could she just take a blood test?"

This didn't unduly alarm Annette and I, but Chris was not happy, not happy at all. You see, Chris and needles did not go well together. His dislike, bordering on hatred, stemmed from the early hurt caused by inoculations etc. every child has to endure. Through a concerted team effort by Annette, the clinic nurse, Dr. Robinson, and myself sufficient blood for a test was extracted from a less than willing arm. We were given an appointment for Dr. Robinson's clinic the following month.

However, about ten days after this first clinic Annette received a phone call at home from Dr Robinson's secretary, asking for us to meet the doctor at the local Health Centre two days later. The state of relaxed calmness was shattered. There must be something wrong for us to be called back so soon. We ran through all the possibilities that we could think of, was it leukaemia?, was it cystic fibrosis?, if not what was it?

The meeting was scheduled for lunchtime, and as I'd only been working for NWS Bank for a short time, I'd gone to work. I came home, picked up Annette and then we made our way to the Health Centre. We did not speak a word, and as we got closer our apprehension rose. The Health Centre was close to Holy Trinity Church in which we had married just over 5 years earlier and was a modern design, but a building that had been attacked by the local graffiti artists. We held each other's hand as we walked in to be met by a pleasant friendly faced lady. She introduced herself as Judith Moulds, a member of the Paediatric Care Team working with Dr Robinson. We looked at one another, as our unease grew further. Judith explained that Dr Robinson would be along shortly, having been delayed at the hospital. We made small talk with difficulty, the usual things, the weather (sunny and bright), the latest local issue and so on. After about fifteen minutes, but what seemed like an eternity, Dr. Robinson dashed in, apologised for being late and invited us into a small consulting room that overlooked a small, unoccupied playground.

"Look," said Dr. Robinson, "there is no easy way to tell you this, but following the blood tests, Christopher has Muscular Dystrophy; there is no treatment and no cure."

I, like Annette, heard the words. I realised it was serious, but I didn't really comprehend what it meant. Up to that point I had not heard of Muscular Dystrophy, I had no idea what it was, no idea of what it meant. The expression on my face must have said it all, for Dr. Robinson proceeded to try to explain. The words swept over me, "genetic condition", "muscle wasting", "in a wheelchair by his late teens", and "limited life expectancy". This was too much for us, tears flooded out. Dr. Robinson and Judith did their best to console us, but what can you say in such circumstances. While many may think that Dr. Robinson was blunt, I have always been grateful for her directness. I think that if she had tried to dress up what she had to say the message would have been even more painful or, maybe worse, lost completely

It transpired that at that first clinic Dr. Jayaram had almost immediately recognised the early symptoms of Muscular Dystrophy, having recently seen another boy with the condition, and had wanted to get a second opinion with out alarming us.

Annette and I returned silently home, before falling into each other's arms and shedding even more tears. That bright future we had thought of just 4 months before now seemed to be unachievable, just shattered and lying on the floor.

We had a couple of weeks to go before we were due to go to Dr. Robinson's next clinic. It was at this clinic, during which Chris was examined further, that we first met Yvonne Bohdanowicz, a relationship that was to last for the next ten years, much to our benefit. Yvonne worked in the Paediatric Care Team and was a colleague of Judith's. She explained that Judith was on holiday and that she would be taking over Christopher's case. Later, when Chris reached the age of 10, Yvonne was supposed to hand Chris over to another social worker in the group responsible for older children however she argued that as she knew him, his requirements and the family she wanted to maintain the continuity.

We decided that we would not tell Chris, at least not in the short or medium term, of the diagnosis. However, it was very difficult to live with the knowledge. Gradually, over a few weeks our whole attitude to Chris changed. We started to wrap him up in cotton wool and let him get away with behaviour that we would never have condoned previously. After perhaps 6 - 8 weeks of this approach, Annette and I agreed that, while perhaps understandable, it was completely wrong and that we should go back to the way we were before. We acknowledged that as time went on we would have to make allowances for Chris's physical capabilities, but there was no reason why his behaviour should not be correct and pleasant, and as we reminded him "It costs nothing to say Thank You". Correcting his behaviour took a little while longer, but it was very much worth it in the long run.

Through Dr. Robinson and Yvonne we were put in touch with another local family who had a son with Duchenne Muscular Dystrophy (DMD) with a view to helping us to understand the issues that we faced. Peter and Sue Herbert, whose son was also called Peter, came to see us several times in those early months and we have remained friends ever since. Sue was at the time the local organiser for the Muscular Dystrophy Group. Their experiences and suggestions were very helpful, some preparing us for what was to come and some giving us useful information that we were able to use to our advantage. Two things that Sue said at the time stand out in my memory. She told us that we would get the most support as the years past from our friends and that family would simply, at best, acknowledge the situation. She also pointed out that in her experience most, if not all boys with DMD never asked about the condition or the situation they found themselves in. As we shall see, she was partly right.

One other conversation from those early days also stands out in my memory. Pam Dowd, a physiotherapist, based at Dorin Park said to Annette and I that throughout the coming years when we were making any decisions about Christopher's care or future we should keep in mind to "do what provides the best quality of life". That simple maxim stayed with me right to the end and was often used.

CHAPTER TWO (Crying and Crawling)

At the end of the day you're another day older.

Les Miserables

Christopher Banks Barratt was born at 00.57 am on 30th June 1985. Although he was several weeks late and the birth was induced, it was a momentous and joyous occasion. The actual delivery had gone reasonably well, although Annette had suffered, mainly from me consistently mopping her brow! The initial Apgar tests were conducted and everything was fine. We had been delivered an 8lbs 13 oz, healthy, handsome little boy, with fair hair (fortunately not ginger as mine was or Annette would have "been sending him back"). While I hadn't minded whether we had a boy or a girl, I was overjoyed it was a boy - train sets, Scalextrics, football and a continuation of the Barratt family all beckoned. Life couldn't get better than this.

Following Mum and Dad, and the Delivery team the first person to meet the new arrival was Auntie Ju. Julie Tilston, our sister-in-law, was an Auxiliary Nurse on the Maternity Ward and as chance would have it she was working that night. So, the first person to be photographed with Chris was his Auntie, it was the beginning of a close and enduring relationship.

Annette had to spend a few days in hospital recovering, but eventually she and Chris were allowed home. For one reason or another Chris was being bottle-fed. For me this was great as it meant that I could get my hands dirty, not literally, and participate in the caring process. However, within days Chris started to be sick, not much at first, but gradually more. Being new parents we were naturally concerned and arranged to see the family doctor, Dr. Kini. Following an examination of Chris, a referral to the hospital resulted, so off we went there and then. It was thought that Chris had a pyloric sphincter, an overdeveloped valve at the exit of the stomach that was not letting the food out and thus making him sick. This is apparently not uncommon in baby boys and can either quickly clear naturally or is solved by minor surgery. Chris was omitted for observation.

Within 48 hours he was home again having been diagnosed as having, not a pyloric sphincter, but a viral infection and in possession of some lovely pink medicine! Now there's a challenge, getting a two-week-old baby to take medicine. Enter a small syringe and lots of care. This was fortunately one of very few problems that we encountered as Chris grew up. All the early indications were that he was perfectly healthy.

Chris was very sharp and quickly 'found his voice'. We decided from an early time that we would speak properly to him, that is no "cudgie coo" type talk. I often had long conversations with him, telling him what I'd been doing, asking what he and his Mum had got up to, and so on. Around this time Chris had a bright yellow reclining bouncy chair in which he would lie. As was often the case when I came in from work, there he was in the lounge in his chair. As usual I went in to talk to him and as was normal he would chatter responses to my questions or observations. Now Julie was in the kitchen with Annette and quietly asked, "Who's that that Mike's talking to?" thinking perhaps that I had brought someone home from work. "Oh, it's Chris," replied Annette. Julie's face was a picture, as she realised who the conversation was between.

Chris's early physical development appeared to be quite normal with him achieving the expected milestones for head control, sitting and rolling on time. By the age of 9 months he was mobile through a very effective bottom shuffle and very soon after he was able to stand. Around the same time Chris said his first words and he quickly developed a good vocabulary. Just before he was eleven months old he took his first steps by holding onto the furniture and then later using his Thomas the Tank Engine walker. Seven days after his first birthday he walked unaided for the first time, a great family milestone. The one area, looking back, where he was slower to develop was in standing up, where he tended to pull himself up on the furniture. Also he didn't climb very much, which in many ways was a blessing in disguise. But at the time they were not issues to worry about.

May 1986 saw Chris's first accident when Dad turned his back for a moment and Chris 'dived' head first out of the pram, bashing his head on the floor and cutting his scalp just above the forehead. It was quite a bad cut and the screaming brought Annette running, she thought it prudent to visit the local A & E to make sure everything was OK. Fortunately, everything was fine (although my health was in the balance for a while!) and as the cut had stopped bleeding Chris didn't need any stitches. The result was a little scar that was always just visible in his hairline.

Our first Christmas together was I'm sure very similar to that of other new parents, the front room was full of presents, ranging from clothes to toys you pushed, toys you pulled, and cuddly toys. Chris's favourite toy that year was a cuddly clown dressed in blue and red with a bell in his hat, who was christened Corky. Corky brought great fun over the next few years and despite the fact that his suit is a bit dirty and thin in some places he remained a favourite belonging and still sits in Chris's bedroom. Despite all the presents the thing that brought the greatest amount of pleasure to Chris that Christmas Day was the wrapping paper. He lay on the floor and flapped his arms about throwing the paper around, making it crinkle and generally loving every moment, smiling and chuckling all the time.

By 18 months Chris had a vocabulary of nearly 100 words. He soon mastered words such as elephant, rhinoceros and television, although he also had his own words such as leela (lights), bock (bottle) and wuzzer (washing machine). By 2 years and 4 months he could talk in sentences and his ability to have a proper conversation surprised many people, but it was that ability that was to sustain him over the following years. Needless to say we encouraged him to talk to people and maintained our insistence that people conversed properly with Chris. Through this he developed, for his age, an amazing breadth of subjects on which he could chat.

We were greatly helped in those early days by Nanny (Annette's mum) and Nana (my mum), both of whom held special places in Chris's life. Of course there was the expected task of baby sitting, but both Grandmothers added a lot to Chris's early development through their conversation, memories and interests. When Annette went back to work at County Hall on a part-time basis Chris would spend the majority of the days with Nanny, happily playing in the garden or accompanying her to the shops.

His reading of fact books (rather than storybooks) and a first class memory aided his knowledge of various subjects. I learnt at an early stage not to promise him something - you could guarantee that whatever it was would come back and 'bite' you weeks or months later! Chris also started to develop an interest in music and not only enjoyed the usual baby tunes, but quite enjoyed listening to the popular tunes of the day. From a very tender age he would sit up and take notice when the EastEnders theme came on the TV.

Chris was like many kids of his age, he was in to everything and anything, and you had to keep a wary eye on him all the time. His favourite occupation seemed to be taking his toys apart and then presenting them to you and expecting them to be reassembled. On one occasion we found that the video player wasn't working, it was impossible to get the cassettes into the machine. To the question "have you been playing with it?" you got an angelic, innocent smile and a robust denial. Having unplugged the machine and removed the cover I found two or three pens and a plastic toy inside, when challenged with the evidence I was told, without a flicker of a smile, that Corky Clown must have done it.

His fingers were always getting him into trouble. Annette worked in Data Preparation in Computer Services at County Hall and so Chris had a room full of 'aunties'. One afternoon Annette was in town and decided to take Chris, who was by now about 3½, into see the 'aunties'. He happily wandered around the room talking to the various girls at their workstations, while Annette chatted to some of the others and trying to keep an eye on him. He'd made his way back to the front of the room when suddenly there was 'Clonk' and all the machines went dead. Chris had found the 'kill' switch on the back of the main processor unit and decided to see what it did. It wasn't clear who was more shocked, Chris, Annette, Liz Jones or Evelyn Nash, the Supervisors. Fortunately, Liz and Evelyn soon had the system back up and running, without any major loss of data, by which time the youngest member of the Barratt family had exited, feet just touching the floor.

Just prior to his third birthday, in March 1988, Chris started Playschool, the Let's Pretend group run by 'Auntie' Carol Cartwright. The sessions were run on a Wednesday morning in a local Primary School, where Annette would drop him off, and initially Chris was unsure about going. After a little while he settled in and established friendships with a number of the other children, especially Peter Carr. They had very similar interests and got on very well. Through Let's Pretend Chris learnt many new things and was encouraged by Carol and her helper Elva to participate in numerous creative activities, albeit his attention span could be limited, especially where painting was concerned. His favourite activity was playing on the bikes and other wheel things in the playground. By and large Chris was well behaved at Playschool, being no more trouble than the other children. We did however have one difficult episode. Annette arrived one day to collect Chris to be met by Elva and a sullen looking Chris and a tale of biting. Chris had apparently bitten one of the girls in the class. This was a quite out of character, he had gone through a period when he was about 12 months old of biting you when you had him in your arms. But as he would tell people much later "I bit my Dad's ear once and he bit me back and I never did it again!" Annette was of course protective, asking if Elva was sure it was Chris. While no one had seen him do it, the *victim* had said it was Chris. The bite mark was apparently on the little girls' cheek and was "quite large". Chris denied it was him. At home that evening I explained to him that biting was not very nice and that good boys certainly did not do that sort of thing. I asked him again if it was him, he was adamant that it wasn't. Around this time he did have a habit of putting his arms around people and giving them a kiss. We suspected that he might have done this to his classmate and been seen, the assumption being that he'd bitten her. We made it clear to him that we would not tolerate biting. The episode was not repeated and was soon forgotten.

Chris enjoyed Let's Pretend and got on very well with Carol, the 21 months that he spent at Playschool prepared him very well for his move to Primary school. A number of the friends that he made also went to Dee Point, but Peter was to attend a different school. Even so, they stayed in contact for some time and they would visit each other to spend time playing together. The last day at Let's Pretend, in December 1989, was an emotional one and Chris and the others were sent on their way with the best wishes of Carol and Elva ringing in their ears.

Annette had left County Hall in 1989 and had started part time work as an assistant in the Pharmacy Department at the Countess of Chester hospital. It wasn't long before Chris was introduced to Annette's new colleagues and quickly became friendly with many of the staff. Whenever we went to pick up Annette, Chris would gain entry to the Pharmacy and wander round chatting to the Pharmacists, asking questions about what they were doing and why. The manager of the Pharmacy was Elizabeth Morgan and she recalled later, "I shall never forget how we all enjoyed his visits - his cheery greeting to each of us and his inspection of sinks, balances and cupboard doors!"

When Chris started school Nanny would collect him on several days and give him his tea, his favourite being Nanny's special stew. He would happily play in the garden with the next door neighbours, Nazeemah and Selena, although he would always want to be in charge organising what they did. Annette would then pick him up and they would walk the short distance to our house. Later, Chris still went for his tea, but was dropped off at Nanny's by Mrs. Burnett in her taxi. When Annette's mum moved to her bungalow, literally a stone throw across the road from her house, Chris was quick to make friends with the elderly neighbours into whose houses he would visit, returning with sweets, fruit or pocket money. One major legacy Chris learnt from Annette's mum was that of caring for other people, listening to what they said and learning from that.

From quite an early age I would take Chris to the park on a Sunday afternoon so as to give Annette a rest, but also so I could spend time with him. Initially, this would be simply a walk with Chris in the pram or pushchair, but as he got older it included sessions on the slides, roundabouts and swings. We would spend a lot of time in the park, me pushing, him swinging, but throughout chatting all the time. The topics of conversation would be many and varied, but always entertaining. To start with, when we lived in Hoole, our walks were to Alexandra Park, but later after we'd moved to Blacon, we would visit one of a number, Chris nearly always making the decision. We still drove over to Hoole, but the parks at Saughall or Sealand Road were also popular. Perhaps, the favourite though was the little park next to the Water Tower Bowling Green. This park had swings, slide and wooden climbing frame in a small grassy area and provided loads of entertainment. Chris would take turns on each of the pieces of equipment, although as time went on he needed more help with climbing. One of his favourite games was scaling the climbing frame and then with a great shout jumping off into my arms. He loved the swings as well, but would only go on the 'baby' swing, the one you sat *in* rather than *on* as he did not feel safe otherwise. But once in the swing he would have you pushing him hard with encouraging shouts of "Higher, higher". On one occasion when Annette was with us she felt that he was going too high. "That'll do, he's high enough". "No, go on Dad, higher. I've been much higher than this". "Well, you shouldn't, and your Dad should know better". So much to Chris's chagrin the pushing was moderated and was kept so whenever Mum was with us, but when she wasn't .... well space travel was a possibility!

The Water Tower Park also acted as the base for our walks. These started as a simple circuit of the Bowling Green, watching the bowlers, and nearby Water Tower, but gradually extended to climbing the steps up onto the Walls. This then extended to descending the steps on the other side of the Walls down to the canal and from there along the canal to the nearby flight of locks. On many occasions we would watch the boats make their way either up or down the locks. Chris was very interested in the way the locks and sluices worked and watching the people off the boats working the locks helped him understand. His adventurous nature led him to wanting to walk across the lock bridge or the walkway on the lock gate, this we would do, but only with me holding on tight. The lock bridge was also the setting for what became known as 'Christopher Sycamore Wings'. This was a silly game we had that was based on the famous 'Pooh Sticks' from the Winnie the Pooh books. In our version we would each hold a sycamore wing from the nearby tree, drop them into the water below and see who's would appear on the other side first.

Gradually, the length of our walks increased, we would visit the numerous towers on the Walls, climbing to the top of the Morgan's Mount (a small tower on the Walls) from which we could see roughly where our house was or sitting in Pemberton's Parlour and pretending we were Roman soldiers. Eventually, we were walking complete circuits of the Walls and on some days this involved diversions into Edgar's Park in Handbridge. When Chris was four or five he could manage quite long walks and showed no signs of the condition that we were told about later, indeed for sometime after May 1990 he was still walking well and could manage quite long distances albeit gradually getting slower. Only later on some of these walks, especially as Chris got a bit older, was it was necessary for me to give him piggybacks on the return walk. It was a good job he wasn't too heavy. Later we would still have a Sunday afternoon walk, although we would make use of the Major Buggy (a large pushchair). Throughout our walks we would chat away, and Chris was always asking questions about various aspects of his home city and was especially interested in the Roman period. He was great company and I was happy to let him choose what we did on those afternoons. It was only when he became fully wheelchair bound that he chose to stop going

to the parks and would prefer to spend his Sundays doing other things. I well remember one afternoon, not long after Chris started using the wheelchair, that we visited the park at Hoole. The park had swings, a large slide and wooden climbing structures and had been a popular venue for our fun. On this particular day the park was quite busy, climbing was out of the question by now and the slide was a risky proposition, but as we approached the swings I asked, "Do you want to have a go?"
"No, I'm OK at the moment," came the reply. So we watched the other kids for a while.
"Should we go for a walk?"
"Yeah, OK," said Chris. We walked around the park, chatting, and then returned a little while later to the swings.
"Want a go now?"
"No, I'll just watch."
After a short time I glanced at Chris and saw that he was watching the boisterous fun on the swings and some boys playing football with a wistful look on his face. It was almost like he was taking part in his mind. A few minutes later he said,
"Can we go home now?"
"If you want," I said and so we returned to the car. We never went to Hoole Park again.

CHAPTER THREE (The Dee Point Years)

No one has yet realised the wealth of sympathy,
the kindness and generosity hidden in the soul of a child.
The effort of every true education should be
to unlock that treasure.

Emma Goldman

Chris had spent 21 enjoyable months at Playschool, under the care and control of 'Auntie' Carol, finishing in December of 1989 when he was 4½.

From Chris's first visit to Dee Point school in November 1989, when he went to see what *big* school was like, he was quite at home, he thoroughly enjoyed his time at school (with, like all children, the odd *hiccup*). In many ways he was quite well advanced as he could read reasonably well, count easily to 100, could tell the time and had an extensive vocabulary - and with great enjoyment used this to talk to all and sundry. However, he did have poor concentration, which initially led him to be disruptive in class, and his writing, caused by co-ordination problems, was not particularly good. Also at this stage there were some concerns over his interpersonal skills, as he wanted to dominate or organise everybody. His first year teacher at Dee Point was Mrs. Mellor and he was to establish quite a rapport with her, which would last right through his time at Dee Point. She would frequently regale us with stories of how Chris did this or that, and how he was often getting into trouble, not serious trouble, but the sort of devilish behaviour that while being amusing does require controlling and correcting. For example, there was the occasion when Chris, aided by a girl in the class, covered the budgie in sand and struggling for air, and but for the timely intervention of Mrs. Mellor, may have joined the great aviary in the sky. Whenever the school went on day trips Mrs. Mellor would enlist the support of her daughter Alison, mainly to look after Christopher. Many years later he would fondly recall her looking after him and as Mrs. Mellor wrote "My daughter Alison remembers him with great fondness for the time she spent with him in my class and especially on the (school) trip to Liverpool. I will always think of him as a very special boy."

Mr. Metcalfe was the Headmaster at Dee Point, he was what would be described as a traditional headmaster. He strongly believed in the conventional ways of teaching and with strong and loyal support of his staff gave all the children in his care the best of starts. He knew all the children by their first names, knew a great deal about each one and in many cases knew their parents as they had been through the school some years previously. The children, both in the Primary and Junior schools, had great respect for him and he would often be seen with the children in tow, holding their hands and providing great encouragement. He was also a strong disciplinarian and could bring an errant child to heal with a roar of his voice. Mr. Metcalfe was obviously told of Chris's situation and in October 1990 Annette and I were invited to the school to discuss Chris's future. We were quite apprehensive at the prospect of the meeting, but we need not have been. He quickly put us at ease, he wanted to understand what having MD would mean to Chris and how it would affect him. But perhaps most importantly he told us that he would do everything possible to ensure that Chris would be happy and accommodated at the school until such a time as he reached leaving age or we decided on other courses of action. Until Chris left Dee Point at the age of 11 in July 1996 he was as good as his word. Mr Metcalfe recommended that we went through a formal process of obtaining a Statement of Special Needs, a process that is prescribed in The Education Act 1981, and was to prove beneficial in the coming years.

This can be a fairly lengthy process and entails reports being sought from parents, teachers and numerous professionals who have contact with the child. The reports are reviewed and assessed and a Statement of Special Educational Needs is produced. In Chris's case this took until February 1991, the recommended provision being that "Christopher should continue in mainstream education supported by a Classroom Assistant and reviewed on a term by term basis". The statement also noted that while his co-ordination and manipulation were poor, needing assistance with self-help skills, as well as help in maintaining his focus on the work in hand, he was academically well above average for his age. As a result of the Statement it was around May 1991 that Miss Liz Newns, a qualified Nursery Nurse, joined the school as Chris's classroom assistant and immediately bonded with him, providing the necessary physical and psychological support.

Dee Point had a great tradition for staging enjoyable Christmas productions, and while the Primary school would put on a Nativity performance, the whole school was involved in the main event. This meant a show performed each night for three nights, to packed audiences, with every child in the school appearing on at least one night as the cast revolved. The themes of the shows changed each year, scripted and staged by the staff, with the preparations interwoven into the school's course work. The first year Chris was at Dee Point the theme was a 'Century of Song' with each class or year group performing a well-known song. Mrs. Mellor's class sang and danced "I'm Forever Blowing Bubbles". Despite this being his first dramatic appearance Chris was more interested in scanning the audience and finding and waving to the family party, but the nonetheless he really enjoyed the experience.

In January 1991 Chris had moved into Year 1 (Class 3) with Mrs Thompson (although the class was later taken over by Mrs Rees). The children making up the class were the same as the previous year so Chris was amongst his many friends. He'd already established many strong relationships and Melanie Carrington, Laura Holmes, Vicky Chard and Paul Jarvis figured highly in the conversations about school life. It was also during this period that Chris's ability at General Knowledge began to emerge. While he could read well, to get him to read story books was a real problem, as he much preferred fact books in which he would bury his head and helped by an almost photographic memory he could recall the smallest amount of detail. As his school report in June 1991 said, "Christopher has very good general knowledge and he always has something to contribute in class discussions. His reading is progressing well and he understands what he reads". It was also during this period that he first embraced computers and quickly established himself as the class 'expert'. The computer advisory unit of the Local Authority at Woodford Lodge recommended the most appropriate systems and monitored Chris's changing needs over the next few years. The use of the computer provided a major help in producing his class work. Although he was encouraged to use a pen or pencil to write it was quite slow and untidy. We tried numerous things to help, larger pencils and special finger grips, and while neatness improved, speed was always a problem. Miss Newns was a great help, especially in keeping Chris focused on what he was doing.

Following the summer recess Chris returned to school, entering Year 2 (Class 5) with Miss Lenham, who was relatively new to teaching. She was a very caring teacher who always had time for her pupils and Chris liked her immensely. He enjoyed all aspects of the schoolwork, the 3 *Rs* and the topic work and with the continued help of Miss Newns took part in the physical projects and joined in the PE. He'd always had a good, clear speaking voice and was given good parts in the Class Assembly. Chris would always learn the pieces by heart and would deliver them well and with passion.

November 1991 marked a first, a night away from home without a member of the family, when Miss Lenham's class took part in a school trip to Burwardsley for a field trip and overnight stay. Although he was quite keen on going, later reports indicated that he had found it difficult being away from home. At least he had Miss Lenham and Miss Newns to look after him!

The school Christmas production in 1991 was Disney Time inspired by Deputy Head Mr. Hodgkinson's visit to Disney World earlier in the year. Chris was also well prepared having had his first visit to that magic place in June of the same year. Miss Lenham's class sang "Little April Showers" from Bambi, which was performed with tremendous enthusiasm and great enjoyment. As with the previous year Chris was very keen on finding us in the audience and once he had his head tilted and a coy smile and wave followed. The school production was always received well by the parents packing the school hall and the children felt a wonderful sense of achievement. It was also a great tribute to the staff who worked very hard to put on an entertaining event.

For one of his earlier birthdays Chris had been given a small two wheeler bike with stabilisers which he had enjoyed, but as his walking started to become affected by the muscle weakness balancing on a two wheeler was quite difficult. Frances Reeve, the Occupational Therapist at Dorin Park, suggested that a three wheeler might be the answer, not a child's trike but a 'proper' tricycle. Dorin Park had such a bike and Chris successfully tried it out. Frances told us that the bike, a Pashley Polo, could be bought through Davies Brothers in Cuppin Street. So in early January 1992 we placed our order, having to wait until mid-March for it to be built and delivered. Chris got great pleasure from the bike and was able to use it for quite some time, although as time went on it did need Annette or I to provide some pushes. Even after Chris was unable to ride it himself it was still utilised by Paul (Chris's cousin) or me in racing Chris, in his wheechair, around the garden.

It had been suggested to us during a clinic in 1992 with Drs. Robinson and Appleton that we should consider transferring Christopher from mainstream school, Dee Point, to a Special Needs school, primarily to afford him the physical and emotional support such a school could offer. Our reaction to this was not positive, as we were keen to keep Chris in mainstream education especially as at this time his physical problems had not fully manifested themselves. Chris was very happy at Dee Point, had a host of friends, good support and he was very capable academically, being rated in the top 4 or 5 in his class. His reading and composition skills were good, his general knowledge excellent, although his maths could have been better.

The school through the efforts of Mr. Metcalfe, made every effort to accommodate Chris's limited physical abilities. Classrooms were reorganised so that the classes Chris attended were generally on the ground floor, he took part in games lessons with help and he was included in all other activities by making the necessary allowances. This was usually done in such away that Chris did not feel disadvantaged or left out, although inevitably there were a few occasions were he could not take part. Generally, he accepted the situation with good grace and as far as I can remember he did not complain, realising that some things just could not be achieved and that Mr. Metcalfe, his staff and fellow pupils made every effort to help.

In June 1992, with the help of the school and Dr Jayaram, the local authority agreed to provide a taxi to and from school. Initially, Mrs Burnett, a very pleasant lady that Chris liked and looked on as another grandma, provided this. It certainly helped in ensuring he got to school on time, as the use of buses had become more difficult.

The year with Miss Lenham had been very positive for Chris, he had done very well in the statutory tests that had been undertaken in English, Maths and Science, as well as getting good reports for Technology, History and Geography. PE remained a problem, but "with encouragement and a lot of help Christopher tries very hard.... He does what he can and always enjoys himself". Miss Lenham summed up the year with "Christopher is a lovely and friendly little boy who always is willing to help in the classroom. He is making very good progress in all areas of the curriculum and has a number of very good friends in our class".

When the school reopened in September 1992 Chris was in Year 3, Mrs Roberts' Class 7, although he missed the first few days of term as we were on holiday in Florida. On his return he quickly settled in to the class and was still accompanied by Miss Newns. Chris found Mrs. Roberts difficult to get on with, she was not as approachable as Miss Lenham had been and the contrast between the two classes was significant. While he did reasonably well during the year, it was clear that he was not as enthusiastic as the previous year.

The school Christmas production in 1992 was 'Christmas Kaleidoscope', based on the theme of Christmas events, happenings, songs and carols down the years, which as usual involved the whole school. Mrs Roberts' class performed "When Santa got stuck up the chimney". By this time Chris was having trouble climbing steps and couldn't manage to get up onto the stage, so Miss Newns lifted him up and sat him on the edge of the stage from where he could join in. Once in place he scanned the audience looking for the family so that he could wave to them. There was no doubt he loved an audience. The children sang and acted out the song, the 'atchoo, atchoo, atchoo' at the end of each verse being performed with great enthusiasm!

At the end of the whole performance all the performers returned to take a bow, Miss Newns put Chris up on the stage, where he ended up in front of Mr. Metcalfe who did his annual Christmas speech. By this time Chris was getting tired, I think that's why he was yawning, rather than at the content of Mr. Metcalfe's speech!

By the middle of 1993 Chris was using a wheelchair regularly. He had no shortage of volunteers to help, all his class mates wanted to take turns in pushing him and as such they would make sure he was involved in most of their activities.

The remainder of the school year passed smoothly and Chris put in another steady year of study and good contribution to the class. On the whole he was still enjoying school and on most days looked forward to going.

September 1993 saw a number of changes. Chris moved into Year 4 (Class 12) with Miss Spark, who was new to teaching, but she was immediately popular with her charges. Miss Newns had left the school as she was expecting a baby (Chris was very sad when she left) to be replaced by Mrs. June Woods, and the taxi arrangements switched from Mrs Burnett to Dee Cars. This meant that on most days there was a different driver and we quickly found that some were helpful, and some found carrying a wheelchair (and all that entailed) a real pain, something Chris noted and got upset over.

Miss Spark was a splendid teacher who was full of enthusiasm and enjoyed a good relationship with her pupils. Chris immediately struck up a good relationship and would often compare her to Miss Lenham. It was not long into the term before planning for the Christmas production started. For 1993 Dee Point were to perform The Gift, written by Mr Savage (a member of staff), which reflected the festive period around the world. Class 12's contribution was to be the 'The Jolly Postman', and Christopher was selected along with Krysta Wood to be a Narrator. This had two advantages, firstly the role would benefit from Chris's loud and clear voice and secondly it meant that Chris could be positioned in front of the stage, rather than on it, thus avoiding getting the wheelchair lifted. In keeping with the theme Chris appeared with his Father Christmas bobble hat (knitted by Annette's mum) and Snowman scarf. The performance was excellent, no wrong words or stuttering. As one of the other parents said at the end of the evening, "Your Chris has got an excellent speaking voice, I wish (daughters name) could speak like that". As always Chris thoroughly enjoyed his opportunity to perform, although he would never actually admit it publicly, preferring to be modest!

The school put on the traditional Christmas Parties, the gatherings for the older years being held in the evening and Annette always made sure that Chris had some thing new to wear. He would always have a good time and even though he couldn't participate in all the games he would give the others encouragement or organise his friends. When we arrived to pick him up he was invariably in the middle of a big group, holding court, many of the group being girls.

By now writing was a big problem for Chris. He had never really got over the problems he had encountered when much younger. While he could write quite neatly when he put his mind to it, he could not write quickly. To overcome this the school gave him access to one of the computers that they had and he was provided an Amstrad laptop in which he could record his work. He was quite a proficient keyboard user and as a result it helped his school work no end, using it to produce one of his first poems.

RED

Red is a deep ruby colour,
Deep as the blood in my body.
The colours of the roses in my garden,
Beautiful to look at.
Red is the colour of fireworks,
Glowing in the sky.
Red is the colour of a danger sign.
Red is a rainbow colour,
Red is a good colour.

The school year passed very quickly and before we knew it was School Reports and Open Night. Chris invariably came with us and would spend the time whizzing around the school playground in his outdoor electric chair, showing off to all those prepared to watch. Chris's report was again good, Miss Spark being very pleased with his performance although he still had a tendency to loose concentration. One area he did excel at was being bossy, as Miss Spark wrote "Christopher works well in a group and is a great organiser..." and "Christopher's involvement in PE is very limited ... he also likes assessing and giving advice to the other children!" She also added that ".. he is a pleasure to teach".

When the new 1994/95 school year (Year 5) commenced Chris was to remain in Class 12, now with Mrs Rogers, still supported by Mrs. Woods. However, at the start of the term Chris was not present as his legs were still in plaster after surgery (see later Chapter) and as a result he missed the first three weeks of school. This set the scene for the year, Chris worked hard, but it became obvious that Chris was not as happy at school he had previously been. We repeatedly tried to get to the reason for this change, but Chris was not forthcoming.

The 1994 Christmas production was to be 'Keep Smiling Through', representing Christmas during the war. This was inspired by project work the school was undertaking to commemorate 50 years since the end of the war. Class 12 performed "The Union Jack", which as in previous years was performed with great enthusiasm by the class.

Throughout each year Dee Point would have a school assembly at which one class would provide the theme and *perform* the assembly. Parents were always encouraged to attend and they were more often or not excellent, providing the audience and the children food for thought. Chris would actively participate in his class production, contributing ideas and words, as well of course as speaking. We would always make an effort to attend, and at least one of us would always go. As she lived locally Annette's mum would go with Annette, she was immensely proud of Chris, never missing an opportunity to tell people how wonderful he was. In April 1995 Nanny attended Chris's assembly, but sadly this was to be her last, as she passed away that June. The loss of Nan was a huge blow to Chris and this only seemed to add to his now increasing unhappiness. In the end of year report, while his performance had generally been good, there were references to him losing concentration and him "giving up all too easily" and "(he) doesn't attempt to tackle problems that he is quite capable of". He was still very much a team player (he took comfort I think from having people around him) and Miss Rogers wrote, "Christopher prefers working as part of a group where he can organise, rather than on his own". To sum him up she added, "Christopher is a cheerful little boy who always has plenty of stories to tell during Registration!"

During mid 1995 it was suggested that Chris spend one day a week at Dorin Park Special School, primarily so that he could go swimming in the school's heated pool and have access to the physiotherapists. This was a good way forward, as it enabled Chris to maintain his existing links and friendship, maintain his academic work, create new friendships at Dorin (ready for a potential full time move) and have a professional exercise programme. So from early September 1995 Chris began attending Dorin Park on Mondays.

The arrangement worked well, Chris would get taken to Dee Point in his usual taxi and then go on, with Mrs. Woods, to Dorin Park. Chris settled in well, in Miss Jones' class, quickly and easily making friends. In many ways he got the best of both worlds, as Dorin would always invite him to the various special days and functions. For example, on one day he participated in the Dee Point School Assembly and then transferred to Dorin Park to take part in their American Themed Day. Miss Jones also noted that he quite liked to talk, writing in the year-end review, "He works consistently well and contributes greatly to class discussions".

It was around this time that Chris did a piece of work, titled 'Interesting Things' at school and wrote:

> My name is Christopher and I am in a wheelchair and I think it is very interesting and there is another little boy in a wheelchair called Kurt, he can't walk like me that is why he is in a wheelchair. I know a School that many of the boys and girls are in wheelchairs and that schools name is called Dorin Park. There are Physiotherapists and I go swimming there and my best friend is Richard Brooks and Paul Jarvis and Mrs Woods. I like doing Maths. My standing frame is made out of metal and rubber and is going to stretch my legs. I have to go in it for 1 hour each day and it hurts very much.

Also in September 1995 Chris started his last year, Year 6, at Dee Point, reunited to his great pleasure with Miss Spark. He'd very much enjoyed his previous year with her and he really looked forward to this one. Mrs Woods was still assisting him, and she also added to the stability that he needed. Soon after term started Chris was provided a Jewel electric wheelchair for indoor use, which meant that he was now much more self-sufficient in terms of getting around. In November Chris's transport arrangements were changed again, so instead of using a taxi (which had been problematic throughout) a place was allocated on a mini-bus equipped with a tail lift. The other passengers, Kirsty Bridge, Alicia Gough, and Peter Herbert were pupils from Dorin Park, so Chris was familiar with most of his fellow passengers and he soon became friendly with Gary, the driver.

Christmas came and went, the school putting on 'An Olde Tyme Musical' in which Miss Sparks' Class performed "The Sailors Return" and soon after the kids enjoyed their Christmas Party. In January, the school visited Theatre Clwyd to see Gulliver's Travels. All the kids went by double decker bus, but because of the limitations this presented Annette and I took Chris in the car (at this time we had a Nissan Serena MPV which allowed us to carry the wheelchair more easily). The production was a modern adaptation and was quite frankly very poor, or as Chris said, "If that's a panto, they can stick it!"

As the 1995/96 school year progressed we formally started the process of deciding to which Secondary School Chris should go. The local choice was Blacon High School, and this was expected to be the school most of Chris's peer group would attend, although there were a few other alternatives. To start with Annette and I were quite keen to keep Chris in mainstream school, as he was easily bright enough to cope with the curriculum. The professional view though was that Chris would be best served, in a Special School, at Dorin Park. The key question for us was whether the mainstream school could cope with a wheelchair. Our enquiries indicated that the only wheelchair adapted school locally was The Bishops (and that was only partially), across the City from where we lived. The answer other schools gave to the problem was to say that Chris's lessons would be scheduled, whenever possible, on the Ground Floor and in those cases where this was not possible he would be allocated a tutor to enable him to work on alone! So much for integration.

For me these issues resolved themselves one night in early January of 1996. Annette and I had noticed that on occasions Chris was becoming withdrawn, not his usual full of beans self. On arriving home from work, as usual I went to say hello to Chris, who was fighting some giant creature on the PC.

"Hi, mate, how are you?"

"Palion!" came the greeting, "I'm OK." (Palion [to rhyme with galleon] was one of a number of words Chris created and where he usually shortened words this was an extended version of pal).

"What've you been doing today then?" I enquired.

"Oh nothing," a not unusual answer, especially when in game play mode.

"I don't send you to school to do nothing," I responded. "What lessons have you had?"

"English, (pause - kill monster) boring Maths." (Collect power-ups).

"Maths isn't boring."

"It is!" (Destroy enemy vehicle).

"What did you do at playtime?"

"Watched the lads play football." (Another monster despatched).

"You mean played football?"

"No, **watched**."

"Is that what you do at each playtime?"

"Yeah, I park in the corner of the playground and watch, keeping score."
"Well couldn't you join in?"
"No, they're too fast for me now."
"Do you mind not playing?"
(Pause) "No, not really." But his voice and face painted a different picture.
I knew then, in that pained moment highlighted by Chris's subdued behaviour that mainstream school was not the place for him in the future. I'd wanted him to go to one for my reasons, to show to others that he was a bright and intelligent lad. But that was not what Chris wanted. What he wanted was to be able to participate in games of football, to compete on an equal footing with his friends. As Pam Dowd (his physiotherapist) had said, "… quality of life". In the quest to satisfy my dreams, I'd forgotten that. Realistically, even if Chris did get excellent GCSEs or A-Levels it was highly unlikely with the level of his disability that he would be able to use them as intended. The key was to ensure that Chris was happy, enjoyed life and had a good education that would equip him for whatever fate dealt him in the coming years.

I told Annette of my chat with Chris and we agreed that we should put Chris's name down for Dorin Park. Before we did that we had one of our little 'three way chats'. We explained to Chris that we had to make a choice about what school he would go to after Dee Point. We explained the choices and some of the issues. Unusually, he listened quietly, as he was prone to interrupting, taking it all in.
"Where would you like to go?" we asked.
"I don't know," he replied, after a pause.
"Perhaps Blacon High," he added quietly.
"Well Mum and I thought that Dorin Park might be a better option," I ventured.
His face lit up, "Yes! Yes! Yes!" came the shouted response.

The course of action was now clear, so during Statementing we were able to express our collective view as to what the next step should be and from there to be offered a place at Dorin Park, which was duly forthcoming in March 1996, much to Chris's relief and pleasure.

February that year was a bit odd, we woke one Monday morning to find that we were under a couple of feet of snow, quite an unusual situation for Chester. After an hours effort to clear the drive of snow I managed to get Chris and the wheelchair into the car. However, the access to the school was just as bad and it very quickly became apparent that there was no way we could get Chris into the school building. So much to his delight he had to spend the next 4 days at home, waiting for the snow to clear while his classmates continued with lessons.

As I have said before Chris had an excellent speaking voice, he spoke very clearly and enunciated all his words very well. Dee Point always made a point of entering speakers in the Verse Speaking at the Chester Competitive Music Festival. Chris was nominated, although it has to be said he wasn't that keen. I think that it ultimately came down to Miss Spark asking and him not wanting to let her down. The selected verse was 'Hugger Mugger' by Kit Wright, a quite difficult piece. The competition was held at Queens Park High School and is open to all schools in the Chester area. In the section that Chris was in there were 16 entrants, and unsurprisingly Chris was the only wheelchair user. Each entrant had to stand in the middle of the room, in front of the judge, the other competitors and the rest of the audience. Around this time Chris was very conscious of his use of a wheelchair and he was having difficulty with people looking at him and so when he saw the arrangements he was not keen to participate. With some *persuasion* from Annette and I he did take part. He did an excellent job, sadly not good enough to win, but well enough to score 83 points, gain a merit (two points off a distinction) and finish 4th. The judge's comments included, "Fine big voice used - you made the complaint really believable". This was not good enough for Chris who as always wanted to win and while he was good he was not as good as the young lad who won. It turned out this young fellow had competed since he was seven and was very experienced in speaking competitions, "He should be disqualified for cheating" was Chris's view on the matter. Despite lots of encouragement from Miss Spark, Mrs Howard and Mr. Metcalfe, as well as Annette and I we could not convince Chris to enter again. "It's a stupid competition anyway", was how he summed it up.

The week after the Verse Speaking competition Miss Spark's class and the other Year 6 classes were booked on a 4 night Residential Visit to The Conway Centre, Menai, on the Isle of Anglesey. The Conway Centre, owned by Cheshire County Council, is in the grounds of the Marquis of Anglesey's stately home and is the former HMS Conway, used by the Navy as a shore training base for Boy Sailors. For field trips it is ideal as it has classrooms, library, dormitories and refectory. However it is not ideal for wheelchairs or their users. In addition by this stage Chris needed turning in the night and to expect the staff to deal with that, plus getting him dressed etc. while looking after over 70 other children was too much to expect. Mr. Metcalfe though was keen for Chris to be involved and enquired if it would be possible for us to run Chris to Menai on several of the days so that he could join in with a number of the field trip activities. Needless to say, that was no problem and having examined the schedule for the week we settled on two days which had activities Chris could join in. On the first day we set off early, accompanied by Mrs Woods, taking about 1½ hours to get from Chester to the Centre. Chris's class mates where all enjoying themselves on the swings when we arrived, but as soon as our car, a Ford Galaxy, pulled up they all came running over, they were genuinely pleased to see him and he them. No sooner was he in his wheelchair than he was taken off to be shown round the grounds and building by his group of friends. In the afternoon it was planned to visit the Oriel Museum and Art Gallery at Llangefni, so it was arranged to have lunch early which was quite a jolly affair. Chris was in great demand to sit at various tables, but the issue was resolved when Mr. Hodkinson (the Deputy Headteacher) pointed Chris to one particular table. Once lunch was over it was out to the waiting bus, although Chris decided he would travel in the Galaxy. We followed the bus through the lanes of Anglesey to Llangefni and the modern building that housed the Oriel museum. The museum had a small number of exhibits, which were quite interesting and stimulated quite a lot of discussion between the children. The art gallery also generated interest, but less than the museum. Chris was quite interested in the landscapes, which showed the various buildings found on the Island, including Telford's fabulous Menai Bridge over which we had driven that morning. He was quite keen to acquire one of the paintings when he realised that they were for sale, although not so keen when faced with the prices!

From the museum the school party moved on to the nearby Langefni swimming pool. We had gone fully equipped for Chris to participate (as he quite enjoyed swimming), but as we were driving up to the Pool he announced that he didn't want to go in the water. He said he would be quite happy to watch the others. I knew that asking why would not elicit an answer, other than "I don't want to, thank you". I concluded that his decision was either because he didn't want me to get him undressed/dressed in front of his friends or that the water would not be warm enough (Dorin's pool was heated), either way there would have been no persuading him. We settled ourselves at the end of the pool, our backs against the changing room wall. We could hear the shouts and laughter of the kids, with Chris giving a running commentary on who said what and when. After a little time the voices started to get closer as the kids, now changed into their swimming gear, headed out of the Changing Room and through the footbath towards the pool. The Pool Attendants got to their feet and awaited the arrival of the group. Their voices got closer, they shot into view led by Timmy Mills, who on seeing the water ran forward and before anyone could say or do anything dived into ..... the shallow end. The inevitable happened, he cracked his head on the floor of the pool. The attendants reacted very quickly leaping into the pool and taking hold of a clearly shocked youngster as he surfaced. They carefully moved Timmy to the side of the pool, where they braced his neck before carefully lifting him out of the pool.

There was little outward sign of damage to Timmy, apart from a small cut on the top of his head, but neither the Pool Attendants or the school staff were prepared to take a chance with such a potentially life threatening situation and an ambulance was called. Despite being no wiser than anybody else around the pool Chris took on the role of medical advisor, telling his classmates, who were quietly assembled on the pool side, about the dangers to head and neck in such situations. Of course Timmy's sanity in performing such a risky move was brought into question, quickly debated and assigned to the 'MAD' drawer.

The ambulance quickly arrived and Timmy accompanied by Mrs. Howard set off for Ysbyty Gwynedd Hospital at Bangor. I volunteered to follow the ambulance so that I could return Mrs. Howard to the school party later. Chris was left in the care of Mrs. Wood, while the rest of the kids got on with enjoying themselves, although now more aware of the potential dangers.

Over at the hospital Timmy was seen quite quickly and it was established that he had done no major damage, although the doctors were keen to check all aspects before releasing him. By the time he was given the green light to go, looking very pale, but otherwise OK, the school had made their way back to The Conway Centre from the swimming baths. Although nervous about being lifted onto the bus, Chris had quite enjoyed the trip, especially being amongst his friends. However, when I got back he was keener to hear about what had happened to Timmy at the hospital rather than tell me what he had been up to. Following a telephone discussion with 'The Boss' (Mr. Metcalfe) it was decided that Timmy should be returned home that evening, just in case. Only

Mr.Hodkinson had a car with him, so I volunteered to ferry Timmy home, especially as we were going that way.

So after tea in the Refectory we loaded up into the Galaxy, Chris, Timmy, Mrs Wood and another pupil who I had previously agreed to bring back to Chester as she had a hospital appointment the following day. Driving home Timmy was very quiet, he still looked pale and was clearly in shock. Chris was concerned about how he was and at regular intervals enquired if he was OK. He did however point out to Timmy that, in his opinion, Timmy was a very lucky person not to have done more damage than just cut his head. I'm quite sure that Timmy realised that himself and had learnt a valuable lesson that day. When we dropped Timmy off at his house Chris felt it necessary to put Mrs. Mills at ease, "Timmy has been fine in the car, he's realised what he's done wrong and he'll probably feel much better after a good night's sleep".

As for us, after a good night's sleep, we were back off along the A55 towards Menai and the second of our two days on the Field Trip. It had been arranged that we would meet the school party in the car park of the venue for that day's visit, The Power of Wales Museum, at Llanberis. After a short wait the school bus appeared and the party organised themselves for the visit. The first part, around the museum itself, was excellent. Not only was the access first class, but the exhibits were of the highest standard, and are complimented by a fabulous film show. The museum is part of the Llyn Padarn Hydroelectric Power Station and shows how the power station came into being, how it was built and how it operates. Nestled at the top of the mountain is a lake, Llyn Padarn, which during the night (when electricity is cheaper) has water from the lake at the bottom pumped up to it. At points of peak demand the sluices controlling the top lake are opened and the water rushes through the turbines (which also act as the pumps) and generate electricity to be added to the National Grid. Having watched the film it was off outside to board a number of buses to take a guided tour inside the mountain to see the Power Station itself. This, of course, being Britain meant that the buses were not wheelchair friendly. Fortunately at this time I was still able to lift and carry Chris, so he was still able to join that part of the trip.

The buses followed the roadway that winds around <u>inside</u> the mountain, occasionally opening out into vast caverns filled with machinery. The tour started at the top of the 'building' and visitors were let off the bus to view the sluice doors and the giant pipes through which the water passes. Fortunately we had brought the wheelchair with us so Chris was able to get off to have a good look, and hear what the guide had to say. Back on the bus and we were taken down one level to where the turbines themselves are situated.

"It's OK," said Chris, "we'll stay here. I can see from here."

"But don't you want to see properly?" I enquired.

"Well, it would be good, but I don't want you to hurt your back."

"I appreciate that, but this is your trip, so come on."

The noise and vastness of the place was incredible and left a mark on Chris's memory for a long time. A couple of years later I asked if he'd like to visit the Power Station again, he said he would, but then remembered the bus trip and decided against it.

After the tour the school reconvened in a room set aside for them to have lunch. It never ceased to fascinate me how nearly everybody wanted to share the table at which Chris sat. One thing was for sure, the conversation was always more animated when he was involved though. With lunch over and everything tidied away there was just time for another quick look around the museum before it was time to depart. The school bus was to return along the coast road, but as we had already been along that three times I suggested that we go home via Betws-y-Coed and the A5. Chris, who always enjoyed going for drives, readily agreed so Mrs. Wood had no option but to come along. Although the route we took was a little bit longer than the coast road we were able to see various views of Snowdon, the station for the Snowdon Mountain Railway, the picturesque Llanberis and Nant Gwynant Passes, as well as Capel Curig and Betws. All in all a very pleasant drive and a nice end to a good day.

Chris's time at Dee Point was now quickly coming to an end, and while he was still going without complaint, he did appear to be coming more remote from some of the activities. For the last three months of the term Chris was looked after by Miss Dalgarno, a change brought about following discussions on the level of support Chris was receiving in relation to other duties Mrs. Woods had. Despite this his final report was quite encouraging; his strengths again being good general knowledge, working as part of a group, his computer knowledge and his ability to converse, even in French, as Mrs. Higley wrote, "His spoken French is showing great promise. He is always keen to join in conversations". His weaknesses remained Maths and written work.

And so, on 25th July 1996, Chris spent his last day at Dee Point School. He'd spent 6½ years, over half his life at the school and had made a large number of friends, a number of which he maintained in the following years, he had no doubt left an impression and influenced many people. Chris had started Dee Point on his feet, walking, and had left confined to a wheelchair, but he'd taken that in his stride. While he had lost some of the things that his peers took for granted, he had developed other capabilities that would hold good in the coming years. The children he grew up with had seen his physical weakness gradually impinge on his abilities and activities, but they had throughout been hugely supportive. It would be nice to think that these formative years will remain with those kids and that their attitude to disabled people, when they are adults will be much more positive than we observe in many grown-ups today. As a final parting gesture Miss Spark presented all her class a small momentum and a rosette wishing 'Good Luck for the Future'.

CHAPTER FOUR (The Dorin Park Years)

A school should not be a preparation for life.
A school should be life.
Elbert Hubbard

On 6th September 1996, Chris started the next phase of his education with his first day in Seniors at Dorin Park Special School, Upton. One of the great attractions to Chris was Dorin did not, unlike Dee Point, have a school uniform and having been attending the school one day a week he was looking forward to going, although a little apprehensive. From the very first day at Dorin his whole attitude began to change, he was much more relaxed and getting back to his happy self. Transport to school was provided by the Parker's bus that he used before along with Kirsty, Alicia, Peter and Anthony. Chris was placed in Mrs. Blackford's class along with amongst others Alicia Gough, Paul Cooper, Laura Stevenson, Nathan Smith, Lyndsey McCoy and Anthony Barlow.

In the first few months of the school year Chris took part in the Harvest Festival, went to a pantomime in Tarporley (although he was not overly happy at having to be lifted on and off the coach) and went Christmas shopping with the school. Annette and I attended the school Open Night and were pleased to be told that Chris had settled in well. It was also during those first few months that Chris came home one evening and told Annette in a quite serious voice, "You know Mum, I might have a problem, but there are children at Dorin who are much worse off than me. Some of them can't even talk."

The Statement of Special Needs at the start of 1996 identified that the transfer to Dorin had been beneficial and that his physical needs would continue to be met with the provisions already in place. However, it also recognised that support could be given to Chris's emotional needs, as he became more aware of his physical disabilities. Furthermore it was identified that support was needed to curb "frequent interjections in lessons (that) are unhelpful and inappropriate".

In April, Chris's class held a 'camp' at the school. This took the form of special activities on the Friday, tea at the school, sleeping over and more activities on the Saturday. Owing to Chris's special sleeping needs and the night care he needed it was not possible for Chris to 'sleep over' so we picked him up late in the evening and returned him the following morning in time for breakfast. The Friday activity was a trip to the Granada Studio Tours and by all accounts at the time a good visit was had by all. Chris particularly enjoyed the visit to the House of Commons set as all the actors were shouting at one another. Of course he had to bring back a gift for Mum, a little jar of jam from The Kabin. We got Chris back the following morning for breakfast and to get ready for a trip to the local Ten-Pin Bowling hall. This was a new experience for Chris and by using a special ramp wheelchair users can easily take part. Actually, taking part is the wrong description, for, as with anything Chris took part in winning was the thing.

Through the school Chris was able to attend numerous events during the year, including a Sport for All day at Chester's Northgate Arena (where he was able to improve his skill at Boccia[1]), a trip to Chester Zoo and to participate in the School's sports, where for the first time in many years he was able to compete on equal terms.

At the Open night that year Annette and I were pleased to be told that Chris was now well settled and was beginning to understand the school's expectations of him. There was also a good summary of his character when Mrs. Blackford wrote, "He is perhaps gaining insights into his own emotions by being more willing to 'view' other people's perspectives". While he was doing OK at Maths, it was still a bit of a weak spot, as Chris wrote in his report, "I sometimes find maths problems quite difficult. I keep on trying hard with them and in the end I get the right answer", although Mrs Blackford gave a clue to the problem, "His only downfall in this area is that he often rushes at the answer and makes careless mistakes". He was still enjoying talking though, as Mrs Karling noted about Geography, "Chris is always an active participant in class discussions" and Mrs. Smith wrote about History, "Chris brings an enthusiasm to these lessons which infects the whole group".

When the new school year commenced Chris was in Mrs Smith's class with mainly the same group as the previous year. Mrs Smith was Head of the Senior Department and Chris was quite impressed that he was in her class, he felt that it was a bit of a status symbol. The school also had a new Headmaster, Philip Kidman, following the retirement of Mr. Jones.

The start of the school year had gone well and half term was quickly reached. It was then that tragedy struck. Just days before school was to re-open we took a phone call from Peter Herbert's father, also Pete, to say that Peter had passed away. He was just 18. Despite Peter being 4 or 5 years older than Chris they had become quite friendly through travelling to school on the bus together. Chris knew that Peter also suffered from Duchenne MD and they very occasionally swapped *notes* on it. Because Peter was older, Chris looked up to him and through these chats it helped Chris enormously in coming to terms with his own problems. Peter was a totally different character to Chris, he was much quieter and so laid back that he was almost horizontal - he was a really nice lad who is sadly missed. Both Annette and I were shocked and deeply saddened by the news, it was the type of news we were dreading as it also brought home to us an inevitability of MD. After a brief chat we decided that we should tell Chris the news, although we were not sure how he would react. Chris was in his bedroom watching TV, Annette took on the task of breaking the news. After exchanging a bit of small talk, Annette grasped the nettle.

"Chris, I've got some bad news," she said quietly.

"What's that?" he asked with a slight note of trepidation in his voice, for as he was well tuned into us he knew from our faces that something was wrong.

"We've just had a phone call, I'm sorry love, but Peter, Peter Herbert has died."

Initially, there was no reaction, he just sat staring at his TV. Then he just 'exploded'; anger and frustration flooded out. He said all the things you would expect, how it was unfair, how Pete didn't deserve to die, how MD was terrible and it was wrong Peter had to suffer from it. His rant went on for no more than a couple of minutes during which he didn't cry. It was heart rending to watch his

1 Boccia is played like Bowls, i.e. nearest the Jack, but the bowler uses a moveable, aimable ramp down which the bowls are released.

outburst, his anger was so intense, but understandable. As quickly as it had started it finished. He asked how Peter's mum and dad were, how his brother and sisters were, he wondered how the people at school would be, telling us that Mrs. Brown "would be very upset, as she was very fond of Pete". Annette continued to hug him and told him that everything was OK, that people would be bound to miss Pete, but that he was now being looked after by Jesus. He seemed to have coped reasonably well with the news and the rest of the evening and most of the following day passed with the odd comment, mainly recollections of events involving Pete. It was perhaps just 24 hours after Annette had broken the news that he appeared in the lounge. He sat and watched the TV for a few minutes and then, without warning, simply broke his heart. He cried and cried, tears streaming down his face, which was contorted with grief. There was nothing Annette or I could do other than hold him tight and try to reassure him. In all the time that we had shared moments of sadness or emotion I don't think that I had ever seen him get so upset or cry so much. It was awful seeing him so upset and with so little we could do to help. Looking back I think that while he was genuinely sad at Peter's passing and deeply, deeply upset by it, he also at that moment understood what Duchenne Muscular Dystrophy meant for him and he was crying as much over that. If that were the case, then it was the only time when he felt sorry for himself and the problems that he had and showed them openly.

School was a sad place when it reconvened after the half term. We knew that Chris was still upset over Peter because of the questions and conversations we had and the first day back on the school bus without him was traumatic. However, we were still surprised when Mrs Smith phoned us one evening to say that Chris's behaviour at school was giving the staff cause for concern. He had become disruptive and argumentative, and generally unpleasant. Mrs Smith advised that the school understood the situation and would help by providing support and some counselling, but asked if we had any other support on which we could call. We were fortunate, and for the second time in a time of need we were able to call upon Dr. Littlewood, who through a series of meetings helped Chris to understand his feelings. We had not let Chris go to Peter's funeral as we felt it would be too stressful. In retrospect that was a mistake, for had he gone Chris may have been able to grieve properly and come to terms with his loss.

Gradually, over the next few weeks the turmoil inside Chris calmed and he returned to his normal behaviour, if not to the person he was before. There is no doubt that during those few weeks he grew and matured significantly. As Mrs Smith wrote in his school report at the end of that year, "After an understandably slow start to the school year, Chris has applied himself well to his work. I have been pleased with the way Chris came through a very difficult, emotional time (after Peter passed away). He listened and learned from advice given to him, both in school and out".

Time, of course, moves on and the school began its preparations for Christmas. There was the Christmas Fair, which was well attended, and Chris was in his element introducing Annette and I to all his friends. Katie Gerrard was there, with her parents Bob and Sandra, and towards the end of the evening we were standing talking when Annette nudged me and nodded towards Katie and Chris. They were sitting facing one another having a conversation in the way they did; Chris talking like a machine gun, Katie's eyes flicking here and there, her face reflecting her thoughts, but they were also playing footsie, with their feet just touching. As Annette whispered, "they're just like an old married couple". Mind you, it was a good job Chris didn't hear that!

The other Christmas activities came and went, including shopping in Ellesmere Port, where armed with his list prepared jointly with Mum he sorted out presents for the family, which always included Meltis Fruits for Grandma as "she really likes those jelly sweets". Chris took part in the school Christmas production where he had a small narration part, but performed with his usual spirit. Gary, the driver of the school bus and Mike, the escort, took all the kids on their bus to see The Borrowers at the cinema as a Christmas treat and there was of course the school disco. Chris asked Melanie Carrington (his friend from Dee Point) if she would like to go with him and by all accounts they had a good time. The school staff also put on a pantomime, Jack and the Beanstalk, for the children and then in early January reprised it for a paying audience of parents. The staff put in a huge effort and were rewarded by a very well received performance, with award winning contributions from Mr Owen and Mr Newton.

During the year Chris did very well in the academic subjects and got good reports, being particularly strong in those subjects were he could bring his General Knowledge to bear. He also developed into being the class and then school computer 'expert', called on to help resolve any problems that were encountered. He also developed his drama skills, both in acting and in contributing to the creativity process. As Mrs Brown wrote in his Record of Achievement, "Chris was excellent in our play (Where the Wild Things Are by Maurice Sendek) in Term 2 .... (he) portrayed the character with gusto" and "Chris helped write and perform our sea chant for our play. He also learnt the words for the song 'What Shall We Do With A Drunken Sailor' which he thoroughly enjoyed!"

Sport also figured highly and a Dorin Park team with Chris a member took second place in an Inter School Football Competition, held at Hebden Green School. Although disappointed not to win he noted at the time that they, the team, "missed the leadership Peter would have given". He also took part in a cricket competition at Kwik Cricket in Warrington and was awarded a Certificate of Achievement. The annual School Sports saw the team Chris was a member of win and Chris himself win a couple of events, although he was annoyed and frustrated to come second in the wheelchair race, an event he regarded as the blue riband of the sports.

Overall the 1997 – 1998 School year had been very good apart from the passing of Peter and Chris nearly being throttled by another pupil pulling his scarf around his throat. Chris had settled well and was enjoying life, he was maturing and starting to take into account the feelings of others. He was quietly impressed with Mr. Kidman, "a nice man, ooh, but he can be very fierce when he wants". The summer holidays provided more good times (days out, cinema, karting and Heswall Boys Camp) and then in September it was back to Dorin, again in Mrs Smith's class. Chris was really looking forward to the challenges of the new year and quickly threw himself into work. There was also his new friendship with Daniel Wain, who was a few months younger than Chris, and had joined Dorin Park from another school. They immediately hit it off and became firm friends, big mates.

As was normal the school term included the start of preparations for Christmas, including learning the narrator's part for Aladdin. Chris was chosen for the narrator because he spoke loud and clear and the part was often quite big. In many ways he was quite pleased to be picked, but he would come home moaning to Annette that he "didn't want to be the bloody narrator, I want a proper acting part". Despite this he again performed well prompting Mrs Sallis to write, "Chris has worked very hard. His performance as the narrator in Aladdin' was very good. A most pleasing term's work".

A few days following the school Christmas Disco Chris was taken ill and he didn't return to school until the middle of January. Unfortunately just two weeks later he was struck down again with an infection and then a virus and missed a month of school. He also missed another week of school in March when he was in hospital. Despite these missed days and the trauma of being ill he worked hard and made up a lot of lost ground.

In late January 1998 we were all invited to a meeting at the school to begin Transition Planning. This is a process where parents and young people begin to consider the options available once the student is old enough to leave school. The student can leave Dorin Park any time between the ages of 16 and 19. Mr. Owen, Mrs Smith, Lorraine Churchman, Carol Watson and Frances Reeve, as well as representatives from the local authority and health service attended the meeting. The meeting began with just Annette and I having it explained to us the process and the options and what we needed to consider. We discussed Chris's physical and emotional needs and talked about the various further education establishments that Chris could attend. Prior to the meeting Mr. Owen had asked Chris if he wished to attend the meeting and listen to the options and express his own personal view. He had said he would, so Lorraine was asked to fetch him. After a short wait, Lorraine returned with Chris. Initially, he appeared to be fazed by all the faces, but quickly regained his composure. Mr. Owen thanked him for coming and quickly summarised what had been discussed. Chris listened quietly, nodding occasionally to indicate his understanding. Mr. Owen then asked if Chris had anything that he wished to say or ask. There was a short pause then he said,

"I really like being at Dorin Park, all my friends are here and I like the teachers," adding, "I can stay here till I'm 19 can't I?"

"Yes, pupils can stay until they're 19, but you don't have to decide today," replied Mr. Owen.

"No, but I'd like to stay till then, please" said Chris, with a set expression on his face.

Later at home we discussed the situation again. No, Chris was adamant he would stay at Dorin until he was 19, thank you.

Chris had been happily travelling to school on the tail-lift bus (now driven by Alan) since he first started at Dorin. However, following a review by the County Transport Co-ordination group it was decided that Chris would travel to school in a black taxi. Our previous experience of this form of transport was not good and Chris wanted to continue to travel with his friends. We had a lengthy discussion with the Transport Co-ordinator, which included an assurance that the firm responsible for the service was not the same as previously used. After a test run we agreed to give the service a try. The taxi also transported Kylie Tench and her mum Sue, who acted as escort, the driver of the taxi alternated, week by week, between 'big' Frank and Matthew. Very quickly Chris settled into the new way to school striking up a close relationship with Kylie and Sue. He also became very friendly with the drivers and would chat to them about all sorts of things, enjoying hearing all the latest news. So despite our initial misgivings Chris was very happy with the new arrangements.

The Dorin Park 'camp' took place in March, and as in previous years we shuttled him from and to school. The visits on this occasion included trips to the recently opened Blue Planet Aquarium in Ellesmere Port and another highly competitive ten pin bowling session! Chris's time at school was not helped through this period by the difficulties he was having with his support jacket, but as was his way he persevered without complaining. Despite this and his earlier health problems he was doing well at lessons, even Maths where he was now thinking things through much more clearly. His relationship with the teachers was very good and he was reflecting this in his work. He enjoyed History, particularly the project work on the Civil War, Geography and Science. His computing skills were proving to be very useful and this was also benefiting him in producing his work in other subjects, "Chris's computer skills are of a very high standard, he is always eager to use new programs," wrote Mrs. Karling. He was also enjoying Music and his French was coming along nicely as Mrs. Roberts wrote, "Chris demonstrates excellent understanding and his spoken French is very pleasing. He learns quickly; he is highly motivated and an asset to the lesson". English was also going well as this gave Chris a chance to get involved in class discussions and show off his creative side. Mrs. Sallis wrote in that year's Record of Achievement, "He has good ideas and strong opinions which he expresses clearly and interestingly. He is learning to use language in an interesting and entertaining way. The dialogue he wrote for the modern version of 'Romeo and Juliet' is excellent".

Besides the pure academic subjects that form part of the curriculum there were numerous other subjects taught from RE and IT to Food Technology. It was the latter that led to the 'Episode of the Chocolate Cake". Through the term Chris was coming home with a list of ingredients for the next culinary delight. We had sampled, amongst other things pizza and sausage rolls, which Chris had cooked with the help of Lorraine. One week the recipe was for Chocolate Cake and Annette duly assembled the ingredients for the appointed day and placed then in a large plastic container. That evening Chris returned accompanied by Sue Tench, carrying a bought cake and with a story to tell. The cookery lesson had gone well Chris and Lorraine apparently baking a splendid example of Chocolate Cake. The cake was carefully placed in the plastic box for transporting home and to be sampled by expectant parents. With school over Chris and the Chocolate Cake headed for the taxi. While Matthew helped Chris into the taxi the Chocolate Cake was carefully placed on the roof for safety. Then they were off, but so was the Chocolate Cake, off the roof of the cab and across the Dorin Park car park. As Chris wrote on the Record of Achievement "My favourite recipe was Chocolate Cake. Unfortunately it fell off the taxi roof before I could eat it!" Oh yes the replacement cake was bought by Matthew as way of compensation. Still the story caused great amusement for weeks in the school.

Sport was still a big part of Chris's life and he was always keen to have a go, participating in Unihoc, Handball, Kwik Cricket and of course football. Even though he, like a number of his peers, were in wheelchairs the desire to win was very much evident, Mrs Smith summed it up, "Chris is always competitive, but has learned to use everyone in his team where possible". In June, along with many others, Chris took part in an Orienteering Course in Chester Park and did very well gaining another certificate. July saw the School Sports, the usual highly competitive affair, with everyone trying hard and wanting to win. Chris went to school on the day in his outdoor chair, charged and spruced up for the occasion. He really set his heart on winning the powered chair sprint. He took part in several other events, winning the driving skill and Boccia events, but it was the sprint that mattered. The event was called and with "it's the taking part that matters" ringing in his ears he drove up to the start. The event was a handicap and because of Chris's ability and the power of his chair he was set to race off 'scratch'. The concentration on his face said it all, Mr. Owen (the starter) brought the field to order and they were off. The four competitors sprinted across the playground and flashed over the line. Chris's eyes darted to his left to see how he'd done and a smile broke across his face as he thought he'd won. But it was not to be, victory had gone in a very close finish to Celyn. Chris was distraught, the smile faded as quickly as it had appeared, he'd missed out again. I was just in front of the finish line taking photographs and I could plainly see the pain in his face. I got over to him and put my arm around him. "Never mind mate, you drove a really good race, and you were only just beaten".

"But Palion, I **wanted** to win," he said. And then, "I'm off, I've got to congratulate Celyn". With that he was off to say "Well done". That night he was very quiet, he had missed out again and he'd have to wait another year to have another go at winning.

The new school year commenced in September with Chris in Mrs. Karling's class. As we now know this was to be Chris's last year in school and in some ways it was a difficult time, but in others it was a triumph.

During 1999, a National Arts Festival competition for schools was inaugurated to celebrate the forthcoming Millennium and to reflect on it being Christ's 2000th birthday. The competition was to take the form of a dramatic production capturing these themes. Dorin Park, inspired by Drama Teacher Mrs Sallis, decided to enter. The school through the term worked hard on the development of their entry, "Don't Worry", writing the words and composing a number of songs, with the pupils offering a line or more each and set to music by Mrs. Roberts. "Don't Worry" is based on Matthew's Gospel Chapter 6: 25-34 and depicts a scene of two teenagers on their way to a pop concert, worrying about their lives and especially their appearance. Some cool dudes confirm their worst fears but their friends tell them what they look like is not important. What is important is being good mates and enjoying life. The first performances of the play were for the pupils themselves and then at Christmas time for the parents. The time and effort that the pupils and staff put into their productions is extremely high, but "Don't Worry" reached new heights. The sheer enjoyment of the participants was clear to see and it was very well performed, and well received by the audience. Annette and I were thrilled as Chris had a major part and from his perspective it was acting and not narrating. As he wrote, in his understated way, "I was the Christ figure in JC2000. It has been good". Mrs. Sallis noted at the time, "Chris's contribution to this production has been enormous. His lyrics for the "If Only" song were beautiful. His performance was very moving".

IF ONLY

If only I could drive a fast chair
Then I'd feel the wind blow through my hair.
If only I could be like Leo, Billy, Beckham or Cher.
Do you believe I'd get somewhere?

If only I could be a millionaire
And spend my money here, there and everywhere.
If I were rich I'd ditch my worries-
I wouldn't have a care.

My favourite words are If and Only
Put them together and you get 'If only'
Then you can make your daydreams in the air.

Christmas came and went with the seasonal activities in the school. By now Chris was suffering, but generally without complaining, with his back and his support jacket rubbing. This meant that the staff were having to give him quite a lot of attention, to sit him up and lean him over to provide respite to his problems. While it was unpleasant for Chris, it must have been tiresome for the staff. Chris was also getting weaker and needed more and more help to undertake some of the activities in the class. Annette and I decided to press for a permanent one-to-one through the Statementing process. As with all these things they take time to work through the system, but the school was very supportive. To help Chris the school had a small bed placed in the class room so he could be lifted out of his chair and lay down, giving his back a rest, but still able to participate in the lessons. Chris was very good about this and would use the bed for about 30 minutes before returning to his chair.

One evening, while telling me the events of the day (in between flying the computer around some distant galaxy), Chris told me that his class had a new French teacher who came in on Fridays to help out, having recently retired from mainstream teaching.

"He's very nice, you know, he speaks French fluently, and his name's Gordon".

"His name's not Gordon Linnel, is it?" I asked.

"I don't know, we just call him Gordon," came the reply, "why?"

"Well, I used to have a French teacher at the Grammar School called Gordon Linnel. You'll have to ask him if it's him."
"But, you can only ask questions in French," said Chris.
"Well, I'm sure you're up to that!"
This, have you asked yet, no I can't ask the question in French, went on for weeks before Chris announced one night that it was Gordon Linnel, and "yes, Palion, he did remember you". Worse was to come, when a week later Chris, with a broad smile on his face, announced that "Gordon looked you up in his records and says that you weren't very good at French and that I'm much better". Thanks Mr. Linnel. Chris enjoyed learning French and got on well with Gordon, who later recalled, "I really enjoyed teaching Chris; he was excellent at French - he only had to hear a word once and he'd got it for good! And he could count up to 1000! I will miss him very much. I was always touched by his concern for others even when his own problems were very great. I also liked his humour, which could be quite offbeat at times! A great lad!"

During the term the school bid farewell to Frances Reeve, the Occupational Therapist, with an often-emotional production reviving many memories. Each of the performers holding a letter spelling Frances' name, except much to her great amusement it was spelt backwards. Chris had a small part reciting one of these episodes, learnt as usual by heart. Frances recalls his 'big' voice, with the words spoken with great clarity and feeling and as a wonderful end to a wonderful tribute.

The school often organised days out in support of project work being undertaken by the various classes. During the Spring Term Chris's class were studying transport and so a visit to Manchester Airport was arranged. Any trip out always involved a great deal of organising and effort from the staff, but it was always repaid by the enjoyment the students demonstrated. For the trip to the airport there was a requirement for a good number of staff or carers, and because of the amount of care Chris needed the school asked if Annette or I could help out. Well a trip to the airport was too good to turn down, so I told Annette it was my turn!

The trip to Manchester was scheduled for 24th May, but a couple of days before Chris rang Annette from school.
"Guess what, Mum?" he said excitedly.
"What love?" asked Annette.
"I've got my one-to-one."
"Oh, that's brilliant, I'm so pleased," said Annette.
"Guess, who it is," he said, hardly able to contain himself.
"Don't know."
"It's Ian Shingler!" shouted Chris. Ian had been at Dorin for a few months doing a placement as he was undertaking a NVQ and he had struck up a good relationship with Chris when he had been helping in Chris's class. Ian was also very much attuned to the requirements of young people with special needs as his daughter, Sam, attended Dorin Park, but brought another male perspective for the boys.
"Tell Ian we're over the moon he's got the job," said Annette.

Although Ian was available to go to Manchester Airport I was asked if I would still go so as to provide a higher number of carers. The school had hired a large coach that provided both standard seating and facilities to anchor wheelchairs. Access to the coach was by hydraulic lift and through a rear door, something most of the kids enjoyed. It is one of the few large coaches that is adapted in such a manner. Chris had gone to school in the taxi as normal and I arrived in time to help(?) load the kids onto the bus. We were soon on our way and as we drove along the M56 it was Chris's voice that I could hear above all the others explaining what it was we were going to see. This included things such as a list of planes that used the airport, the airlines and the destinations you could get to from Manchester, this was punctuated every now and then with "Isn't that right, Dad" or "I've been there (or seen that), haven't I Dad."

We were dropped off close to Terminal 2, where a Guide met us. From there we made our way to the Check-ins where our Guide described what went on. We saw a few other aspects of the airport, although Mrs Karling and Mrs Brown were unhappy that the kids did not see as much as they had hoped. We ended up on the upper concourse level where we had lunch. From there everybody was able to see part of the apron and the planes coming and going on the runway. Chris kept up a running commentary on what this plane was and what that one was, describing its engines and speed. I had learnt not to disagree with him on this sort of fact, as he was invariably right. However, every now and then I sereptiously had a quick look in one of the Aircraft Reference books Chris had in his bag. Of course, stupid me he was right. We were sitting just above the British Midland gates and throughout the conversation I would get, for everybody else's benefit, "That's the plane you fly to Edinburgh on, isn't it Dad?", "You go from this Gate don't you, mate", and "You fly British Airways most times though". Anybody listening might have thought I was a real jet setter.

As Ian was keen to ensure that he looked after Chris as well as he could, we spent some time chatting over what Annette and I did to make Chris comfortable. He accompanied us to the loo so that he could observe how I lifted and manoeuvred Chris and how we used the bottle. Of course it was Chris who wanted to explain most of this and an occasional "Shut up, while I tell Ian" was required. It had the desired affect, for probably all of 30 seconds.

On the 26th May Chris had arrived home from school, proudly in possession of the school's Determination Award. As the citation said "Staff have nominated Chris for this award for the personal determination that he has shown when in school. He has responded well to the suggestions that staff have made and to the extra support he is given. He also deserves this award for the important role he played in JC2000". Chris had been at the school for over three years and we, as his parents, had felt for sometime that it would be nice for Chris to have won one of the awards before. Whenever there was an award ceremony at school Chris would come home with a report of who had won and why, he would be bursting with pride if one of his friends had won. If either Annette or I suggested that it would be nice if he won, his response was immediate, the winners were much more deserving than he ever was. Even now with him having won this award he felt that the whole of the JC2000 "Don't Worry" cast should have won the award not just him, but underneath we knew he was quite proud of having won. The photograph taken at the time shows that very clearly.

In May, Chris became a published author as through the school poems written by the students were submitted to Young Writers for inclusion in an anthology. Chris was quite good at writing poems and over the years had written a few, but like many things he had to be encouraged to actually 'put pen to paper'. And generally he would produce the work without too much apparent thought and very little reworking after! The poem[2] he chose to be submitted for publication was Friendship', about, who else but Daniel.

During the Summer Term a letter was sent home from the school asking parents their views on the adoption of a school uniform for Dorin Park. Chris was very forthright in his view on the matter - No. No amount of discussion or persuasion was about to change his mind. In the end we managed to convince him that the democratic process should take precedence and that he should adopt the majority view, however he insisted that we vote against. "Its OK for the Juniors," he said, "but the Seniors should be able to wear what they like". In the event the vote was for the school, from September 2000, to adopt a uniform sweatshirt, "Well I'm not wearing one," was Chris's reaction, democracy in action. Of course, in the event, Chris didn't wear the uniform - that probably gave him quite a laugh.

The Dorin Open Night in June was very positive, Chris despite his discomfort caused by his support jacket had done very well, Mrs. Karling wrote "He always wants to succeed in whatever he attempts and tries his very best to do so. Chris shines in class discussions and never fails to have something interesting to say". There was of course a lot of talk about 'Don't Worry', not only the performance but also the creation and development of the production. Mr. Kidman summed it by writing, "The highlight of the year must be the JC2000 performance at the Bridgewater Hall. Wonderful!"

The summer of the year 2000 was generally very good, with a number of sunny, warm days including Wednesday 24th July, the day of the Dorin Park Sports. For several weeks before Chris had started the build up, he was adamant that this was to be his year. He was now in possession of the Quickie F55, a Formula One wheelchair, which was not only fast, actually very fast, but accelerated very quickly as well. On the morning of sports day he went off to school with the annual warning ringing in his ears, "It's the taking part that matters, not the winning". I suspect that under his breath his response was "The hell it is!" In the afternoon, parents and supporters assembled around the playground and the various races and competitions got underway. As is the case there were the winners and those that took part, Chris won Boccia and took part in the barrel rolling (won I think by Kurt). In between the competitions in which he was competing Chris was busily speeding around encouraging his team-mates to raise their game, oh yes, winning <u>was</u> important. Eventually, the sprint race was called. Chris made his way to the start, the concentration already etched on his face, although it was partly hidden by his by now ubiquitous black cap and sunglasses. Mr. Owen, in his role of Starter, ordered Chris to start at the back eventually making him move right back against the wall of the playground, "With that chair Chris you should be starting in the car park of the Library (half a mile down the road)," he added. I'd suggested to Chris that once he was in position to check that the front wheels, which work like castors, were ready to go forward otherwise there would be a slight pause while they straightened. I saw him edge

[2] 'Friendship' is included in Chapter 13 - Friends.

forward and check they were right, he was watching Mr. Owen like a hawk and was keyed up ready to go. Staggered in front of Chris were Kurt, Alicia and Celyn, all in their own fairly powerful chairs. The stagger Chris had to overcome was pretty big and I was beginning to think that it was too much even for the F55. Annette and I knew how much winning this race meant to Chris, **this** was the Olympic 100 metres final and British Grand Prix all rolled up into one.
"Ready."
"Steady."
"GO!" shouted Mr. Owen. All the chairs shot forward almost as one, but the acceleration of the F55 and the almost perceptible lunge from its driver, had the green machine hurtling across the playground. By half distance the stagger was closed down and with Mr. Owen watching opened mouthed Chris took the lead by three-quarters distance and then crossed the line a delighted winner to a good round of applause. The disappointments of previous years were forgotten as Chris celebrated with an excellent set of *doughnuts*! The smile on his face said it all, it was a moment to savour. The first words he said to me were, "Palion, **I** won". As Annette said later, "I'm really glad we bought him the Quickie, at least he was able to achieve the one thing he really wanted to do - win." It was as it turned out a very poignant moment.

Four days after the Sports Day the school broke up for the Summer Holidays, little did we know at that time that it would be Chris's last day at the school and he was saying good-bye to his friends.

Dorin Park was very, very important to Chris (and Annette and I), it provided for Chris stability and he was amongst friends and people he could (and did) trust. Dorin Park was an extension to his family. He never, well rarely, complained about going to school and although he would moan about certain things and some people, these were generally transient moments. He was very protective about Dorin, he would sing its praises and tell people about all of its benefits; he was protective about the children there, especially his close circle of friends and he was very loyal to all the staff, he would have nothing said against them, having great respect for them all. He obviously had his favourites, but that was in relative terms, and that was generally because they shared his interests or got to know him that little bit better. He had established a friendly relationship with Mr. Owen, the Deputy Head, referring to him as Mr. O. Mr. O provided a strong guiding hand to an enquiring mind. They would have regular chats about most things and Chris would come home very often and tell us what Mr. O had been up to, being particularly impressed when he took part in the Three Peaks Challenge. Mr. Owen said of him later, "Chris showed great strength and determination each and every day. I will miss his humour and company."

In Mrs. Brown he had a friend, who through the teaching of science, fed a mind that just loved facts and a desire for knowledge. In return she enjoyed Chris's presence in her class, always ready to ask the questions (some which she admits she had to look up), always ready to help his classmates and ready to have fun. They also had a mutual interest in Formula 1 and shared support of Mika Hakkinen. Mrs. Karling, who was Chris's class teacher in his last year, also taught maths and ICT. She spent many hours chatting with Chris about holidays,

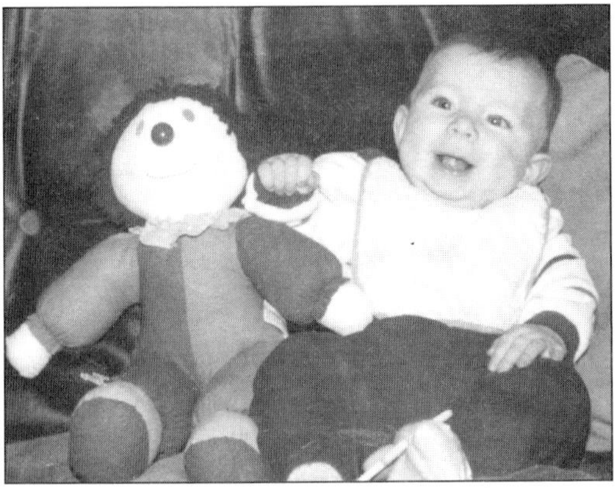

Chris, 6 months old, with Corky Clown
and two teeth!

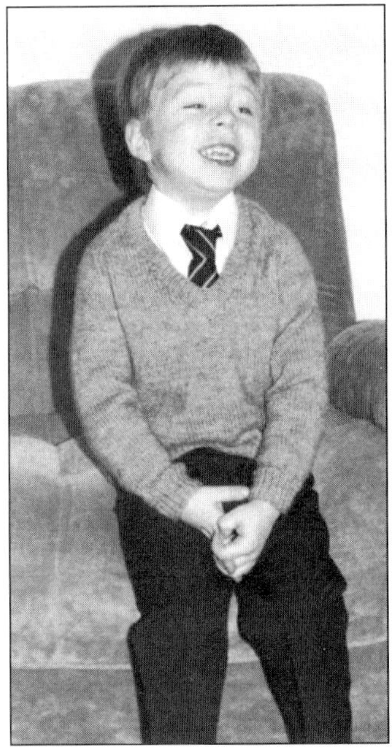

"Here I am". Ready to start school. 9th January 1990

"Je suis un rock star!". Age 21 months
Christmas 1987

Mum, Nanny, Chris, Grandma and Nana. Christmas1989

Chris was non-plussed to be taken for a walk by Pluto during his first visit to Magic Kingdom. 1st June 1991

"Ooh, I do love you Mum". Mickey's Starland Barn, Magic Kingdom.
20th September 1992

Uumm, I love those Shamu bars, but they are a bit messy!
Sea World
23rd September 1992

Annette was dispatched to just beyond the Finish Line of the London Marathon and the two great athletes representing Great Britain trotted up to the line hand in hand, raising their free hands as they *won*! 23rd August 1991

"Thanks Mickey". Mickey Mouse comes to say good-bye at Orlando Airport. 29th September 1992

especially their respective trips to America. As with others, Chris wanted to know about her family and was known to exchange conspiratorial thoughts with her son, Mark. Karen Flynn was the classroom assistant during Chris's final year and Karen bore much of the lifting and moving of Chris to get him comfortable. He was very aware that this constant need to be moved was an inconvenience and was grateful for Karen's help. The classroom assistants become close to the children and Karen wrote, 'Chris was a very special young man who touched everyone that he met. I feel privileged to have known him and will miss him'. Throughout his time at Dorin Chris would turn to Lorraine Churchman for advice and she provided a constant stability. Chris was also friendly with the non-teaching staff and could often be found chatting to them; Joan and Julia; the physios and OTs; and school nurse Sue Johnston ('I remember taking Chris around the school when he came to Clinics before he started with us - showing him the guinea pigs which he liked as long as he didn't have to hold them! He was apprehensive over starting at Dorin Park but soon settled and grew up a lot. One thing I will always remember is the fact he would never use one word when ten would do!')

Perhaps the card we received from the school in September 2000 summed it up, "Words always seem so inadequate. However Chris has left his mark with all at Dorin Park".

CHAPTER FIVE
(Cause and Effect, Clinics and Experts)

When you close your eyes
there's a frightened pride that lives for you
That your mother's life and your father's eyes can't hide
You had no choice didn't ask the dice too fall for you
Still your courage comes like thunder through the skies

C.Macdonald/R.Macdonald - Run Rig

"Muscular dystrophies (MD) are a group of progressive inherited neuromuscular disorders. Some conditions are severe and life-threatening, others are milder, a few are treatable.

All these conditions are characterised by muscular weakness though its degree is variable. All these conditions are defined as disorders of the motor units (i.e. functional units comprised by motor nerve cells in the brain stem and spinal cord, motor nerve fibres linking the nerve cells with the muscle fibres, the neuromuscular junction where a chemical is released to activate the muscle and the muscle fibres themselves). Dysfunction may occur in any part of the unit.

Different disorders affect different levels of the motor unit: for example, peripheral neuropathies affect the nerve fibres to the muscle, while myasthenic conditions affect the neuromuscular junction.

Muscular dystrophies are characterised by progressive necrosis (death) of muscle fibres. Regeneration of the damaged muscles is inadequate and muscle is gradually replaced by fibrous tissue and fat." (Source: CAF)

That describes the medical view of MD, but from a parent's view MD is a despicable condition that robs boys and young men of many things that the rest of us take for granted. Having allowed the person to have led a normal life walking, playing football, climbing and fighting, MD slowly and deliberately steals those functions and capabilities, and gradually reduces the sufferer to almost soul destroying incapacity. And this mainly to boys of 8 through 18 years. To watch your son go through this dreadful degradation is amongst the most awful things that can be encountered, especially as there is nothing you can do about it. Helplessness, as a dad you shouldn't feel that. To overcome this, as Chris did (and many other sufferers do), is a testament to their strong will and joy of life. They may be weak in muscle, but weak in heart - no.

I read a piece recently about how Jackie Stewart, the famous racing driver, had dealt with his son Paul's diagnosis and treatment for cancer of the colon. He talked about positive thinking and the benefits that he believed that brought. Annette and I remained positive throughout with Chris, but deep down you know that there is a finality, somewhere out there in the future. That is one of the reasons that we tried to cram in as much as we could into each year. The testimony though to positive thinking is from Chris himself. He very, very rarely dwelled on his circumstances. He looked at life, told it as it was, enjoyed it, and got on with it. He could be uncompromising, but that simply helped him deal with what life had dealt him. He didn't want pity, absolutely not, he hated that. As, our friend Lesley Harrison said, "He simply said, 'what you see is what you get – and if you don't like it, sod off!'" Of course some did, they couldn't handle the situation, but those that stayed were more than adequately rewarded.

Following the initial diagnosis in May 1990 Chris's life was interspersed with almost constant visits to one clinic or another. There were the regular 3 monthly visits to Dr. Robinson's clinics where Chris's progress was monitored along with his general health. This was mainly very good, although during 1990 it became necessary to have his adenoids ("the largest I've ever seen" said the specialist) removed as these were causing a number of problems with his nose, throat and ears. We also visited Dorin Park, where some of the clinics were held. As part of these visits we were seen by Frances Reeve, the OT, who was helping to improve Chris's co-ordination and the resident physiotherapists, who were providing us with exercises to help the various muscle groups and especially the legs.

During our early visits to Dorin Park to see the physiotherapists we were under the care of Pam Dowd. Pam was a very experienced and pragmatic physio, who got on very well with Chris. It was essential that we kept Chris's legs as mobile as possible and much of the exercise regime focused on this. It was mainly stretches of different types, but included the use at home of a standing frame. This was frankly an horrendous contraption. Chris had to lie down in the frame and then have his abdomen strapped in, before pushing his knees (which had slight bends due to the contractions of the tendons) flat and locking them in place with shaped and padded bars. Having completed this process, Chris and the frame were stood upright. Initially, Chris was expected to spend as much time as possible in this frame, but in reality this was no more than an hour at best. Chris just hated it. He was so limited in what he could do while in it, and he moaned all the time he was in it. Over time the standing frame became a major point of confrontation – Chris hated going in it as it was uncomfortable/painful and hugely restrictive and Annette and I hated putting him in it as he would always get upset, although we clearly understood the benefits of persevering. Pam pointed out the benefits of regular use of the frame, but understood not only the physical, but mental, trauma one gave. It was while we were discussing these issues with her one-day that she made the comment about "quality of life" and how important it was to consider that when making decisions.

Sue Herbert had told us that Chris would probably never ask about the 'whys' and wherefores' of Muscular Dystrophy, which at the time had been a comfort. However, Chris as we were to find out was no ordinary person. Not only was he reasonably bright, but he was also very inquisitive. He had developed a technique whereby he would ask questions around the main subject and then, when he was ready, ask the question to which he really wanted the answer. This process could last a few minutes, days or weeks depending on the subject. I just knew that at some point he would ask about MD. I discussed the possibility, and how we might deal with it, with Annette. I was strongly of the opinion that we should not lie to Chris, if and when he asked, but we just couldn't see how best to deal with it. Annette, not for the last time, turned to Yvonne Bohdanowicz for help. After a short time she suggested that we meet with Dr. Steven Littlewood, a child psychologist, who she was sure would be able to help.

The meeting took place in December 1990 at Dr. Littlewood's office in Ellesmere Port. We explained to him the situation and described Chris. He listened carefully, every now and then asking particular questions, which eventually led us to understanding the situation more clearly and understanding the best way forward. Dr. Littlewood agreed that we should tell the truth, but to consider being conservative with it. We should consider the questions we were asked and try to understand what it was Chris really wanted to know. He also suggested that we should think about developing strategies to deal with the type of questions he may ask. All in all Dr. Littlewood's advice was tremendously helpful and Annette and I both felt much more prepared.

In late 1990 we all attended a clinic run by Dr. Fielding, who was an expert in genetics, to determine both the extent of the genetic problem and, for future reference, if Annette was a carrier. This involved us all having a blood test. Now Chris and needles just did not get on, so to try and show him that there was no problem I went first and then Annette gave her sample. Chris watched this impassively, but when Dr. Fielding suggested he might like to give some of his blood, Chris suggested otherwise. We tried all ways to persuade him, but in the end brute force was called for. Dr. Fielding had clearly been here before advising that Chris was held nice and tight as "I don't want to get kicked into the next parish!". I sat Chris on my knee with his arms held tightly against his body, while Annette held his head. Dr. Fielding knelt down in front of us, moved the needle towards Chris's arm and then issued a sickening "Oooph" and stood up quickly. Chris's leg, which had been between mine had risen at a rapid rate and caught the good Doctor in an area that hurts considerably! So much for precautions. After a short delay while Dr. Fielding composed himself and Annette and I took a tighter hold of all parts of Chris the task of taking a sample was successfully completed, albeit to loud protests.

It was some time later before we received the results of the tests. It had been explained to us how in many cases MD is passed on from the female, as the missing gene is held on the X chromosome. However, the tests had shown that Annette was not a carrier and the MD that Chris had was almost certainly caused by a spontaneous genetic mutation. Dr. Fielding also explained that the tests showed that there was an almost total gene deletion, which would lead to a significant deterioration in Chris's muscular development over time. To start with we were positive that a 'cure' would be found. Significant research was underway and the failing gene had been isolated, several programmes testing gene therapy were undergoing field trials. Our optimism at that time knew no bounds. With the right care, exercises, diet and fruits of the research perhaps after all Chris would have a long life.

Initially, Chris was seen regularly by Dr. Robinson, then in 1991 it was suggested that Chris might benefit from seeing Dr. Richard Appleton, a neuromuscular specialist, based at Alder Hey. Keen to ensure that we were optimally advised we agreed and after an initial session in Liverpool Chris was seen in Chester at a clinic held jointly between Drs. Robinson and Appleton. Things were progressing well. We were advised on what we should be doing to keep Chris healthy, we should endeavour to keep him active, but not to tire him unduly, we should strive to keep his weight down, not to become obsessed, but to ensure he ate sensibly. Chris was very good about it all, he enjoyed walking and would often walk quite a distance and while he didn't eat many sweets anyway he was weaned off them almost totally, eating raw vegetables instead, carrot being a particular favourite. Annette strived to ensure that Chris kept healthy generally and was keen to keep him free of colds and similar ailments, keeping him well wrapped up in winter.

During the second half of 1991 and into 1992 the first real signs of the effect of Muscular Dystrophy started to become evident. Chris started to show the *classic* walking style of MD, the raised heels and shoulders forced back causing the back to be curved to compensate for the raised heels and to maintain balance, which led to a waddling type gait. Chris also began to find that walking long distances tired him out. To help us on days out we were provided with a McLaren Major buggy, a larger and more substantial version of a baby's pushchair. Initially, we tried to keep its use to a minimum and didn't take it with us all the time, trying to find the right balance between keeping Chris active and not over doing it. When he did get tired, he also got irritable and then he could be just a tad unpleasant! The exercise and standing frame regime were still in place. Leg and hip stretches took place every morning and every evening, while the standing frame was used in the evening (still much to Chris's upset and annoyance). It was during this period of time that Annette and I were really hit by the enormity of Chris's situation.

Prompted by Yvonne, Annette as Chris's carer applied for Disabled Living Allowance in January 1992 and set about filling in a myriad of forms. Within a month we received a rejection, Chris did not meet the criteria on which the allowance was paid. The professionals that were associated with Chris's care were dumbfounded and encouraged us to appeal, which we did. More forms, supporting letters from Dr. Robinson and the physios, a visit from an independent doctor (who told us that he had not heard of MD!) and more forms later we were, in September 1992, eventually awarded the allowance. It helped enormously, as Annette had reduced the hours that she worked, but we were still able to get the various items that Chris required. On an almost annual or bi-annual basis we had to complete the same myriad of forms to ensure that Chris retained his right to receive the allowance.

During 1992 we were asked if we would consider travelling to Alder Hey to see Dr. Appleton in his clinic there, primarily as he would have his team available, as well as continuing to see Dr. Robinson in Chester. Obviously keen to ensure that Chris received the best support and advice we readily agreed. So commenced a series of regular trips across the Mersey. The clinics at Alder Hey were in many ways more intense than in Chester as the consultation would take place in a room of up to 5 or 6 people. Chris was very uncomfortable with this feeling that he was on show. However, we did convince him that it was for the best. What did cause a problem though was that we would go to Alder Hey where they would advise a particular course of action, for example certain exercises and stretches. We would then attend the clinic in Chester where we would get different advice. Back to Liverpool a month or so later and their advice would be repeated. It was all very confusing and frankly irritating, there seemed to be no

willingness for the two groups to converse.
As 1993 progressed Chris had become more and more unstable on his feet and as a result he had had a number of falls, one or two quite heavy, causing injury to his knees, elbows and face. These falls were often caused when he was accidentally bumped in the school playground and as he was unable to get his arms up to protect himself he would drop like a sack of potatoes. He would generally only walk anywhere if he could hold someone's hand, and along with Miss Newns the children in his class would be very supportive. As Chris gradually became weaker and walking became more of a problem it was suggested to us by the care team in Chester that we consider having a wheelchair. Annette and I knew that this day would arrive at some point, but we just wanted to delay it as it seemed so final. After some further discussion we eventually agreed to have a wheelchair. It was arranged for the chair to be delivered while Chris was at school, so one evening when I got home from work Annette pointed me into the dining room. There in the corner was what was to be Chris's first wheelchair, silver with reddish covers and child sized. I looked at it and just felt sick, I could tell from Annette's face that she felt the same. Our deepest anxiety was there in front of us, it was a manifestation of what the future held for our son. The door of the dining room was firmly shut and its contents not mentioned for several days. It was perhaps a week or so after it arrived that Chris went into the dining room to get something or the other. He came back in to the lounge as fast as he could,
"Quick," he said, "come and look at this".
"What?" we said.
"Just come and look". We followed him back into the dining room, looking at one another with apprehension. He waddled across the room to where the wheelchair was.
"Look at that," he said almost triumphantly, "Whose is it?"
"Well, its yours," said Annette hesitatingly.
"Can I sit in it?"
"If you want to," Annette replied. We moved it out of the corner and he eased himself into it.
"It's very comfy," he said, smiling and with a little laugh. "Let's go for a walk in it." Not for the first time (or the last for that matter) he knocked us sideways with his ability to take things in his stride.

While Chris could still move around on a flat surface, managing stairs had become a real problem. To get down stairs he simply resorted to a technique he'd used as a toddler, sit down and bump down the stairs one at a time. Climbing a staircase was a completely different kettle of fish and it wasn't long before we had to carry Chris whenever he went to bed, had a bath or wanted to go to the toilet. This soon adds up in a normal day (you count how many times you go upstairs) and as he got heavier it became more and more difficult, especially for Annette. Chris was very aware of this and would wait until I was around before asking to go to the toilet. The long-term implications though needed consideration. We could move Chris's room to what was the dining room and build a bathroom downstairs (but that would mean at night we would be on different floors), or we could have a lift built. We were fortunate that the house we had was probably big enough for such a project, but the thought of having a huge lift shaft in the house was not very palatable. The alternative was to move to a bungalow. After much discussion and weighing up the various alternatives we settled on the idea of moving, being fortunate that we could undertake a move. It was sad really as we were happy in the house and also had good neighbours. Of course, a house sale, house purchase and move doesn't happen overnight and it took quite some time to complete. As we were keen to move we priced the house quite competitively, but ultimately as time was going on and Chris's situation getting worse we had to accept an even lower price. We'd spent quite a lot of time, effort and money getting the house sorted and the bungalow we moved to needed a lot of work as it had been owned by a elderly bachelor whose tastes did not quite match ours!

Moving day, 27th May 1993 arrived wet and got wetter, typical of our luck just then. Chris was despatched to spend the day with Nan while we set to completing the packing. After a last minute delay when the funds transfer process wasn't initiated properly (further good fortune!) we eventually moved the 1000 yards (as the crow flies) to our new home. With the help of the removal men and sister-in-law Julie we gradually got sorted. Due to the delay in the funds transfer the whole moving process was several hours behind schedule, so when I went to pick up Chris from Annette's mum's he was grumpy to say the least. "Where've you been?" he snapped, "I'm getting bored". Ten or fifteen minutes later we were at the bungalow. He walked slowly around his new home, accompanied by Nan, carefully studying each room. He found his bedroom in which we'd put most of his favourite items which prompted a favourable response, but it was the location of the bathroom that impressed the most, "Going to the loo's going to be a lot easier now". He soon settled into the new house and for all of us it was much easier to manage without the stairs.

The issue of conflicting advice between Chester and Alder Hey was resolved in mid 1993, but not in the way we would really have liked. Chris had taken to using the wheelchair, initially not all the time, but he was quite happy to use it when we went out. At Alder Hey the walk to the clinic from the car park was quite a distance so it was sensible to take the chair, or so we thought, especially as the team in Chester were quite happy for us to use it. We arrived in the clinic and waited our turn, eventually getting called in. As usual there were a large number of people present, Dr. Appleton and an assistant, a physiotherapist and the Care Officer from the Muscular Dystrophy Group.

Once the initial pleasantries were over we were greeted with "What's he doing in that?" meaning the wheelchair, "We don't encourage that so early at Alder Hey". I tried to explain that we didn't use the chair all the time and that it had been suggested by the professionals in Chester, but there seemed to be a lack of willingness to listen. Chris was a little bemused by all of this, but the next thing that happened took him completely by surprise. The physiotherapist, who was sitting on a stool, and was examining his legs suddenly grabbed hold of him under the arms, lifted him out of the chair and sat him astride her knee. Then in a loud aggressive voice demanded that he stand up. Chris responded by saying that he couldn't. "Can't or wont?" came the reply. By now Chris was getting upset, tears welled in his eyes. "I don't think that's going to help," said Annette in a controlled manner. There was an almost theatrical sigh of indignation and the physiotherapist roughly put Chris back into the chair. His face was bright red and beads of perspiration covered his forehead. The tears now quietly rolled down his face, despite him trying hard not to cry. His face was set, with a look of indignation, as it did when he felt aggrieved. There followed a short exchange during which Dr. Appleton pointed out that they liked to keep boys out of wheelchairs until they were 10 or 11, Chris at this stage only being about 8. I pointed out that we would be very pleased for that to happen, but having followed all the advice we were given the fact of the matter was that Chris was still falling over and hurting himself, finding walking progressively more difficult and could manage less and less distance. The clinic was brought swiftly to a conclusion.

Both Annette and I were very annoyed about the way Christopher had been treated, whatever the view of Dr. Appleton, and especially the physiotherapist there was absolutely no need to manhandle him in such a way. Chris was very quiet on the way home and indeed didn't say much about it for a long time after. He was, even at this age, aware that people were doing their best to help him. Having talked the matter through together, Annette and I arranged to speak with Dr. Robinson to explain what had occurred. As a result of our meeting it was agreed that we would terminate visiting Liverpool and put Chris back fully under the care of the team in Chester, at least ensuring that we got a consistent approach. Over the next year Chris attended Dr. Robinson's clinics roughly every six months and with her care and the support of the physiotherapists (Pam Dowd and Carol Watson) and occupational therapist (Frances Reeve) at Dorin Park Chris maintained reasonable mobility.

It was also around this time that the moment Annette and I had dreaded arrived and it really hit us of the blue. Over the months Chris had been asking a series of what appeared to be unlinked questions, but not following them through. Suddenly one evening he said, "I'd like to have a meeting in my bedroom".

"OK," we replied, looking puzzled, so we followed Chris down the hallway to his room, where he fell onto his bed and got us to straighten him out. He smiled nervously and chuckled in an engaging sort of way.

"You two sit here," he said, chuckling again, "I need to ask you a question".

"Right," I said nervously.

"You know I have Muscular Dystrophy," he started, "well I want to know what it means and .... if my legs will get better". Oh, God I thought, my heart raced, Annette had gone pale. We knew it would come, but not so soon, but here we were faced with it. He was just over 8 years old, how do you communicate the effect of a complex condition and the potential scenario. A condition that we as adults struggled to understand fully. And most importantly I wasn't going to lie. I thought back to the advice Dr. Littlewood had given us, I searched for something to say, my mind raced, I wasn't really prepared.

"Well mate, it's like this," I stumbled. "You know that your body is made up of lots and lots of cells, well each of those cells contains something like a computer programme which tell it what type of cell it is and what it is supposed to do. So cells in the eye contain an 'eye' programme and muscle cells have a programme that tells them what to do." Chris looked serious and nodded. "The programme in the muscle cells in your legs have a fault in them, so the pro-

gramme doesn't work properly and the muscles don't do what they're supposed to," I said.
"Right, ... But, will they get better?" he asked again. I paused, this was the moment of truth, how would he react, what should I say? Could I lie? Should I lie? I swallowed hard, my palms sweated, my heart beat even harder.
"No, Chris, I'm afraid they won't," I heard myself say, "but you'll be able to do lots of things". There was a pause, the room fell quiet.
"I see. You and Mum will look after me, won't you?" he eventually said without a flicker of emotion on his face.
"Of course we will," we replied in unison. We told him he was our son and we loved him.
"I'll get up now".
It was like he was dismissing us. He went back to what he was doing earlier and never asked a similar question again. Indeed he hardly ever spoke about the condition except when he was in his teens to tell people what he had and then that was very much in a matter of fact, clinical sort of way, never seeking sympathy. Perhaps we should have seen the signs at various points in time, but Chris was different, Sue Herbert was wrong, he did ask.

In January 1994 we took delivery of a Nissan Serena MPV, which I had managed to convince Capital Bank to let me have as a company car. While it was not the most comfortable of vehicles, it made life moving the wheelchair and other equipment around a lot easier so we could get out and about, visiting people and places. I will always be grateful to the Bank for their generosity in allowing me this benefit.

As part of the ever-expanding number of people looking after Chris's well being Yvonne had introduced us to Kath Law, a Community Occupational Therapist, who worked for Social Services. Kath came to see us many times over the months and had recommended the installation of a second hand rail on the stairs at the house in Wavertree Road. Having moved to the bungalow she visited us again to assess the facilities and how we *managed* Chris. Kath's main concern was the way in which we gave Chris a bath as this involved one or both of us lifting him into the bath, and then lifting out again. She felt that this lifting was likely to lead to back problems for us and possible injury to Chris. To start with she arranged for us to have a bath lift, a seat that sits in the bath, lowering and raising the occupant, although she believed that it would be more beneficial in the long term to have the bathroom converted to have a roll in shower and shower chair. After some discussion and consideration of alternatives we agreed to have the work done. So after obtaining the necessary funding and getting plans approved the work was undertaken in March 1994. The end result meant that it was now much easier and safer to give Chris a shower, rather than a bath, and the shower chair also doubled as a toilet chair so access to the loo became easier as well.

In early 1993 Chris had been referred to Mr. Campbell, an orthopaedic consultant, to review his posture, muscle and tendon progress. The main concern that we had was the shortening of the Achilles Tendon, which was causing his toes to point down and his heels to lift, and the constriction of the tendons behind the knees, which meant Chris couldn't fully straighten his legs. We had tried to keep on top of the problem by using the standing frame and regular stretching exercises, but over 12 months the problem gradually grew worse until Mr. Campbell recommended that Chris had surgery, Bilateral Tendo-Achilles Lengthening and Hamstring Release to give it its full name, to ease the constriction. Chris having surgery was something that we had always pushed to the back of our minds and there is no doubt that Chris was reluctant to go ahead. While he was quite use to hospitals and he'd had his adenoids removed just before he was five (after which he was up and about an hour after the operation), this was a completely different proposition. The benefit would be that he would have straighter legs with less tension that would assist with his posture, but the downside was that he would no longer have any prospect of standing unaided. By this time Chris was largely confined to the wheelchair anyway so we determined, in conjunction with the professionals, that the surgery was the best course of action and it would help maintain his quality of life.

The day of the operation, 22nd August 1994, dawned and we duly presented ourselves at Ward 29 of the Countess of Chester Hospital at 10.00 am. Chris was introduced to the nurses who would look after him, Barbara and Suzanne, both of whom he 'clicked' with straight away. Predictably Chris engaged them in conversation wanting to know everything about them and their families! With the necessary paperwork completed the major task was keeping Chris occupied until he was called to the theatre. During the wait the anaesthetist came to see Chris and explain the procedure. Oh no, this would require a needle. Panic. After much calming and soothing the nurses persuaded Chris to have a canula inserted. Having used 'magic' anaesthetic cream the canula was deployed into the arm of a tightly held Chris. Sometime in mid-afternoon the porter arrived to take Chris over to the theatre. His generally carefree attitude collapsed in a heap and the tears flowed. At times like this there was only Mum who could provide the right support and Annette took him in her arms and gave him a big kiss and cuddle. Worry and fright were etched all over his face as our little group made its way via corridors and lifts to the pre-op suite. Suzanne talked to him all the way doing a great job to keep him calm. As the anaesthetic was administered we told him he'd be fine and we'd see him soon and that we both loved him. He was quickly asleep, he looked so peaceful lying on the trolley, a little smile on his face, but as he was wheeled into the theatre my stomach churned and Annette and I gripped each others hand. Not for the last time we shed a tear about him.

Suzanne suggested that we go and get a cup of tea as the operation would take a little while, even so we were back at the theatre waiting room well before they came looking for us. We were led into the post-op room where Chris was just coming round and being tended by a Theatre Sister. Chris was lying on his back and was partly covered by a sheet, but his legs encased in plaster from the very tips of his toes right up to his groin were visible. His eyes opened, saw us standing there and smiled. A huge flood of relief surged through us.

Back on the ward Chris drifted in and out of sleep as the anaesthetic wore off. We had known that his legs would be in plasters, but the extent of them was a bit of a shock. A little while later Mr. Campbell called by to see how Chris was, explained that the procedure had gone well and that the plasters were to keep the legs straight. They had been put on so that the toes were held pointing at the knees and the knee was held as flat as possible. It sounded very painful.

Annette and I had decided to stay the night with Chris, which as it turned out was a good decision. In the bed opposite Chris was a young girl who'd also had surgery on her legs and throughout the night she screamed and wailed. The night staff tried all manner of things to calm her down, but to no avail. The problem was that the other kids in the ward (and their parents) could get no sleep. Added to this Chris's legs had started hurting from the operation and from having his legs held straight, so he was not in the best frame of mind. His comments about the young lady across the room are not really repeatable here!

During the following day the plasters on Chris's legs were reinforced with a special epoxy type material that made them almost 'bullet proof', and incredibly heavy. Chris was supposed to stay in hospital for a day or so, but he was adamant that he wanted to go home. Hospitals are OK, but home is better. As there was no real reason for him to stay the staff gave him permission to be discharged. The only problem was that there was no ambulance available. But Chris was not to be put off by that, saying that he'd go home in the Serena. Now this presented a number of problems as the seats in the Serena are quite high up off the ground and because of the plasters Chris would not be able to bend his legs. In the end we compromised and sat him in the back on the floor, suitably padded and with Annette holding on to him. This was just the beginning of the problems we encountered over the next few weeks.

The weight of the leg plasters made it extremely hard to move Chris easily, they nearly doubled his body weight. When we sat him in the wheelchair we had to support his legs, although we eventually sorted out an adaptation with a board which extended the length of the seat. Sitting like this however was not very comfortable and so was only used to move Chris to the bathroom, the majority of the time he spent lying in bed. For ease we moved Chris's bed from his bedroom into the dining room, moved the TV in as well so we could all be together. The cumulative effect of the operation, the straightened legs, the weight and length of the plasters (which he was expected to have on for at least four weeks) and lying in one position really caused Chris a lot of discomfort. While appreciating it must have been an awful situation, it has to be said that he was a dreadful patient. Chris constantly wanted his legs moving and his bum repositioning, this went on day and night. After the first night Annette and I took it in turns in sleeping on the sofa in the dining room so that only one of us was disturbed in the night. After a few days I went back to work, leaving Annette to cope with the (not so) patient, which she managed to do with the help of her mum, who in her usual controlled manner kept Chris in check (and entertained). The lack of sleep eventually caught up with me though and after suffering a bout of headaches, sickness and stomach cramps I was signed off work for a week. During the time Chris was confined to bed he had plenty of visitors, family and friends. We were particularly grateful to Carl Scourfield, a friend of Chris's from next door but one. He not only came round most days to see Chris and entertain him, but also lent him videos and his Nintendo games console and games.

Towards the end of the second week after the operation Chris started to complain that his feet were sore. Initially we just put this down to another thing to complain about, but he was very persistent. About the only thing that could be seen of his feet though were the very tips of his toes. I thought perhaps that his toes were looking a bit swollen, but wasn't sure if this was just imagination. We were due to see Mr. Campbell at the Royal Infirmary a few days later and so mentioned Chris's concerns. Reluctantly, as they were supposed to be on for another 10 -15 days, he decided that the casts should be removed as a precaution. The cutting process took a long-time mainly because of the reinforcement. When the plasters were eventually taken off it was very clear that there was a problem, Chris's feet were a darkish colour and very swollen. The nurse who was in attendance examined his feet. Very quickly she located the problem, on both heels there were what looked like blood filled blisters larger in diameter than a 50p piece. The nurse looked shocked and said she'd never seen pressure sores as bad. By the time we got back to see Mr. Campbell Chris's feet had swollen even more and the swelling had spread to his lower legs. Annette made it quite clear to Mr. Campbell that she was less than impressed with the situation, it was a good job that we had listened to Chris regarding his sore feet, what would have happened had he not had the plasters removed just doesn't bear thinking about. As it was he had to have a lengthy course of anti-biotics and have the wounds bathed twice a day.

As the plasters had come off early Mr. Campbell was keen to ensure that we did everything to maintain the stretching of the tendons behind the knee (the Achilles Tendon release was very successful) and so a programme of physiotherapy was organised. This was entrusted to Carol Watson from Dorin Park. Her early visits were a bit traumatic, for Chris and Carol. Chris found the stretching really painful due to the operation and the swelling and screamed and shouted throughout the session (despite Mum remonstrating). Poor Carol went home with a headache. During this period Chris saw an orthotist to be cast for ankle splints that would hold his feet and ankles in correct position and maintain the good work of the Achilles surgery.

About a week after the plasters had been removed the blood blisters on Chris's heels burst during the daily treatment we were giving him. As a result he ended up with huge holes in his heels, at the bottom of which you could see the heel bone. With the help of the District Nurse, Sister Marion, Chris started on the long road to recovery. For a lot of the time he had to wear sheepskin wrap over slippers, as wearing shoes was impossible. In fact it was well into January of the next year, nearly five months from the date of the operation before he managed to wear shoes again. Chris received his ankle splints in mid-October and took to them very well, and once he got used to them (and the pressure sores allowed) would wear them all-day and everyday.

One of the effects of the dystrophy in weakening muscles is to lead to a curvature or scoliosis of the spine and an imbalance or obliquity of the pelvis. Active exercise and stretching helps delay the onset, but at some point the professionals associated with the case recommended the use of a support jacket. Dr. Robinson was well aware of the ongoing trauma the standing frame was causing and told Chris that if he wanted to stop using it then he would need to wear a support jacket for his back. As Chris hated the standing frame with a passion he readily agreed to Dr. Robinson's suggestion. The support jacket is made by an orthotist taking a body cast using plaster. The casting was done at Dorin Park, with the help of Carol, and a couple of weeks later, in October 1994, Chris received his first jacket. After a week or so of getting used to it, he took to wearing it, generally without complaint. Getting Chris into a support jacket became a daily ritual that Annette and I became quite adept at. Chris wore it whatever, even when we were holiday and it was only in the last year that wearing it really became a problem.

There is an alternative to wearing a support jacket and that is to have what is known as a Luque Rod inserted. This is a major surgical procedure in which the patients back is opened up, the spine exposed and a stainless steel rod attached by pins and wires, thus keeping the spine straight. This option had been discussed with us quite early after Chris's diagnosis, as an option to consider for the future. We knew at the time, and nothing over the next few years changed our minds, that this was not something we could put Chris through, even if it did offer an extension to his life expectancy.

Through 1995 we were provided, with the help of Kath Law and Yvonne, various aids to help with the management of Chris. Firstly we got a small mobile hoist to help us transfer Chris from his chair to bed, which was subsequently replaced towards the end of the year by a permanent ceiling mounted electric hoist. We were also provided a Baltimore electric bed, which raised and lowered and tilted in three separate places. This made life much easier, especially as following the operation on Chris's legs we now needed to get up in the night to turn him over. Being able to position the bed at the right height made this an easier operation and less stressful on our backs. To Chris though the bed was magic and he would have great fun getting it into all sorts of angles with him somewhere in the middle. For a long time it was something he had to demonstrate to all visitors. Put simply it was his pride and joy..... well at least one of them. During the year he also took possession of an indoor electric wheelchair, which was slower and more suitable for use in school. The bungalow was gradually getting taken over by appliances of all shapes and sizes.

In August 1995 Annette and I were invited to a meeting with Dr. Robinson at which she told us that she was retiring and that Chris's care was to be transferred to a new paediatric consultant, Dr. John Gibbs. We were sorry to see Dr. Robinson go as she had been very supportive of us as a family since our first meeting in 1990. We were introduced to Dr. Gibbs, who explained his background and aims for the future, we immediately felt comfortable with him and felt Chris would too, although the first clinic was sometime off. Chris was quite sad that Dr. Robinson was not to look after him anymore and insisted that we buy a small gift and send a card as a 'thank you'.

From earlier in the year Chris had been having trouble with an ingrowing nail on his big toe, which was partly due to him not walking. After treatment a number of times by a chiropodist it was recommended that the nail was removed. Our GP, Dr. Kini referred Chris to a specialist - Mr. Campbell. Now Chris, who had not really forgiven him for the problem with the leg plasters, was not too happy about this, especially as whenever he saw Mr. Campbell he would try to stretch Chris's legs and end up hurting him. It was not an easy task convincing Chris to see Mr. Campbell over his toe. Eventually, Mum prevailed. So in November Chris was a day patient at the Nuffield Hospital. By a strange coincidence the anaesthetist that day was a Dr. Robinson, our Dr. Robinson's husband. Chris was quite impressed by this and happily chatted away about how Dr. (Mrs) Robinson had looked after him. Dr. (Mr) Robinson had heard of Chris from his wife and was happy to chat with him, keeping him calm while he sent him off to sleep, using the mask and not a needle. Chris's toe soon healed, but that success still did not alter his opinion of Mr. Campbell.

1996 was a fairly uneventful year as far as the medical side was concerned, Chris was seen regularly by Dr. Gibbs and with his general health being good the only concern we had was in maintaining control of his weight. Generally, he ate very few sweets or crisps and did not drink much fizzy drinks. Annette ensured that his diet was well balanced, and he still ate his raw carrots and potatoes. Although his weight was increasing it was nothing to be alarmed at. As Chris was getting bigger he was assessed during the year for new wheelchairs and was moved up into adult sized chairs. The bungalow also entered the space age when, again through Kath Law, we had installed the Possum system. This is a very clever set of equipment that allows the user to turn on/off lights, open doors, use the phone, operate TVs, hi-fis, computers etc. and any other electric device all from one console by the use of infrared. Needless to say Chris was over the moon with this contraption and found it very useful.

In early 1997 Dr. Gibbs asked us if we would consider Chris being seen by a neuromuscular specialist at the Robert Jones & Agnes Hunt Orthopaedic Hospital, Gobowen, near Oswestry. Our initial reaction was not positive as we well recalled our previous experiences with shared care. Dr. Gibbs was familiar with this issue and moved to put our minds at ease, by saying that he would remain in close contact with the specialist at Oswestry. After some thought the opportunity to provide Chris specialist care was too good to miss, Dr. Gibbs suggested an initial meeting with Dr. Quinlivan at Oswestry.

Our first visit to Oswestry was in March 1997. Gobowen is just like an old cottage hospital, although it is gradually being modernised, it has a very pleasant feel about, not like a hospital at all. Chris quite liked it, not least because of the long central corridor along which he could whizz in his chair. In the clinic, before seeing the doctor, Chris was weighed, measured, had the volume of his lungs checked and had an ECG (a bit of panic here as he thought a needle was involved). We were last in to see Dr. Quinlivan, a small, bespectacled lady doctor with a lovely soft-spoken voice. She had had a letter from Dr. Gibbs and was aware of our concerns over dealing with two centres, she assured us that she would keep Dr. Gibbs fully informed with progress. She wanted to know Chris's history, which between the three of us we were able to furnish. She explained to us her knowledge of MD and that Chris was one of several boys with MD that she had under her care. Amongst the points that she made was for us to maintain Chris's good sitting posture and to keep control of his weight, but at the time she felt that generally things were good overall. We came away from the clinic feeling quite positive.

April saw us attend a meeting at Moston Lodge, on the Countess of Chester Hospital campus, which was organised by Yvonne to discuss with a team of professionals various aspects of Chris's care. One of our main concerns at this time was that Chris was not sleeping well. After the operation on his legs and the gradual muscle weakening he was unable to turn himself over in the night, this resulted in him becoming uncomfortable, waking up and shouting Annette or I to turn him over. On a good night this could be 5 times, but was more likely to be 7 to 10 times. As a result of the meeting Sister Jenny Jones, the District Nurse, was asked to investigate alternative mattresses. After contacting the Muscular Dystrophy Group a Tempur mattress was suggested. We took one of the mattresses on trial and found it made a considerable difference, reducing the disturbances to 3 or 4 a night. After a bit of a fight the necessary funding was obtained and Chris was able to have a Tempur permanently.

Another issue of concern were certain aspects of Chris's emotional balance. He'd been using the wheelchair for about 4 years and appeared to have adapted quite well to the circumstances. Initially it had been a relief for him as he felt safer, no more falling over and hurting himself. But for a little while we had noticed that he had become very conscious of people, especially other children, looking at him. We tried to explain that it was because people saw him as special that they wanted to look, but he was still not happy about it. To start with he would just mutter to himself or whoever was with him, but gradually it got to the point that if we were out and about he would just say, "I want to go home" or "Let's go now". No matter what we did or said we were unable to change his outlook. Through Yvonne it was arranged for us to see Dr. Littlewood again. The initial meeting was between Dr. Littlewood, Annette, Yvonne and I and was to allow Dr. Littlewood to catch up with what had happened since we last spoke and to understand the latest problem on which we needed his help. Dr. Littlewood suggested that a meeting with Chris would be beneficial, but he was concerned about ensuring there was no erosion of his self-esteem. As Chris was nearly 12 Dr. Littlewood felt that Chris should decide whether he should come to see him. He suggested that he would write a letter to Chris inviting him to a meeting, the meeting to be just between the two of them and that their chat would be between them unless Chris decided otherwise.

A few days after our meeting Chris received his letter. He was quietly impressed that he had received such a letter from an important doctor. The letter asked if Christopher would like to meet, without Mum and Dad, to talk about things that were important to him. Chris considered the invitation for some time, asking various questions of us, including would we be upset if he went without us. We explained that he was old enough now to make his own mind up and there were some subjects that he might find easier talking about to Dr. Littlewood than to us. After further consideration he decided, to our relief, that he would go. The meeting took place a few days after his 12th birthday and lasted for quite some time.

"Everything go alright?" I asked as we made our way out to the car.

"Yes thanks," came the reply.

"Did you find it helpful?" asked Annette.

"Yes thanks," came the reply.

"What did you talk about?" we asked.

"Several things," was the reply in a voice that said I've finished that conversation. We never did find out what was discussed.

This was the first of a number of meetings with Dr. Littlewood, which generally followed a pattern of Chris; then Mum, Dad and Yvonne; and finally all of us over a period of 12 – 15 weeks. There is no doubt that Dr. Littlewood helped us all enormously, helping us to understand our emotions and how to deal with events. As for Chris, whatever they spoke about seemed to have a positive affect. After that first meeting Chris gradually came to terms with people staring at him. One technique he adopted was to stare back and make the other party feel uncomfortable, but eventually he simply accepted it. There were more important things and people to be concerned about than what people thought of him. Dr. Littlewood was also very helpful to Chris in helping him overcome the traumatic loss of his friend Peter Herbert. When Annette and I saw Dr. Littlewood in September 2000, after we had lost Chris, Dr. Littlewood told us that Chris was always very open and seemed to enjoy their discussions. However, he had raised the issue of Muscular Dystrophy with Chris on numerous occasions only to find the *road* blocked or diverted ("Look at that aeroplane, it's a Boeing 737 etc. etc.). There was no way he was going to talk about that. He was, Dr. Littlewood said, quite unique, quite mature in his outlook and quite remarkable.

In October we made our second visit to Dr. Quinlivan's clinic at Oswestry, where we were introduced to Carolyn Evans, a Care Officer, from the Muscular Dystrophy Group. Also working in the clinic supporting Dr. Quinlivan was Kate Fox usually in *residence* at the Neuromuscular Centre in Winsford. After Chris's weight and so on had been checked we were in to see the doctor. In conjunction with Kate, Dr. Quinlivan gave Chris a full examination – lung volume (lower than average), pulse and blood pressure (slightly up), and posture (we were aware that there was a slight bending in Chris's spine and that he was leaning over slightly). Chris was then asked to go for an x-ray on his back and then come back to see the doctor. Having the x-ray taken is a fairly simple procedure, except it did involve us having to remove Chris's support jacket and get him comfortable on the bed. With him well padded to stop him rolling, and his legs bridged the x-rays were soon taken. The x-ray was developed while we sorted Chris out and then we were back to the clinic. We could see from the x-ray that the scoliosis of Chris's spine was quite pronounced in the bottom third. Dr. Quinlivan and Kate studied the x-ray, before Dr. Quinlivan said, "I don't think that, with the reduced lung capacity and your views that Chris would be a candidate for the (Luque) rod". Chris, who hadn't been listening properly as he was chatting to the nurse, went pale and suddenly burst into tears. We managed to calm him down, unsure what the problem was. Eventually, he told us that he didn't want to have the rod operation. Dr. Quinlivan was taken aback, and quickly explained that she had said he wouldn't have it and that they were recommending a different course of action. He was still unsure and listened closely to the next part of the discussion. Dr. Quinlivan and Kate were keen to ensure that the scoliosis did not develop any further and so wanted some pads inserting into Chris's jacket to counteract the bending of the spine. Kate was also keen to improve Chris's sitting position as the leaning was being caused by the pelvic obliquity that was associated to the scoliosis.

The Orthotist Department at Oswestry was unable to see us that day so we made an appointment to return a few days later. The appointment was with Mr. Williams and after reviewing the existing fit of the jacket and the new requirements defined by Dr. Quinlivan the jacket was taken off to be changed. This was going to take a little while so Mr. Williams suggested that we went and got a cup of tea. When we returned, about an hour later, the jacket had just been returned from the workshop and now had three pads neatly stuck inside effectively forming the points of a triangle so as to exert pressure and oppose the curve of the spine. The Examination Room was very small and putting the jacket back on Chris was like performing gymnastics in a wardrobe, but we eventually completed the exercise. Once on Chris was uncomfortable, which was both expected and understandable, and had a bit of a moan, although his biggest gripe was about the smell of the glue used to fix the pads! Within a few days Chris was used to the jacket and was back into the routine of wearing it with out complaint and the smell went away.

Having had the jacket changed we could now adjust Chris's posture. To save us another trip to Oswestry Kate Fox kindly offered to visit us at home. This also gave her the opportunity to see Chris in the various wheelchairs that he used. At this stage Chris was using a Tempur cushion to sit on, which we had bought for him, that he found much more comfortable than the standard foam cushions previously used. Kate suggested a number of changes that we could do there and then. One was to try out a Roho Quadtro 'dry floatation' cushion. This cushion is made up of 4 sets of 20 air sacs that are inflated and each quarter can be set to balance the seating of the user. Chris very quickly found the Roho to be, as he said, "brilliant". The effect of setting the Roho was to have Chris sitting upright and no longer leaning, which in turn meant that he was much more comfortable and he didn't need repositioning all the time. Following the visit Kate prepared a letter for Dr. Quinlivan recommending a variety of changes to the wheelchairs, such as wider arm rests, adjustable head rests and firmer bases. Kate was happy to loan the Roho cushion to us, which was a good job as it was nearly three months before we got referred to the Wheelchair Clinic in Ellesmere Port for assessment.

We arrived at the Clinic in plenty of time for our appointment, but it was one and half-hours later that we were called in. Chris, not the most patient of people, had been all for going home .... after 10 minutes. Had it not been so important then I think we probably would have. Eventually, we got called in. We explained to Dr. Kiteroot the reason for our appointment, essentially wanting the clinic to provide a Roho cushion, which in the previous few months had proved to be extremely beneficial. To start with the doctor told us that he was not aware of Roho Quadtro cushions and that as he was an expert on wheelchair seating he would make a judgement on Chris's needs. I asked if he had received a letter from Dr. Quinlivan (which he had), but received a lecture on how the medical profession worked. Doctors referred patients to him to be assessed, they did not make recommendations to him, and used an analogy of a GP sending a patient with diabetes to a consultant. Frankly, I was to put it mildly not happy with his attitude, which bordered on the unprofessional. I pointed out that Dr. Quinlivan was a specialist in neuromuscular conditions, especially Duchenne Muscular Dystrophy and had wide experience of treating the condition and this was not at all similar to his analogy. I suggested that he telephoned Dr. Quinlivan and discuss the matter with her. The debate went on for some time, mainly revolving around his role as an expert. I pointed out repeatedly that I was not questioning this and we were quite prepared to listen to or try out any alternatives. During this time I was acutely aware that we were talking about Chris, in front of him. So suddenly I said,

"Why don't we ask Chris, as the patient, what he wants?"

"What do you think Chris? What do you want?" asked the Occupational Therapist who was in attendance.

"Well," said Chris, with a mischievous smile just about evident, "I like my Quadtro, it's absolutely brilliant".

With that the doctor nodded to the OT, who fetched from behind a screen a box containing a Roho cushion. Chris smiled, we said "Thank You" and an hour and a bit after we'd gone in we left the clinic. The Roho was of tremendous benefit over the next years, Chris found it very comfortable, especially once his natural padding on his bum began to get thinner and it allowed us, by readjusting the cells, to keep him well balanced and straight.

By and large 1998 ticked on without any real major issues health wise. We continued our regular visits to Dr. Gibbs in Chester and Dr. Quinlivan in Oswestry. Chris's general health was good, with him suffering the odd cold, and by this time Annette had started an interest in aromatherapy so Chris benefited from the use of essential oils and was also regularly taking echinacea. The only problem that Chris was having was caused by him growing and putting weight on. We had tried hard to control any weight gain without becoming obsessive and making his life dull, but as 1998 progressed he was loading up a bit. This in turn meant that his support jacket no longer fitted well and we couldn't get it fastened properly which in turn was causing him some discomfort during the day. So at a visit to Dr. Quinlivan in mid-August we discussed this problem with her and Jenny Whitall (from the NMC, who had taken over from Kate Fox when she retired). At this stage the scoliosis appeared to have stablised, but it was decided that Chris needed to be cast for a new jacket, one that fitted better. As we were going on holiday to Florida we wanted to have it done prior to going so that if possible we could take it with us. So we were dispatched to the Orthotics Department where we were seen again by Mr. Williams, who as the last time we'd seen him was very pleasant and happy to chat to Chris, especially about cars.

The casting involves wrapping plaster bandages tightly around the abdomen while holding the patient upright and then before they set cutting them off. From this casting a 'body' is made around which the jacket is moulded. This process is both messy (from the plaster bandages) and uncomfortable (as Chris needed to be held upright underneath the shoulders) and takes about 15 - 20 minutes. Mr. Williams worked quickly, but ensuring that the plaster was pressed into the body form. Next came the bit Chris hated, having the plaster cut off by running a sharp knife down the breast. This wasn't actually as bad as it sounds as the orthotist inserts a metal plate the length of the cast down which the cut is made. However to Chris there was still a major risk he was going to get cut!

Making the 'body' takes time, especially as it needs to cure before the jacket can be moulded, however we arranged to have the jacket fitted on 1st September, just after Chris returned from his third visit to the Heswall Boys Camp. We were shown into Mr. Williams' fitting room, there was Chris's jacket on the floor in a bag. I nodded in its direction drawing Annette's attention to it. "That looks far too big," I whispered. Mr. Williams came in, greeted us and asked how Chris was. He picked up the jacket off the floor and studied it with a puzzled expression. We got Chris on the couch, removed his old jacket and helped Mr. Williams put on the new one. It was immediately clear that the jacket was too big. So big in fact that I could have probably got in it at the same time! The look on Mr. Williams' face grew more puzzled. He didn't know what had happened, but taking the jacket set off to the workshop to try to find out. He was gone some time, eventually returning to apologise and say that it was not clear what had gone wrong, but as they still had the body (which was from Chris's casting) they would make another jacket.

The new jacket now wouldn't be ready until after we returned from holiday and as Chris was also going to Hope House it wasn't until the end of October that we were able to get to Oswestry again for the jacket to be fitted. As before we saw Mr. Williams and as before the jacket didn't fit, this time it was too long and even with trimming would not be suitable. There was no other option, but to make another body, so we got Chris ready to be cast and Mr. Williams set to, ensuring that the plaster bandages fitted snugly against Chris's body. Considering that it is an unpleasant and tiring process Chris was well behaved and maintained his humour throughout. Once the casting was finished we cleaned Chris up as best we could, but a shower was the order of the day when we got home to get rid of the flakes of plaster that somehow found their way into all the creases of the body and if left can become very irritating.

Once the jacket was ready we got a phone call to arrange for a fitting, as I was busy at work it was not until the end of November that we could go. Unfortunately, on the morning of the appointment Annette was not feeling well. Rather than postpone the appointment and as it was for a fitting only I said I would take Chris, besides Mr. Williams would be able to assist in moving Chris. Leaving Mum in bed we had a pleasant run down the A483 to Oswestry, arriving at the Orthotics Department in plenty of time for the appointment. We reported to the Reception, only to be told that Mr. Williams wasn't in, but that we would be seen by one of the other orthotists. After a short wait, during which Chris started fretting over how we would manage without Mr. Williams to assist moving him, we were shown into a small fitting room by the orthotist, a young lady. A student accompanied the orthotist and with the wheelchair it was quite crowded in the room. I took off Chris's jumper and shirt, removed his old jacket and lifted him onto the couch. The orthotist fetched the new jacket, which <u>looked</u> much better than last time. We eased it onto Chris and pulled it up across his chest, it fitted quite well. The orthotist studied the fit of the jacket, explaining to the student what she was doing as she went along. It was clear that she was not particularly happy with the fit, although to me it looked fine. Eventually, after repositioning the jacket several times, she declared that it was simply not long enough, would not give Chris's back the right support and he would end up slouching in it. The expression on Chris's face said it all, "this is bloody stupid" and "what are we going to do now" and "Mum'll go mad".

The orthotist excused herself and disappeared, jacket in hand. While she was gone Chris occupied himself chatting to the student, finding out where she was from and explaining that he was a veteran of this process. Despite the uncertainty he was still cheerful. The orthotist returned and explained that making another jacket from the body was not possible, as it had been damaged, there was no alternative, but to take another casting. Chris was mortified by this, "How are we going to manage without Mum?" he wanted to know. He was even less pleased when the orthotist said she wanted to do a front and back casting. This entails the patient firstly lying on their back and having the plaster laid across the chest and down the sides, which once the plaster has gone off is removed, and then the patient lying on their stomach while the back is cast. The first part of this is OK, but for Chris the lying on the front was very, very uncomfortable as because of the constrictures in his legs he couldn't get them straight, he couldn't lift his head and he was just generally uncomfortable on his tummy. Added to this he was worried about how we would manage the process without Annette and was all for going home and coming back again. I was more conscious of us still not having a good fitting jacket three months after we arranged for one and as I was running out of holidays from work the impact of having to come back again would be problematical.

I bit the bullet, overrode Chris's opposition to the idea and agreed to carry on. I got Chris ready, putting on the gauze vest which stops the plaster sticking to his skin and easing down his trousers and shorts ("not to far, please"). The casting of Chris's front went well, the orthotist explaining what she was doing for the benefit of the student. The need to ensure that the plaster forms exactly to the body, the need to ensure measurements are taken and with this process that the mid-line down each side is clearly marked so the two half can be put together correctly. Then came the back cast. Turning Chris over was no easy task due to the fact that he was quite heavy, was quite floppy and the couch was quite small. After a struggle we managed to get him over and into the right position to be cast. I held his legs so that they were not straining, but he was still very uncomfortable, a state not helped by all the bits of plaster and water lying about, which seemed to get everywhere. As the orthotist set to work it wasn't long before it all got too much and having got redder and redder Chris started crying. Of course, holding his legs there was little else I could do but try to reassure him, seeing him in such a state just made me feel completely inadequate. After what seemed like an age, but was actually only 5 or 10 minutes, we were able to roll Chris onto his back. His face was bright red, his eyes streaming tears were red, his nose was running, his hair was all over the place and he was covered in plaster. I calmed him down and gave him a hug, then with the help of the student, I cooled him down and cleaned him up as best I could with paper towels. If I'd found the whole episode traumatic, heaven only knows how Chris felt. It was awful to watch his anguish and not having Annette there to comfort him made it even worse. After a further struggle to get his old jacket back on and his shirt and jumper on we were in a position to leave. Rather than go home straight away we went to the Coffee Shop for a drink and as a reward some chocolate ("don't tell Mum though!"). Unfortunately it was to be the end of January before we were able to get back to Oswestry for a fitting of the jacket as in the interim period Chris was taken ill.

Annette had worked part time in the Pharmacy of the Countess of Chester

Hospital for about 8½ years, gradually reducing her hours over the years as Chris needed more care (and earning thresholds dropped affecting carer benefits). She had found her time there generally enjoyable, but over the latter years a number of her friends had left. Eventually, as Chris needed more attention she decided to leave, finishing in November 1998. Annette was then offered a part time job, a couple of mornings a week, by Lee Barrett at his hair dressing salon, Barrett's Classic Cuts, starting in early December.

December had seen the usual activities in the build-up to Christmas, shopping and parties, as well as a brief stay at Hope House and a visit to Dr. Gibbs. Chris was really looking forward to Christmas, the list of wanted items had gone in early (July if my memory serves me well). Chris had enjoyed the Dorin Park Disco, but had come home feeling tired from his exertions and the heat in the school. His general health through the year had been good and apart from the discomfort from the jacket everything was going well. The day after the Disco Chris had a bit of a sniffle, so Annette swung into action with the various medicines we kept to hand. Previous experience had shown her that if you could 'get on top' of the cold early then the cold often subsided before developing fully. During the day, Friday 18th, he seemed fine, but during the night he was quite restless, needing more turning than usual. On the Saturday he got up as usual, although the cold had taken hold and he was now coughing and wheezing. Annette had called the doctors and we were asked if we could get him to the surgery. Chris was seen by Dr. Kini, who thought Chris had bronchitis gave us a prescription for medicine and a *spacer* to inhale through. We were also seen by Sister Jones, who said if we wanted any assistance to give her a call. When we got home Chris just wanted to go back to bed and rest. We started the treatment advised by Dr. Kini, but Chris did have a bit of trouble using the *spacer*, although he did persevere, helped by Sister Jones who called in to see him on her way home. Through the night Chris was very restless and as the night wore on he was having trouble breathing. Because of the scoliosis Chris's chest and therefore lung capacity was impaired and this meant that he was unable to get his lungs fully filled and unable to give a big cough to get the phlegm off the lungs. First thing Sunday morning and Annette called the doctor. Fortunately, Dr Kini was on call and was soon at the house. He listened to Chris's chest and then said that he felt it best if Chris went in to hospital for treatment, especially some physiotherapy to help get the fluid off his chest. Chris was not too impressed with this suggestion, but Annette and I knew there was no alternative.

The ambulance was a while in arriving, so we had time to get Chris's gear together and also to get our own bag packed as we knew that one or both of us would have to stop overnight to move him etc. The ambulance eventually arrived just after midday and Chris was admitted to Ward 30 (of the Countess) and put in Room 8, which although a two bed room was previously unoccupied. The nursing staff efficiently went through the admission procedure, including taking blood, which caused the usual panic at the sight of the needle. Chris was 'attached', via a probe over his finger, to a device that monitored his pulse rate and blood oxygen level. Chris was prescribed some anti-biotics, which as with other medicines he took without complaint. As time went on Chris's breathing was becoming more and more laboured, so he was put on a low flow of oxygen to help him, although the physio we had expected had not yet materialised. The results of the initial tests came back in the early evening and as a result it was decided to increase the strength of the anti-biotics and to administer them intravenously. The first problem was to introduce the line, but by now Chris was so poorly that he did not have either the strength or willingness to object to the needle. The monitor was also reflecting the situation with Chris's pulse rising and the blood oxygen level falling. The oxygen flow through the mask was increased and the bed tilted to try and help drain his chest. The night of Sunday 20th was one of the longest nights of our lives, the situation seemed to be getting worse, his pulse was regularly over 160 and the blood oxygen level down to 30 or less. Even with the oxygen Chris's breathing was becoming shallower and shallower, we couldn't believe how quickly the situation had deteriorated from a simple cold the day before last. It was clear from the staff's concern that the situation was not good. As midnight Sunday came the situation was very grave, Chris's pulse was even higher, oxygen sats lower still and I was helping him breathe by massaging his chest. We felt that we were looking into the abyss, I can not describe how we felt. I just couldn't sit and watch him fade away, so I found the nurses and asked for them to fetch a doctor. She was having forty winks and was bleeped, coming to see Chris almost immediately. As a result they introduced an even stronger anti-biotic and some other drugs. There needed to be a reaction within an hour or so. Chris kept drifting in and out of sleep, but was generally fairly peaceful. The staff kept popping in and providing us with a constant flow of tea. For the next hour or so we just kept watch either on Chris or the monitor, watching for the slightest change, looking for any positive sign. Eventually, as morning took over from night the situation had not got any worse, the figures on the monitor were pretty stable and Chris's temperature had eased slightly. Chris himself was very lethargic, the sparkle and fight seemed to be missing, when he opened his eyes they simply seemed to be saying, "Why me?", Goodness knows where he'd been in his mind during the night, had he looked over the fence between the here and there and decided it wasn' t time to go?

Dr. Gibbs told us later that it was touch and go whether they had put Chris on a ventilator on the Sunday, and if the stronger anti-biotics hadn't worked they would have had to. He went on to say that if they had it was possible that Chris would not have come off it, as the lungs would not have been able to recover sufficiently to support his needs. The rest is unthinkable.

There was still concern evident from the doctors when they did their rounds on Monday 21st and this was quickly followed by the arrival of the physiotherapist to help get phlegm off Chris's lungs. This involves some fairly heavy beating on the chest and lots of rolling from side to side. Just the thing you want when feeling under the weather. Chris was pretty good about it, but you could tell from the stony look on his face that he was not overly impressed, but I was able to take some comfort that if he could react in even that way things must be improving. The process was quite successful as quite a lot of 'muck' was brought up. Through the rest of the day the medication was maintained and there were further visits from the physio, and more 'muck' removed. As the day wore on the monitor indicated that progress was being made, Chris's pulse rate was dropping from the worrying heights of the night and the oxygen sats were gradually climbing as the anti-biotics and physiotherapy got to work on the lungs. The course of strong anti-biotics had been completed early in the day, but he was kept on a lower dose for the rest of the day. He had a reasonable night, although he did want turning quite often, another good sign was the impatience when we didn't respond immediately.

Through Tuesday 22nd Chris continued to improve, regular physio from the physiotherapists and Annette and I, as well tilting the bed to drain his chest, helping enormously. During the day Chris had something to eat for the first time since he'd been admitted, he was off the oxygen and by now we felt that he had turned the corner, but there was still a long way to go. As the evening came he actually looked a lot brighter, and must have felt so as he started to be cheeky and even chat up the nurses! However, another problem was brewing. Chris was well aware that Christmas was just around the corner and he didn't want to be in hospital over the festive period. The nurses tried to convince him that it wasn't so bad, there were lots of things to do, but he wasn't having any of that. As the day wore on he was building himself up into a real state and this was having an adverse effect on his well being. Dr. Gibbs came to see Chris during the afternoon and reasoned with Chris in a 'grown up' way. He told him that he would review the situation the following day, but if he continued to get angry and frustrated his recuperation would take longer. Chris always listened to Dr. Gibbs and calmed down, but I also knew that he had set his heart on going home.

Wednesday 23rd brought a major improvement in Chris's condition, his breathing was now significantly better although we were still draining his chest. His tactic for going home had also changed, rather than getting upset he was talking positively about what he would get for Christmas, how he was looking forward to Nana coming for lunch, what was on the TV and so on. He had a real knack for putting those around him on a real guilt trip. Dr. Gibbs saw him in the morning, but said nothing about going home, which left the patient slightly confused. It wasn't until late afternoon that Dr. Gibbs returned, looked at the notes, examined Chris and eventually said he could go home, as long as he took it easy. "YES! YES! YES!" probably said it all.

Chris did get home later that evening and went straight to bed, but it was very clear from his behaviour and the expression on his face that he was glad to be back in his own bed, with his own 'stuff' around him. I knew that Dr. Gibbs had really wanted to keep him in for at least another day and that Annette was worried that if anything went awry Christmas was not the best time to get support. Chris was happy enough to stay in bed the next day, Christmas Eve, and during the morning he was visited by Lin Wakley, one of the physiotherapists, and by Sister Jones to check he was OK. We needed to maintain the procedure of chest beating and pressure to help bring up the phlegm. Having the electric bed also helped in the draining process as we could tilt it down at the head end. Chris had had a few visitors (Auntie Ju, Nana, and Josie) while in the hospital, including one from a good colleague of mine, Paul Forrester. He'd brought Chris some videos about Manchester United (a bit of a struggle this as Paul was an avid Everton supporter) and during the day Chris watched them all, which kept him occupied while Annette and I ran round trying to get Christmas organised at the last minute. During the early evening Chris said he would get up for a while so we got him up and sat him in his chair. He stayed up for a while, but found breathing more difficult while sitting up (we hadn't put his jacket on as that would have made breathing harder still) and after about an hour asked to go back to bed. He'd not been in bed long when he was paid a visit by the whole of the Carrington family, this really cheered him up as he always enjoyed seeing Mel, and he enjoyed the occasional rude word or joke from Sharon. It was Sharon who'd told him his favourite joke - 'How do you make a door laugh? Tickle its knob!'

Unlike previous years Christmas Day did not start at some unearthly hour, it was lateish when Chris woke up, he'd had a reasonable nights sleep, only being turned the normal number of times. As was normal, Chris was excited about the prospect of what was waiting for him in the lounge. Christmas was always a special time, the sparkle in his eyes seemed brighter and the smile on his face seemed wider, but this year having been through so much in the previous week it meant so much to us. To get things rolling he opened a few small presents in bed, but was keen to get to the meaty ones. Before we got him up we undertook the physio on his chest and drained as much phlegm as we could. We got him up and settled in his chair, and then he was off. His eyes were nearly as big as the mound of presents, which he set to opening with a little help. After each one was opened there was an expression of gratitude, a study of the item and then .... onto the next one. Needless to say what he wanted most was to try out a couple of new games on the computer (after all he hadn't played it for a week). He did quite well, he managed to keep going to just after lunch, but then decided he wanted to go back to bed as he was tired and his back ached. At the end of a long day Chris summed it up, "Thanks Mum, for a great Christmas".

Chris's actual recovery took a long time, but he was helped enormously by the regular visits of physiotherapists Lin Wakley and Carol Watson. It was not until January 6th 1999 that Chris's chest was clear, he was breathing properly and was staying up all day. During his illness he had lost almost two stone in weight, which on one hand was a bonus, but was also a nuisance as many of his bony bits were now more exposed. Having missed a week of school Chris returned on 11th January pleased to be back with all his friends and they were all pleased to see him.

With Chris recovered and back to school we were now able to arrange to go to Oswestry to have the new support jacket, cast at the end of November, fitted. While we had set off for the appointment with trepidation, amazingly, everything seemed to be OK. The jacket fitted reasonably well, albeit a bit on the big size due to Chris's weight loss, but at least we returned home with a new jacket. We decided that we would break the new jacket in slowly, so for the next few days Chris used his old jacket (which we had started padding with bits of sheepskin) and planned to try the new jacket over the weekend when we could change jackets if needed. The best laid plans......

On Friday 29th January Annette phoned me at work to say Chris had been sick at school and was not well, could I go and pick him up. Fortunately, I was able to

and arrived at the school about 15 minutes later to find Chris waiting with Joan (the Receptionist) by the door looking as white as a sheet. "Hi ya, pal," I said, "what's up with you?"
"I don't feel well, Dad. Can we go home?" came the downbeat reply. I quickly got him into the Galaxy and we were home in another quarter of an hour, and a short time after that Chris was in bed. Whenever Chris felt sick he nearly always gave us plenty of notice so that we could be prepared, I can only remember two occasions when he threw up on the floor. So it was this evening, each time he felt unwell he would let us know so we could sit him up in bed and get a bucket ready. It was well past midnight before he settled and went off to sleep. Even though it was late when he went to sleep, Chris was awake at his usual time the following morning. As was normal, he wanted a wee. Since Chris had been in his wheelchair we had been using a toilet bottle and so I went to fetch it from the bathroom. As soon as Chris started weeing it was obvious something was wrong, his urine was dark, almost treacly brown. Fortunately (sic), Annette had a sample bottle that was available when the doctor called. The diagnosis was a urinary tract infection and Chris was prescribed another course of anti-biotics and told to drink regularly. Chris was feeling under the weather for all of the weekend and despite the best efforts of Annette he hardly had anything to eat, however from the Monday he began to feel better as the anti-biotics 'kicked' in. As the week went on his wee cleared, Chris got up and resumed a more normal day. Then on the Friday morning his wee was almost as bad as it had been the previous Saturday. Annette called the doctor and we were asked to take a sample to the doctors for testing, the outcome another dose of anti-biotics. Thankfully, over the weekend everything cleared up and we looked to be back on course.

Wrong. Come the Tuesday morning Chris is feeling and being sick again. Annette calls the doctor, who duly calls and diagnoses a virus. This results in more time in bed, more being sick and more lost weight. During the first few days Chris was really quite unwell, although as usual in these circumstances there was little complaint, fortunately by the Friday he was recovering which continued over the weekend. By this point Chris had been ill almost continually for two months, so by the end of February 1999 he had lost almost 3 to 3½ stones in weight.

By this point in time it was clear that Annette was not going to be able to continue working, having not been in work since Chris had been admitted to hospital just before Christmas. So she advised Lee (who along with his wife Nikki had been very supportive of our family during the previous months) that she would not be returning to work.

Because of all the weight Chris had lost we found that the 'new' jacket that he'd been fitted in early January was now too big, so we returned to using his old jacket, which we could at least get firm on him. The only problem was that it began rubbing him, due to the fact that his shape had changed. With the help of Carol Watson at Dorin Park we found that by padding the jacket with sheepskin or towelling we could get Chris reasonably comfortable.

Annette was obviously keen to *build* Chris up, although we were keen to keep his weight in check if we could. We were pleased as over the next week Chris's appetite returned. Chris had always been a regular user of the loo, but he began to be uncomfortable on the loo seat, so it became an issue. Combined with this Chris started to have the odd *accident*, which we initially put down to the fact that he wasn't using the loo regularly. Over the next week his appetite began to recede again. Sue Johnston, the nurse at Dorin Park suggested to us, that Chris might be constipated. Following her advice we tried a number of approaches, but without success. There was no alternative, but to call the doctor, and so a locum duly arrived. We filled her in with both Chris's condition and recent history and Sue Johnston's suggestion. The doctor examined Chris and firmly discounted constipation, suggesting he had an infection. Over the next few weeks the situation didn't improve, meals went half eaten and *accidents* happened more frequently. Eventually, in desperation Annette called Dr. Gibbs, explained the situation, and an appointment was made to see him a day or so later. We were shown into Dr. Gibbs' examination room and got Chris up onto the bed. Dr. Gibbs carefully placed his hands on Chris's abdomen and almost immediately said, "I know what's wrong". Annette and I looked at him, both in apprehension and anticipation. "He's totally bunged up, right up to the gunwales," announced Dr. Gibbs. For an instance we were both dumbstruck, "But, the doctor told us he wasn't," one of us eventually said. In reality we were both feeling pretty stupid, if we had consulted Dr. Gibbs earlier the situation may not be as bad as it clearly was now.

Dr. Gibbs gently explained to Chris what needed to be done. Chris needed to come into hospital for a few days and take large doses of Cleanprep, a purgative. It would be easier to have this administered through a nasal tube, as he would not be able to drink the volumes required, and besides Dr. Gibbs explained it tasted horrid. Chris was not keen on this. Dr. Gibbs continued to explain what the situation could lead to if not treated, he told Chris that for the sake of a few days unpleasantness he would be fine. He suggested that Chris went away, thought about it and discussed it with Mum and Dad.

Over the next few days all the parental persuasion skills were brought to bear, against some firm opposition. Eventually, Chris relented but was adamant that he would drink the liquid, no nasal tube for him. As it happened Chris was booked into Hope House and while there he had the opportunity to take counsel from his friend David. On his return he was slightly more amenable to the idea of the tube.

So on Monday 8th March Chris was admitted to hospital to be, as he put it later, 'dyno-rodded'. He was still adamant that he was going to drink the mixture, but having tasted it he quickly changed his mind. The next step was to get the nasal tube inserted, which was eventually accomplished, but not without quite understandably, a struggle (literally) and some upset. As we had often witnessed, Chris shrugged off adversity and was soon back to his cheerful self and was interrogating the staff as to what they were doing and why, as they connected the tube up to the drip. Fortunately Chris had been given his own room, complete with TV and video so we were at least able to keep him reasonably occupied. Dr. Gibbs had suggested that Chris might be in hospital for perhaps two or three days so we had gone prepared for a lengthy stay. Chris was quite embarrassed about the procedure he was about to endure so we were under strict instructions from him not to tell anybody. This of course was very difficult as we explained to him, so he modified his position so we could tell those that needed to know, but he didn't want any visitors.

As he would need turning in the night, it was necessary for either Annette or I to stay. It was easier for me to stay at night (for one thing Annette wears contact lens and without them can't see). This wasn't too bad as there was a spare bed in the room and the staff were happy to let me use it. The first night was reasonable as Chris slept quite well, but not having his own mattress he did need turning a bit more than usual. When Annette arrived to take the 'day' shift I was able to go home to top up my sleep, ready to return in the afternoon. The Cleanprep, while being given through the tube, had started to make Chris feel sick, so the rate of flow was slowed, and he managed to remain fairly cheerful. Dr. Gibbs called in to see how things were progressing and stayed for a little while to chat with Chris. During the day there had been plenty of rumblings from Chris's stomach and he was confident that things would soon be happening. During the afternoon Yvonne called in to see Chris and Annette and to see if there was anything she could do.

Anne Bolton also called in to see Chris and keep Annette company. It was bad timing. It was then that the Cleanprep finally worked. To describe the results of the Cleanprep in a book such as this would not be appropriate. Suffice to say that the nursing staff soon christened the room 'Poo Corner'. Good progress, if that is the right description, was made over Tuesday and into Wednesday with the staff of Ruth, Kath, Jeanette and Jan being kept very busy! Dr. Gibbs examined Chris during Wednesday and thought that things were going in the right direction although he could still feel a number of blockages in the guts. However, conscious that Chris had been in bed for two and half days he asked if Chris wanted to go home and come back in a few days later. Chris considered this for a short time and then said, "No thank you Dr. Gibbs, I'll stay here until it's cleared up". As Dr. Gibbs told us later he was very impressed by Chris's resilience and maturity in making that decision.

The embargo on visitors was still firmly in place, Anne had been in again (to make sure Annette was alright, not to see Chris you understand!), and Chris had also had a visit from Josie Harpley. Now this was perfectly OK, as in Chris's eyes Josie could do no wrong, he would hear nothing bad said about her. "What," I said when I arrived back at the hospital late afternoon, "I thought visitors were banned. I'll have to phone Crossroads (for whom Josie worked) and complain". "**You**, will do nothing of the sort. Josie is **my** friend".

Things kept moving over the next few days, Dr. Murphy saw Chris on the Thursday and advised that things were almost clear, which cheered Chris up considerably. Then on Friday Dr. Gibbs examined Chris in the morning, returning later in the afternoon to announce after a further examination that Chris could go home, which was greeted by huge cheers and not just from Chris. The effect of the Cleanprep was felt for a few more days, but this was a minor inconvenience in comparison to what may have been. Yet again Chris had taken a major problem in his stride, and on this occasion one that must have been highly embarrassing for a 13-year-old with good humour. For months after he did enjoy a laugh about it, one can only imagine the descriptions that he used when relating the story to his friends! Chris did return to the hospital a few days later, but that was only to take a Thank You card and box of chocolates to the staff, at 'Poo Corner'.

The net result of Chris's stay in hospital to be 'dyno rodded' was not only to clear him out, but also for him to lose further weight and for his back muscles to weaken further. Consequently, the problems we had had with his jacket not fitting and rubbing were now even worse. Even so, by and large he remained positive about things and through various tactics we kept him as comfortable as possible. Having almost lost the first quarter of the year through one illness or another Chris pitched himself back into his school and social life, greatly enjoying the things he did and enjoying the company of his friends. Of course we still had clinic appointments and April saw our first visit of 1999 (other appointments had been cancelled due to Chris's ailments) to Oswestry, although Dr. Quinlivan was on holiday. The doctor we saw made some helpful suggestions on how we could try to keep Chris's bowels working using natural products. From these suggestions we created a cocktail of Prune Juice, lactulose syrup and orange juice which Chris drank every night from then on before going to bed. As constipation never reared its head again we have to conclude that the mixture worked!

We visited Oswestry again in mid May and naturally, Dr. Quinlivan wanted to know what had happened to Chris since the last time she had seen him and was also very concerned to hear about the issues with the support jacket and was shocked at his loss of weight. It had been agreed that we would stay at the hospital and attend the Orthotics Department that afternoon where Chris would be cast again for a new jacket. Dr. Quinlivan was to arrange for the head of the Orthotics Department to undertake the work. Carolyn Evans suggested that we went to the restaurant to get lunch and then get to the clinic on time. Having enjoyed fish and chips we took the short walk to the Orthotics building, where we met Carol Watson (the physio from Dorin Park) who had very kindly agreed to accompany us so that we could get the cast right. After a short wait we were approached by the head orthotist, who we will refer to as Harry Horse.

"Christopher Barratt?" he asked.
"Yes," we replied.
"Right, where's the jacket?" asked Harry.
"Erh, we don't have it with us," I answered hesitantly and slightly confused.
"Well, how do you expect *me* to do anything with it then?" asked Harry in a sarcastic manner. With that he turned around and started to walk away.
"Excuse me," I started.
"What!" snapped Harry, continuing to walk away.
"Well firstly you can stop walking away. *You* are supposed to be casting my son for a new jacket".
"I'm not arguing with you in public," came the increasingly angry response, "I don't have time to do a casting, do you know how long one takes?" By now I was striding after Harry.
"Don't walk away from me while I'm speaking to you," I said in a fairly controlled manner.
By now he was in his office so I followed him in. I was then subjected to a tirade about how people expected him to just drop everything for them, that the Muscle Clinic was useless and so was everybody that worked there. I eventual-

ly managed to explain that we had been seen by two orthotists and had three jackets, none of which fitted. This simply led to another outburst during which we were blamed for seeing different orthotists ("You've seen the entire department"), despite the appointments having been set by his department, and "do *you* realise how expensive these jackets are to make, *you* just can't waste them". This guys attitude was by far the worst we had encountered in any and all our visits to hospitals and clinics - he may well be a good orthotist, but as a departmental manager and a public servant, he was a disgrace. Harry sarcastically told us to go back to "Quinlivan's Clinic" and to come back that afternoon, informing us that "I suppose I could see you at 2 pm". With that we decided to return to Dr. Quinlivan's clinic to see if we could speak to her. We explained what had happened and the doctor was both shocked and annoyed, intimating that this was not the first time this had happened. She asked us to speak to the director in charge of the department, which we did. I find situations like this very difficult, on the one hand you want to make your feelings known, put your case forward that seeks to improve the situation both for the person affected most and for other patients, but on the other recognising that you may need to call on the skills of this department or individual to achieve those objectives. We explained the background to what had happened and described the 'meeting', and described the impact both in the short and long term on Chris. The director apologised on behalf of the hospital, undertook to speak to Harry, and then asked if we wanted to formalise our complaint. We decided at that point not to do so, in hindsight perhaps we should have done so. While not looking for 'a pound of flesh' a formal review may have led to more and better improvements, and an apology to Chris.

After some further discussion with Dr. Quinlivan, Carolyn Evans, Jenny Whitall and Carol Watson we decided not to return to the Orthotics Department that afternoon, we were all too upset, but to make another appointment. Before we left the hospital that day a call was made to the Orthotics Department and a new appointment arranged for the following Friday. In the meantime, Jenny Whitall and Carol Watson had discussed matters between themselves and being concerned about the deteriorating position of Chris's back had agreed that a two pronged approach should be undertaken. We would continue to get a jacket made up at Oswestry and Carol would arrange for a jacket to be cast in Chester, this would mean that there was a good chance one jacket would be right or, if both fitted, Chris could take his choice of jacket.

Chris was not very keen on returning to Oswestry as he did not like Harry and "I don't think he should speak to you like that", adding, "If he does that again I'll tell him what I think". Mum suggested that it would be best if he kept quiet and let Dad deal with it. As it turned out Harry was in a completely different mood, and although he didn't apologise for the previous week's episode he proceeded to chat to Chris about a trip he was about to make to the Spanish Grand Prix at Barcelona and watch Manchester Utd. in the European Cup. The front and back casting was done with the minimum of fuss, much easier this time, as Annette was on hand to help, although as usual the bits of plaster got everywhere. We were given an appointment for 5 weeks on to have the jacket fitted, being told by Harry that because he was the Manager we would have to wait that long as he was so busy.

In the week following the Oswestry visit Chris had another casting in Chester (supervised by Carol) and a week later the new jacket (coloured with a planetary scene) was fitted, Chris coming home that day wearing it. This jacket as with most of the others had internal padding and rounded edges for comfort. For the first time in many weeks Chris was reasonably comfortable and sitting up much better. From the point where we had first raised the issue of a new jacket, to getting one that fitted properly and comfortably had taken **10 months**. In that 10 months Chris had had to put up with a considerable amount of discomfort (with very little complaint from him). While it is true that his illnesses and hospital stays, plus his weight loss, had not helped the situation during the period that he waited for a new jacket the fact remains that the scoliosis of his spine got significantly worse. So much so that his rib cage was now badly out of position, which contributed to his discomfort in the jacket. It also meant that he hated people seeing his deformed abdomen and he would insist on being covered up when he had visitors.

Although the Chester jacket was a good fit and Chris found it reasonably comfortable, we attended the Orthotics Department at Oswestry on the appointed day to have the other jacket fitted. It was a good fit, but to Chris's horror had no internal padding (like all his other jackets). Chris quickly pointed this out. Harry explained that the jackets he made were such a good fit that the padding wasn't needed. Chris was not convinced. He did make the effort to wear it, keeping it on for the journey home, but once in the house he wanted to take it off. "It fits OK," he said, "but my legs've gone numb". The reason was soon obvious - the bottom of the jacket that was like a knife-edge was digging into his thigh. We made several attempts to ease the problem by flaring the edge out, putting foam under it and so on, but to no avail. So after a while, Chris decided that he would wear the 'Chester' jacket.

During one of our visits to see Dr. Quinlivan she suggested that Chris underwent a 'Sleep' Test or Polysomnogram to determine how he was breathing during the night. A poor intake of oxygen while sleeping can lead to a number of problems, for example, morning headaches, restless sleep, etc. With Chris's spine problems his chest cavity was reduced and the working of the diaphragm impaired which in turn affected his ability to inhale and exhale. The test was scheduled to take place towards the end of the saga of the jackets at Shrewsbury Royal Hospital, under the direction of Dr. Rees. We arrived at the hospital mid afternoon and Chris was shown into his room. As he wasn't being admitted as such, once the booking in was completed, we were free to come and go as we pleased, but had to be back at the hospital around 8.00 p.m. so Chris could be fitted up with the electrodes for the test. We decided to go and get something to eat, so set off for a local Beefeater that we knew. By sheer coincidence my cousin Patricia's son, Paul, was working in the restaurant and a little while late Patricia called in to see him. As she wasn't in a rush we were able to have dinner with her and catch up on events. Patricia suggested that one of us spent the night at her house, which was fortunate, as the hospital room was quite small and only had a little 'crash' bed. As it was easier for me to look after Chris during the night I volunteered to stay at the hospital.

We returned to the hospital in plenty of time and got Chris into bed and waited for the doctor. The equipment for the test was already in the room and was contained in a medium sized case. It wasn't long before the doctor arrived and began to connect Chris up; there were electrodes to monitor heart rate, blood oxygen levels and blood pressure, and sensors that detected airflow into the nose and mouth. Apart from the device that recorded the inputs from the sensors that was it. The only other aspect of the test was to record manually whenever Chris needed turning. We'd taken Chris's mattress with us to the hospital so Chris had a reasonable nights sleep, although he did need turning more than normal, not helped by the room being so hot. Early the next morning the nurses disconnected the equipment and packed it away. When the doctor arrived he suggested we went to get some breakfast (by now Annette had arrived) and when we returned he would have the initial results of the test. The analysis showed that Chris's breathing and oxygen uptake during the night was perfectly OK and that no changes were required at the time. The doctor said he would write to Dr. Quinlivan with the more detailed results. Some time later when we discussed these with her and they confirmed the initial review and no further action was needed. We were quite reassured by this as it showed that Chris's lungs, while not working at full capacity, where working efficiently in oxygen transfer and not putting an undue strain on his heart (although his heart rate was higher than a healthy lad of his age). Dr. Quinlivan suggested that we repeat the test again in 12 - 14 months, May to July 2000.

After all the difficulties of the first part of the year Chris's general health was now back on an even keel and his prune juice mixture was keeping his bowels regular. Our biggest concerns were keeping him upright and comfortable, and as the autumn and winter approached, trying to ensure that he didn't get a cold with the inherent risk of it affecting his chest. The prune juice mixture was augmented with drops of echinacea and Annette continued her use of aromatherapy so the house benefited from vaporised essential oils such as tea tree, eucalyptus, lemongrass, peppermint, orange and bergamot. Appropriate essential oils were also mixed and used as rubs on Chris's chest, feet and stomach. To start with Chris thought this a bit of a fad and initially humoured Mum, but became quite used to the massages especially as he found it quite relaxing.

With the loss of weight Chris had suffered and the effect of the scoliosis on his pelvis the Ischium bone in his bottom made it uncomfortable for him to sit on most things other than his RoHo cushion. This meant that going to the loo or having a shower was a trial for him. We tried numerous ways to ease the problem without success. Annette had contacted Wendy Sutton who was responsible for Occupational Therapy for Chris to try and find an alternative to the existing shower/loo chair we had. Annette also contacted Philippa Harbin, an OT working for the Muscular Dystrophy Group, to see if she could help. She suggested something called a Sutton Shower cradle, in which the person reclines so transferring some of their weight off their bottom. Annette arranged for us to have one of these cradles demonstrated to us. Chris was a bit wary of trying it out as he thought he might fall out of it. The chap from the company assured him that it was perfectly safe, there were sides and straps to provide support, and pointing out his young nephew used one. Having tried it out Chris was sold on the idea. The problem was getting one. We eventually persuaded Social Services to provide one, but not without a struggle and not before it had caused enormous friction between Annette and I. The shower cradle was eventually delivered in mid-November and immediately made life easier for us all, although it did mean that Chris was back to having a regular shower which he would preferred to have avoided. Showers were a major chore and something Chris disliked, probably for good reason as the whole operation took ages. We would have to get him undressed on his bed, transfer him to the chair or cradle, wheel to the shower room and then between Annette and I give him a head to toe wash (how many teenagers would be happy for their parents to do that?), then dry him off, wheel him back to the bedroom, transfer him onto the towel covered bed. While Annette got him properly dry, especially the creases, and started to get him dressed, I would wipe down and dry the shower chair or cradle. The whole operation would take between 30 and 60 minutes. While Chris would moan about it, it was generally good humoured, and once dressed he would be off to do something else and it was soon forgotten about – until next time of course.

With school breaking up for the Christmas holidays Chris had gone to spend a few days at Hope House, but a couple of days after his return he started with a cold. With the first signs Annette swung into action, aromatherapy was stepped up, and the medicine that was kept to hand administered. With Christmas approaching and not wishing to get caught like we did the last time Annette called the doctors to arrange for a nebuliser, which I was eventually able to collect, although not before one doctor suggested that we could boil a kettle in Chris's bedroom! Our worst fears were soon realised as the cold moved onto Chris's chest and his breathing became difficult. We were determined that it wasn't going to get as bad as the last Christmas, and Chris was already building up his case not to go into hospital. So with use of the nebuliser, anti-biotics, tilting the bed to aid drainage and physiotherapy we managed to keep on top of the condition. Even so, the effect of impaired breathing, coughing and the exercises took their toll on Chris and he spent most of Christmas in bed. Despite this his resilience and good humour shone through; he was determined to enjoy Christmas, made an effort to get up and open his presents, returned to bed and then got up again for Christmas lunch, albeit that he had to go back before the meal was over. Although he was clearly unwell he kept cheerful throughout the day, enjoying watching a number of new videos (especially Only Fools and Horses) and laughing out loud at the jokes. I sensed that at times he was putting it on for our benefit, not wishing to spoil the special day. He even kept apologising for being ill at Christmas again. The physio and breathing exercises really took their toll on him and by the end of the day he was very, very tired.

Come the following morning and he was much brighter and having had a lie in, watching videos or listening to CDs on his new Personal Player, he made the effort to get up. The lure of the computer too much to resist. For his comfort it was necessary to put his support jacket on, but this itself caused him some breathing problems, so we compromised by leaving it on, but loosening it off. Once on the computer and with his mind taken off the situation he settled down and was more his normal self. In mid-afternoon though his day was really made when Josie dropped in accompanied by her husband Chris, son Pete, daughter in law Natalie and best of all (sorry folks) baby Sam. Their visit really cheered

Chris up, meeting Josie's family was good, but getting to hold Sam was better. He was keen to show everyone around, especially his computer and electric bed. The whole thing was a bit much for him and after about an hour he asked if he could go to back to bed. Even so, once in bed he still held 'court' wanting to hear what Josie's family had done on Christmas Day, what "little Sam" had had on the day, what they were up to next. And, of course, he wanted to share with them what he had had, including showings of particular scenes from his new videos. The Harpley clan visit was a great fillip, and he continued to recall it for months after.

Although it took a week or so for Chris's chest to completely clear he was back to his normal self before the end of the year and was therefore able to enjoy the start of the Millennium. His general health remained good for the rest of that year up to when he was poorly in his last few days. The biggest problem that he had to contend with was caused again by his jacket. Despite wearing the jacket everyday the scoliosis appeared to be getting worse all the time, and the way the bottom of his rib cage on his left side stuck out was becoming more pronounced. Both of these problems led to further rubbing of his skin and despite our best efforts Chris ended up with an ulcer like sore on one of his ribs. With the help of Sister Jenny Jones, the District Nurse, we were able to stop matters getting worse and then gradually to get the wound to heal, although it was a lengthy process, not made easier with Chris having to continue to wear the jacket.

Very early into the New Year it had been necessary for Chris to wear incontinence pads, to minimise the impact of accidents, as muscle control was lost. This was a major embarrassment to him and only a very, very select group of people, those who **really** needed to know were told. Otherwise, it was simply a taboo subject.

Also into the New Year and despite our best efforts Chris had another bout of getting bunged up, possibly caused by the anti-biotics taken over Christmas. This time we knew what we were looking for and asked for Sister Jones to give Chris the 'once over'. Having confirmed the problem the remedy was not pleasant, but as with most things Chris took it in his stride and was even able to joke about it. Annette keen to do everything possible to keep Chris well, and encouraged by the positive effect of aromatherapy, decided to follow up some information on Reflexology. Initially, Chris wasn't sure he was going to like this, but there again he wasn't actually sure what it was, still that didn't stop him arguing against it. However, Annette was in full flight on this one and there was to be no argument. It was arranged for Dee Kelsall, a local Reflexologist, who made house calls to come one Saturday for an initial consultation. To start with Chris was in a non co-operative mood, reflected by the expression on his face, which gradually thawed as Dee chatted to him and told him what she did and how she did it. From when he was about four or five Chris had never been very happy about people touching his feet, Dr. Robinson had said he just had sensitive feet, and washing his feet nearly always led to an outburst. So as Dee started work massaging the sole of his feet, all you could hear was, "Ooh!", "Ow!", "Uuh!" and so on. This was interspersed by the odd giggle and "It doesn't hurt" from Dee and "Chris! Just cut it out!" from Mum. As the session went on the *objections* became fewer and by the end I think he was quite enjoying it. After Dee had left I asked him how it was, "It was OK, but my feet are aching".

From then on Dee came about every 6 weeks and as time went on Chris was quite happy to have an hour's reflexology, especially as this generally coincided with his afternoon lie on the bed. From early in the year Chris had taken to have a brief period, perhaps 30 minutes, sometimes an hour, lying on his bed, with his jacket off to give his back a rest. We had tried hard to delay this, as we realised it was another step down the ladder. Many of these 'little' things had happened in the last few months, Annette and I had observed them and independently seen the ominous direction we were heading, fearing to mention it to each other. In the week in February that Chris went to Hope House we shared our fears one tearful evening, little knowing that time was so short.

During the spring and summer months Chris's decline became noticeable, even to those people, including Annette and I, that were close to him. His eating remained good, but not as good as it had been, he began to 'chew' words, the tendons in his wrists shortened causing his hands to turn outwards, and he continued to get thinner, his bones ever more pronounced, especially his back and ribs. This in turn caused more problems with his jacket rubbing and yet again we reverted to a Heath Robinson approach using foam to provide extra protection. In mid-March it was decided to cast another jacket, which Chris was to submit to with little complaint. While the process was quite rough he did recognise that people were trying to help him. Throughout this period Chris remained generally happy and positive, socially many things were happening, relationships blooming, the smile we knew and loved was nearly always there and he seemed not to be noticing his physical problems. I say seemed, because looking back I am sure now that he was probably more aware of his problems than we were. To my eternal regret I got cross with him over small and inconsequential things, which caused him upset, as the stress of watching this decline surfaced.

Chris's sleeping had also gradually become more disturbed. Annette and I were now sometimes getting up 7 - 10 times a night to turn him over or reposition his legs. During visits in early 2000 to Hope House Chris had tried out a Talley air mattress which was set to the users weight and slowly 'rippled' so changing the pressure points. When using the Talley it was found he slept much better. It was suggested that we tried to get one for home use. Through the efforts of Julie Rawlinson and, not for the first time, Yvonne Bohdanowicz, Annette managed to get the funding for one. The new mattress was delivered in early July and immediately made a huge difference. While it was still necessary to get up in the night to roll Chris the number of times reduced to between 3 -5 times, a major benefit to us all.

Chris's decision not to travel to Florida, a trip that Annette and I had already realised would probably be our last trip to the States with him, was a huge shock and disappointment, but was testimony not only to how he felt; a clear understanding of his limitations and also a reflection of his maturity. Duchenne Muscular Dystrophy has a lot to answer for.

There was one final irony. Support jackets had become the beign of all our lives. Chris was cast for his new jacket in April, many weeks after it had been agreed he needed one. The delay this time was because the company providing the orthotics service to the Countess of Chester Hospital was being replaced in the new financial year and (officially) did not believe that they should produce a jacket that the new company would need to fit and maintain. The real reason of course was that they didn't want to spend the money on a contract that they were losing. Clearly, a well negotiated change of contract - not! And the losers, well not the NHS administrators (who were probably congratulating themselves on saving a few quid here or there), but as usual the long suffering patients. Administration of the NHS is clearly very distant from the actual 'coal face', from the consultants, doctors, nurses and patients so that the real requirements just get forgotten or lost. S H A M B L E S.

CHAPTER SIX (Caring and Helping)

For the universe and the stars are around you now
But the healer in your heart is only a breath away

C.Macdonald/R.Macdonald - Run Rig

During 1996 Yvonne Bohdanowicz approached us with the idea of finding a Respite Family, who would have Chris to stay for short periods of time and allow Annette and I to have some time to ourselves. I was not at all keen on this idea, I was strongly of the view that Chris and Chris's care were our problem and for better or worse we had to deal with that. Additionally, I wasn't at all sure that I wanted strangers to be looking after Chris. After a two-pronged offensive from Yvonne and Annette I reluctantly agreed that Yvonne could commence looking for an appropriate Respite Family. I privately consoled myself with the view that she was unlikely to find a candidate family, as they would need to have the right physical facilities for a wheelchair, have appropriate bed and bathroom facilities and be prepared to get up in the night to turn Chris. The chances of that were pretty slim I thought. Chris was aware of the idea, but unusually for him was quiet on the subject. In fairness to Yvonne she didn't give up trying, but her search was proving fruitless.

Then in mid 1997 Yvonne was invited, in her professional capacity, to see Hope House and meet Jon Mills, the resident Social Worker, and the team that worked there. Even during her visit, she thought of us, recognising that this might be what would be right for us. So prompted by Yvonne we arranged to go to Hope House one Sunday in November to meet Jon Mills, look at the facilities and have lunch.

Driving to Hope House for the first time along the A483 I was sceptical that this was the right thing, Annette on the other hand could see the positive side, whereas Chris was apprehensive as he didn't really know what to expect and was quite quiet on the journey.

Hope House is actually located on outskirts of the village of Morda, a couple of miles south of Oswestry, in beautiful rolling Shropshire countryside. Annette describes it as being at the edge of the world. From the main road it is approached up a side road that climbs the hill, before taking a lane that climbs a little more through a small modern housing estate. As you reach the top of the rise Hope House opens up in a small dip to the left. It is quite imposing on first sight, a fairly large building of a modern, chalet-like design. The campaign to build the respite home was initiated in 1990 by the mother of a severely disabled child named Hope Peachy and Hope House opened for the care of children on October 23rd 1995.

We were met at the door by Jon who, without being rude, had the quintessential appearance of a Social Worker. "Hello," he said, "you must be Christopher. Welcome to Hope House, come in. Would you like drink, a cup of tea or glass of orange." When meeting people for the first time Chris always preferred to be slightly behind Annette or I and would answer questions by saying something

like, "Are you having a drink Dad?"
Inside Hope House is just like a large private house, there are pictures by the children on the walls, cuddly toys in corners and, as we entered, the smell of Sunday lunch cooking. We followed Jon through the short hallway and into the large Dining Room, pausing only for Jon to point out the Games Room in which there were several games consoles and an IBM compatible PC, which immediately caught Chris's eye. "What specification is that?" he enquired of Jon. "Sorry, Chris," he replied, "but I only use them. I think it's quite *big* though". Then he added, "You can have a go later if you like". A smile appeared on Chris's face.

The Dining Room is a large room with four large oblong tables, with plenty of room for wheelchairs, adjacent to an open plan kitchen in which the cook (who we were introduced to as Fran) was toiling away. The atmosphere was very homely and made you relax. Jon made some tea and on rejoining us at one of the tables explained that the Dining Room was at the heart of Hope House, everybody came together at lunch and dinner times.

Jon gave us a brief overview of the services offered by Hope House and then suggested a tour. The House is built on a split-level and the children's bedrooms are on the lower part, reached from just outside the Dining Room by a gently sloping, curving corridor. The walls of the corridor are decorated with lots and lots of photographs of the children and the carers, nearly all without exception smiling. As the corridor reaches the lower level it opens out into a medium size open space, referred to by the staff as 'Piccadilly Circus'. This is where the night staff sit, just outside an office, and ideally located between the two sets of bedrooms. Jon showed us the bedrooms, each with its own name, well equipped with electric beds and hoists and nicely decorated as well as providing good views across the garden and the Shropshire countryside. Jon explained that where possible once a room was allocated that was the room they tried to provide each time the youngster came to stay.

From the children's bedrooms we visited the parent's rooms, a number of which are just along from the children's, while a number more are upstairs; we visited one of the small lounges for use by parents and then returning up another sloping corridor saw the main lounge (TV, video, satellite), Play Room, Multi-sensory Room and Swimming Pool. Chris was itching to get in the Games Room, but before he could do that it was lunch.

The Dining Room was filling up with children, some parents and the carers. There was a general hubbub and happy chatter that seemed to sum up the atmosphere. My reservations were gradually being eased as the visit went on. Lunch was roast pork, with crackling and applesauce, roast potatoes and carrots followed by apple crumble, which was very enjoyable.

Once lunch was over Chris was very keen to visit the Games Room and so he and I went off, leaving Annette to chat with Jon about the workings of Hope House. Visits can be arranged approximately every 12 weeks, for weekends or weeks, and parents and, if applicable, other siblings can stay as well. Hope House levy no charge to the families, nearly all funding (Hope House costs £1.5 million per annum to run) is provided on a charitable basis with only about 4% being provided by the local authorities who refer the children. Scandalously, bearing in mind the service Hope House and similar homes provide, central Government does not contribute at all, the necessary finance being achieved through a core group of fund-raisers and dedicated volunteers. New contributors are welcome all the time[1].

After a little time Annette and Jon joined us in the Games Room, where Chris had been quite impressed by the equipment. Jon went on to ask if we'd like to make a booking. Before we could answer Chris interjected with a very firm "Yes, please". As it would be our first visit we made a family booking for a weekend in late January. The next major hurdle was to extract Chris from Hope House in general and the Games Room in particular. He had, by now, mastered the 'in a moment' or 'can I just do this first' approach. So, eventually after another quick walk round, including selecting the bedroom he would like to use, and a final go on the PC we managed to bid Jon good-bye. For most of the journey home Chris was full of what Hope House could offer and how he would be able to enjoy the Games Room.

At Christmas time we received a Christmas card from David Riffel and Pauline Evans who introduced themselves as being the prime contacts for us at Hope House. They would wherever possible be on duty to look after Chris on his visits and would provide a link between Hope House and the family. Just prior to our first in January 1998 David phoned us to see if everything was OK and that we were still coming.

Even though our introductory visit to Hope House had been very positive and successful we were still apprehensive at the thought of our first stay. So when we set off one Friday evening we were still not sure how we and particularly Chris would find the experience. The bottom line was that Chris needed a lot of physical care, much of it of a personal nature, and not only did we feel that was our responsibility, but entrusting his care to others was a big step. On the journey Chris was quite relaxed, he did take a lot of things in his stride, and although we had explained how Hope House worked I'm not sure that he fully comprehended what it meant for him.

On our arrival we were met by David, who showed us to Saturn, Chris's room. On the door was a personalised sign of an aircraft and a message 'Welcome Chris', which quite impressed their guest. It was necessary to go through the 'Booking In' process during which an inventory of belongings is recorded, medicines etc. are handed over and logged and the Care Plan is written up. This covers likes and dislikes, specific routines and handling regimes, all the information that the carers need to ensure that the guest is well looked after. This is a fairly lengthy process, especially the first time, and Chris was becoming fidgety, wanting to be off and doing things, well actually playing on the computer for which he had brought some of his games from home. So while Annette and David finished 'Booking In', Chris and I paid a visit to the Games Room.

Once these initial activities had concluded, Annette and I were shown to our room, which was just around the corner from Chris. Of course, never one to miss out, our room had to be *inspected* by the younger member of the family and passed as being acceptable. David suggested that he and Chris leave Annette and I to unpack and go and use the computer, for as David said, "I need you to show me how these things work." It was also suggested that we all meet up again an hour or so later to get a drink before bedtime. When Annette and I arrived in the Games Room the first thing Chris did was to ask to go to the toilet.

[1] Hope House, Nant Lane, Morda, Nr. Oswestry, Shropshire, SY10 9BX.

"You could have asked me to do that," said David.
"Oh, its alright, Dad'll do it, won't you Palion." It's very difficult to say no in those circumstances, but I knew where David was coming from. Chris had to get used to other people helping and staying at Hope House was also about giving Annette and I a rest.

David was very keen to understand Chris's requirements and the way Annette and I looked after him. So getting Chris ready for bed that night was a bit of a team affair. Chris was very good about it, explaining to David all the things that we did and in what order. It was not long before he was in bed and watching a video on the TV. Annette and I retreated to the Dining Room, leaving David with Chris. A little while later David joined us and suggested that we should spend the following day shopping in Shrewsbury. "It'll give us chance to get to know Chris and for him to be more comfortable with being looked after. Pauline's also in tomorrow, he'll be fine with us."

When we told this to Chris he was not so sure it was a good idea, but David and Pauline convinced him that it was fine and that they would look after him and that there were loads of things to do. Early Saturday evening when we returned to Hope House we found Chris doing his favourite thing, playing on the computer.
"You haven't been in here all day?" asked Annette.
"No," came the indignant reply, "we've been doing loads of things." There then followed a list as long as your arm of the activities in which he'd taken part. He'd clearly not missed us and it was like he'd been coming to Hope House for years.

David and Pauline had made an immediate impact and both of them struck up an enduring friendship with Chris. Pauline and David clearly got on well with each other, with David taking the Mickey out of Pauline, which Chris was soon joining in with.

By the time it came to leave on Sunday Chris was all for staying a bit longer and it took a combined effort to prise him out and into the car. However, before we did we were asked if we would like to book a future stay. Chris was all for this, as long as Mum and Dad came too, so a weekend in April was entered in the diary.

In the week leading up to our second visit Chris was quite excited and this was added to when David called to see how he was and say that he would be on duty. David also suggested that Annette and I took ourselves off during Saturday, as we had last time, so that Chris got more use to others looking after him. The weekend was another success, with Chris being happy to let David and the other carers look after him with less input from Mum and Dad. Although the one thing he still wouldn't let anybody else do was look after him in the swimming pool when we tried out the facility on the Saturday evening. By now my reservations about passing Chris's care to others had been completely overcome, I was sure we could trust Hope House with his care, and it was very clear that he was already enjoying his visits to Hope House. So much so that at the end of the weekend as we were encouraged to make a further booking Chris was happy to agree to a week long booking, without Annette and I.

The week's visit was scheduled for the school half term, around June 1998, and

Chris was quite happy to go, although he did find it quite difficult to say goodbye to us on the Friday night as we left for home. It was clear however from the phone calls that we got from him during the week that everything was fine. He had gone well equipped with computer games, favourite videos and music cassettes, but by all accounts was finding many other things to do in and around Hope House. It was also the time in which he struck up a number of friendships with other youngsters that were staying at that time. Also, while David and Pauline were not on duty at points during the week, there were other carers who looked after Chris and this was the beginning of good relationships with Mary, Gilda, Lesley, Kim and Annie. When we picked him up the following Friday he was full of tales of the week's activity, he introduced us to his new friends and of course was reluctant to leave. One of the stories was of being looked after during the night by Ganda.
"Ganda?" asked Annette.
"Yes, Ganda" replied Chris.
"But, I don't think that's right," said Annette, "Do you mean Gilda?"
"Oh, yes, that's right," came the response.

Sometime later Pauline told us of an amusing aside that had occurred during the week. In a quiet moment Chris had taken her aside and asked if she was married to David. Apparently, the question was prompted because they argued all the time! Once she got over a fit of the giggles she explained that they weren't, but were good friends, that she had a husband and two children and David had a wife and three children. It is not recorded whether Chris was relieved by this or not.

On the day of Chris's birthday at the end of June he was delighted by a surprise visit by David and Pauline, who were able to share his Birthday Cake, although as he'd now become a teenager he wasn't having a party! He was quite in his element giving both his guests a tour of the house, especially his bedroom. After that he wanted to demonstrate a number of the games and other facilities he had on his computer, which David was happy to do. Pauline meanwhile drank tea and ate cake with Annette!

Before the end of 1998, in October and December, Chris enjoyed a couple more visits to Hope House. Each time he looked forward to going and he would come home having enjoyed his stay, often having made more new friends. It was during this time that he first met Matty Ford and his brother, Richard, and sister, Emma. Matty was suffering from a very rare degenerative disorder that was gradually robbing him of his faculties. Even so, Matty continued to enjoy life and they would often be found in each other's company, Chris would chat away merrily, both of them laughing at the slightest thing, as they seemed to share a similar sense of humour. Chris also built up a friendship with Rich (like his Mum Chris would shorten everybody's name) through a common liking of things computing and football.

Of course, one of the attractions of Hope House was being away from the rules set down by Mum and Dad and an ability to *con* (to a degree) the carers. Amongst other things this meant late nights and on his visit in the October of 1998, Chris, Richard and Emma were still watching videos well passed midnight while Jean supplied them with bowls of popcorn. This activity was supposed to be a secret, but Chris was not very good at keeping that type of secret and within 30 minutes of us arriving to pick him up he'd spilled the beans and 'grassed' Jean up.

Whenever Chris stayed at Hope House one of the first things that took place was to update the Care Plan; changing any medication requirements (for Chris thankfully very few), updating any care processes, activities, likes and dislikes. At home we had a good routine that involved weekly showers, which it has to be said were not Chris's favourite pastimes, so when he was at Hope House he generally managed to avoid them by careful manipulation of whoever was looking after him. Avoid them that is until his Mum and Pauline conspired to include a weekly shower in the Care Plan. What's more Pauline ensured that the Plan was executed, she had no messing where that was concerned! On future visits when the Care Plan came out Chris would wait for the bit where showering was discussed and say, "Well, as it's **my** Care Plan that can be taken out". Mum had a different view and in the Plan it remained.

At the end of 1998 and during the early part of 1999 Chris had been very poorly and had needed a lot of care and attention. It had not been planned for Chris to go to Hope House until early Spring time, but a vacancy was found for him towards the end of February, primarily to give Annette and I a rest. By now we were happy to entrust the care of Chris to the wonderful team at Hope House, secure in the knowledge that they would look after him as well as we would. Having spent so much time either in hospital or at home his visit to Hope House surrounded by a different group of people and doing different things helped his recuperation enormously and he returned home much brighter.

Chris's special friend Katie Gerrard had been one of the first people to stay at Hope House when it was opened. He would often proudly tell people that she had her name on the Foundation Stone, so he was over the moon that during his weekend stay in March 1999 Katie was to be there as well. We had also booked in, as had Katie's dad, Bob, although Chris was far too busy to be bothered with his parents. There was looking after Katie to be done, helping David with the other children, computers to be used, and painting in the Play Room with Sandy. Still, the adults managed to amuse themselves and despite being 'rejected' we had a pleasant weekend!

At the end of March, through Hope House, Chris was invited along with Matthew, Ben and other children and accompanied by Stuart from Hope House for a day at the Granada Studio Tour in Manchester, organised and funded by students from Manchester University through the Prince's Trust. We all met up at about 11 o'clock and after lunch we were taken on a guided tour during which we saw many aspects of how a TV program is brought to our living rooms. At one point we assembled in the 'front room' of the Tate household on Emmerdale Farm and were treated to a little scene acted out by two of the characters, Eric Pollard (Christopher Chittel) and Stella Jones (Stephanie Schonfield). Chris quite enjoyed the use of (slightly) rude words by Eric Pollard, which were greeted by "Arhhh!" and a little chuckle. After this little performance the audience had an opportunity to ask questions,

"Go on Dad, ask a question." "You ask one." "No, go on Dad you ask."

Following the Emmerdale set we passed through a number of other areas, including one showing behind the scenes of 'Stars in Their Eyes' ("I've met Matthew Kelly," Chris told anybody who'd listen), Coronation Street costumes, a mock up of Downing Street and a room from The Borrowers (massive furniture and fittings, small guests). With that the formal tour finished it was time to explore the remainder of the 'theme' park. This included a London street from Victorian times and the inside of the House of Commons (although Chris declined the opportunity to watch a mock debate, "that'll be boring") and the highlight - Coronation Street. This is actually the set on which the outdoor shots of the famous soap are filmed. We had a good look round, including a quick visit to the Rovers Return (much smaller than on the TV) and knocked on the door to see if Jack and Vera were home (sadly not). The ubiquitous *team* photograph was called for and this was taken outside the Rovers Return and now adorns the wall of the Hope House dining room. As with all good themed attractions there is plenty of opportunity to acquire mementoes of the day. As always Chris was keen to ensure that Mum was well catered for and having looked around the Coronation Street shop selected a jar of Rita Sullivan's Kabin jam and a key ring.

Through the rest of 1999, in April, July, September, October and December there were further visits to Hope House for different periods of time. Each time Chris was welcomed with open arms by the staff, and while he loved the company of David and always looked forward to him being on duty, he also enjoyed being looked after by many of the other carers. Each person brought a different perspective and approach and this gave Chris the chance to have many different conversations and extend his interests and knowledge. With Kim it was an interest in films, especially James Bond, and Formula One motor racing; with Annie it was Lotus cars and football, "I was quite close to him and looked after him quite a few times. He was a great lad and I was hoping that my friend from Norfolk who has a Lotus Elise would get up to give him a ride in it, but unfortunately it didn't happen in time. However Chris did get to see some photographs of it that I brought in for him. Chris had a lovely caring side to his nature and he always worried about the other children especially those most vulnerable. I always admired the way in which he often thought about them before himself. He was a very "instant" person and I remember feeling immediately comfortable and at ease with him, and as he got to know you more he became more cheeky and often asked for a kiss"; with Mary it was, amongst many other things, what Dr Nigel was up to!; with Lesley it was wanting to know about the other children; with Sandy it was stories and adventure in the Play Room; and with Pauline well just about everything and anything. He also liked chatting to Anne 'Wicked' Williams about her sports car and loved her dog Spar-ci who was a *regular* at Hope House. Of course he always had time for Jane and Fran, who shared cooking duties, ensuring that his needs were fully met!

There were regular special activities put on either by the staff or invited guests. One such event was put on to celebrate Hope House's 4th birthday and featured a performance by a lady ventriloquist. Chris had apparently been less than interested to start with but his curiosity eventually got the better of him. One of the dolls was a cat that spoke French and much to everybody's enjoyment and amusement Chris chatted to the cat in French which got him a round of applause.

During his visits he got on well with the other children and was able to relate to both those younger and older than himself. His visits brought him into contact with a few other boys who had MD, and while it was obvious from what he said they had spoken about their problems, issues and concerns no amount of coaxing could get him to discuss it with us. One lad had a Luque Rod to help with his posture, it was partly as a result of these chats that Chris was convinced the rod was not for him.

Throughout Chris's visits in 1999 and 2000 he was helped enormously by Alex, the resident physiotherapist. She would help get his jacket right, help with padding and provide stretching exercises. Alex also helped by providing information on various appliances and other equipment that we were able to use to make life easier and safer. She also liaised with Jenny Whittal and Carol Watson in helping to keep Chris comfortable. Julie from Hope House, who now worked 'in the community' also helped us in getting the Talley air mattress for use at home, after Chris had successfully tried one while staying at Hope House.

When picking Chris up from his visit in July David took us aside and slightly apologetically said, "I hope you don't mind, but as he asked I showed Chris the Snowflake Suite". Hope House have a special self-contained wing that has provision for a family who have lost their son or daughter to be able to spend time together and be provided with support, if that is what the family want. It is accessed from 'Piccadilly Circus' and is generally out of bounds. Chris had always been aware of the Snowflake Suites existence and one day had asked David what it was like and what it was for. David knew that we were open with Chris and that simply fudging the answer would not be enough so he had explained the reason and purpose. He'd then asked Chris if he wished to see it and had shown him around. David told us that Chris had asked very sensible questions, which he'd answered as best he could, but he felt that Chris was quietly moved by his visit. Interestingly, Chris never mentioned his visit to us and never raised the question again, but I have no doubt that the significance of the Snowflake Suite had been stored away within his memory.

In September, through Hope House, we were invited to a car race meeting at Oulton Park by Martyn Woodley of the 2CV Racing Club, who were to compete for the Hope House Cup. Despite Chris's interest in motor racing we had never been to an actual race meeting, for one reason or another, so he was quite excited at the prospect. The 2CV Racing Club made us and other guests from Hope House very welcome, with a number of the drivers taking time to describe their cars and the racing. Chris was also invited, during the lunch break, into the Pit Lane by the marshals and shown into a number of the garages where the Pirelli Porsche cars were being readied for their race. The main races of the day were for the Formula Palmer Audi cars, but they turned out to be a huge disappointment; crashing at the first corner twice and then being stopped because of a downpour and then in the second race another crash caused the race to be stopped! The 2CV guys thought that this was most amusing, all that money and no racing. Their race in contrast was tremendous with good dices right through the field, with the Hope House Cup being won by Richard Dalton.

Hope House is fortunate not only to have wonderful nursing and caring staff but also many other staff who help to ensure the house operates safely and to its high standards. David, the General Manager; Kath, the Care Manager; Jenny; the House Keeper; Brian, the gardener; Eric, the handyman; Kay, in the office and the fund raising staff. They all pitch in to help. Eric often has a team of *assistants* (especially to test the fire alarms) and the fund-raisers attend many of the events. At Oulton Park it had been Claire and at Chris's next stay in October she was to share a secret with him. She was expecting a baby and Chris was the first person outside of her family that she told. Claire had not planned to tell anybody quite so soon, but it was she said almost like she felt compelled to tell Chris. It was a secret he was overjoyed to keep, but first he wanted to know when it was to be born, did she want a boy or a girl, was her husband pleased and a dozen other questions.

Despite its role, Hope House, is a warm, often noisy, vibrant place. It is a comfortable and embracing environment that creates a strong sense of well being. It is staffed by people who are caring and trusting, to whom you can turn for support and understanding, in a quiet and unassuming way. While that support is available at any time, many people turn to Hope House and its staff at the darkest moment of their life. That became clear to us at the time of Chris's visit in December 1999. Annette and I were aware from contacts that there had been a bereavement at Hope House, but we did not know who, so on the Friday evening as we arrived to drop Chris off it was not at the forefront of our minds.

As was normal we parked the car, got Chris into his chair and he set off to the door with Annette in tow. The door was opened by Sharon, who welcomed Chris with a hug and a kiss and asked how he was. Just then Richard Ford came out of the Computer Room, pleased to see him Chris said, "Hello, Rich, how's Matty?" Richard looked sheepish, made an excuse and slipped away. Sharon took Annette aside and quickly and quietly explained that Matty had passed away the weekend before. It was quite a shock and Annette knew how badly it would affect Chris.

"Chris," she said, "I've got something to tell you". He turned round, an almost knowing look on his face. "I'm sorry, but sadly Matty's died". Chris took in what had been said, his eyes filled with tears and they silently trickled down his face. Annette put her arms around him and whispered things that Mums do at times like these. He sobbed quietly for a little while in his Mum's arms, there were no histrionics, no outburst, just quiet sadness and mourning, eventually composing himself.

"Would you like to go home?" Annette asked, "we'd understand if you did".

"No, I'll be fine," he replied with a little sigh, "but what will I say to Jackie (Matty's mum), and Richard and Emma?"

"Oh, don't worry about that, you'll *just* know," I offered. With that he set off with Sharon to his room so we could book him in.

Once through that process we headed back to the top, Chris to the Computer Room, Annette and I to the Dining Room for a cup of tea where we found Jackie Ford, in the company of Mary. As best we could we expressed our condolences, asked how Richard and Emma were and Jackie asked us to join her. We chatted about Matty and laughed at some of the memories. I became aware of the whirring noise of Chris's wheelchair approaching. As he entered the Dining Room there was a *click* as he stopped, a very brief pause, a moment of composure and then another *click* as he started off again. He swept across the Dining Room, looking serious, turned and parked in the gap between Jackie and myself. "Hello, Jackie," he said, "I'm dreadfully sorry to hear about Matty, **he** was my friend. How are you Jackie?" A serious, but compassionate look on his face. Jackie put her hand on Chris's arm and said, "All the better for seeing you, thanks Chris". With that the serious expression on his face changed to a smile and his chest puffed out slightly. He went on to ask how Richard and Emma were and how they were coping. Satisfied with the answers he sat quietly for a short time, listening to the conversation, and then was off, back to the Computer Room.

When we picked up Chris at the end of his stay, "Ooh, I have missed you" was his greeting, he was full of what had been going on. While Chris made his last visit to the Computer Room, Annette and I adjourned to the Dining Room with David. Over a cup of tea David told us how Chris had been over the weekend and what a splendid job he'd done helping Richard start coming to terms with the loss of his brother. When Richard had wanted to talk about Matty, Chris had chatted away; when Richard wanted to talk about other things, Chris had chatted about computers, football, motor racing and whatever; when Richard wanted to be on his own, Chris had given him space. It was David said as good a job as any social worker could have managed. On other occasions I have been proud of Chris's achievements, but perhaps none more than at this time. On the way home I asked Chris what he had been up to, we got the a run down of the usual activities, but no mention of Richard, so I enquired if he'd seen Richard. "Oh, yes," came the reply, "we just played on the computer and chatted". No need to embellish what had gone on, no need to brag, no need to explain.

Through one of the parents at Hope House, Peter Bone, Chris was nominated, during the year 2000, as a recipient of the Round Table Children's Wish. After the Wish organiser, Wendy had contacted us, we set Chris off thinking what he would like to do. After some thought he announced that he would like to visit an aircraft carrier. This was duly passed on to Wendy, who advised that it may be possible and that she would come back to us as soon as possible. Chris was quite pleased at the thought of visiting one of Her Majesty's vessels, but the logistics and access with the wheelchair might prove problematical. It occurred to me that the aircraft carrier perhaps was not the main reason for Chris's visit. "Are you expecting to see the planes take off?" I asked one evening, knowing that this was a major point of interest in a video he had. "Oh, Yes", was the reply, "it'll be fabulous!" I explained that the ship would be most likely in port and the planes would not be allowed to take-off. The expression on his face summed up his thinking. As it turned out Wendy was having a problem sorting something out and called to explain. Annette related the conversation I'd had with Chris, so it was suggested that Chris might like to think of something else. Over the next few days suggestions came and went before he decided what he'd really like to do - meet David Jason, Del Boy Trotter and Jack Frost himself. When told, Wendy thought that this would be possible and so she set the wheels in motion. Within weeks Chris had a letter from David Jason, saying he would be delighted to meet Chris and that he'd got his people working on a suitable date, Chris was well impressed. Ian Shingler (Chris's one to one and a great fan of Only Fools and Horses) was beside himself with envy, and pleaded with Chris to let him go with him, I suspect bribery may have been in the air. Eventually, it was arranged that Chris would meet his hero while he was filming a new series in September 2000. All things were arranged, but sadly the meeting never took place, Chris's Wish didn't come true. David Jason sent us a very nice letter later saying how sorry he was that he had not been able to meet Chris, I'm sure they would both have had a lot of fun and enjoyed their meeting, especially as planes were a common interest. Chris, undoubtedly would have taken it in his stride, playing the meeting down, but secretly, inside, bursting with pride at having met "a star".

On a few occasions Chris's frustrations would bubble to the surface and the carers at Hope House would help him work his way through them. Each had their own way to help, but none perhaps as unusual as that employed by, well perhaps they should remain nameless. This activity had the three of them, ensconced in Chris's room, thinking up rude words, one for each letter of the alphabet! As you can imagine by the end there was much laughing and conspiratorial looks.

In 2000, Chris was to have another three stays at Hope House, prior to August, and including the two weeks he had when he decided not to go to Florida. It was during this stay that Chris had *words* (that started as a disagreement over football) with one of the carers, which led to an unpleasant situation and had quite an adverse effect on him. He didn't tell us about it immediately, leaving it for a few days. He was very clear about what had happened, recognising and admitting that he had been wrong in saying certain things, but was unhappy about the way the carer had responded and treated him. His biggest worry though was that he would be stopped from going again to Hope House. That was a dreadful thought as Hope House and the people there were just so important to him.

When Chris participated in the University of York Sharing Value project, looking at what *quality* service meant he told the Researchers, "I go to the hospice .... They have a brilliant care team there, I think it's about 35 carers and they're all very, very, very pleasant". He also told the Researchers, "They (the hospice staff) ask <u>you</u> what you want to do every day."

Annette and I are enormously grateful to everyone at Hope House for enriching Chris's life. The folk there are like family and remain our friends.

We were also fortunate to benefit from the support of other organisations being introduced to Sue Gale, manager of the Crossroads organisation, which provides 'carers for carers' by Yvonne Bohdanowicz. The service was named after the television 'soap' opera of that name popular in the 1970s (and recently revived) after the programme makers, ATV, donated £10,000 to set up a respite care service. Today there are 200 schemes nationwide, providing 3 million care hours a year, allowing carers to go shopping, go to the hairdressers, socialise, go to the doctors and so on. The service celebrated 25 years in 1999. When we first met Sue there were no mutual grounds for support, but we were kept on 'file' and some time later, in November 1997 we were able to start to take advantage of their wonderful service. Chris had generally gone everywhere with us, but visits to the supermarket for the weekly shop were becoming boring. Crossroads were able to provide us two hours, on a Thursday, so that Annette and I could go and do the shopping and Chris could stay at home. To start with Chris was looked after by Claire, who Chris already knew through Saturday Live!. Claire was with us for six weeks before she moved on to another full time carer's job. So on 29th January 1998 Josie Harpley entered our life and soon became one of the family. To start Chris was not sure about Josie and the first few weeks he was very reserved during the evening. Josie's approach was just to allow Chris to do what he wanted (within reason of course!). Over a short time Chris warmed to Josie, drifting in and out of the lounge to chat, to tell her his news and to hear what Josie and her family were up to and how the cat was. Highlights were hearing about Josie's holidays that generally were to exotic places. When Josie was away Chris would always receive a postcard, which was met with great pleasure. When we were away Josie was always towards the top of the list for a present.

During the school holidays Josie arranged for extra hours so that Annette could get in to town, an arrangement of which Chris approved. In the periods when Chris was ill Joise was a tower of strength, always being positive and providing enormous support to Annette and I, both helping to look after Chris and cheer him up. Chris was very fond and protective of Josie. I would occasionally wind him up by saying that I was going to complain to Sue Gale about Josie for doing this or that. This would lead to an indignant outburst and various threats of physical violence upon my person.

One of Chris's favourite programs on the TV was Eastenders. Josie recalls one Thursday night when watching a particular episode in which Phil Mitchell was up to 'no good' Chris was swearing at the telly. Josie was reading a book, but was conscious that Chris was sereptiously looking at her, and clearly waiting for her to react. Josie allowed this to go on for a short period and then said, "Chris, that type of language doesn't bother me, I've heard it all before, but Mum and Dad wouldn't like it". After a very short pause, he said, "Sorry, Josie" and never swore again, even when he was uncomfortable.

On the occasions that Josie wasn't available as she swanned off around the world ("shut up Dad!") Crossroads provided other carers who were all very nice and friendly and got on well with Chris. There was Pat, Sharon (whose daughter Chris had gone to school at Dee Point with), Hazel and Trish who all provided help and friendship. But Chris was always pleased when Josie returned. In the last few months Josie was kept busy on her visits trying to get Chris comfortable, as his jacket caused him problems. Even so Josie thought that Chris was only asking her to move him as a last resort, as conscious that he was heavy and difficult to lift, he was reluctant to trouble her. Josie's last visit to look after Chris was on Thursday 24th August when he was in bed with stomach pains. As was normal, Josie cheered him up and when she said good night and that she would see him next week she left him in reasonably good spirits and with a smile on his face.

Another organisation that provided very welcome support was the Barnardo's organisation. Our first involvement came about when the service provision for children with special needs became a joint venture between them and the NHS. Barnardo's is probably best known for their children' homes, but as this requirement had reduced in line with social needs Barnardo's had evolved to provide a set of services in the community. From an initial suggestion by Yvonne Bohdanowicz Chris was provided in early 1997 with a Project Worker, who came to visit Chris for a few hours one evening a week, and acted as a companion, chatting, playing games or watching TV/video. The first Project Worker was James and Chris was just getting to enjoy the visits when James told us that he was leaving to take up a post elsewhere. James was replaced by Wendy and after a couple of weeks the relationship was warming when she too announced that she was moving on. Chris was quite concerned and asked me if the Project Workers were leaving because they didn't like him. I tried to reassure him that he wasn't the reason, the folk were just moving on to other jobs, with probably better pay. However, through Yvonne we made it clear that unless Barnardo's could guarantee some stability we didn't think it worth while to carry on, it was not helping Chris.

As a result of Yvonne taking control Chris was assigned Trena Salmon in the autumn of 1997. Chris quickly built up a friendship with her and after a few weeks of getting to know each other Trena suggested that they used the time to go out together, as she would be able to get the Barnardo's accessible minibus. Chris was not sure about this, but Trena persisted and so their first trip out was to go Christmas shopping in Chester. They were accompanied on the trip by another Barnardo's worker, Jane. Two things stick out from the trip. Chris regaled Jane about various aspects of flying aircraft, after he had been dropped off Jane apparently said to Trena that she was impressed that Chris could fly a plane. Trena had to explain that he was talking about a computer based flight simulator! The other thing was that Trena couldn't believe how many people Chris knew. She said that nearly every corner they went round he would be saying "Hi" to people and progress was very slow, as they had to stop and chat. Over time there were other trips out, to the cinema (some with Trena's husband Steve, a "good guy as he had a V6 Mondeo"), ten pin bowling, Chester Zoo (with Mel from Barnardo's "there's not many people I'd take there on a freezing November afternoon") and so on. Trena also sat with Chris on a few evenings when Annette and I went out and on one of those occasions they both cried their way through 'Titanic'.

Towards the end of 1998 Barnardo's were looking to reorganise the way they provided their services and this coincided with Trena announcing that she was expecting a little Salmon. Chris was both sad and delighted. Happy about the baby, getting Trena to promise that he would get to have a hold of the new arrival, and sad that she was leaving. Trena's role was taken over by Norma Hellon, who Chris had previously met on a Barnardo's Summer Scheme. Norma quickly filled the void left by Trena and established a deep and lasting friendship. Initially, Norma would take Chris to the cinema to see whatever was 'flavour of the month' and then other social outings. Trips to the cinema also involved popcorn, which Norma would scoop into Chris's mouth, the only problem being that in the dark of the cinema it was difficult to see the *target*. The end result was almost as much popcorn in the wheelchair as in Chris. Chris had been going, on Saturday mornings, to age related activity groups and had enjoyed that, however he was getting to the point were he would need to move on again. Norma suggested that Chris might find Choices in Ellesmere Port good fun, especially as many of his school friends attended. Never one to rush into things Chris wasn't sure, so Norma pulled some strings and arranged for Chris to go one evening and see for himself. From then there was no turning back. With Norma's help Chris was accepted at Choices and from then on he went nearly every week. Norma would come to our house, jump into the taxi with Chris and off they would go. Norma's influence on Chris and how he matured and coped with his increasing disability cannot be underestimated, she always knew what to say, and she never made decisions for him, but helped him to come to one for himself.

Norma carried on from where Trena had left off, but also introduced new things. She was determined to ensure that Chris had the opportunity to have a full social life. There were the visits to the cinema, more often than not accompanied by Norma's daughter Abigail, a visit to the Blue Planet Aquarium, shopping, the Saturday Night socials at the Croft and of course Choices Youth Club. Norma's influence was significant and she enhanced Chris's life immeasurably.

The Neuromuscular Centre, which is located in Winsford, is a facility for everyone within the region directly or indirectly affected by muscular dystrophy. There is a full physiotherapy service available by appointment. For young school leavers with muscular dystrophy, there is the chance to train in computer based graphic design to a recognised standard, with an opportunity to take up a place in the associated Design company. For all those in the north-west who have muscular dystrophy, their families and their friends, the Centre offers information, practical advice, social contact and emotional support. The Centre is the first of its kind. In time, it is hoped, there will be others like it throughout the UK. It was founded by Sarah Kelly and Kate Fox in 1990 and has as its President, Matthew Kelly. We were first introduced to the NMC by Sue Herbert in 1995 and maintained contact over the years. Both Kate and, latterly, Jenny Whitall provided Chris with specialist physiotherapy support and other sound advice relating to the management of muscular dystrophy. During 2000 we had visited the NMC to show Chris around, as it was one of a number of potential places that Chris could consider for further education. He had been quite impressed by the computers available, but as he re-iterated on the way home he would only consider it after he left Dorin Park.

All of the groups that provided help to Chris and the family rely heavily on independent fund raising and to assist that they require publicity. In early June 1999 Stuart from Hope House called us and asked if Chris would be prepared to help raise their profile as they were suffering a severe funding shortage. This would involve an interview and some pictures for the paper. Chris was happy to say 'Yes' and was secretly quite chuffed to have been asked. So there we were one Friday in June, featured on the front page of the Chronicle, the local paper, explaining the importance of Hope House to families like ours. Almost at the time that picture was printed Sue Gale phoned to ask Chris if he would help Crossroads publicise their 25th anniversary. Chris was more than happy to say 'Yes' again, getting quite a taste for being a 'celebrity'. This time the feature and photograph, which included ("my friend") Josie, was printed in the Daily Post.

Chris examines 'big' Chris Bolton's glider. 14th August 1993

"Beat yer!" Just past the Finish Line, Chester 10K. May 1993

Presentation of Chris's first powered chair at Helsby Golf Club by Liverpool footballer Ian Callahan (back right), with Bert Dyson (back left), Peter Herbert (front centre) and John Brassington (front right). 10th June 1993

Chris and Dee Point friends. Melanie (in front of Chris), Laura (to Chris's left), Jordan (to the right), and Vicki (behind Chris). Mel's 9th birthday party, 14th September 1994

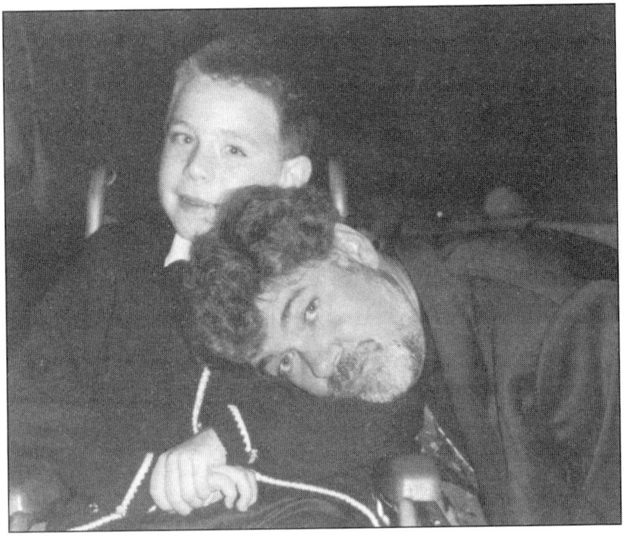

At the NMC Fund Raising Celebration with Mathew Kelly (president of the NMC). 23rd September 1994

"Right Chris, don't touch." "OK John". Preparing for take off. North Wales Gliding Club. 14th August 1993.

Chris, achieving one of his aims. Top of the Empire State, NYC.
Wrapped up, 'cos Mum worries. 30th April 1997

Inter School Football Competition, held at Hebden Green School. 21st May 1998

CHAPTER SEVEN (Home and Away)

You can waste a whole lifetime
Trying to be
What you think is expected of you
But you'll never be free

Chris Rea

Our first proper holiday as a family had been to a house in Charmouth, Dorset just after Chris's third birthday. The house was next to a caravan site owned by the same people, so we had access to the site facilities. These included a small children's playground equipped with swings, slides and roundabout. In addition there were a number of old farm tractors on which the kids could climb. These were a great attraction to Chris and he would spend most of his time in the playground on one or other of them pretending to be the farmer, although it was my job to be the sound effects man.

The weather was reasonably good while we were away so several days were spent on the beach nearby or somewhere along the coast. Chris liked nothing better than building a castle (or watching Mum and Dad do it) and then smashing it down by running through it. We also visited Lyme Regis and walked out on the Cobb harbour wall, but did not recreate the scene from 'An Officer and a Gentleman'. We visited Cricket St. Thomas, home to the setting of TV programme 'To the Manor Born' and also a small zoo that Chris enjoyed, up to the point a large macaw behind him screeched and frightened him to death. However, I think his favourite part of the day was running or rolling down the big grassy banks that formed the garden.

Over the years we made many trips down the coast to Prestatyn, Rhyl, Colwyn Bay, Llandudno and Criccieth, as well as to the local attractions such as Chester Zoo, Knowsley Safari Park, Jodrel Bank and the Boat Museum at Ellesmere Port amongst others. However, once walking was either difficult or impossible and the wheelchair came into regular use days at the beach became less interesting for Chris. One of his favourite places to visit though was the Museum of Science and Industry in Manchester, where there is a whole variety of things to do and see with good wheelchair access. The museum is split across two sites, one covering the history of the area as well as the technology and science aspects and the other site covering aerospace. While the latter was of great interest to Chris he always enjoyed the former. The technology and science section has many 'hands on' exhibits dealing with light, sound and so on and Chris would happily try out all of the experiments making sure that it was Dad who looked the fool in front of the optical effect mirrors. The history section of the museum is well laid out with a number of working exhibits. This includes steam engines, used for various tasks, recreations of the turn of the century Castlefield area, featuring a period setting railway station, a gas works and a walk through sewer, complete with smells, which appealed to Chris's humour.

On the way home from the museum we would often call in at the Viewing Area at Manchester airport to watch the aircraft taking off and landing which would satisfy Chris's interest in planes and give him the opportunity to demonstrate his knowledge of the various aircraft.

During one visit to the Museum Chris said he wasn't feeling very well and wanted to go home. We set off and were soon speeding along the M56, he suddenly announced that he felt sick. Fortunately there was a plastic bag in the front of the car so I passed that to him just in case. I pressed on hoping to get home, but without luck. As we approached the end of the motorway he was sick, thank goodness for the plastic bag I thought, until that is I realised that it had small holes in it!

In 1990 we had a holiday in a caravan at Saundersfoot, near Tenby, in South Wales. It was a really enjoyable week, the caravan site had a large playground with big swings on which Chris could indulge his low level flying as well as a swimming pool and evening entertainment. We visited many of the local places including St David's for the Cathedral, Pembroke for the castle and Haverfordwest for the shops. Chris quite enjoyed the visits to castles and over the years before the wheelchair arrived we got to see quite a few. I have to say that they were tiring days, as for Chris to enjoy the tour of the rooms and towers it would involve me piggy backing him around. To start with this was no problem, but as he got older and heavier the task became more difficult. Still there was no doubt from the enjoyment he got it was well worth it.

During the school summer holidays of 1991 we spent a few days in London, although the hotel, the London Ryan that was supposed to be close to the tube station turned out to be quite a walk, or for Chris a piggyback. Nevertheless we had a very good time showing Chris all the sights that he had previously only seen on the TV or in pictures. One of our first stops was at Tower Bridge and a visit to the newly opened viewing area at the top of the bridge, between the two towers. This affords great views up and down the river and over the Tower of London. We also visited the Bridge museum to view the original steam engine that was used to open the bridge and also viewed the original design drawings. Even at this age Chris was interested in how things worked and would often ask questions that we found difficult to answer. After Tower Bridge we visited the Tower of London and then took a boat trip up the river to Greenwich to see the Cutty Sark and Gypsy Moth. Later we visited St. Paul's and walked down Fleet Street.

The next day we took the tube to Westminster, as Chris wanted to see Big Ben. As we exited the underground station Big Ben, which was almost opposite across the road, was just beginning to strike. Chris just stopped, his wide open eyes tracking the tower from street level to the clock face, and stood there with his mouth open and quiet. I don't think that he had realised how tall or how loud Big Ben ("it's the name of the bell and not the tower," he told us) was. We stood for sometime admiring this symbol of our country, "It's great" was about all he managed to say.

By this time I had run the London Marathon a couple of times and Chris wanted to know where the course went and was always looking for bits of the 'blue line' that the runners follow. He knew the race finished at that time on Westminster Bridge and he wanted to see the finish line. "One day," he said, "we'll run the race and finish together." We walked up onto the bridge, "I'll tell you what," I suggested, "if Mum goes ahead with the camera we can run across the line now and Mum can take a photo." So Annette was dispatched to just beyond the Finish Line and the two great athletes representing Great Britain trotted up to the line hand in hand, raising their free hands as they *won*!

We returned across the bridge (recovering a lot quicker than the last time I ran across it) and walked round to the front of the Houses of Parliament, Chris being disappointed not to see any famous politicians. From there we walked up Whitehall, pausing to peer through the gates of Downing Street (further disappointment as no Mr. Major) and then onto Trafalgar Square. We admired Nelson on his column and the fountains, but it was the lions that attracted Chris most, particularly when he realised that other kids were climbing up and sitting on the big bronze heads. Not wishing for Chris to miss out this meant that Annette or I had to 'accompany' him, and I drew the short straw. Getting him up the plinth and then the lion itself was no easy feat, but getting down was a doddle as he was simply able to slide down. As you can imagine this became a great game, so we were up and down, up and down. Chris thought it was great fun, I thought it was very tiring and Mum thought it was very dangerous.

Chris had always fancied himself as a bit of a photographer so he had taken his little camera with us to London. At all the right times he would get it out and shoot off a couple of snaps. When we got home we put the film in for developing and looked forward to the results. We were not disappointed. There was the windowsill on Tower Bridge, the railings at the Tower of London, the rail of the riverboat, and several of the seats on the boat. Admittedly, he did take a few descent shots of some of the sights.

We were back in London in the April of 1992 for the marathon in the company of Hugh Griffiths and his fiancee, Jeanette. We arrived around midday on the Saturday and having checked in to our hotel we went across the Thames to Registration close by County Hall to get our race numbers and sign on for the race. Chris was in his element, you would have thought it was him that was running the race. We wandered around the exhibition and then did a bit of sight seeing, including Big Ben, the Houses of Parliament and, yes you've guessed it, the Lions in Trafalgar Square. The trouble was eight months had passed since our last visit and climbing was much more difficult, so although Chris did manage to get to the lion's head he was not up and down like the previous time. We had the Major Buggy with us on this visit so when he got tired we could sit him down and keep moving around.

The next morning Hugh and I had to be up early for breakfast and then to set off to Blackheath for the start, leaving Annette and Chris to have breakfast with Jeanette a little later. Hugh and I were of slightly different running standards so we had agreed to run our own races, and we had arranged for Jeanette, Annette and Chris to watch the race in the Victoria Gardens on the Embankment. Chris was full of himself when he got up and was into everything and anything. After breakfast Jeanette, Annette and Chris set off across Trafalgar Square to make their way down to the Embankment to get a good position to watch. Chris's behaviour was not getting any better and as Annette said later, "He was a right little sod". He continued to mess about and play up so much that the group missed me running past, although they did see Hugh and give him a big cheer. As Hugh and I were running to raise money for the Muscular Dystrophy Group we had arranged to all meet up at the MDG Reception that was to be held at the Queen Elizabeth Hall on the South Bank. I got there first and after a difficult run was absolutely shattered, so found a corner and sat down.

A while later the others found me, led by Chris and Hugh, who despite this being his first marathon looked great and flushed with success. I recall getting a big hug and kiss off Chris and a request to have my medal. The MDG Team always had a non-running captain and that year it was the boxing commentator, Harry Carpenter, assisted by actor Ronald Magill (Amos Brearley of Emmerdale Farm), so Hugh, and I ably supported by Chris were able to get our commemorative 'team' photograph taken.

While Annette's mum helped us out by having Chris after school and during the school holidays, my mum would help out at weekends and also during the school holidays. Trips into town on Saturdays were quite regular, with visits to Edgar's Park in Handbridge and a small wooded area of the park on a sandstone hill that Chris christened 'The Magic Secret' onto which he would climb and play 'hide and seek'. During this time Nana was the secretary of the Kings Lea House Residents Committee, the sheltered accommodation where Chris's Great Grandma lived. For the residents Nana organised a number of social events during the year and whenever the trips were in the school holidays Chris would be invited along. He really enjoyed these days and visited places such as Llangollen, Llandudno, Southport, and Stapley Water Gardens (!). He was very popular with all the ladies and was happy to entertain them. He would go off on these day trips with his pocket money, but invariably come home with a bag of goodies and more money than he started with. Although, the trips did continue after he started using the wheelchair it was only possible as the bus driver would kindly lift him on and off the bus, he eventually became too big to manage easily. As he only really felt safe when I carried him, he reluctantly told Nana he wouldn't be going on the trips anymore. It was quite a shame really as not only did Chris enjoy the days out, but he also kept the many ladies who went on the trips entertained with his chatter and jokes.

Chris also enjoyed an annual trip to Chester Fair, which more often than not involved an invitation to Nana. To start with Chris would go on quite a few of the rides, amongst his favourites were the Big Wheel, the Dodgem cars, the Ghost Train and the Octopus. The Fair was also a good place to meet people and as we walked around Chris was always saying hello to folk he knew, many of which were from Dee Point School. As time went by the rides became fewer and fewer, but he still enjoyed a visit to play the slots, eat candyfloss, enjoy the sights and smells and, of course, meet people. Eventually, he decided that he no longer wanted to go and would rather stay at home playing on the computer. Every now and then he would talk about the Fair and recall some of the rides he had been on and the fun we had had, never in a sad way but happily recalling days gone by.

My running had continued and in May 1993 I was preparing to enter the Chester Half Marathon. Chris was keen to take part in an event himself so I suggested that we did the 10K that was run in conjunction with the Half Marathon. Chris was over the moon. Obviously he wasn't going to run the event, as we were going to press into service the recently arrived wheelchair. He also decided that he wanted to run the race for charity so we set about getting sponsorship. The Sunday morning of the race arrived, a nice sunny day. Chris chose to wear my 1991 Muscular Dystrophy running vest and I wore the 1992 version. So suitably attired we toed the line ready for the start, well actually as the start is on the grassy Roodee I toed the line and Chris waited with his Mum by the gates to the

Roodee a few hundred yards away, where I could 'pick' him up. The course runs through the city centre and then out down the Parkgate Road and up through Blacon, before returning to the Roodee. The race has always attracted good public support and Chris really enjoyed the crowd cheering him on, by the end he'd perfected quite a good royal wave. The course is not that easy as there are quite a few gradients and although I was relatively fit it was hard going, but Chris being a hard task master kept shouting to go faster, targeting competitors in front of us to overtake and cheering as we did so. As we ran down the hill on Saughall Road we were moving fairly quickly and as we crossed over where a new road was being built we hit the crest of the road and Chris very nearly flew out of the chair, despite being strapped in. Still that kept him quiet for a few minutes! The run went very well and about 45 minutes after we started we were running down the finishing straight to a good round of applause from the crowd, the royal wave working overtime. Chris was very impressed by his performance, the commemorative mug and was even happier a few weeks later when the official results were produced as that showed C. Barratt had finished in front of M. Barratt. For a long time after he didn't let me forget that.

As a result of his efforts Chris raised several hundred pounds and was able to make donations to Dee Point and Dorin Park schools, as well as the Neuromuscular Centre in Winsford.

By October 1993 we'd been using the wheelchair a little while, but had not been too far from home only using it in familiar areas, so we decided to have a weekend away. Chris wanted to go to York to see the Minster (he'd seen a TV programme on the renovation of the Rose Window after a fire), so with that in mind we booked a suitable hotel and off we went. Initially, things didn't work out too well as we got stuck in a traffic jam on the M62 caused by a lorry shedding a load of glass. Chris was a good passenger, but not the most patient, so as we crept along he was not at all complimentary about other road users. He was all for leaving the motorway at the next junction and finding our way through the A and B roads. Eventually, just to stop him moaning I did just that, but whether or not it reduced our journey time I have no idea, at least we were moving and the nagging had stopped! On journeys he generally sat in the front otherwise he would have been an excellent example of a 'back street driver'.

We eventually arrived in York, found the hotel and got settled before taking a walk to get orientated. We stopped at one point at a café, checking that it was OK to bring in the wheelchair and that there was a disabled toilet. We were told it was OK and there were appropriate facilities. Having enjoyed a nice tea Chris wanted to go to the loo, so off we went. Sure enough there was a disabled toilet, the only problem was that its location off a small corridor made it impossible to turn the wheelchair in through the door. As you can imagine Chris was not too impressed by this, still with a bit of imagination we eventually managed. Still, we did learn some valuable lessons about access, people's attitudes and how to 'drive' the wheelchair.

The following day we paid a visit to the Minster, having walked up the Shambles and admired all the medieval houses. We were pleasantly surprised that there was wheelchair access to the knave and so we were able to enjoy a tour inside the Minster and appreciate the sunlight streaming in through the magnificent Rose Window. Chris was also interested in the bells in the tower, especially how many there were, and kept asking me. Well, I had no idea, so I told him to ask one of the Guides. Initially, he was reluctant to do so, wanting me to ask, but eventually his curiosity got the better of him and as a Guide walked past he said, "Excuse me, but could you tell me how many bells make up your peel?" I'm not sure who was the most surprised, me or the Guide, with Chris using the word peel.

From the Minster Chris and I made our way to the Railway Museum, while Annette went off to do some shopping, a mutually acceptable arrangement for all parties! The Museum is a great place, especially if you like all things connected with railways. Chris especially loved Mallard, but found many of the other static exhibits fascinating as well. Outside, on the day we visited, there was a large steam locomotive being shunted back and to to demonstrate the noise, smell and power of these wonderful beasts. After each pass visitors were invited up a ladder and onto the footplate to view the fire and controls. Naturally, Chris wanted to look, but it was quite a climb and there was no way he would manage it. My reaction was to say no, but he asked and asked to go, and it was made harder as kids younger than him took their turn. I went to walk away, but he began to get upset so I gave in. After considering the options I decided a piggyback was the way to go, so I lifted him up and climbed the steps and onto the footplate. Aware of the effort he used the time very well asking a lot of sensible questions that the driver and his mate were happy to answer. Getting down was not easy, but we managed it safely. Once he was back in his chair the expression on his face said everything and it was an experience he talked of for some time to come.

The next day we paid a visit to the Jorvik Centre and were very impressed by the disabled facilities. For a start as we queued up we were approached by a member of staff and shown in through a suitable entrance, briefed on the procedure and then shown to the boarding point for the tour buggies. After a short wait a wheelchair accessible buggy arrived and we were invited to board. The chair was strapped down and away we went. A very good example of what can be done; it's a pity that other places in the UK don't follow suit. Chris thought "the ride was really good, although it was a bit pongy!"

All in all the weekend to York was a great success, we had learnt a number of things about using the wheelchair and how to get about and what to look out for, and Chris had seen all the things he wanted to and learnt a whole load of facts. Some time later, after we were Internet enabled he found a web page about the Minster and the peel of bells, including a sound file which he enjoyed playing from time to time.

One of Chris's favourite things was his annual visit to the local Fireworks display on or around November 5th. To start with we attended the Lions display at Chester Zoo accompanied by Nana and then after a few years went to the Fire Brigade's display at the Deeside Leisure Centre with Paul, John and Julie and Nana. While he loved the displays he would make a terrible fuss about all the bangs and insist that you stood behind him and covered his ears, what a wimp. We would get to the displays in plenty of time to get a good front row view, but it never ceased to amaze me how many people would then ease in front of us, despite the fact that Chris was in the wheelchair. Chris would nudge me and look at me as if to say "What a plonker!". People's attitude when you asked them to move so Chris could see was also beyond belief. We didn't miss a year until 1999 when it was teeming down with rain and Annette, rightly, was reluctant to let Chris go for fear of him getting a chill and it affecting his chest. He wasn't happy and he let his feelings be known. But he did see sense when Paul described how wet he'd got!

In 1994 Chris decided that he didn't want a birthday party as such, but wanted to do something different. "What have you got in mind?" asked Annette. "I want to go to Blackpool, to the fair," he replied. So on the Saturday after his birthday we set off up the M6, accompanied by his friend Melanie and with a plan to meet Eve and Dave Nash, her sister Pauline and Pauline's son Stevie. As planned we all met up and began a tour round the fun fair. There were loads of rides for the kids to go on, accompanied by the 'big' kids, of course. We stood and watched the roller coaster type ride that you do on *horse*back, before a small group led by Chris volunteered to have a go. Needless to say I had to go with Chris to hold onto him, which was no mean feat as the *horse* jumps fences. From there we went to the Pepsi Big One and walked past. Well, as Chris said, "the queues too big" and anyway it was lunchtime. After lunch we continued our tour of the Pleasure Beach taking in further rides. Eventually, we arrived at the Grand National, a large twin tracked wooden roller coaster on which two trains race one another, classed by roller aficionados as one of the best in the world. Being a roller fan myself I announced I was going to have a go, Dave was game as well. Then Chris, who'd cut his teeth on Thunder Mountain in Disney and the Scorpion at Busch Gardens, said he wanted to go as well. I explained what the ride was like, but he was adamant he was going to have a go. Melanie wasn't sure, but didn't want to miss out, so the four of us paid our money and headed towards the train station. Naturally, there was no wheelchair access so Chris had to put up with a piggyback. Before we got in I checked again he wanted to ride. So, there we were, Chris and I sitting behind Dave and Mel. We settled in, pulled down the safety bar and waited in anticipation. Out of the station we slipped and started the climb to the top of the first peak. Chris was shouting to Melanie and was putting on a show of bravado. We got closer to the top, admiring the view across the amusements and out towards the Tower. Suddenly, the click-click-click of the pulling mechanism went quiet, there was a pause, I pulled Chris closer to me and held on as we hurtled down the slope towards the ground. The chatting had stopped now, I felt him stiffen and a breathless "Bloooody Hell!" emitted from Chris. That was the last he spoke for the next 2 or 3 minutes as the carriages clattered their way around the ride. At one point there is a very quick section that goes up, down, up, down rather like going over fences and as we hurtled over the second rise I could feel Chris shooting upwards. I had visions of him flying backwards out of the carriage, but managed to grab his jacket and pull him back alongside me. As we shot under the bridge there were Annette, Eve and Pauline waving, but I'm not sure Chris or Melanie saw them. Once back in the station we exited the carriages, Melanie looking a little on the white side, Dave a bit flushed and Chris just quiet. "Fancy another go?" I asked. "On your own," said Dave, "No chance," mumbled Chris, "No thank you," whispered Melanie. Ah well never mind. Still, the experience was useful, as for quite sometime Chris would impress people with the story of how he had been on The Grand National roller coaster at Blackpool.

As with all good things they have to come to an end and the fun day at Blackpool was no exception and so with the sun going down it was time to set off home. Chris who normally travelled in the front decided on this occasion to sit in the back with Mel. They spent the whole of the return journey recalling the events of the day, telling silly jokes and stories and eating sweets. In fact one of the abiding memories of that day was spending ages cleaning all the sweet papers and other rubbish out of the back of the car the next day. "Nothing to do with me," came the response when challenged.

The Neuromuscular Centre had run a special fund raising campaign during 1993/4 to raise money for a new building. We had contributed from my marathon effort and Chris's 10K and so we were invited to a special event, held in September, in the Manweb Ballroom to help celebrate reaching the target. The President of the NMC, Matthew Kelly, was present, greeting all the guests as they arrived, along with a number of other celebrities for what was a very enjoyable evening. Chris was still suffering from the operation on his legs, but had a really good time and particularly enjoyed the verbal jousting with Matthew. Perhaps the highlight of his night was meeting Kate Copstick, the star of 'Marlene Marlowe Investigates', one of his then favourite TV shows. She was also the 'star' of the evening's entertainment, a special version of 'You Bet!', in which she ate a plate of chillis in 5 minutes. Chris also enjoyed rushing around in his wheelchair with Daniel, a nearby neighbour, bursting balloons.

Suzanne and Barbara, two of the nurses at the Countess who'd looked after Chris during the short time he was in having the operation on his legs, remembered him in early 1994 when they sent him some tickets for a circus which was planned to take place on the Roodee. Although it was only a small troupe the entertainment was really good, featuring high wire, trapeze and ladder balancing, as well as an act where two guys held a large flexible pole between them and a girl was bounced into the air and did various twists, turns and somersaults. The height that the girl went into the air had the audience gasping in anticipation. The highlight though for Chris was the band of clowns that just got up to all sorts of mischief, some of which involved the audience. There was lots of water and much of that went down each other's trousers. Chris laughed so much at some of the antics that he nearly fell out of his chair.

Chris had had an interest in aeroplanes from when we had prepared him for flying to Florida in 1991. Over the following years he read more and more about planes, watched videos and visited the airport. One of his ambitions was to fly on Concorde, and while we never managed to arrange that for him, the next best thing was to see it. So one Sunday in April 1996 we headed off to Manchester Airport, accompanied by cousin Paul and Nana. We set off we thought in plenty of time, but when we arrived at the public viewing area on the east side of the airport it was full. We drove round to the terminal side and eventually found a spot close to The Airport Public House near the end of the runway. We got out of the car and took up a place by the perimeter fence from which we could see the taxiway and the end of the runway. As it turned out it wasn't a bad spot, we were able to get good views as the various planes taxied past us, lined up and then set off down the runway. We could also watch the planes as they arrived and headed down the runway to land. Chris kept us fully informed with all the necessary information on which plane was which. As the expected time for Concorde's departure drew nearer the size of the crowd grew and the anticipation increased. Concorde's appearance was heralded by the loud noise of its Rolls Royce SNECMA engines and its small size was put in perspective as it followed a Delta Airlines Boeing 747 along the taxiway. Our choice of viewing place couldn't have been better, Concorde ("Isn't she beautiful") stopped right in front of us and stayed for several minutes while an inbound plane approached and landed. Concorde was then cleared for take off and eased out onto the runway. What happened next had us gasping for breath, almost literally. The Captain increased the thrust on the four engines, held her on the brakes and then she was off, slowly at first and then quicker, the engines absolutely roaring, the noise was deafening, your ears throbbed with the noise and the vibration made your chest resonate taking away your breath. Chris summed it up, when we could speak and hear again, "God, that was fantastic, wasn't it Paul? Wasn't it fantastic".

Having enjoyed the circus early in 1995 Chris asked to go to see the Moscow State Circus when he saw it advertised in May 1996. This was a much bigger circus than the one we had seen before and was perhaps more traditional (except there were no performing animals). The Ring Master was a tall imposing chap, who was actually English, and he kept the show moving along at a good pace so that the audience had no chance to get bored. One act that fascinated us was the girl who was able to spin rings on her arms, legs, neck, waist and chest, with the rings spinning in different directions. As Chris asked, "How the hell do you do that?"

Through Sue Johnston, the nurse at Dorin Park, Chris was nominated in 1996 to attend the Heswall Boys Camp in August, although he was yet to start at Dorin full time. Initially, Chris was not too keen on the idea, especially as it meant being away from home for a week, which would be the first time for him. We encouraged Chris to go, but he was not positive. This has to be seen against a backdrop of knowing the level of personal care that he needed. He knew that we, his Mum and Dad, provided what he wanted and how he wanted it, entrusting that care to strangers was a step into the unknown and therefore a potential problem. Eventually, after being encouraged by Sue and others at Dorin Park, and in the knowledge that his friends Anthony and Paul were going, he agreed. However, this was only on the understanding that if he didn't like it or he was uncomfortable we would go and pick him up.

The Boys Camp, is funded and organised by Heswall Handicapped Boys Camp Committee and their hard working members led by Michael Byrne, takes place in the middle of the school summer holidays and is based in the Kingsmead School in Hoylake. As the weekend approached we could sense that he was getting nervous and privately Annette and I expected him to say he wasn't going to go. Chris had received a timetable of the activities and was quite encouraged that there would be lots to do and places to visit. Saturday arrived and we were packed and ready to go, "Don't forget," said Chris, "if I don't like it you promised that you'd come for me".

"Yes," responded Annette, "we will, but please give it a chance."

The journey up the M53 did not take long and we soon found the school down a side road. It was quite an old building, set in quite extensive grounds which were already a hive of activity as boys, helpers and parents milled around. When Chris was nervous or anxious he was quiet, and that how he was now, his eyes darted here and there taking everything in, then with relief evident in his voice he said, "There's Anthony, at least he's here". We unloaded and made our way up a very substantial ramp and into the school building. It was a bit like stepping back in time, the school was just like you see in Billy Bunter's School Days. We turned into the Refectory where registration was taking place. While the necessary information was noted down, we were offered tea or juice and biscuits, and then Chris was introduced to his main carer for the week, a big, friendly guy called Pete. With initial pleasantries over Pete took charge and accompanied us to one of the dormitories. The corridor down which we walked was covered in old school photos and various shields showing old sporting and educational success. The 'dormitory' was actually a classroom in which iron framed beds had been arranged. Chris seemed quite happy and chose a bed near the door with good access for his chair. Annette was a bit more concerned, worried if Chris would be able to sleep on such a bed and mattress. Her concerns were not helped when she saw the toilets, there was very little room in the cubicles. "How are they going to manage Chris?" she whispered. After a short discussion we agreed that the best thing would be to bring his toilet chair from home. We checked with Pete that this would be OK, and arranged to return later that evening with the necessary equipment. By now Chris was itching to have a look round and find Anthony and Paul. The facilities were actually quite good, the sports hall was large, airy and modern, the swimming pool likewise, although the water was pretty cold. Outside we joined up again with Pete, who introduced us to some of the other helpers, including his sister Heidi, Caroline (who looked after medical matters) and Ian.

The time was approaching for Annette and I to leave, so having made sure that Chris was reasonably well settled, we said our good-byes. There were some big hugs and a little tear followed by "Now don't forget you promised to come and get me if I don't like it".

"You'll be OK with us," said Heidi, "you'll have a great time".

So with that we left. As we drove out of the car park we could see Chris looking after us and waving. Once home we had some tea and then put the toilet chair in the Serena and headed back to Hoylake. By the time we got back to the school it was dusk and we were able to see the group through the window in the Refectory. They were all having what appeared to be a good time, it was certainly noisy, and as we approached the door it was Chris's voice that we could hear above everyone else's! We parked the toilet chair and quietly and quickly left, not wishing to interrupt the group's evening.

It was most unusual not having Chris at home, this was the first time in ages that we had not looked after him (our visits to Hope House had not yet started). Annette and I were constantly wondering what he was doing, if he was alright and if he was enjoying himself. Then, early Monday evening the phone rang. We looked at one another apprehensively. Annette answered the call.

"Hello, Chrissie, how are you?" I studied her face to see if I could gain any idea of what the answer was. Gradually, Annette's face broke into a smile. Relief. Oh yes, he was having a good time, it was great, he was eating well and everyone was really nice. Yes he would speak to Dad (briefly) and yes he would phone again (he did and everything was still OK). Bye.

The 'campers' had to be collected mid-Saturday morning, so we set off in plenty of time, arriving in a stream of other parents. We soon found Chris, holding *court* in the middle of a group of other campers and carers. It was clear from the beaming smile that he had enjoyed himself. We were introduced to a number of his new friends (including Ronie the cook) and Phil (one of the carers), who all agreed it had been a great time. Chris had struck up a good relationship with Phil, who flew in every year to help from Seattle, where he worked for Boeing. As Chris explained they had had long chats about various aircraft and airports around the world. We collected his belongings and the bag of sweets, fruit and mementoes of the camp, but as usual getting Chris away was a real battle. Eventually, after thanking all the helpers and organisers, we managed to get him in the car and with a wave, a shout of "See you next year" and a toot on the car horn we were on our way home. The journey took perhaps 40 minutes and for the whole time Chris provided us a day by day commentary on what had been happening. There had been trips to Llangollen, Chester Zoo, Anfield Football Ground (a bit of a low point for a Man. Utd. supporter!), Blackpool, and Granada Studio Tours along with bowling and a camp barbecue and disco. All in all Chris had had a really, really good time and yes he would go again if he could. A few days after getting home he asked if he could write a letter to Michael Byrne and all the helpers to say thank you for a great time.

Later in 1996 we took a trip to the Nynex in Manchester to see Walt Disney on Ice, despite the fact that the areas set aside for wheelchairs were some distance above the rink we had a good time. The show was really good, all the main characters were present, although Mickey Mouse was the star of the show. The highlight for us though was watching Tigger bouncing around on skates (don't try that yourself) and the antics of Chip 'n' Dale, who were up to their usual naughtiness and involved the audience in some of the *fun*. Chris was a bit disappointed that we were well away from the rink, as he would have liked the opportunity to join in and, as he saw it, meet up with old friends.

As Chris became weaker it was a problem to find things for him to do, although we still went swimming a lot of sports were out of the question. He quite enjoyed watching various competitions and through Jill Smith at Dorin Park went to watch the Chester Rockets Wheelchair Basketball team at the Northgate Arena. He knew a few of the players, either through school or clubs, or in the case of Stuart Ramsey as he was the father of two kids that had attended Dee Point. We went to see a couple of games, but while he enjoyed them he was not keen on going too often. I suspect that he really wanted to play himself and watching was no substitute. If that were the case he would rather not go.

Chris did attend a Sport for All day at the Northgate Arena in June 1997, but he found that most of the sports needed arm strength, something that he just didn't have. However, one game he was pretty good at was Boccia, which he'd learnt to play at Dorin Park and he had a number of goes, as always played to win, beating most other players.

August 1997 saw Chris attend the Boys Camp at Hoylake for the second time. Again, Sue Johnston had put forward his name, only this time he was relieved when he got accepted and he was very much looking forward to going and re-establishing old acquaintances. We were better prepared this time as well, packing all the necessary creature comforts, including the toilet chair. We arrived mid-afternoon along with everyone else, but this time Chris was away and greeting his friends, while Annette and I went and registered his arrival. Chris soon reappeared and with Ian we went and selected his bed for the week. Even knowing what to expect after the previous year Annette was still concerned over the beds and whether Chris would be comfortable. Initially, Chris was a bit disappointed, as Phil was not at the camp. He was much relieved when Ian told him that he would be flying in the following day and they were picking him up from the airport in the morning. After a cup of tea and a chat with various people we said our good byes and set off home, with Chris bordering on the keen to see us go. How things change in twelve months!

The week was another great success and Chris had another great time, perhaps more so this year, as he knew what to expect. There were the days out to the nearby Bowling Rink, the Ellesmere Port Boat Museum, and of course, Blackpool, as well as many activities in the camp. These included games, a visit from the local classic car club, with some fairly exotic and exciting machinery, and a barbecue and disco. We did get a couple of phone calls during the week, but these were fairly short and provided a very brief update before Chris was off to join in with something or the other.

Sadly, for Chris, the week soon came to an end and we arrived along with other parents to collect the 'campers'. More friendships had been made, more good times had been had and there were many sad faces as people set off for home. Chris said his good byes and thank-yous; arrangements were made to see everyone again next year and with a wave and a toot of the car horn we were off. As with the year before the journey home provided Chris the opportunity to give us a day by day review of the camp's activities, it was very clear that he had really enjoyed himself. For sure there were a few niggles, meals that he didn't like (although alternatives were always found) and minor disagreements with other campers (mainly because they didn't want to do what Chris wanted!) to name a few. There were some high spots, like the late nights, the dormitory chats, the rude jokes and the beer drinking (well a sip or two from the helpers' cans). One of the major things about the camp was the sense of independence it gave Chris, time away from Mum and Dad and doing other things.

October saw us visit the circus again, another of the small touring groups, but still good entertainment. The highlight again were the clowns, especially their little vintage car which amongst other things squirted water at the performers and the audience, much to Chris's great amusement, until that is he got caught!

Chris's great passion was of course aeroplanes and fortunately for him the bungalow in which we lived was right under the approach into Hawarden. So he was able to *enjoy* the arrival of the Beluga transport plane, various medium sized jets and a host of Biz jets on a daily basis. Every other year British Aerospace hold an Open Day at the airfield, we had missed the one in 1996 as we were otherwise engaged, but Chris won tickets through The Chronicle for 1998. He'd entered the competition some weeks before, well actually I did the entry, he just provided the brains to answer the questions! He was delighted when the letter came to say he'd won. Chris had arranged for our friend Chris Bolton to come with us, as he too is fired up by things with wings. When the Saturday arrived we waited for big Chris to arrive, and we waited and we waited. Eventually, I called his home, only for his wife Anne to answer the phone. Chris had gone gliding, he'd got the dates mixed up. "Dipstick" was Chris's summation.

Once Chris got over his disappointment we set off to Hawarden, arriving in plenty of time before the flying display. I parked the car close to the static displays and got Chris out of the car. After some thought he said he didn't want to look round the factory, but did want to go and see the Beluga which was parked close by and was being loaded with wings. Sitting with its cargo doors wide open it was a fabulous sight and seeing the wings loaded using the special carrying trolleys was fascinating. It was a sight that Chris would describe to many people in the following months. There was plenty of time before the flying exhibition started and so we were able to take in a number of the static displays, watch a display of rally cars (some doing doughnuts) and get some chips. As the flying display commentator began the build up to the display we moved up to a good viewing place, making sure that Chris would have a decent view of the activities, on a little rise in the grass and slightly away from the other spectators. As we waited patiently Chris excitedly said, "There's Mr. Lalek (a teacher from Dee Point School, which Chris had left a couple of years before)", before adding "I didn't know he was interested in planes". The said teacher walked right up and past us, Chris looked up expectantly, preparing to engage into conversation, only for Mr. Lalek to walk straight past without even acknowledging him, "Guess he didn't see me," said Chris slightly crestfallen. Even a 'Hello' would have been well received.

As the flying started the incident was soon forgotten (although it was the first thing he told Annette when we got home). The show got off to a great start with the Beluga, which we had watched being loaded earlier, taking off by almost trundling down the runway, to be followed by the appearance of a couple of Spitfires and a Hurricane. The sound of the Merlin engines in the Spitfires is absolutely fabulous and Chris watched enthralled, this being the first time he'd seen one flying. From that moment on the Spitfire remained one of Chris's favourite aircraft, second only to Concorde. The display moved on at a good pace and featured passes by both a BAE 146 and a Airbus 320. To see a passenger type jet doing low level passes and pulling tight turns was breathtaking, "I'm glad I'm not on that", said Chris, "I think I'd be sick". The Royal Jordanian airforce provided a formation flying show, complete with smoke and close proximity passes, a single aerobatic plane did things that shouldn't be possible in something with wings and the 'Crunchie' sponsored Stutz provided a demonstration of wing walking. "I think they're just mad," was Chris's considered opinion, although he thoroughly enjoyed watching. Perhaps the most amazing sight however was of the 'Utterly Butterly' sponsored Antonov An2, a Russian aircraft with a huge radial engine that takes off in the shortest distance possible and can fly just off the ground no faster than walking pace.

After the flying there was time to take in a little more of the static displays, but eventually Chris said he wanted to go as he was getting tired and starting to get cold. It had however been an enjoyable day and one that stayed with Chris for a long time.

The last week in August saw Chris's third attendance at the Heswall Boys Camp, as yet again he was lucky to have his nomination accepted. Considering his hesitance at the prospect of his first visit, he now looked forward to going with a great deal of enthusiasm. Arrival on the Saturday afternoon was a special moment as his face lit up as he renewed acquaintances, both with campers and carers. It was also good to see the reciprocated smiles as Chris was greeted by Peter, Heidi, Ian and Phil (in again from Seattle). As in previous years there was a comprehensive activity programme and everyone was looking forward to the week. Annette's concerns over the sleeping arrangements had not gone away, and were perhaps more so this year as by now Chris now needed more attention in the night and was using a special mattress. Chris was very aware of his Mum's worries and after choosing his bed in the temporary dorm said, "Ah, don't worry Mum, I'll be fine. And anyway it's only for a week. Phil'll look after me".

Of course he was fine, in many ways he was quite resilient and just got on with things. There were a lot of things to do, and people to talk to, and a good time to be had. The Classic Cars visited again, there was a visit to the Merseyside Police Station were the police horses were stabled and a visit to the bowling alley. The day out to Blackpool was of course the highlight, although he did admit later that the trip on the bus had been a bit more arduous this time. There was a Sports Day in the camp and for which Chris was awarded a certificate for being 'Wet and Wild' in the water games (we never did get a proper explanation - but it had something to do with soaking girls!). For Chris the other good thing about the week were the late nights and the dormitory chats "until 1 or 2 o'clock". The week passed quickly and we arrived in good time to pick Chris up. When we arrived it was easy to find him, listen for his voice and look for the biggest group, there he was holding court. He just loved being with people and sharing his jokes, his thoughts and passions. As in previous years there were new friendships, where as others had been re-established, one young lad from Liverpool, George, had attended the camp each year Chris had and they had got on well. As it was time to go there were a few tears, Chris edged forward, put his hand on George's arm and said, "Don't cry mate, we've had a good time and we'll be back next year". And then laughing he added, "I'll have some more jokes to tell". George was soon back into good spirits, put his arms round Chris and gave him a big hug. The carers came along to say 'good-bye' and we were off, another successful and enjoyable week completed.

Sadly, this was to be Chris's last time at the camp, for although he was allocated a place in 1999 he decided not to take it up. By then he was having trouble with his back, needed even more care, was beginning to find some days to be tiring and we were concerned about his general health. The three visits to Heswall had, for Chris, been greatly enjoyable and fun times. There was always a good crowd of boys who through the week got on well. The carers, all volunteers, did a really splendid job and were well liked by the boys. The organisation of the camp must have been a mammoth task, as must the fund raising to allow the camp to take place every year, at no cost to the participants. As parents we were very grateful to everyone involved for giving such a great time to the boys. Chris perhaps summed it up best in a letter he wrote on his return from the camp in 1998.

> *Dear Mr Byrne,*
> *Thank you very much for inviting me to the boys camp this year.*
> *Would you please pass on my thanks to all the brilliant helpers especially Phil, Ben and Ian who helped me throughout the week. I enjoyed all the days out, especially Blackpool, one of the best bits was the singing on the coach there and back.*
> *Once again many thanks to all my friends old and new, who helped me to enjoy myself so much. It was great.*
>
> *Best Wishes*
>
> *Chris Barratt.*
> *(E-mail: Chrisat193@aol.com)*

Through the early part of 1999 there were not many social outings as Chris suffered a number of setbacks following his chest infection. January though did see the arrival of his new computer, which cheered him up no end, and meant he could now play a number of games that required more processing power.

As Chris hadn't been too well through the year we had not been away during the year so during August Chris arranged with cousin Paul for a day out to the Camelot Theme Park in Lancashire. So one Saturday morning we piled into the Galaxy and set off. Fortunately the weather was quite good and while it wasn't sunny, at least it was dry. Chris had decided to take his electric outdoor chair, rather than be pushed about and meant he could run around as he pleased. For theme parks Camelot is quite small, but packs in quite a lot of entertainment and once you've paid to get in, apart from food and drink, most of the attractions are included in the price. Once in we got our bearings and headed into the park. Camelot is built in and around a small valley and some of the climbs are quite steep, thank goodness Chris was in the electric chair, although on one particular slope even that struggled. The first ride we came to was a sort of slide down into the valley below. Paul wanted a go, so that meant John did too. Chris took one look and said, "No thanks, I'll go and wait at the bottom with Auntie Ju," adding with a slight smile, "Go on Dad, you have a go". That was the way he was, he knew his own limitations, but seemed to get pleasure from watching others and then asking what it was like after. He amazed me, as there was never, not even a hint, of frustration at not being able to take part, he had gone through that and now seemed very much at ease with his situation. That set the tone for the day, Chris would encourage us to go on the rides, sit and watch, and then enter a full debrief. Often he would find the outcome very amusing, especially when John (conned into it by Chris) and I went on the roller coaster that loops-the-loop (Paul initially bottled out) and he saw John's face and heard how he'd gone nearly the full ride with his eyes shut, "Wimp". Later in the afternoon we paid a visit to the Karting track. Chris stayed with Julie to watch while we went off to have a go. Julie and Chris found a good spot to watch, but then found themselves with other people in front, obscuring the view. Julie went 'ballistic', while Chris tried to hide and placate Auntie Ju by saying, "It's OK, I can see, I can see" in embarrassed tones. All in all we had a good day, which was rounded off when we bumped (almost literally) into a friend, Wally Rumsden and his family, who as always made a fuss of Chris.

With the school summer holidays coming to an end I was keen to get a day out with Chris doing something he wanted. I suggested various things, but the one that really fired him up was the idea of a visit to the Museum at RAF Cosford. We set off early morning as it takes about an hour to get to the museum, which is located just past the M54 motorway. Having parked the car we took the short walk into the entrance hall, paid our money and got down to some serious plane spotting. Many of the exhibits are outside, but we were very lucky, as it was a really sunny day, so we had plenty of time to examine the planes. There is wide selection of military and commercial planes, most with interesting histories. We gradually made our way around the exhibits and were amazed at the size of the Victor tanker plane and the Vulcan bomber, in their day they must have been awesome sights, enjoyed the old passenger planes like the Boeing 707, VC10 and BAC 1-11. Chris particularly liked the old military planes like the Javelin, Buccaneer and Meteor and was very interested in the TSR2. As we visited each plane Chris would have me find the right entry in one of his books that we had brought with us and read out the necessary information, although in some cases that wasn't necessary, as he already knew the facts.

Following a brief pause for lunch in the museum's restaurant we resumed our tour through the indoor displays. We marvelled at a Rolls Royce RB211 jet engine (as used in a Boeing 747 Jumbo jet), the engine is the size of an elephant, and at the Rolls Royce SNECMA Olympus as used in Concorde. In another hall there were examples of various types of missiles, for which I had to read out all the pertinent technical information, which was carefully lodged away for later use. To finish the day off we had to revisit certain exhibits, the engines, the Vulcan and the Trident. Eventually, we departed, agreeing that we should come back at some point in the future as it had been such a good day.

As the last year of the old century drew to a close Chris mustered together John, Paul and I to go to the local cinema to see the new James Bond film, 'The World is Not Enough'. He'd been a Bond fan for sometime and had been waiting to see the new film for a while, growing more and more impatient. Needless to say, we had to go and see it in the first few days of it being shown in Chester. Our trip to the cinema to see it wasn't Chris's last, he got Norma to take him a couple of weeks later as well! Norma's recollection of the film being that Chris kept saying, "Watch this bit Norma, such and such happens".

At home of course Chris's main interest was his computer through which he was able to play all sorts of games, design certificates and birthday/thank-you/Easter cards etc., (as well as do some of his homework - "ugh"). He'd been on the Internet for quite some time to help satisfy his thirst for knowledge and stay in contact with numerous people. One of the many games he had was 'Age of Empires', which I was also in the process of playing. This game involves the player controlling a civilisation, feeding and housing it and where necessary fighting enemies. I was gradually working my way through this and was more advanced than Chris. After a little while though he'd passed me and was well in front. Chris Bolton takes up the story, "On one occasion when I called in to see all at 193 (our house) on my way home from Chester. Mike was at his mums and Netty was 'buzzing' around the house so Chris and I retired to the computer room. Chris showed me some of his latest games where he was blasting 'alien spaceships'. He got fed up with this and asked me if I wanted to see the game he and Mike were currently playing, called 'Age of Empires'. Apparently, Chris volunteered that his Dad spent hours getting to level 8. But Chris could do it in a quarter of an hour! "Do you want to see how" he asked. "OK Chris away you go" said I totally perplexed. Those 'lightening fingers' minimised the game and we were on the Internet. " I've found this great site with 'cheats' on it " says Chris. We return to age of Empires, festooned with Egyptian Galleys and army's armed with swords, bows and arrows and siege machines with what can only be described as a 'tank from the future' with laser guided guns and young Chris does battle (or was it just annihilation). Never before have I seen someone reach level 8 of a game so quickly! "Does your Dad know about this?" I quizzed. "Don't think so" came the reply " but it gives him something to try and beat, doesn't it." Smile, little laugh.

Other than the computer the TV and videos provided a lot of enjoyment. He was an avid Soap Opera fan (taking after his Mum) and also enjoyed comedy and music programmes, as well as particularly liking "You've Been Framed". He was the proud owner of a raft of videos, ranging from Disney classics, old and new, through Fools and Horses, Home Alone, football and motor racing, adventure stories to James Bond. The complete set of the latter being probably his prized possession. Most of Chris's books were fact books covering General Knowledge, planes, motor racing, James Bond and numerous other topics. He would sit and read them time and time again, these being the basis for his outstanding knowledge. He much preferred storybooks to be read to him, insisting that the reader gave the characters different voices!

About the house his ability to help was limited, but that didn't stop him asking and some jobs as a result could take an age to complete. When in the garden his main occupation was running back and too between Annette and I, chatting, asking questions, giving advice (lots of advice) and pointing out bits that we'd missed! After a while though he'd get fed up and return to the computer. Having a big garden, races from one gate to the other were often a feature, featuring wheelchair against wheelchair or bike. He would generally win either fairly or by knocking his opponent off and boy, did he hate losing!

He was generally well behaved and polite, but there were times when bossiness took over - get this, pick that up, do this, do that. We had never objected to helping him, recognising that he clearly had limitations, but we did insist on the use of 'P and Qs'. If he forgot I would just say to him, "Just hang on while I go and put my servants suit on" which would elicit a tut and a stare, but also a 'please'. Annette would just point out to him that "manners cost nothing".

CHAPTER EIGHT (Other Events)

Once, as my heart remembers,
All the stars were fallen embers.
Enya

Finding things for Chris to do, keeping him interested and providing a social environment always presented problems once Chris started to use the wheelchair. Not for the first time Yvonne Bohdanowicz came to the rescue suggesting that Chris might like to go to the Saturday morning Youth Club Group, for 8 to 11 year olds, at The Croft, a partly converted house owned and used by Barnardo's. Predictably Chris was not sure if going was the right thing, would he like it, would he like the people, would they like him? Annette told him the best way to find out was to go and see, so one Saturday morning we paid our first visit and of course he quite enjoyed it. The other kids were a friendly bunch and he quickly got friendly with Jack and Mark. There were lots of things to do and the helpers were skilled in keeping children with a wide range of disabilities occupied. Chris went to The Croft most Saturdays for the next couple of years, but having turned 11 he needed to move on to the next stage, Saturday Live! at the Square One Youth Club in Vicars Cross. Mark had been attending Live! for sometime so Chris at least would know someone. Again, he was unsure if it was the right thing to do, but gave it a try. As before he quickly settled in, established new friends and seemed to be quite enjoying Saturday mornings. There were a number of special mornings arranged including a trip to Chester Fire Station ("brilliant"), theme mornings, Christmas lunch etc. all of which were well received and enjoyed. During 1998 Mark moved on to the next stage and Chris was quite disappointed not to see him any more on Saturday mornings and occasionally would make an excuse not to go. Then one day Annette and I arrived to pick Chris up to be met by Soraya, the club leader. Chris had had an accident and had cut his head. Apparently what had happened was the club had organised a birthday party for one of the members, a young lad with autism. As everybody gathered round to sing 'Happy Birthday' he had got over excited, flapped his arms about and in the ensuing melee had caught Chris quite hard across his face. Chris having little arm movement had not been able to protect himself and took the full force of the blow by his eye. Apparently, he'd been very good about it, the helpers had put a cold compress on his face and he'd accepted it as an accident. He did have a little cry when he saw Annette, but soon cheered up. However, the incident did have a marked affect on him. The cut and bruises soon healed, but the fact that he wasn't able to defend himself in such a situation really worried him. We explained that it was a one off event but the excuses for not going to Live! became more frequent and eventually he stopped going, preferring to go shopping and for coffee in Chester with Annette and I.

It was during 1999 that Norma Hellon suggested that Chris might like to try 'Choices' in Ellesmere Port, particularly as many of his friends from Dorin Park also went. After a little bit of persuasion from Norma he agreed to give it a try and so Wednesday nights (in term time) became Youth Club night. 'Choices' was very popular with Chris and on the nights it wasn't held he was quite miserable. Going to 'Choices' opened up a complete new chapter for Chris, there were new people to befriend and chat to, new people to impress with his knowledge, new things to do including regular discos. 'Choices' provided a safe environment where young people, both disabled and able bodied joined together to have fun. 'Choices' was (and still is) wonderful, much of the success is down to the club leader Ena Blocksidge and her band of helpers. When working with the University of York on their 'Sharing Value' project Chris specifically mentioned 'Choices' and how it was important to him, it gave him an opportunity to do things without Mum and Dad, and to be himself (and as we were to find out later, he certainly was!). After Chris's passing Ena wrote, "The young people and staff (at Choices) will miss him zooming around in his wheelchair and talking to everyone. If it is alright with you we would like to make our Halloween Disco this year a Charity Night and all the money raised will go to Hope House in memory of Chris. We would also like to buy a trophy, which will be named the Chris Barratt Memorial Trophy[1] and given to a club member each year. It really was a pleasure knowing Chris and the way he lived his life is an example to us all".

By mid-1993 Chris had been using his push wheelchair for a short while and was visiting Dorin Park to attend clinics, where he was seen by Frances Reeve. In mid-May Annette received a phone call from Frances asking if we would like her to nominate Chris to receive a powered wheelchair from Helsby Golf Club. Needless to say we were delighted and were very happy to accept. The Golf Club has raised money annually for many years[2] to provide chairs for children from local special needs schools. Although at that time Chris wasn't actually at Dorin Park Frances had asked if he could be nominated as he was under the care of the school. So, on the evening of June 10th we made our way to the Club House in Helsby for the presentation, where we were introduced to the Appeals Secretary Bert Dyson. There were three chairs to be presented that night, one to Chris, one to Peter Herbert and the final one to John Brassington, a lad the same age as Chris from Crewe. The Club members made us very welcome before the presentation by ex-Liverpool footballer Ian Callaghan. Chris had chosen a blue chair and was really excited at receiving it. He was less pleased though when he realised that we couldn't take the chair home with us as the chair was too big to get in the boot of the car. He had to wait a couple of weeks before it could be delivered.

He was very excited on the day it was due to come. Les from Ross Care explained how it worked and that it was important to drive carefully. As Chris was a novice Les gave a short lesson in how to drive a powered chair. Chris was itching to have a go and following Les' suggestion he tried it out on slow speed in the garden. However, once Les had gone, round went the speed controller to 'fast', off shot Chris and the chair, and pinned me by my legs to the fence. The look of shock on Chris's face was matched only by the look of pain and anger on mine. Fortunately for Chris his Mum was on hand to calm down the situation and suggest an apology was required. It's fair to say that he very soon mastered how to drive the chair and he was quickly pulling all sorts of stunts. One of his favourites was to blast down the drive at full speed into the (empty) garage and flick the chair into a 180° turn and power back up the drive without stopping. Within six months the rear tyres were worn through to the canvas and we had

[1] The Chris Barratt Memorial Trophy was presented for the first time at Christmas 2001 to Kirsty Bridge.

[2] By 2000 Helsby Golf Club has raised about £220,000 and provided 117 powered wheelchairs for young people with physical difficulties.

to order a new set!

Mind you even with this clear demonstration of driving skill he could still be dangerous. On Sunday afternoons we would go for a walk around the local roads and it was on one of these that he stopped and asked to be moved in the seat as he was toppling over. I moved up to the side of the chair and repositioned him, but before I could move he switched on the chair and moved forward .... running right over my toes. Now, as I'm sure some people know, powered wheelchairs are not light, plus Chris was weighing in at around 6 stones. To make matters worse I'd been running that morning on a long training run for the forthcoming London Marathon and had suffered a number of blisters on my toes. As the wheel rolled over my foot I could feel each of the blisters burst, I was not best pleased and told my son exactly that. Chris, when told off, sort of shrugged his shoulders and buried his head, then he shot off and made for home. When we arrived home Annette could sense 'an atmosphere'.

"What's the matter with you pair," she enquired, "I can't leave you alone for five minutes".

"Stirling bloody Moss here only ran over my feet, blisters and all," I replied.

"Well I'm sure it was an accident," said the voice of reason.

"It might have been an accident, but it still bloody hurts," said the sore party.

"Well you should have moved your feet before I moved," said the driver and with that drove off.

The chair had been very reliable and apart from new tyres on a couple of occasions and a new control box when sand mysteriously got in it ("I don't know how that happened") the chair was in quite good condition despite a lot of use. However, after 4 years Chris was growing a bit too big for the chair and when wearing his support jacket and outdoor coat it was a bit of a squeeze to get him into it. So at the start of 1997 Frances Reeve came to our rescue and nominated Chris to Helsby Golf Club to receive a new chair. We were very pleased and grateful when his nomination was accepted, Chris with the help of Frances decided on a change of colour selecting a pleasant turquoise.

So almost four years to the day after the presentation of the first chair, accompanied on Chris's request by Chris and Anne Bolton, we attended another presentation evening at the Club House. The presentation this time was performed by a young local actress, Emma Cunliffe, who caused our eleven year old some embarrassment by giving him a kiss (in public too) as she presented the chair. Once he officially had the chair Chris was keen to demonstrate his ability to drive fast and proceeded to do so around the car park. After a little while we were able to persuade him to stop and on this occasion he was happier as we were able to get the chair into the back of the Galaxy and take it home there and then. The following night he went to Melanie Carrington's birthday party in the Saughall Village Hall and was able to show off his new chair to all the other kids. It's always surprising how a wheelchair is such a draw to able-bodied kids who want a go in it.

A week or so later, when we were chatting, Chris asked what were we going to do with the old blue chair. I said I hadn't thought about it. Quick as a flash Chris said, "Well we could sell it and I could have the money for computer games".

"I suppose that's one option," I said.
"But," said Chris, "perhaps we should just give it to someone who needs a chair like I did."
"That's a very good idea, I'm very proud of you for suggesting that". So, Chris went to see Frances and suggested that the chair could be returned to Helsby Golf Club, repainted and re-presented. Frances thought that a good idea and asked Chris to write to Bert Dyson, the Appeals Secretary, with his suggestion. So in his Thank You letter for his new chair he did just that. The Club were pleased to accept his offer and a couple of weeks later Ross Care collected the chair, which we understand was presented to a young girl a few months later.

At the start of 1994 Chris was delighted to receive an invitation to the wedding of Hugh Griffiths & Jeanette. This would be the first wedding to which he had gone and so he was full of anticipation. As the day in May approached he got more and more excited. Annette ensured that he was smartly turned out in shirt and tie, along with a colourful waistcoat. We arrived at the church in plenty of time, chatting to other guests before taking our seats. When Jeanette entered the church Chris twisted round to see, the expression on his face as he saw her dress was a picture, "Oooh, she's lovely", he whispered. For once he was quiet through the service, even during the hymns! After the service he waited patiently to present the lucky horseshoe and key that Annette had brought for him, although I think he was a bit embarrassed to get a kiss off the bride. Once some photographs had been taken the bridal party moved on to the Reception at Rosset Hall. As with all weddings, the activity of taking the photographs is a long drawn out affair, especially if you are a small boy and it wasn't long before he was telling us that he was bored. This was relieved to a degree by introducing him to as many people as I knew and letting him chat for a while. Eventually, we moved into the reception itself and shared a table with a number of colleagues from work, Paul Forrester and his partner Julie and John and Jan Humphries. Chris was extremely well behaved through out and chatted politely, especially to Paul who he was quite impressed by. He insisted on taking a number of photographs, which came out very well, but perhaps his highlight was the profiteroles for dessert. By the time everybody on the table had donated one to him he'd probably had twice as many as anybody else. How he wasn't sick I just don't know. All in all he thoroughly enjoyed the day.

One day during the half term in June of that year I was taking Chris to spend the day at my mum's and was stopped at the end of Victoria Road by the Northgate Arena. I'd been stopped sometime waiting for a gap in the traffic. Chris was sitting in the front of the Serena, quietly watching the traffic, when all of a sudden there was a tremendous bang from the back of the car as it shot forward. Fortunately, the seat belt stopped both of us being thrown forward. Before I could do or say anything, Chris shouted, "What the bloody hell was that!" He always felt justified in swearing at such times. What it was was a Vauxhall Astra assaulting the back bumper and rear door of the car. When I saw the damage on the Astra I thought, 'Oh, no', but amazingly the damage to the Serena did not appear too bad. Having exchanged particulars and checked the other driver was OK, "I didn't see you (the big blue van thing that is!)" being the reason for the collision I carried on my journey. Chris was perfectly alright and used every derogatory word he knew to insult the perpetrator. The irony of this incident was that the driver of the Astra was the brother of a work colleague of Annette. The biggest inconvenience was not having the Serena for a week while it was repaired. The Astra was nearly a write-off, "Serves him right for attacking my Serena," was Chris's final view on the subject. So much for sympathy.

Chris's interest in planes was fuelled by big Chris, who himself had been a plane enthusiast since he was a boy (a bit longer than he cared to say). He indulged himself by gliding, something that increased his status in the eyes of our Chris. Needless to say it was not long before an invitation for Chris to go gliding was forthcoming. So in May 1993 we made our first visit to the North Wales Gliding Club that was based at Rhuallt, near St. Asaph. Having met up with big Chris he gave us a quick tour round, explaining the finer points of a glider and introduced us to his fellow members. He explained the procedure for launching the gliders, both from the launch end and from the winch end. Chris was quite interested in the winch and spent quite a while sitting in the cab watching the proceedings. The club members share the various tasks around the field, amongst which is retrieving the towing cable from where it lands and pulling it back to the launch point, as well as retrieving the gliders from where they come to a halt on landing. When big Chris took his turn, driving up and down the field in an old Land Rover Chris was happy to join in and thoroughly enjoyed zipping back and to. However, when the question of Chris going up in a glider was raised he politely declined, "I'm OK just watching, thanks Uncle Chris". As with all enjoyable days they eventually have to come to an end and as the members began packing up we headed for home, but not before big Chris had got Chris to agree to come again.

It wasn't until the following August that we were able to arrange another visit and the day we chose turned out to be a really lovely day, sunny with a light wind, ideal for gliding. When we arrived big Chris was in the process of helping to move a glider from the hangar onto the field. Chris insisted that we hurry up so that he could help. The moving operation involved the glider being towed slowly behind a car while a number of people keep it upright by holding the wings. So when we joined it must have been quite a bizarre sight with a young lad in a wheelchair holding on to the tailplane. As with our earlier visit Chris was happy to spend time in the winch and also helping to retrieve the cable and gliders. However, this time when asked if he wanted to fly he said, "Yes, please". Chris was introduced to John, the club's Chief Instructor, who was to pilot the glider. He took Chris through the controls, in both the front and rear cockpits, explained the procedure for taking off and then landing. Finally John checked that Chris still wanted to have a flight. There was no stopping him now, so with big Chris's help I lifted Chris into the well-padded seat of the rear cockpit. Further padding was provided to keep him upright and the headrest positioned carefully. Finally, he was strapped in for his maiden glider flight. I told him to behave and enjoy himself, a little smile came to his face, "Oh don't worry Palion".

John climbed aboard and the canopy of the cockpit was slid into place. John ran through the necessary safety checks, the launch cable was attached and checked. The Flight Director gave permission for the launch. Coded signals were exchanged between the ground crew and John, the cable tightened, Chris gave a little thumbs up, and with one final hand signal from the ground crew the winch hauled the glider down the field. Within a few yards the glider was in the air and rapidly climbed into the sky. The rate of climb is phenomenal and the glider very soon reaches the point at which the cable is released. I watched the glider as it quietly soared through the sky, wondering how Chris was finding it. Length of flight depends on many factors and big Chris expected this maiden flight to last 10 or 15 minutes, so he suggested we get a cup of tea.

We'd just had time to finish the tea when big Chris pointed to a glider heading towards the field, saying, "Here he comes now". John made a perfect landing and Chris and I rushed down the field to where the glider stopped to see how things were. By the time we got there John was already out of the cockpit and chatting to a smiling Chris.

"How was it?" I asked excitedly.

"Palion, it was absolutely brilliant. Thanks Uncle Chris, Thanks John," he bubbled. Once we got the glider back to the top of the field we were able to lift Chris out; he was still excited by the experience and had clearly enjoyed it, giving a detailed review of the experience.

"What was the take off like?" I asked, "it looks pretty frightening from the ground".

"Awh, no, it was fine," replied Chris, "it's just like being in a lift".

Big Chris came over to join us, smiling broadly, and as he recalls, "Chris was flown around for a while by an instructor who told me after the flight about the many questions he was bombarded with during the flight. What's this for, how does that work, what are you doing that for, what happens if you push this lever? And during the flight how mysteriously the trim tab would edge itself forward and backwards (moved by the small hands in the rear cockpit - no doubt). When he had landed how he wanted to see everything else to do with gliding, the winch, and the tow out tractors. A very inquisitive mind our Chris."

For one reason or another it was to be nearly twelve months before we visited Rhuallt again and it was just a few weeks before Chris went into hospital for the operation on his legs. In the days leading up to the visit he was very keen on the idea of flying again, particularly as he hoped that big Chris might fly him. Big Chris by this stage had also bought a share in a glider and Chris was keen to view the acquisition and cast a critical eye over it. It got off to a good start, it was blue. Chris was very impressed, especially as the glider was equipped with a radio and oxygen. Big Chris had lined up John to take Chris up again, but each time big Chris suggested flying Chris would say that he was happy doing whatever we were in the middle of and he would do it later. Of course, as I knew from his prevarication, later would never come. "Are you going to go up? You know Uncle Chris has arranged it for you," I said.

"I'd like to go, and I want to go, but I won't be comfortable with my legs," he replied.

"That's OK," I said, "but you need to tell Uncle Chris".

"Can't you do it?" Chris asked.

"No, I don't think so. You must do it. Uncle Chris will understand".

"Well come with me". So with that we found big Chris and Chris explained the problem. Big Chris suggested ways of getting Chris in and making him comfortable, but once he'd made his mind up there was very, very little chance of changing it. In some ways it could be very exasperating, but you had to admire the way he stuck to his guns. I'm sure that this attitude helped him deal with his disability. Having made up his mind there was never any sign of regret, he just moved on to the next thing. Just like now, maybe he wasn't going flying but there was the fetching and retrieval of the cable and gliders and sitting in the cab of the winch, chatting to who ever was operating it. Life offered many different opportunities.

It was some time before we were to go gliding again. This was not for the want of trying by big Chris who frequently issued invitations. When we did go again in June 1998 Chris had moved Gliding Clubs and while Chris was able to do a few things it was not as much fun as the site at Rhuallt. He helped out with a few things and was genuinely excited when big Chris took his glider up and flew a few circuits. The day was brought to an early close by unsuitable weather, and this was to be the last time that we went gliding. That's not to say that Chris wasn't interested as he was always telling people "that my uncle has his own glider" and "my uncle flies gliders, he's very good" and "I've been flying in a glider you know".

Following Chris's diagnosis we had quickly got into a round of clinics with experts in various fields. Through this it was recommended that Chris went swimming so as to keep his muscles toned. Carol Watson, the physio, suggested going to Dorin Park as the pool there was heated and he wouldn't feel the cold so much. As part of the Evening Schools programme there were swimming lessons held at Dorin Park on a Thursday evening and Carol arranged for Chris to go. So on 27th September 1990 we arrived at Dorin Park and introduced ourselves to the tutor, Andy Howie. It was to be the start of a lengthy and happy association.

The 6 o'clock session that we attended was for Parents and Youngster and was to teach youngsters how to swim. Andy, who was also a teacher at Dorin Park, was absolutely brilliant, getting the kids confident in the water and then gradually introducing the basic concepts of swimming, before developing their capabilities. In the hour of the lesson it wasn't all teach, teach, teach, but Andy allowed free playtime in which the kids gained confidence in the water and had some fun. In all the time Chris and I went every child was capable of swimming at least one length of the pool by the end of the term. Chris was quite successful in the first year and could swim OK, but as time went on he found swimming on his front very difficult, as he couldn't lift his head up out of the water, so swimming on his back became the preferred method. Most of the kids would attend two, or perhaps three terms and then having learnt to swim well would move on. Consequently there was always a turnover of children and parents and Chris enjoyed making new friends. One of his favourites was a little lad called Mikey, who came with his sister, Mum and Dad. The thing that Chris liked about him was he was an absolute devil, into everything and Chris, much to his mum's dismay, was constantly encouraging him to do things.

As the end of each term approached Andy would enquire if we wanted to come the following term, and with an affirmative answer, Andy would very kindly allocate us a space on the course. As time went on it became difficult getting Chris dressed and undressed in the main changing rooms so we were able to use a small side room that had a bed in it on which I could get Chris changed. Gradually this operation became longer and longer and in the winter months was something of an ordeal. Even so, Chris was still keen to attend and enjoy his swim. The class we attended was the middle one of three that Andy ran, the preceding lesson was for Parent and Toddler while the lesson that followed us was for Adults who wanted to learn to swim. By the time we finished getting changed the adult group were in the pool and as we exited through the pool area Chris would insist on stopping and watching for a while. Needless to say he became quite popular with many of the ladies who would come to the side of the pool to chat. Andy eventually would have to politely remind everybody why they were there!

During the Spring Term of 1997 Andy approached us after the evening's lesson and said that at the end of the term he was stopping teaching swimming, as he wanted to concentrate on some other things. He said that the classes would continue and he would ensure that Chris could have a place if he wanted. One Thursday evening as the end of the term approached Chris said as we were driving up to the school, "Dad, I hope you don't mind but I've decided to stop swimming when Andy gives it up". I wasn't really surprised, he was finding it much more difficult, getting changed was hard work and he felt the cold terribly while changing, he was also becoming aware of the scoliosis of his back and felt people were looking at him.

"Look mate, it's up to you, but I don't mind taking you, you know," I said. "I know Palion," he said, "but we've been going a long time and if Andy can stop so can we. It's been good fun and I've enjoyed it, but I've done it enough". As always I knew that arguing would be fruitless, it was Chris's decision and that's all there was to it. So, on 22nd May 1997, almost seven years after we first started and well over 150 *lessons* we said thank you and good-bye to Andy. As a parting gesture Chris wrote Andy a card and bought him a small memento. Andy was by now teaching on a supply basis at Dorin Park, but he remained one of Chris's friends and Chris was always grateful for the time and effort Andy gave to him.

Chris was friendly with most of his peer group at school and would regale us of what they had been up to, either at school or at home or on holiday. During the early part of 2000 he would occasionally inform us of the latest situation with one particular friend who was having a difficult time. He was quite guarded in what he actually said, but it was clear that the situation was weighing heavily on his mind and in around about way was looking for advice. This went on for some time until some action was taken, although he remained concerned as to how his friend was and felt.

We were told later by Norma how Chris had approached her about the issue. He knew that Norma was acquainted with his friend and had taken her out. He also knew that Barnardo's provided support for his friend. So, one night while returning from Choices Youth Club in the taxi Chris told Norma, "You know X, well she has been very upset at school, she's been crying. I've been talking to her and trying to help, but..... You know Norma, she's said she's so unhappy she wishes she was dead."

He was clearly upset by this thought. As a result of Chris telling Norma how X felt Norma was able to advise her managers who looked into the situation. As a result of Chris's intervention further support was provided and other actions were instigated later.

From time to time with my colleagues at work I would go indoor kart racing at the local tracks. Apart from the first time Chris would always accompany me. He was quite interested in motor racing and knew a fair amount about the subject. Consequently, while he was a vocal supporter, he was also my coach and chief critic. To Chris winning was everything, even in the heats, and it was woe betide if I didn't perform as well as he expected. Whatever the result though he was first to my side with the withering comment or, if merited, glowing congratulations. I guess that if I was winning then so was he.

I'd been fortunate enough to win the finals at the first two or three events when during the summer of 1995 we went over to The Circuit at Sandiway. Ray Hall had organised the evening and had invited his brother, Barry, along. Now, Barry like Ray raced motorcycles and was quite good. Chris would watch the various heats and try to spot who the danger men were in terms of being tough opponents, Barry was quickly identified and this was duly reported back to me. The evening progressed with Barry doing well and accumulating points from the heats, enough to take pole position in the first semi-final and then go through to the Final. I also qualified for the Final having won my semi and so lined up alongside Barry. I knew this was going to be tough as Barry had beaten me earlier in the evening. I warned Chris that a win was not going to come easy, "Oh, you'll be alright Palion, you can beat him," was all he had to say. Sadly, Chris's optimism was not well placed and Barry easily held off my challenge. Chris was mortified, he did manage a begrudging "Well Done", but was close to tears. He was convinced Barry must have cheated, he felt it was the only way he could have won and beaten his Dad. My suggestions that the better man won on the night, wasn't good enough and "there's always next time" fell on deaf ears.

Of course, there was a next time, and we all assembled for another race night on a cold night in early December. "I hope that Barry's not going," was Chris's observation. "I think he is," I said, "but we'll have him this time." Having got Chris out of the car and into his wheelchair we entered the warehouse in which the circuit was laid out.

"There's that Barry," said Chris, "I'll stop him winning." and with that he was off at great speed towards Barry (and his legs). Fortunately, I realised what he was up to and just before he reached Barry I managed to switch the chair off. "Hello, Barry," said Chris, in a slightly hypocritical sort of way. "Hi, Chris, how are you?" said Barry, without realising how close to disaster he'd been. As it turned out Chris needn't have worried as Barry had a poor night and encouraged by Chris I was again the winner.

After the racing had been completed and the awards handed out, the owner of the track came over and asked Chris if he'd like a ride round on one of the karts with this chap driving. Chris thought for a moment and then politely declined, but asked if he could drive his chair round the track. The track owner said it was no problem and so off Chris went. From the smile on his face he was clearly enjoying himself and as he came towards the end of the lap the owner stepped forward and waved the chequered flag. A few of my colleagues had stayed behind to watch and gave a loud round of applause as Chris was handed a *winners* trophy by the track owner. When we got home that night it was his trophy that was shown to Mum first.

There were other karting nights and other wins, all keenly supported and all enjoyed by Chris as much as by me. I shall always be grateful for that unswerving support and that undiminished expectation that I would win. If there are future events I know that they will not ever be the same.

CHAPTER NINE (Music and Other Entertainment)

And still I stand this very day
With a burning wish to fly away
I'm still looking
Looking for the summer

Chris Rea

From an early age Chris, like most children, developed an interest in listening to music. One of his earliest likes was "One, two, three, four, five once I caught a fish alive" and "Old MacDonald's Farm". He also liked the traditional tune Greensleeves, which was guaranteed to send him off to sleep when he was a baby. Some of his other early influences were the Theme tunes to Coronation Street and Eastenders! We like many parents had the complete collection of The Early Learning Centre tapes, which featured all the well-known songs such as "The Wheels on the Bus", "Nellie the Elephant", and "Frere Jacques". These were supplemented by the Postman Pat songs, but perhaps his favourite tape for a long time was the one containing songs from the Rainbow programme featuring Zippy, George and Bungle with Geoffrey and helped by Rod, Jane and Freddy. All the tapes were carried around in a blue cassette box and it travelled everywhere with him. Although he had started listening to more 'grown up' music these tapes continued to provide entertainment until he was seven or eight. A number of the tapes Chris had were 'educational' and contained things like the Times Tables, or simple sums and one even had General Knowledge set to music!

As he grew older Chris's choice in music began to be influenced by what Annette and I listened to. He therefore quickly became a fan of Dire Straits and the guitar work of Mark Knopfler, although he really liked Abba, and their tracks were regular plays at home and in the car. Other favourites were Run Rig, Gerry Rafferty, Cat Stevens, Lindisfarne, The Kinks, Simply Red, Barclay James Harvest, Genesis and The Mavericks. Most of the songs he was able to sing along to after one or two plays. Having heard the Moody Blues on the radio it was Chris that suggested we bought one of their cassettes, which duly became one of the favourites. As a result we took it with us on holiday to California in 1997, two of the tracks "Question" and "Your Wildest Dreams" still invoke memories of driving down the Pacific Coast Highway, the wonder of that place and the excitement Chris got from it.

Perhaps his favourite artist though was Chris Rea, of whom we had numerous cassettes and CDs and who was probably played the most frequently. He went on all our journeys and went on all our holidays. As soon as a new LP came out we had to have it. There were many tracks that Chris enjoyed, such as 'Johnny Needs a Fast Car', 'Windy City', 'Auberge' and 'I'm Ready' and many, many more. Two tracks that he particularly enjoyed were 'Black Dog ' and 'Boom Boom' and he would sing and whistle along, encouraging us to do the same.

In my youth I'd been a fan of Supertramp and for one birthday Annette bought me their Greatest Hits. Chris was not that impressed the first time he heard it, until we came to 'Bloody Well Right', which contains almost limitless reference to the B-word. Now here was a golden opportunity to be able to swear, legitimately. So from then on whenever the song was played (and that was quite frequently) all you could hear was "Right, right you're **bloody** well right, you've got a **bloody** right to say" and so on. Any remonstration from Mum would be met by, "but I'm only singing the words to the song", "Yes, but perhaps not quite so loud". It was funny because despite not liking Supertramp too much to start Chris actually grew to like them. I guess from small *bloody* acorns oak trees can grow.

Of course, he did develop his own tastes in music the first perhaps being M-People through their hit record 'Moving on Up' and he also quite like Back Street Boys, Black Box and Eiffel 65. However, in the last couple of years he particularly liked Shania Twain, attracted purely by her music and nothing else he assured his mother. The disco at Choices Youth Group provided plenty of opportunity to hear the latest music and a popular record was 'Sex Bomb' by Tom Jones, who Chris thought "was ace". Abi and Norma Hellon bought him a copy of the CD for Christmas and it was quite amusing when he played it on his Walkman with the head phones on as Chris would sing away while the 'audience' could hear no music.

Thankfully Chris's tastes did not include the Spice Girls, indeed when the girls at school played their music at breaks during the school day he would encourage the other boys to sabotage the cassette player, which often led to conflict that the teachers had to sort out. Music played a great part in the life of Dorin Park School, there were often musicians of all types visiting and there were sessions playing and composing music (led and inspired by Mrs. Roberts). Chris was very proud of his contribution to a number of pieces, especially the lyrics used in the JC2000 production 'Don't Worry'.

While Chris enjoyed listening to music he was not naturally musical and he'd attempted to learn a few instruments at school but this was not very successful. However, spurred on by experiences at Dorin Park he asked for a keyboard for his birthday in 1998. After a short look we chose a Yamaha keyboard which, if needed could be linked to the computer, but most importantly had the capability of reproducing the sound of countless instruments. While Chris never mastered playing, with the exception of very simple tunes, he got a lot of pleasure from selecting the various sounds and playing them. During the year 2000 using the keyboard became harder for Chris as he was unable to lift his arms across the keyboard to push the buttons and so it gradually it made fewer and fewer appearances[1].

Chris had enjoyed the film 'Men in Black' starring Will Smith and also enjoyed the films eponymous title song. As was usually the case when he had money he wanted to spend it. He decided that he wanted the cassette with 'Men in Black' on it and found the film's soundtrack. I pointed out that he didn't know any of the other songs, so I suggested that he buy another cassette that MIB was on, with perhaps some other songs he'd like. No. He'd made up his mind, the money was burning a hole, so the cassette was bought. On the way home he insisted that we played it. The first track was the one he liked and that was great, from then on it has to be said that the song quality went rapidly down hill. Chris put on a brave face, but as far as I'm aware he never played it again, some lessons do come costly!

[1] In keeping with what Annette and I believe would have been Chris's wishes the keyboard is now in use at Dorin Park for the benefit of all his friends there.

Chris's taste in music was quite diverse and quite a lot of the music he listened to came about through hearing it on the TV. He liked Ladysmith Black Mambazoo after one of their records was used on a TV advert and he played their cassette quite often. Through Groundforce, the gardening program, he found that he liked Brass Band music and would listen to the compilation CD of the music featured on the program. And of course there were the James Bond Themes. I don't know what started it, maybe it was seeing the location of a Bond film while on holiday, but Chris began a fascination with James Bond. To start with we recorded the films off the TV and Chris would watch them again and again to the point he knew the dialogue off by heart. We bought him a number of books about Bond and the films that he would read and commit to memory. He had several CDs and cassettes, which contained the theme music and these became the most listened to recordings during 1999 and 2000. Then when the films came out on video under his instructions we set about acquiring the set. It was a good investment as he watched them all time and time again, usually when he had gone to bed to rest. You could always tell if the film was at a point when James Bond was enjoying, should we say female company, because if you walked into his room he would switch the video off, whereas he would allow any other scene to play on. The videos were a key part of his kit that he took to Hope House and all the carers had to suffer at least one session with the suave secret agent. For Kim that wasn't a problem as she was a Bond fan as well. By mid 2000 he had all the videos, all that is apart from 'The World is not Enough' which was due out for Christmas 2000. He has the complete set now.

From about the age of four Chris had enjoyed watching Disney films on the telly and so after a while we started buying the films on video, gradually building up quite a collection. As with many of his possessions they were not one off wonders, he would watch then again and again, although he did have certain favourites. Early favourites were 'Pinnochio', 'Sword in the Stone' and 'Robin Hood' and later on 'Aladdin', 'The Lion King', 'Toy Story' and '101 Dalmatians'. Besides the videos Chris also had Disney Story Books, audio tapes and music cassettes. The tape with a compilation of Disney Songs was a regular travelling companion with 'When You Wish Upon A Star' from Pinnochio being a particular favourite. Other videos also provided a source of entertainment, with the Home Alone trilogy keeping us laughing over a long period. Chris would often just play the bits where the baddies "get it" and we would roll about laughing. The Star Wars videos were also part of Chris's library, augmented by various computer games, so not only did he watch the action, but to all intents and purpose he was part of it. From early 2000, after Annette bought him one of the videos, he had become a fan of Dad's Army enjoying the antics of Captain Mainwaring, Corporal Jones et al. It wasn't long before "You stupid boy" became a regular saying in our house.

However, it was another long running TV series that really caught Chris's attention, 'Only Fools and Horses'. The stories of the Trotter family from Nelson Mandela House really caught his imagination, Chris being completely in tune with the humour. Del Boy (and his alter ego, actor David Jason) became heroes to Chris, and he was quite good at mimicking Del and his sayings. Phrases such as "You plonker", "Dip stick" and "Fabrique en Belgique" were often heard about the house (and elsewhere). As a result of this Chris was gradually establishing a collection of videos. It did make buying Christmas presents easier. For Christmas 1999 Chris received a Fools and Horses alarm clock, in the shape of the Trotter yellow 3-wheeler, which woke you up with 'Rodney, Rodney, wake up you dipstick'. When Ian Shingler became Chris's one-to-one at Dorin Park there was a meeting of like minds as Ian is also an OFAH fan (he **has** the t-shirt) and they would re-enact scenes from the programmes as well as exchanging insults! All in the best possible taste.

Chris had quite a good line in mimicking, other than Del Boy, he could do Rodney, Granddad and Uncle Albert, as well as quite a good copy of Boycie's laugh. From other programmes he did a good version of Pauline Fowler, had a passable version of Captain Mainwaring and Corporal Jones from Dad's Army and was good at Jim Royle (from the Royle Family). His greeting of "Ooh, I have missed you" could easily bring a tear to your eye as he used the voice of Shadow the dog from the film Homeward Bound.

One of the music cassettes that we had in the car was an original cast recording of 'Les Miserables'. Many of the tracks are quite inspiring and Colm Wilkinson's singing is absolutely fabulous. Chris immediately took to the music and it became one of his favourites. One of the songs, 'Master of the House' is sung by the characters Monsieur and Madame Thenardier, who provide the comic relief and contains a number of rude words. When Chris first started listening to the cassette he wasn't very old, no more than five or six, so when these came up in the song Annette or I would discretely cough or whistle or fast forward through the track. Eventually we started to forget and Chris got to hear the words. "Arhh, ah," he laughed, "they used a rude word. He said a**e". "Yes, well there's no need for you to repeat it," snapped his Mother. "Rewind it Dad, let's listen to it again". Of course, that track soon became very popular.

A number of years later, in 1996, Chris bought me the video of the Les Miserables 10th Anniversary concert at the Albert Hall. Although it was mine it soon ended up in Chris's room and was a popular video to watch while he was resting in bed. He also found it amusing to find 'Masters of the House' and play it through for his friends. All you could hear would be howls of laughter from his room as the *offending* words came up. At the end of the concert all the actors playing Jean Valjean from around the world appear on stage to sing 'Do You Hear the People Sing?'. Every time it came on Chris would have me say the name of the actor in the accent of their country. It has to be said that I was not very good at this, but it seemed to amuse Chris. One night while watching the video I asked, "Would you like to see Les Miz in the theatre?"
"Oh, Palion, that would be great".
So I set about trying to get tickets for a performance. The first place I tried was the home of the London production, The Palace theatre. As with many London theatres wheelchair access is pretty poor (not surprising I suppose given their age) and The Palace is no exception, there are several places to negotiate steps and it is necessary to transfer from the wheelchair to standard seats. Chris wasn't very keen on that idea, so it was back to the drawing board. A few months later it was advertised that there was to be a short run in Liverpool.

Great, I thought. Not so, as again wheelchair access was limited. More time passed, we were still enjoying the video, when it was announced in the papers that Les Miz was coming to Manchester, but again enquiries drew a blank. I was beginning to sense that getting Chris to see a live performance was not going to happen. Then in early 1999 while looking at the Les Miz web-site I saw that there was a forthcoming touring production, which included amongst its venues the Sheffield Arena and the NEC in Birmingham. I looked up the Sheffield Arena on the Internet, it looked promising, describing good disabled access, so I fired off an e-mail asking for information about the Les Miz production. Less than 30 minutes later the phone rang, on the other end was the Disability Access Co-ordinator from Sheffield Arena. I ran through our requirements and 15 minutes later had booked tickets for the production. I waited for the tickets to arrive before I told Chris.
"What are you doing on the 24th of May?" I asked.
"I don't know, nothing as far as I know," replied Chris.
"Well, how about watching Les Miserables?"
"Oh, brilliant, brilliant," he shouted, before shooting off to find Annette.
"Mum, Mum, we're going to see Les Miz. By the way Dad, where is it we're going?"

Leading up to our trip to Sheffield Chris was becoming progressively more uncomfortable due to the problems with his support jacket not fitting and sitting in the car, so the prospect of the journey to Sheffield was causing Annette and I some concern. We decided that we'd drive over to Sheffield during the afternoon, thus giving Chris sometime to get comfortable in his wheelchair before the performance. We had to stop a couple of times on the way over to Sheffield to readjust Chris's position in the car and ease his discomfort. Having arrived in Sheffield we located the Arena and then drove the short distance to Meadow Hall Shopping Centre to get something to eat and drink. In the Food Court there was plenty of choice ("It's just like Florida Mall," observed Chris), but it was Colonel Saunders finest that Chris decided he (we) wanted. Having got tea out of the way we had a short walk around before finding our way back to the Arena.

The Arena's statements regarding access were spot on. The disabled car parking places are within yards of the door, the access is flat, the doors automatic and wide enough for wheelchairs. Once inside we bought our programme and made our way to the loos - accessible and clean. Chris was getting more and more excited, more so when he realised that Jean Valjean was to be played by Phil Cavill who appears as the British Valjean at the end of the Anniversary video.

After a short wait the doors to the auditorium opened and in we went. The stage, set at an angle, was about half way down the arena with huge curtains either side blocking the rest of the arena off. We were shown to our seats, again with flat access. There were two rows allocated for wheelchair users and their party and the set-up was quite simple - you chose where you wanted to sit, they removed a chair to provide a place for the wheelchair and you settled down to watch. As we were first in we were able to make sure Chris had a clear and unobstructed view of the stage, with Annette and I either side of him. He was almost bubbling over with anticipation, chatting incessantly, "You know, you need to be quiet during the performance," he was told by both of us. "Yes, yes, I know that," came the indignant reply.

The house lights went down, the overture played and the performance commenced. The chain gang appeared and the first lines of 'Look Down' drifted from the stage. "There's Phil Cavill," came this loud whisper. "Sshhh!," came the response from either side of him.

As the production unfolded it was clear that Chris was very much enjoying it. As each song came up you could just about hear him singing along, although occasionally it got a bit louder and either Annette or I had to remind him that there were other people listening and to be quiet. Of course 'Master of the House' was greeted with "Arhh" and a laugh. At the interval we had ice cream, repositioned Chris in his chair (his back had started to give him some discomfort and he needed a few *leans*) and then settled down for the second act. The well known songs kept coming 'Little People', 'A Little Fall of Rain', 'Drink With Me' and 'Bring Him Home' all well performed and accompanied by an occasional small voice. Chris had been amazed at the way the scenery moved to form the barricade against which many of these songs were performed. The performance moved on to the portrayal of the Final Battle, when the soldiers attack the students. The noise of *battle* is very loud, the depiction of the pride and belief that the students have and their ultimate slaughter is very intense and seeing it is very moving, much more so than just hearing it. Out of the corner of my eye I noticed Annette's arm appear around Chris, I looked across to see a steady stream of tears running down his face, the power of the performance clearly having had its effect. He soon regained his composure and enjoyed the rest of the performance. At the end as the cast came out for their curtain call, Phil Cavill was greeted by an enormous cheer from my left and shouts of "Brilliant, Brilliant".

Considering the discomfort that Chris was suffering at the time due to his badly fitting support jacket he had done very well and thoroughly enjoyed his evening, the trip back to Chester was a lot easier than our journey over. Buoyed by the thrill of the evening Chris reprised the entire show for us singing along to the cassette, oh and saying "Arhh" to 'Master of the House'.

Of course anybody who knew Chris was well aware of the pleasure and enjoyment that he got out of his computer, as he was quite able to talk for hours about it! Being well aware of the benefit of computers we had bought Chris his first machine in September 1993, which as they were in use at Dee Point was an Acorn A3010. He got a lot of fun out of the machine, using it both for school work and playing games, and it taught him the basics of how to use a computer confidently. One of the great things about the Acorn was that it was quite portable, using the TV as a monitor, and so Chris was able to take the computer with him when he visited Nanny and Nana although it has to be said that both struggled with the technology. During 1995 Chris started making noises that he wanted one of the Sony or Nintendo games consoles. After discussion with Annette (she says she just listened to me) we decided that it might be better to spend the money on a PC as this would allow Chris to use it for school work, play games (which are arguably better than the consoles) and at some point gain access to the Internet.

After some research we settled on a Gateway PC which was ordered to arrive by Christmas. Chris had no idea he was getting a PC as a present so after he'd gone to bed out came the boxes and the system was wired together and placed in the dining room under wraps. As usual we were up early Christmas morning, anticipation getting the better of him, and he set about working his way through a near mountain of presents. It was clear from his demeanour that he'd expected something else, a games console? Annette asked him to go into the dining room to get something for her, "Aw, do I have to?". "Yes, you do". So with a whirr of the motors off he went, there was a pause, "Oh my God", and a whirr as he reappeared, a great beaming smile across his face. "Oh my God," he said again, before turning round and going back into the dining room. It was a wonderful moment, he was just so excited, we helped him pull off the wrapping paper and powered it up, to a chorus of "Thank you, thank you, thank you" he was at the keyboard and away, a love affair had commenced.

Chris quickly built up a library of games, his favourites being either of the adventure type or flight sims, although he did have a few 'shoot 'em ups'. Whatever they kept him entertained. As his physical capabilities deteriorated over the following years the computer provided him with a great deal of benefit. For many children it may be considered that spending too much time on a computer is not good, perhaps they should be out riding bikes and playing games. Annette and I were very conscious of this and for some time limited Chris's time on the PC. However, as time went on we did relax that rule. There is no doubt that the PC provided Chris with many things; it was a complete entertainment system, a source of knowledge (through Reference CDs) and his window on the world. In early 1996 we hooked up to the Internet for the first time and that opened up even more sources of information and access to quite a few people around the globe. One person Chris conversed with was James Adkins, who lives in Arizona and is a test pilot for McDonnell Douglas, flying Apache helicopters. Chris made contact after James Adkins was asked to provide some information by our friend Dave Park during the Dubai Air Show. The black baseball cap with 'These Colors Never Run' badge, regularly worn by Chris was one of the gifts.

Technology moves on at a tremendous pace and although we had bought a top of the range machine in 1995, by the middle of 1998 it was running out of steam, especially in being able to run the new games that were coming to the market. This of course caused Chris considerable annoyance as quite often when wanting to buy a new game he couldn't as it wouldn't run on his machine. So in January 1999 we invested in a new machine, another Gateway, with a faster processor, bigger disk, more memory, faster CD drive and faster modem. Sufficient to keep him happy for a bit more time. With the new machine's arrival came the demands for many of the games that he'd not been able to run before and his game collection grew even bigger. To be fair, he would play many games again and again, even those he had from day one and there is no doubt he did get his money's worth from them.

CHAPTER TEN (Disney Time)

When You Wish Upon A Star
Makes no difference who you are

Having holidayed in various places in the UK in previous years Annette and I decided that we should do something special in 1991, especially as we didn't know how long Chris would be on his feet. We decided therefore to visit that great playground in the USA, Walt Disney World. A number of my work colleagues had previously visited Disney World and so I set about gathering information and their views on what to do and where to stay. At the same time it became common knowledge at work about Chris's diagnosis and I was approached by Kate Williams, who worked in the Administration Section of Management Services, to ask if we would be offended if my colleagues raised money to send Chris, Annette and I on holiday. I said we would be very grateful, but that we would only use the money to pay for Chris, Annette and I would pay our own way. I felt that it was unreasonable to expect colleagues to pay for my holiday. I added that any money that was left over I would happily put by until Chris may require it for a wheelchair, electric bed or similar equipment. Kate was aided in the money-raising venture by Karla Jones and they set up a small trust fund in which the money was held. Another colleague of Kate and Karla recommended the Christopher Barratt Fund to her brother who worked at the Shell Refinery at Stanlow. The workforce there raised money through their safety record and donated the result to local charities. As a result we were invited with Karla to an afternoon at the refinery at which the fund was presented a cheque for £300. Through the efforts of Kate, Karla and the staff in Management Services the fund exceeded £2,500.

Independently of Kate and Karla's wonderful and much appreciated effort Annette's colleagues at the Pharmacy Department of the Countess of Chester Hospital undertook a number of fund raising events, including a sponsored swim, organised by Lesley Harrison. As a result of this the Pharmacy presented a cheque for £624 which was gratefully added to the Fund. In addition, Cheshire Kart Club, of which I had been the Secretary for many years, organised a raffle at a kart race meeting in April 1991 the proceeds of which were also added to the Fund. Over the years further donations, as well as some of Chris's own money, were added to the Fund and this help pay for all Chris's holidays, some computer equipment, some special equipment and other items to helped support Chris's well being. Chris never forgot everyone's effort, especially Kate, Karla and Lesley. Everybody's kindness and caring left an everlasting mark with us all.

Our first holiday to the Sunshine State and the home of Mickey Mouse took place during the first two weeks of June 1991. In what was to become a tradition Chris Bolton took us to the airport. This was Chris's first time on an aeroplane and we had spent sometime preparing him for what was to come. We flew out from Manchester on an American Trans Air Lockheed Tristar chartered by Airtours. The flight to Orlando, via Bangor, Maine, was fairly uneventful apart from Chris wanting to know how much further it was to go every 5 minutes. Chris was fascinated by everything from the airport, to the plane and flying itself. It was an interest that was to last throughout his life. We arrived in Orlando in the early afternoon, disembarked and passed through immigration and baggage collection with no problems. It was then necessary to board a bus to travel to the Dollar rental depot to collect a car. From the moment that you board the plane in Manchester right through to exiting the airport in Orlando you are in an air-conditioned, temperature controlled environment, so when the doors of the airport open and you step out its like entering an oven. Within minutes you are soaked in sweat as you struggle with the suitcases (which in our case always contain the proverbial kitchen sink!) and a 5-year-old that's getting tired. A valuable lesson was learnt on this first trip, not to wear denim jeans to travel in as they definitely are not helpful in Orlando's hot and humid conditions. Once at Dollar the car was sorted quite quickly (a bit of a disappointment as it was a Toyota Tercel and not a true American car) and we were on the road to the hotel. After much research and comparison we had chosen the Holiday Inn Maingate East in Kissimmee as the general facilities were good and the rooms contained coffee making facilities, a fridge and a microwave. Chris could be quite choosy about what he ate and we were not sure what he would like in America, so having a fridge and microwave meant that we would at least be able to give him something to eat.

The first day, being new to Florida, we attended the Welcome Meeting at Medieval Times and a little while later, back at the hotel, fell for a timeshare sales pitch at Orange Park Country Club. Towards the end of the sales pitch Chris was getting really bored so to keep him occupied it was suggested that he play miniature golf with another little lad, but this nearly ended up in a fight, as they had a disagreement over the use of the clubs!

On the next day we made our first visit to the Magic Kingdom in Walt Disney World. While planning the holiday, Terry Padget the Systems Development Manager at NWS Bank, had told me that the best way to reach the Magic Kingdom on that first day was to go across the Seven Seas Lagoon by boat (rather than using the monorail), as it added to the excitement and anticipation as the Magic came closer. We took his advice and positioned ourselves at the bow of the boat. Off we went across Lagoon, leaving the dock and the Polynesian Resort Hotel behind. The magnificent pink and white Grand Floridian hotel appears and you gaze at its beauty, before the wonders of the Magic Kingdom open up before you. The warm breeze, caused by the boats motion, ruffles your hair and clothes and brings with it the sweet smell of the popcorn stalls at the entrance to the park. Chris was transfixed by the sights of the castle, Thunder Mountain, Space Mountain and the Main Street Station and became more and more excited, as the landing dock grew nearer. If Annette hadn't kept hold of him he'd have been off and into the water in his rush to get there. The thing about Disney is that they live the magic, you actually feel like you're on a Southern River steamer, the crew and the announcements make it so. The boat docked and it's "All Ashore!". The short walk to the turnstiles, under blue skies, in the hot sunshine and you can feel the hairs on the back of your neck stand on end. As we knew that Chris would not be able to walk around the park all day we hired one of the Disney strollers, light blue pushchair, and then it was under the Main Street Station, a pause to put on sun-block, and out into Town Square and Main Street USA. Chris was just mesmerised, the shops, the trees, the castle,

all the people, there it was happening all around us. Magic.
We were fully prepared for our trip to Walt Disney World, we had watched most if not all of the Disney videos and as such Chris was quite familiar with the characters, our favourites being Tigger and Chip 'n' Dale. What we hadn't thought about though was the size of the characters in real life, Goofy, for example, to the top of his hat is well over 6 feet tall. Initially, Chris was very reluctant to go anywhere near them, he was quite happy to sit in the stroller and watch, leaving the autograph hunting to Annette and I. At one point, while in the Town Square, we were watching Mickey Mouse when I sensed the stroller moving. I turned round to see a non-plussed Chris being pushed around by Pluto.

We spent quite a lot of time in Mickey's Starland where there were climbing frames and slides (which Chris could still manage with a little bit of help, although the big concern was him getting knocked, losing his balance and falling) as well as water sprays in a maze where he could get wet. During that first day we went around the entire park taking in many of the rides and attractions as well as most of the shops. We bought the first of Chris's Disney hats, this one the Goofy hat with the teeth on the peak and the long floppy ears.

By late afternoon, we had had enough for the day and returned to the hotel, although we did return to Magic Kingdom later to see Tinkerbell's Flight and Fireworks. Having taken up a viewing position close to the Crystal Palace we patiently waited for the show to start. Even at 9 o'clock at night the temperature was quite high and Chris, quite comfortable, in his stroller was soon asleep. We decided that the best thing to do was to move back down Main Street and get ready to get the boat across the lagoon thus avoiding the crowds after the show, but while still being able to see the fireworks. We watched Tinkerbell *fly* from the top of the castle and then walked down Main Street reaching the dock just as the fireworks started and Chris woke up. There is really nothing else like Disney fireworks, it is a truly spectacular show, and fully enjoyed by Chris.

The following day we had decided to take easy and spend by the hotel poolside. The day was most enjoyable, splashing in the paddling pool or being pulled around the main pool was great fun for Chris. While in the pool he was able to get quite a lot of exercise and we encouraged him to kick his legs or to walk around the shallow end. Having returned to the room later in the afternoon Chris said he felt unwell and was promptly sick! We thought initially that maybe he had had a touch too much sun, but as the rest of the day wore on he became more and more lethargic. There was nothing else for it but to call a doctor, which the hotel kindly arranged. This being America there was nothing to worry about, the doctor visits your hotel room, is fully equipped and able to dispense most drugs on the spot and is then paid! The doctor examined Chris and diagnosed a bout of bronchitis, which he felt he may have picked up on the plane. We were always very careful to ensure the doctor knew the underlying condition Chris had, but having prescribed and dispensed some antibiotics, he said that he should be up and about the following day and that it shouldn't spoil his holiday. Sure enough after taking the tablets, a good nights sleep and a day's rest Chris was ready for action again. It was during this time that the fridge and microwave came into their own as we were able to keep Chris going with cereal, toast and jam butties!

We tried to do most things, but also ensured that we had rest or less active days. We took in Gatorland and watched the alligator jumperoo, went to Water Mania and toured the shops, including Disney Village Market Place. We went to Sea World and enjoyed the dolphins, loved the Shark Encounter and thrilled at the Shamu show while avoiding getting wet. Chris particularly enjoyed the Clyde and Seemore Sealion show, including the pre-show entertainment. As you entered the auditorium from one side or the other you were greeted by a white faced clown, if you were lucky that was as far as it went. However, for certain unsuspecting guests they became part of the show. The clown would mimic people's walk, would point out certain features of the guest or just clown about behind them. The best one though was when he took one guest, whom was looking for a seat, by the arm and deftly accompanied him out the other side of the show area. Chris laughed and laughed; he very much liked that sort of zany humour. It's a hard act to follow, but Clyde and Seemore surpassed it and Chris loved the otter that kept, literally, stealing the show. One of the other things Chris enjoyed about Sea World was the Shamu bars. These were chocolate covered ice cream lollies in the shape of Sea World's biggest attraction. My abiding memory is of Chris sitting astride a Shamu stroller eating one of the said bars, with a paper napkin bib and chocolate all over his face.

We also took in a trip to Busch Gardens in Tampa. The 2-hour drive is well worth it as Busch Gardens have some good rides and attractions. Perhaps not quite as good as Disney it is still a fun place, the mix of thrill rides and exotic animals blends well. In 1991 Chris wasn't tall enough for the rollercoasters, but absolutely loved the Stanley Falls log flume ride. He and I must have gone on it at least half a dozen times, and the big drop at the end really got him excited. To ensure his safety he would sit in front of me so that I could hold onto him and as the drop approached he would give a running commentary to be followed by a huge yell as we went over the top and then a cheery wave to waiting Mum. Chris also enjoyed the Umbongobongo Bumper cars, where we had great fun and loads of laughs piling into other cars and drivers.

But it was Disney that gave him his most fun, he simply loved the whole thing, eventually overcoming his apprehension of the characters and shaking hands, hugging and kissing them. On this holiday we mainly visited Magic Kingdom, with a brief tour of EPCOT. We saw the afternoon parade and sang along to the songs, we watched the lights parade and were amazed by all the lights. Of course no trip to Disney is complete without buying a cuddly toy character, for Chris there was no other option but Tigger. Each year after we had to celebrate Tigger's 'birthday', that being the day he was bought! One of the many highlights of the holiday was the trip to the Disney Extravaganza. This was a giant bar-b-que held in a large marquee in the Fort Wilderness area of WDW. We travelled on a coach from the hotel, during which Chris met Robert (and his mum and dad, Viv and Chris) who was also on his first visit to Florida, through the back roads to close to the Hoop-de-Roo Revue. The marquee was set out inside with long tables and benches, covered in red and white chequered tablecloths, with a stage on which a country and western band played and an area in front for dancing. To one side was a large serving area at which you could get burgers, hot-dogs, ribs, beans, salad, coleslaw etc. as well as drinks of various types. The marquee was packed with holidaymakers and once the food had been consumed the real visitors arrived. Dressed in Wild West gear nearly all the major Disney characters led by Mickey and Minnie came in. They walked slowly up and down the aisles of tables, happily being photographed with the guests, signing autographs and generally joining in the fun. Chris could hardly contain himself, he shook hands with Mickey and had his photo taken with him; did *high fives* and played with Chip and Dale who in typical fashion caused as much trouble as they could; shook hands with Goofy; got a cuddle and kiss off Minnie; was almost as tall as Donald (in his Davy Crockett gear) and got as many autographs as he could. Once the characters left the group played and the guests danced and just enjoyed themselves. Then just before it was time to leave all the characters returned for one last round of fun, joining in the dancing and, in some cases (Chip 'n' Dale), being naughty. Chris just loved their antics and so the evening finished on a huge high, with a huge smile across his face.

As with all good things it must come to an end and so we spent the last morning of the holiday at Water Mania with Chris's new friend Robert and his mum and dad. Chris, in his usual way, took over the leadership and happily organised Robert, which pool they would go in, where they would sit, what ice-creams they would eat and so on, Robert seemed happy to comply. So came to an end an absolutely wonderful holiday.

Having returned to the normal world Annette and I agreed that Florida had been superb and we would try and go again in 1993. However, as 1992 unfolded it came clear to us that Chris was gradually becoming more and more unsteady on his feet and was having greater trouble getting up off the floor and walking. We had taken to using the Major Buggy when we went out for the day so that Chris could cope with the physical demands. As July approached I said to Annette that we should consider going back to Disney so that Chris would be able to enjoy the rides and attractions while he was still able to walk and get on them. After further thought and discussion we booked to go in the last two weeks of September.

As with the previous year we had booked with Airtours, only this time the flight was, with British Caledonian albeit on a Tristar again. While a nice plane and quite quick in the air, it did need a refuelling stop in both directions at Bangor, Maine. This meant that the journey seemed to go on forever and Chris was not the most patient of passengers. Based on our experiences of the previous year we went prepared, or so we thought, with books, games and cassette player. What we found was that we spent most of the journey switching from book to game to cassette to game to book and so on every ten or fifteen minutes. Over 9½ hours this can become, shall we say, very tiring.

By the time we arrived in Orlando Chris was quite tired, having been up early and having kept active throughout the flight. While Orlando airport is very modern it does have an annoying process; passengers have to collect their bags twice. Firstly at the point of arrival where bags are simply moved from one location to another, and then again in the main Baggage Hall. Add to this the immigration and customs checks, the trip from the arrival point to the central hub of the airport and the whole process takes ages. We had taken with us the Major Buggy, but of course this was carried as hold baggage and so was not immediately available to us. As a result I had to piggyback Chris from the plane to the Immigration Hall. The queues for Passport Control are quite long and while standing in line, without warning, Chris suddenly collapsed in a heap on the floor. His legs had simply given way underneath him, primarily as he was so tired. Annette and I sat him up, fortunately as he'd fallen on some bags he hadn't banged his head and seemed OK. A very nice Immigration Officer rushed over and inquired if we had a problem. Annette explained the situation and having got Chris a drink of water the Officer ushered us to the front of the queue. As a result we were soon on our way to collect our bags, the buggy and then on to get the car.

Having collected the car from Dollar, we were much happier this time, as it was true American one, a Chrysler Grand Prix, we set off for the hotel. As we had booked almost on the spur of the moment we had decided to stay at the Holiday Inn Maingate East again. The hotel is built in the motel style so there are rooms at ground level and one storey up. To ensure that Chris didn't have to climb stairs I had written to the hotel to request a ground floor room. On checking in we were surprised to find we had been allocated the same room we'd had the previous year.

After getting something to eat and a good night's sleep the traumas of the previous day were forgotten. We attended the Welcome Party at Cattleman's Steakhouse and then at Chris's request we spent the best part of the day at Water Mania. As he was that bit older (7) Chris wanted to try most of the pools and slides, although he did draw the line at the big drops. He particularly enjoyed the wave pool and the water guns, especially when soaking anybody in range.

The next day was what it was all about, a trip to WDW and Magic Kingdom. As the previous year we travelled across the Seven Seas Lagoon on the boat. The anticipation and excitement was no less than we had experienced 16 months before, Chris was so excited to be back he almost burst. Chris, being that bit older, was definitely up for the rides. But before all that it was hat buying time, on this occasion it was the Donald Duck example, blue sailor hat, ducky eyes and big yellow beak. We went on Jungle Cruise, Pirates of the Caribbean, Swiss Family Robison Tree House (Chris piggy-backed around as he couldn't manage the stairs), Peter Pan's Flight, It's a Small World (oh no the song stays with you the rest of the day!), Thunder Mountain (Chris's first ride on a roller coaster type ride), took in the show in Mickey's Starland and more, but the highlight of the day was our first ride on Splash Mountain. Splash Mountain, based on the Brer Rabbit story, had only opened a few months earlier. We had seen it on one of the TV travel shows, but it surpassed everything we expected. From the pre-ride queuing area to the loading area the atmosphere is great. The small drops give a taste of what is to come later, the chipmunks house makes you laugh and the views across the park towards the castle are fabulous. The animatronic scenes of Brer Rabbit being chased by Brer Bear and Brer Fox have you chuckling out loud and the song in 'The Laughing Place' has you joining in. But it gets more serious as you pass under the vultures dressed as Undertakers and climb the hill. I held on tight to Chris, the anticipation of the drop was almost too much for him and then another view of Cinderella's Castle and whoosh down we went into the briar patch and a bit of a wetting. Chris laughed and laughed. The finale of the ride is a trip past the Zip-A-Dee Lady, a paddle steamer, with ostrich dancing girls singing what else but Zip-A-Dee-Doo-Dah, which of course

Chris and I had to join in with. When we arrived back at the loading point Chris was all for staying in and going round again.

With the previous years experiences behind us we were much more comfortable with holidaying in Florida. Whereas in 1991 we had eaten mainly in the hotel, on this visit we tried many different establishments for both breakfast and dinner. We liked the Ponderosa and Denny's, but rated the Kettle Family Diner (with the circulating model train) in Kissimmee our favourite. Chris had established a liking for hot-dogs (no relish or mustard of course) and as long as they were on the menu we were OK. As we were more familiar with the area we also did more things on this visit and ventured further afield. We drove up to Ocala, 80 miles north of Orlando, to Silver Springs, a natural water spring that was also a zoo-like attraction. A lot of the animals were seen from a variety of rides on glass bottomed boats, from which it was also possible to see the source of the spring. One fact that interested Chris was this was also the location for the filming of one of the James Bond films. He also enjoyed the family of racoons that darted through the trees and chased the boat, with their black eye markings they looked like masked highwaymen trying to ambush us.

We had planned to visit the Magic Kingdom the day after our trip to Silver Springs. So we were up reasonably early and went for breakfast at the Ponderosa, just down the road from the hotel. After breakfast we needed to return to the hotel as Annette had forgotten something ("Ah Mum, come on"). We parked the car outside the room, Annette went in and as she was a little while I followed to see if everything was alright. I told Chris to stay in the car, as I wouldn't be long. I came back out a minute or so later to find Chris climbing out of the car, and before I could say anything he shut the door. Now Chris being Chris he had put the lock on the door, which on this particular model caused all the locks to shut. No problem? Except I'd left the keys in the ignition. Now you're probably saying that's my fault, except that's not how I saw it.

"I told you to stay in the car," I said.

"But I wanted to see where you and Mum were," came the reply.

"I told you to stay in the car, now look what you've done."

"But I wanted to see where you and Mum were."

Had it not been for the fortunate intervention of Mum the younger member of the Barratt family may well have been in orbit.

"Use the spare key," said a helpful Chris. But therein lies a problem. Hire cars in the USA don't have spare keys for security reasons, but the hire companies thoughtfully provide you with a telephone number of firms who will 'break' into your locked vehicle. Apparently this is big business as we were told the operative would be with us in about an hour. Sure enough the guy arrived about 60 minutes later, took 30 seconds to open the door and relieved us of $100. For the second time that morning the intervention of Annette saved a small person becoming an astronaut. Having been saved from physical damage by his Mum Christopher then suggested that it was all Annette's fault, as she'd wanted to go back to the hotel! So about an hour and a half later than we expected we set off for the Magic Kingdom – so much for an early start. Still we made up for it, with more rides on Splash Mountain, Dumbo, Pirates, the Haunted Mansion and the paddle steamer on Rivers of America. The one problem with Disney is the length of the queues and it was while waiting in line for Thunder Mountain that

Chris took up chatting with three ladies, who were accompanied by their husbands. The three, who were probably in their late fifties, were fascinated by Chris's knowledge of the rides, he happily shared with them what was good and what was bad. "Are you on holiday with your grandchildren?" I enquired. "Oh no," they replied, "we're here on our own and we've been on all the rides and loved it." Ah, the magic of Disney.

We stayed in the park quite late that night, bagging a good spot by Sleepy Hollow, to watch the new night-time parade - Spectro Magic. We'd thought the Light Parade in 1991 was good, but this was fantastic. It was led by Mickey, resplendent in a long white cape illuminated by hundreds of lights, with a huge glass globe in which light beams danced. It seemed that each float that went past was better than the one before, there was Roger Rabbit, the Little Mermaid and her father Trident, along with Flounder and Sebastian. There were scenes from Fantasia, Snow White and the Seven Dwarves, plus the usual characters of Goofy, Pluto, Donald, Chip 'n' Dale and our favourite, Tigger, who made our night because as Chris said he knew where we were and waved at us.

The following day saw a late start and a morning spent by the pool, even on holiday we needed to keep Chris's stretching and exercise regime going and the pool provided a good excuse to stretch the legs. After the pool we ventured to the local Kartworld, a large double figure of eight track, where they had two seat karts which looked, with the bodywork, a bit like racing sports cars. The passenger side had a dummy steering wheel fitted so Chris could 'drive'. Being so low to the floor it really felt like you were going fast and Chris really enjoyed it as we outbraked our 'opponents' into the various corners. Although it wasn't a race as such Chris concluded that we had won easily.

Having returned to the hotel for a rest we attended, later that evening, the Disney bar-b-que at Fort Wilderness. Now called the Star Time Jamboree, it was essentially the same format as we had enjoyed the year before. Having enjoyed the meal and the drinks and listened to the group, the characters, led as usual by Mickey, arrived. As in the previous year they made their way up and down the aisles between the tables shaking hands, being photographed and signing autographs. I don't think the smile on Chris's face could have got much bigger, he was in his element. After a while the characters went off to get a drink and the group struck up again. The dance floor filled and Chris and Annette went off to show the world a mean shake of the body! Unlike the previous year the characters did not come back to dance (apparently some people at previous evenings had taken to picking them up while dancing resulting in injury). However, they did return to just outside the marquee, where guests could queue up for autographs etc. It had been a long and tiring day for Chris and it needed Annette to hold Chris up while he got the autographs he wanted. Even so he was determined to meet his favourite characters and kept going until they left.

The following day we visited the Disney-MGM Park, which had been opened since our last visit. This park is themed around the movies and in some parts is a working film lot, but is also great fun with a mix of good attractions. We saw the Muppets show and met Mickey Mouse, Pluto, Beauty and the Beast, and Chip 'n' Dale (who were their usual naughty selves). Chris was using the Buggy while we moved around the Park and one of the great things about Disney is the excellent awareness the characters and cast members have for children with special needs. At the time of our visit the Teenage Mutant Ninja Turtles were all the rage and Chris was keen to meet them and get their autographs. They were performing at regular intervals at the end of the New York Street set, so we got there in good time to watch. Afterwards they were available for autographs, but this meant queuing. We got in the line, but we were some way back, and it did not look good for meeting them. I warned Chris that we might not reach them in time, which was not what he wanted to hear. We edged closer, only to hear from one of the minders that the Turtles would only be signing autographs for another few minutes, it was definitely not looking good for us. Then quite unexpectedly a cast member approached us, he asked Chris who he wanted to meet. "Donatello, please," replied Chris. "Right young man, please come this way." and with that the guide rope was undone and we were ushered forward to meet the Turtle. Donatello was great, he knelt down to Chris's level, shook hands and happily signed (stamped!) the autograph book. It was some time before we stopped hearing about how Chris had met the Turtles.

We had enjoyed Sea World so much in 1991 that a return visit was high on the To Do list. As previously the day was hugely enjoyable, the Shamu show, Shamu ice cream bars, the Whale & Dolphin Show and the sea lion show, this time Hotel Clyde and Seemore. The ingredients were the same as the previous years show, the sea lions perform, the humans get wet, the otter steals the show and the walrus spits water, but all in all a tremendous laugh. And, oh yes, the white faced clown was the pre-show entertainment. We also paid a return visit to Busch Gardens in Tampa Bay, which in the 16 months since our last visit had been updated with more animal attractions, including a 'Gorilla's in the Mist' viewing point. Close up the huge silver-back gorillas are an incredible sight. Chris and I went on the Congo River Rapids and got very wet, as well as having a number of rides on the Stanley Falls log flume. This was still Chris's favourite ride, the shouts of delight as we slid down the big drop will always stay with me. I think he would have stayed on the ride all day if he could. We drove the Umbongobongo Bumper cars again, showing all those Americans how to drive, and watched everybody getting soaked to the skin on the bridge over the Tanganyika Tidal Wave, although Chris passed on a ride. Busch Gardens has a number of good roller coasters and I'm a big fan of that type of ride. As the queues weren't too big I said I would ride the Cobra, which includes a corkscrew element.

"I'm coming as well," announced Chris, much to his mother's surprise.

"Are you sure?" I asked.

"Are you absolutely sure?" asked Annette. Chris assured us he was.

"He'll be OK," I said, "if he bottles out when we get to the cars, I'll bring him out." As we made our way slowly down the path I told him what it would be like, I pointed out that once on board and harnessed in there was no going back, you were in for the ride. We reached the loading station.

"Are you sure you'll be OK?"

"Yes!" There was no further chance to debate it, the train pulled up, I lifted him in, pulled down the shoulder harness and settled myself. As the seats had side headrests I couldn't see Chris, but was able to hold his hand and hear his chatter. The train began to move, rolling slowly out of the station before beginning to climb. At the top of the rise there is a small pause and then the rush, down, back up, right, right, down and up into the corkscrew, over twice and then several more corners and minor ups and downs. The hand gripping mine squeezed tighter through the ride, but all I could hear was "Yippee! Yippee!" The train came to a stop, the shoulder harnesses moved up and it was over. "Dad, lets go around again." I explained that we had to get out, and maybe we could come around again if there was time. Sadly, the queue had built up and there wasn't time, but we now knew that Chris was a roller rider.

You can't go to Florida without doing some shopping, or so Annette would tell Chris and I. These were not Chris's favourite days, especially once he'd bought what he wanted. However, visits to Mercado, Belz, Florida Mall and the Flea Market were interspersed with ice cream, Coca-Cola and at Belz a go on the giant carousel, with magnificent horses. While Annette would indulge herself in the shops, Chris and I would wander round chatting. I actually quite enjoyed this as we would talk about anything and everything, watch people go by and generally have a laugh.

There was still time for one final trip to Magic Kingdom and that meant a chance to go on all the favourite rides. Pirates of the Caribbean was first, then Thunder Mountain and then Splash Mountain, and after much cajoling and encouragement Mum came too. So coached by Chris, who pointed out all the important aspects as the ride progressed. Annette didn't take much of this in as she was already focusing on the big drop at the end of the ride. Chris kept telling her it was fine, if he could do it so could she. Down the small drops, past the tableaux and through the Laughing Place (not many laughs from Annette though!) past the vultures and on towards the climb and the drop. As the log boat crested the rise, teetered on the top and began its descent all that could be heard was "Oh my God" followed by a scream, Annette squeezed my hand and Chris just laughed.

Chris had decided this year that he would get a cuddly toy friend for Tigger (who incidentally had travelled to America with us) and so having studied all the options in the many shops around the park he settled on the last day for Chip. By late afternoon Annette had had enough and suggested that having got something to eat we went back to the hotel so we could start packing. However, being a good Mum she then suggested that Chris and I return to the Magic Kingdom for a short time while she got on with the job. So for just over an hour and a half Chris and I ran (well I ran and Chris bounced in the Buggy) between Thunder Mountain, Splash Mountain and Pirates. As there were relatively few people about getting on the rides was straightforward and so we must have ridden Splash and Thunder at least a total of ten times. Time was now moving on and it was time to go. I asked Chris if he wanted one last ride. "Pirates of the Caribbean" came the reply, so a sprint across Adventureland was necessary. Into the entrance of Pirates we raced to be greeted by a cast member pulling the gate shut.

"Oh, well," I said "just too late." From the Buggy came a huge sigh of disappointment.

"Is it just you two?" asked the cast member. I nodded. "Go ahead, I'll radio down to say you're coming."

Through the winding dungeon corridor we hurried to the loading dock. Into the boat and onto the ride – just Chris and I. As you can imagine he thought this was just great and he was the bee's knees. Being the only two on the ride, especially as you pass the galleon, is quite spooky.

The following day started with the traditional end of holiday photo with the car, before checking out and making a last visit to Florida Mall for some last minute shopping. From Florida Mall we took the short drive to the airport. Annette felt that it was wrong to only have Chip, so a visit to the airport's Disney Store to find Dale ensued. So we headed for the plane with Chris in the Buggy almost hidden by two furry chipmunks. But this holiday had one final twist, for there in the departure lounge was Mickey and Minnie Mouse. "Mum! Dad! Mickey and Minnie have come to see us off!" came this excited voice. Indeed it was almost as if they had, for showing that amazing awareness the characters have for children with special needs, Mickey and Minnie headed in Chris's direction. They shook his hand, they ruffled his hair, Minnie kissed him and they generally made a fuss and as it was time to go they stood and waved good-bye. I think that Chris was so happy he probably could have floated home without the plane.

It was to be a while before we went to Florida again, as in the meantime we moved house to the bungalow. Our third visit to Walt Disney World came in September 1995 and followed soon after the death of Annette's mum, but she had wanted to go for Chris's sake. We again travelled with Airtours, although this time on a Boeing 767 of their own airline. Just for a change we stayed at the Holiday Inn Maingate East, now this may sound boring, but this was the first time we had been to the USA with the wheelchair. We knew that the Holiday Inn was predominately flat and accessible for disabled travellers, so would cause us no problems.

As usual the first day was taken easy to recover from the long flight and to come to terms with the jet lag (which never seemed to affect Chris). The following day we woke to a black sky and rain. Our plans for a Disney day were put on hold so we paid a visit to Church Street Station and then, as the rain had stopped, the Scenic Boat Tour in the Maitland area of Orlando. This is a little known attraction and involves a boat trip around a number of the lakes and their interconnecting canals viewing places such as Rollins College and houses belonging to the famous. Although the tour was quite slow paced Chris enjoyed the boat ride and the amusing commentary from the skipper.

The next day was our first visit to the Magic Kingdom. Unfortunately, the holiday took a downward turn. Having travelled across the Seven Seas Lagoon on the boat, we paused under the Main Street railway station to put on sun cream and while doing so Annette mislaid a gold chain and ring belonging to her mum. As soon as she realised we went to City Hall on Main Street to report the loss and see if anyone had handed them in. The Disney folk were very helpful, explaining that property handed in was taken at the end of each day to the Lost Property office, situated near to the Ticket & Transportation Centre. So the following day we headed there hopeful that some kind person had handed in the jewellery. Alas, we were not fortunate, but we went back numerous times, mostly prompted by Chris who never lost his faith in people, believing that whoever had found his Mum's chain and ring would hand it in. The loss of such sentimental items needless to say took the shine off the day. I'm not sure who was most upset, Annette having lost the items, or Chris who was upset for his Mum.

In the time since our last visit there were a number of new attractions. We loved the Lion King show, a mixture of characters and puppets set against a background of the savannah, complete with authentic smells, and music from the film. We were amazed by and laughed at Timekeeper, a 360° film show that takes you back in time with Jules Verne. Timekeeper is a robot, which looks, sounds and acts like Robin Williams and controls the time machine in which you travel.

Of course we did some of the usual things, but Chris would not go on all the rides. Generally, the access for wheelchair users within the Disney parks is very good, often the queue can be bypassed by the use of special entrances or entering through the normal exit. All the information a guest requires is set out in a special booklet. The Cast Members are very helpful and understanding, and continuous loading rides will be paused so disabled guests can board. Some rides have special wheelchair accessible cars. However, in some cases it still meant that Chris needed to be lifted into or onto the ride. He needed to feel confident that it was safe or no amount of persuasion would work. So we didn't go on Pirates of the Caribbean, but we did ride It's a Small World and Dream Flight (both with the wheelchair), Thunder Mountain and Splash Mountain (no Annette this time though!) and both needing Chris to be lifted from the chair to the ride. Thunder was no problem, as having once picked Chris up it was straight into the carriage, but Splash needed a big step down into the log, made more hazardous by the wet floor. However, once aboard the log the ride was magic. Chris was always great company on the rides, you could sense the excitement and anticipation, he would chatter about the ride, he would sing the songs, he would ooh and aah, but most of all he would laugh. I truly loved those moments and for me riding Splash with him was like nothing else, nothing can surpass those rides around that fantasy mountain.

In keeping with one of the now traditional activities we had to scour the shops for the Holiday 1995 cap. On this occasion Chris chose a cream number with a green peak featuring Timon and Pumbaa, amusing characters from the Lion King. Having left the park to have dinner we returned later that evening to watch the Spectro Magic night parade, which was the usual Disney magic. We then boarded the boat to return to the Ticket and Transportation Centre, timing it so that we could watch the fireworks, something Disney excels at.

Orlando and its area continues to be developed, with new roads, new hotels and new attractions, all benefiting from the draw of WDW. Since 1992 one such new attraction was Splendid China, located in Kissimmee West Gate. As its name suggests it is wholly centred on all things China, from restaurants, through live shows to splendid models of famous Chinese buildings. For some reason Chris had always been interested in China and so a visit was on the cards. The models vary in size and scale, but are all beautifully detailed and have signs (in English!) explaining what they are and where they are. Tiny soldiers populated the model of the Great Wall, the various palaces are exquisite and clearly illustrate their size and magnificence, and the Forbidden City even in model form is incredible. Chris took all of this in, we had to view the models from various points and read the signs. Perhaps the most breathtaking model is that of the famous terra-cotta warriors. The model portrays only a portion of the real exhibit, with the soldiers being two-thirds actual size, but it is still fabulous to see. The real thing must be breath taking.

On this visit while still enjoying visits to Denny's and the Ponderosa, sadly we found that the Kettle was no more – it had been lost in a new shopping area development. However, having visited Splendid China we had found a new place, the Sizzler, which was to become a favourite, both for dinner and breakfast. Amongst the reasons for this were the ample buffets, wide choice of meals (including hot dogs), good access and the availability of A1 steak sauce. It became a marker for Chris for how good a restaurant was if it provided (or not) A1.

On this trip we had upgraded the car to a mini-van, a Plymouth Voyager, so that it would be easier to lift Chris in and provide plenty of room for the wheelchair. Of course Chris needed to know everything about it, he read the driver's manual from front to back, had the bonnet (or hood) up to examine the engine and was able to explain all the interior controls. It was sensible therefore to make the most use of the vehicle and so we thought we'd go a bit further afield. After much discussion Annette and I discounted Busch Gardens, as we knew that wheelchair access was limited and most of the rides would be beyond Chris. We therefore planned a trip to the Weeki Wachee springs on the Gulf Coast. The drive over to the coast was really pleasant and gave us all the chance to see a little bit more of Florida. To make access easier Chris sat in the front passenger seat with Annette relegated to the rear. This was a mutually satisfactory arrangement as Annette could stretch out and relax, Chris could act as navigator (at which he was very good) and I could drive! Weeki Wachee, while being a natural water spring, is famous for its 'mermaids'. You do get used to the grand Orlando and Tampa theme parks and so Weeki Wachee is a quite a contrast. It is set in a lovely wooded area and very tranquil. The 'mermaids' perform in part of the spring, with the audience seated in a subterranean theatre watching through a giant window, like viewing a huge fish tank. Access to this theatre was, as is generally the norm, in America very good and provided good views. The production we watched was "Little Mermaid meets Pocahontas" and was most enjoyable. The 'mermaids', complete with tails, act out the story and *sing* songs to a backing track. They are able to maintain the action underwater by taking air from strategically placed pipes. After the performance there is an opportunity to meet one of the mermaids, an opportunity Chris didn't want to miss. There were also boat trips up the small river to view the local fauna and flora. Watching the herons and pelicans gliding over the river before plunging in to spear the fish was very relaxing. All in all Weeki Wachee was a very pleasant afternoon.

Rather than return to Orlando the way we had gone we decided to drive south towards Clearwater and return along Interstate 4. The drive along US 19 gave us further opportunities to see more of Florida, you get quite used to the high rise hotels around the theme parks, but rural and coastal Florida is quite a contrast. Many of the houses are ramshackle, some seemingly in the middle of nowhere and then you get a pocket of luxury houses, apartments or condominiums. Having taken in the Gulf Coast down to Clearwater we turned inland towards Orlando. The sky had been progressively getting blacker and blacker, a fact not lost on Chris, who was no lover of thunder and lightning. As we headed across the Causeway and towards the darkening sky he was becoming more and more nervous suggesting that we find another way. This was not practical I pointed out and in any case it was nothing to worry about. We had just got onto the Interstate when the heavens opened, we had never seen rain like it. Within minutes the road was flooded and the windscreen wipers could not cope with the volume of water, so in common with all the other cars we stopped. By now the chance of thunder and lightning was forgotten, this was a great adventure, although I'm not sure Annette saw it that way. After a short time the rain eased off and the Interstate traffic sprung back into life. It had rained so much that the service road alongside the Interstate was under about a foot of water though.

The next day we visited the Disney-MGM Park under a now brilliant blue sky. We took in the Great Movie Ride (and got slobbered on by an Alien), went on a Voyage with the Little Mermaid, and went on the Back Stage tour to Catastrophe Canyon. Now this was great fun, Chris had a great time almost acting out the disaster with all the necessary nervous laughs and screams (although I suspect that when the tram rocks some of the screams were for real). We went to Muppets 4D, a 3D film with added action, which was hilarious particularly the various objects that jump out of the screen. From there it was on to the Tower of Terror, a new attraction since our last visit. This is based on a hotel which supposedly was hit by lightning one night in the 1920s destroying a lift in which a number of people are travelling. The ride consists of a pre-show, held in the library of the hotel, during which the story is explained and then its on to the service lift and the ride; a serene climb through several floors before plunging at breakneck speed down, up and down again. In keeping with Disney the cast members wear appropriate costume and solemn faces to add to the atmosphere. A lot of the rides have 'walkthroughs' so that guests can enjoy the pre-show, but bypass the ride - Tower of Terror is no exception. There was no way either Chris or Annette would ride the Tower, but Chris did want to see the inside of the hotel. We confirmed that there was a 'walkthrough' and walked up the misty path between the trees, onto the patio of the hotel and in through the door. We entered the library and shivered to the story and the music of the Twilight Zone. The room goes dark, Annette and Chris panic, thinking that the room is going to drop, but the wall opens and you exit into the basement of the hotel. You wind your way around the boilers and then queue to enter one of two service lifts. The Lift Attendant steps forward and indicates our party towards the lift.

"We're doing the walkthrough," chirps Chris.

"I'm sorry, sir, but we don't have an exit," replied the Attendant, through a dour face.

"But, we don't want to go on the ride," said Chris, a slight panic edging his voice.

"No, we don't," added Mum, also with panic in her voice.

"I wish I could help, but you need to take the elevator," the Attendant intoned.

"But, I can't ...." stammered Chris.

"Then you'll have to go in that elevator over there which takes you to the exit," chuckled the Attendant, with a now smiling face.
The relief on the face of two people close by was almost touchable.
While I carried onto the ride, Chris and Annette headed for the elevator indicated by the Attendant, where another cast member joined them. The lift door opened, in went Chris and Annette. "You're very brave going on the ride," said the cast member. More panic and stuttered words before the door opened in the post show area. After a shock like that there was only one thing to do, go and watch the stage shows of Beauty and the Beast, and Pocahontas, much less stressful.

The following day we needed to be up early, as we had a breakfast date with Pooh Bear and Tigger. We drove over to Disney Vacation Club (now Key West), found the restaurant and were shown to a table. The restaurant quickly filled up and breakfast was being served. There was quite a mix of people; family groups, young and old couples, and much exciting chatter. Getting Chris to eat his breakfast was difficult, there was so much to see, so much to listen to and so much to say, as well as so much anticipation. Then without warning, Pooh and Tigger entered, immediately joining guests at their tables, happily giving autographs and being photographed. They slowly moved through the tables, eventually Pooh arrived at our table. He shook hands (paws?) with us and generally made a fuss. The photographs were taken and then he was off to the next table. A few minutes later and Tigger arrived, Chris greeted him like a long lost friend, busily telling him that they'd met before in 1991 and 1992, and that he was his favourite. Tigger obliged with hugs and his characteristic hand moves etc. Autographs were obtained, photographs taken, sausages stolen. Despite all the people you didn't seem rushed at all and it was fun to watch the characters with the other guests. Having completed the round of the tables, Pooh and Tigger left only to reappear a short while later and do it all again. This time the visits to tables were a bit quicker, but having completed this round of visits they stayed a while and danced and frolicked, with Tigger getting up to 'naughty' tricks. The kids (and the adults) thought this great and the whole place was filled with laughter. Eventually it was time to go and with a final wave Pooh and Tigger were off, back to the Hundred Acre Wood presumably.

Breakfast the following day wasn't quite as entertaining, but the Sizzler in Kissimmee is always good value and accommodating with the wheelchair. It was a leisurely start as this was to be a shopping day. Having filled up with coffee, or hot tea in Chris's case, we got up and left. In the car park a number of people had gathered in small groups, all looking in a Northeast direction. A brief enquiry told us that the Space Shuttle was due to launch, and moments later there it was. Despite Orlando being 50 - 60 miles from Cape Canaveral the Shuttle, with its rocket flame, could be clearly seen hurtling skywards leaving its vapour trail behind. Even at that distance its an awesome sight and it must be fabulous to see close to. Needless to say this prompted a barrage of questions most of which Annette and I were unable to answer or answer satisfactorily.

No trip to Florida seemed complete without a visit to Sea World. Whereas the other major theme parks provide a diet of fantasy and film Sea World puts you in the heart of nature. Chris enjoyed watching the animals perform and the risk of getting wet was an added attraction. Indeed he would insist on going just that bit closer, but not close enough to get soaked. The dolphins were most often or not the first port of call, although on this visit it was a bit more difficult to see over the wall into the tank from the wheelchair. Visits to Hotel Clyde and Seemore, Shark Encounter, the Whale and Dolphin Show and the Shamu Experience were made, along with a ride up the Sea World Tower (fabulous views across the park and out towards Epcot) and the new Manatee Encounter. Manatees are lovely creatures, apparently what sailors of old thought were mermaids (they must have been at sea for a long time!), and have in recent years suffered from injury caused by speed-boats. Sea World have a programme to nurse injured animals to health and to release them back into the wild.

Another new attraction at Sea World was the Mermaids, Myths and Monsters sound and light show, shown late evening. This was spectacular using a curtain of water onto which laser images were projected to a classical and rock music sound track. To Chris and my delight, but not Annette's, it was interspersed with fireworks. After a visit to Epcot the following day, Chris and I took in more fireworks at Illuminations, which is a spectacular display set against a musical background.

In previous years we had not ventured to Universal Studios as we felt that Chris was not old enough to enjoy the rides, but as he was now 7 years old we paid a visit. We got zapped by Ghostbusters, attacked by a giant white shark in Amityville, shaken and scared by an Earthquake, flew with ET and were entertained by, amongst others, the Blues Brothers. Chris was very impressed by the ET ride, as we were able to get the wheelchair onto the ride. He also liked the bit towards the end when ET himself said "Good-bye, Chris". "How did he know my name?" he asked. It was sometime later that I told him that they type your name in as you go through the entrance.

The penultimate day meant another visit to the Magic Kingdom, still Chris's favourite place. We went on the accessible rides and to the shows, visiting the Lion King twice, watched the afternoon parade and enjoyed the park in general. The Lion King was very much the attraction of the moment and this inspired the choice of cuddly toy, Simba being added to the growing list back home. Of course we went to Splash Mountain, but no amount of persuasion would coax Chris onto it. We went on Thunder Mountain one more time, but he was not prepared for me to lift him into the Splash Mountain logs, he said he just didn't feel safe. He told me to have a go and he would stay with Mum and watch. I did go, but somehow it wasn't quite the same.

So Florida 1995 came to a close, in many ways it was the best holiday we had had to then, we'd done such a lot, we'd had a great time and Chris looked very well, the sun and air had done wonders. There was one last thing to do, the by now traditional photograph of Chris and I besides the car or on this occasion mini-van. Then it was off to airport and home. While sitting on the plane waiting to leave Annette announced to Chris and I that she was fed up with Orlando and that when we came again we would do a fly-drive and visit several places in the State. However, by the time we got back to the UK this had changed to a fly-drive in California!

CHAPTER ELEVEN (California Dreamin')

Between the silence of the mountains,
And the crashing of the sea.
There lies a land I once lived in,
And she's waiting there for me.

Justin Hayward

Following our return home from Florida I spent the next few months researching where to go in California and what was the best time to visit. It became clear during this research that flying to and from the West Coast of America was not going to be possible as Chris would not be able to manage an eleven hour flight. Chris had always been interested in many different things and probably through reading his various books of facts and things like the Guinness Book of Records he had developed a fascination for tall buildings. Based on this Annette and I decided to theme the holiday on "The Biggest and The Tallest". It was obvious therefore that New York and Chicago should be the places to break the Californian journey. It was also clear that the normal two-week break would not be long enough, so a three-week vacation was planned.

With the holiday planned in detail I put together a small computer based presentation of what the itinerary was, and gave it to Chris. He went quietly through it slide by slide and once it was finished I expected him to be very excited. Instead he simply said that it was very interesting. Perplexed, I said, "But that's where we're going on holiday." Eventually, the penny dropped - and so did Chris's jaw.

So in late April 1997 Chris Bolton chauffeured us to Manchester airport to catch the British Airways shuttle for the first stage of our journey to London Heathrow. Despite all the planning, including letters and phone calls regarding travelling with a wheelchair, boarding the aircraft caused problems - no aisle wheelchair was available at the Gate. The shuttle needs to leave on time and as the minutes ticked away the cabin crew were becoming more agitated. After considering the options I told them that if they could make seats close to the front of the aircraft available I would carry Chris on. This was not how we wanted to start the holiday and it's very uncomfortable for Chris (and me), but it did seem to be the only answer. Having moved people on the plane I was just about to pick Chris up when, to Chris's great relief the aisle wheelchair arrived, and we were able to board properly. The flight to London was aboard a British Airways 737 and with Chris's interest in aircraft he was soon deep in conversation with one of the stewardesses (the good looking one of course) about the plane. He told her that his favourite plane was Concorde and he hoped to see one in London. The stewardess, who introduced herself as Carrie King, told him that she normally flew Concorde and Carrie was able to provide a lot of information (which Chris *filed* away for later use). Towards the end of the flight she returned and presented Chris with a card, signed by all the air crew wishing him a good holiday and also gave him a pen inscribed with Concorde's insignia, normally only available to people who fly on BA's flagship aircraft. Chris was overjoyed with the pen and it remained one of his prize possessions, with pride of place on the unit in his bedroom.

Heathrow was very well organised, we were met off the plane by a helper, who guided us through the airport to the American Airlines check-in, pushing Chris in his wheelchair. The helper remained with us until the flight was called and took us to the door of the plane. To our relief an aisle wheelchair was ready to hand, and with the assistance of the helpers and cabin crew we were efficiently boarded on to a McDonnell Douglas MD11 for the flight to New York's JFK airport. The flight was generally uneventful, the American Airlines crew being helpful and considerate, and we arrived around 4.30 p.m. local time after what can be described as a *long* flight. Disembarking was handled with well-practised efficiency, once the other passengers had filed off, the aisle wheelchair was immediately to hand and two ground staff helped move Chris, with tremendous consideration and care.

Once through immigration, customs and baggage collection it was a case of calling the wheelchair accessible transport we had booked. A phone call to the New York Gray Line, a wait of about 30 minutes and then we were on our way into the Big Apple, a drive of about 45 minutes. This was fantastic, the views and the sights were brilliant, "Look there's the Empire State", "There's the Chrysler, that's beautiful", "Oh, my god, look at the WTCs, they're magnificent!", "Look at this", "Look at that" and so on. In many ways just hearing the excitement in Chris's voice in that first hour made the trip worthwhile.

All the accommodation on the trip had been pre-booked as the last thing you want is struggling to find a room, especially with the wheelchair. Pre-booking allows you to ensure that the hotel is accessible for the wheelchair, or so the theory goes. Our hotel in NYC was to be the Best Western Manhattan on 32nd Street and it wasn't long before the van pulled up outside the property. Problem, the entrance to the hotel had three huge steps into the lobby. Fortunately the doorman was a big guy and between us Chris was soon sitting in the tiled hall. Over to check-in, quoted the name and the booking reference. The Receptionist typed away at the computer, typed something else, and checked the booking confirmation slip, then typed some more.

"I'm sorry," she said, "we don't have a reservation for you."

"Well I have a booking," I replied politely, but firmly.

"I'm sorry, but the hotel is full. There will be rooms at our sister hotel."

"That's good, but we're staying here. My son is in a wheelchair, we've just had a seven hour flight and come from the airport in special transport which has now gone." With that she retreated into the back office.

"Do you want me to come and sort the problem Dad," came a voice from behind me. "No thanks, I think I'm OK at the moment," I replied. The Receptionist reappeared, with what transpired to be the Manager. More checking of the booking confirmation and more typing. Eventually he pronounced that he'd found the problem – the computer had the booking for the 30th May (not 30th April). Well that's alright then. It was pointed out that I was hardly likely to make a booking for the end of May when all the other bookings were consecutive from 30th April and the booking confirmation with them clearly showed the 30th April. Eventually, after further discussion, including mutterings from behind me (and not just Chris!), a small suite suddenly became available.

The first thing Chris had to do was check out the facilities on the TV, including any in-room movies. Having satisfied himself on what he could watch and freshened up, it was off to get a bite to eat (via the big steps) and then a visit to the first of Chris's objectives - the Empire State Building (the world's tallest building for over 40 years). What a fabulous place, it just oozes atmosphere and the view from the 86th floor observation terrace is fantastic. While it was quite warm and calm at street level out on the viewing area it was windy and chilly, Annette insisted, despite protestations, on Chris wrapping up. The views of the East and Hudson Rivers, Central Park, Macy's, the Chrysler Building and down Manhattan to the twin towers of the World Trade Centre leave a tremendous impression. Chris was really excited to have achieved one of his aims. We couldn't have timed our visit better, for having taken in the views the light started to fade and we were able to watch as the city lit up. As Chris said, "It's like watching fireworks from above."

Although we were tired after a long day sleeping was a problem, they say that New York is the city that doesn't sleep, and they're right. The noise from the streets is incredible, a constant cacophony of shouting, car horns, refuse collection, emergency sirens and more. Fortunately, Chris sleeps through most things (except plane flights) and so was reasonably refreshed when he woke early. Of course with all those things out in the big city to do all he wanted was to watch 101 Dalmatians on video on the TV as it had yet to be released in the UK. This was not the last time we saw this film during the next three weeks, as nearly each time it was available we had to have it on. So much so that by the end of the holiday Chris knew virtually every word of the film.

We had breakfast in a typical New York diner just around the corner from the hotel and then we were off to the bottom of Manhattan to catch the Staten Island Ferry to view the Statue of Liberty and Ellis Island. Having the wheelchair meant the subway was a no-go option, so the bus was the best solution. We found the nearest stop for the route we wanted and waited. The bus arrived, indicating it was wheelchair accessible. The driver got off the bus and went to the rear side door, opened a small panel and then proceeded to hydraulically change the steps into a lift onto which Chris was pushed. Up we went and then while Chris was parked and locked into position (a set of seats tip up to make space) the driver reset the lift/steps, climbed aboard and off we went. Chris was most impressed, an impression that was to remain with him and one he would recount some years later at a conference[1] he was invited to. The bus ride was great as we passed places and names we had only previously seen on films, such as Wall Street, Fifth Avenue, the Flatiron Building and the American Stock Exchange.

Having taken a round trip on the Staten Island Ferry (great value at 50c each) and taken in the wonderful sights, we walked up, via Fort Clinton, to Chris's main attraction in New York - the World Trade Centre or WTC as he would say. The WTC being the second tallest building in the world at that time. Having queued a short while for tickets we were shepherded into one of the express lifts that shoot visitors to the 107th floor, nearly 1,350 feet up, of the South Tower, at breathtaking speed. The observation floor provides awesome views, augmented by the floor to ceiling windows, which allow you to look at the people way below milling around like ants. We slowly walked around the four sides taking in the views that each face of the building offered. Sadly a trip to the very top of the building was not possible as it was reached by escalator, but as Chris said he

[1] 'Care and Health Needs of Disabled Children in Recreational and Informal Settings', see Chapter 14.

probably wouldn't have liked being outside that high up.

Once back on the ground we took a final look around and walked north on West Broadway taking in the sights and sounds of Lower Manhattan, before catching a bus for the journey to 34th Street and Macy's, the world's largest department store. Now this is more Annette's territory than mine or Chris's and the first real moan of the holiday was soon forthcoming, quickly put in place by a "This is my holiday as much as yours". The excitement (sic) of Macy's was over reasonably quickly and we returned to the hotel via a family diner and after an amazing thunderstorm, which flooded Broadway. As Chris observed, "they do things big in NYC".

The following morning we were up early for our transfer, by accessible van, to JFK and our flight to San Francisco. The drive out of the city was a bit of an anti-climax and we strained to keep the views of the buildings in sight. We checked in with American Airlines, advising that we would need pre-boarding and grabbed some breakfast, before heading for the gate. We approached the staff at the gate to ensure that they knew we needed wheelchair assistance. The young lady confirmed that they were aware, but that as the plane was a McDonnell Douglas DC10 it would be easier if we travelled in Business Class as it was closer to the door. Now who's going to argue about that, certainly not Chris who almost floated onto the plane in excitement. As a result the 6-hour flight across continental America was very pleasant, Chris fully enjoying the attention from the stewardess!

The approach into San Francisco airport was across the Bay, providing us good views of the Bay Bridge and in the distance the Golden Gate, but of more interest to Chris was the Virgin Boeing 747 on approach alongside us. Flying with Chris was always a memorable experience as he gave a running commentary on what the pilot was doing, including flap angles, engine speed, and discussion with the control tower. To those who did not know him you would believe he could fly, although his ability was actually limited to computer based flight simulators.

The off airport car rental location meant a shuttle bus trip for me and a wait at the airport for Chris and Annette, before we loaded up and set off into the 'City by the Bay'. Chris was very impressed with our transport, a brand new silver coloured Ford Windstar people carrier. Our base for the next few days was to be the Holiday Inn on Fisherman's Wharf, which we easily found. Chris was quite impressed by the location of the hotel at the end of Columbus Avenue as it afforded an excellent view of the futuristic looking Transamerica Pyramid building at the other end, which at 853 ft is San Francisco's tallest building.

Once we were checked in, unpacked and freshened up it was out on the town, well actually out onto the Wharf and the Piers, with great views of Alcatraz and the Golden Gate. A trip to the island prison would have been good, but we were advised that it was not really suitable for wheelchairs (not surprising I suppose). Chris said Annette and I could go, and he'd wait for us, but we said that was kind, but we'd leave it, thanks. It was quite chilly on the waterfront so we found refuge (and dinner) in a Denny's - different state but good old Denny's.

The next day, once breakfast had been eaten, we set off on San Francisco's 49-Mile Scenic Drive, a well signposted route that takes in most of the main sights of the city and surrounding area. Our first stop was Fort Point directly under the Golden Gate Bridge. When you're that close the sheer size of it is breathtaking, this was the biggest single span bridge (4,200 ft long, 746 ft high towers) in the world until surpassed by the Verrazano Narrows Bridge in New York (already viewed from the top of the WTC). For Chris to be in possession of such facts, or to have a source for them, was an important aspect of any holiday or day out. They were taken in, mulled over and at some point, in some conversation, would be brought out generally correctly. While admiring the scale of the engineering we were treated to nature's own amazing ability as one of San Francisco's mists formed and engulfed the bridge. We returned to the route of the Scenic Drive passing through Crissy Field, past the Cliff House (and our first view of the Pacific Ocean – the world's biggest), past San Francisco Zoo and around Lake Merced, before entering Golden Gate Park (one of the world's largest city parks). The 49-Mile Scenic Drive proceeds to wind its way through the park on its many roads allowing views of the Dutch Windmill, Japanese Tea Garden, several museums and numerous lakes. From there the route takes you past part of the University of California and the climb up to Twin Peaks, from which there are superb panoramic views of the city. From here we were treated to splendid views of the Golden Gate and the sea fog, the Transamerica Pyramid ("a really lovely building" noted Chris), the Coit Tower and the Bay. You could also clearly see how hilly San Francisco is. Having stretched our legs and had a good breath of fresh air, Chris was all for moving on. So we returned to the route descending from Twin Peaks down a bit of a hairy route before passing the historic Mission Delores and on to the Embarcadero and the route through the city centre. It was here that things went a little pear shaped. I lost track of the route and took a wrong turn, realised I'd gone wrong and turned round, returning to the junction of Beale and Harrison, where I waited at traffic lights to turn left. The lights turned green and off we went, as I started to turn I glanced in the drivers door mirror to see a Toyota speeding up alongside me. Now the inside lane is for left turn only, not for going straight on, but that's what this car was doing. Unfortunately, I didn't react fast enough and the Toyota clipped the front driver's side wing with an almighty bang. The shock and surprise caused a noisy reaction from the two passengers, much of which isn't printable! Chris was quick to realise that the car should not have been going straight on and made his views on the driver very clear. The driver turned out to be a young girl, of Chinese origin, who having stopped came back to our car, which after a bit of a struggle I had moved out of the junction. She apologised for the crash, and admitted that she was rushing to classes (despite this being Sunday), but as soon as I spoke and she realised I was not American she said, "that of course being a stranger I did not understand the layout of American junctions". I was quick to point out that I had driven for many years in the US and was very familiar with the road layout and pointed out that she was in the wrong, as she should not have gone straight on. Despite this she was very helpful allowing me to use her mobile phone to call Alamo and report the accident and to sort out a replacement vehicle. We had to wait about an hour before the replacement arrived, a Chevrolet Astro van (which is similar to a Ford Transit); Chris was much less impressed. We set off to complete the Scenic Drive, passing through Japantown, Chinatown (the largest Chinese community outside of Asia), Little Italy and past the Civic Center, Grace Cathedral, Cable Car Barn and the Coit Tower (a memorial to the city's volunteer firemen) on Telegraph Hill.

The route also passes through Union Square, the heart of San Franciscan shopping and this fired up the "taste buds" of Annette. So, to the stifled groans of Chris, we found somewhere to park the car (not easy in San Francisco) and took to our feet. Now Chris and I were well practised at filling in time while the shopaholic went to work and in Union Square and Market Street there was plenty to do. We watched the cable cars clanging and ringing their way back and to, in Nordstrom's we studied the unique spiral escalators (sadly unable to use them with the wheelchair), and in Mason Street watched a film crew making an advert for a car. Actually, most of the time was spent watching the film crew measuring, wetting the road from a large water bowser, moving props and generally doing everything but film, to which Chris observed "what a boring job!"

The following day we took a walk around the Ghiradelli Square area. Ghiradelli Square is now a shopping centre, built in a converted chocolate factory and a nice, pleasant place with views across the Bay and home to a number of performing musicians. The nearby Cannery, once a fruit processing plant, is also a shopping centre with a number of novelty shops and coffee bars. Close by is a cable car terminus for the Powell-Hyde line and we sat and watched the cable cars arrive and depart. The cars are turned around on a turntable that is rotated by the driver and guard pushing the car. Cable cars are not wheelchair friendly so a ride on one was not possible, to Chris's huge disappointment, but as usual it was a passing moment before he was on to something else. That something else was to go and see Lombard Street, the 'crookedest street in the world" which was five blocks up from the cable car terminus. Now on the face of it this seemed like a good idea so off we set. Now, as I've said before, San Francisco is hardly flat and Lombard Street is some way up Russian Hill. Initially I could manage to push the chair, then it needed both Annette and I, and then about half way between the second and third blocks we ground to a halt. Despite much encouragement from Chris we were going nowhere. "Come on, keep pushing - what are you weak or something" came the helpful words from the chair. Annette and I decided it was no good, a trip to Lombard Street by car was called for, so we turned the chair round. It was then that the steepness of the hill (especially to the incumbent of the chair) became apparent. "Bloody hell" was all that was said. We actually negotiated the hill backwards, as we were afraid that Chris might fall out forwards, although the prospect of him rolling down the hill did cause a few titters, which I hasten to add, were not well received, from the subject of the mirth.

We returned to the hotel for the car and the short trip to and down Lombard Street, which at least we can say we did. From there we passed across Filbert Street, the steepest slope (31.5 per cent gradient) and then onto the Golden Gate Bridge. While looking at the bridge from below is amazing, driving across it is a memorable experience. At the North end we pulled into the viewing area and completed our experience by walking out onto the bridge. The noise from the traffic is incredible and even though it was a warm day the breeze blowing in from the sea made it quite chilly. Peering down to the water from the bridge you can clearly see the strength of the currents as the water sweeps past the bridge. Having made it as far as the first tower, a long walk, but only a short part of the bridge we turned around and headed back to the car. From the bridge we drove the short, but twisty, distance to picturesque Sausalito. We found the 'centre' of the town and somewhere to park the car. We had just finished getting Chris out of the car and into his wheelchair when he said "Uh oh". I turned around to see a policeman, we'd passed a short while earlier, approaching us on a motor trike.

"Good afternoon, folks," came the cheery welcome.

"Good afternoon," we replied, in chorus.

"I guess you folk are visitors to our little town." We nodded in agreement.

"Well we're very keen on maintaining good order," he went on "and so we get all the young folk to help." And with that he presented a replica Sausalito police department badge to Chris.

"Thank you, sir," came the smart reply.

A short walk and we were in the town centre, actually a small collection of tourist type shops. One particular shop caught our attention, as there was a considerable queue outside. As we got nearer we identified the cause of the popularity, ice cream. Needless to say we were not going to be allowed to miss this. The queue was moving quite quickly so we soon reached the front, to be greeted by probably the biggest choice of ice cream flavours we had ever seen. One option was to have a *special*, which meant you could have three different flavoured scoops. So between us I think we ended up with nine different tastes. The rest of the day in Sausalito was very pleasant, admiring the shops, the craft fair, the little harbour and the pretty houses, all watched over of course by the special deputy!

Having returned to the hotel Chris decided that we should have dinner that night in the nearby Denny's, always a popular choice. It was while eating that Chris drew our attention to a lady who was in a wheelchair. Despite his own problems he was always concerned about other wheelchair users, how they were, how they managed to travel about - did they have a van or car? The lady and her husband had been in the restaurant before us and so finished their meal before we did. As they left, making their way past our table, Chris smiled at the lady and said "Hello." This was quite unusual for him, for although he was generally friendly, he more often or not did not make the first move. The lady and her husband stopped and asked how Chris was and if he was enjoying his holiday. A lengthy conversation then took place about what we were planning to do and where we had already been. It turned out that Linda and Gordon were from Gateshead and were stopping over in San Francisco while returning from Hawaii. There then followed an interrogation of what Hawaii was like; who were they flying with (Virgin); and what was the Virgin service like? (very good for wheelchair users). After Linda and Gordon left Chris said, "Oh dear, did you see that lady's hands (Linda was an arthritis sufferer), it must be very difficult for her to manage."

The following morning we departed San Francisco on Highway 101 passing through Silicon Valley, recognising as we went numerous familiar names from the world of computing. That said, it's not the prettiest of places. Having briefly stopped for lunch at a roadside diner we arrived early afternoon in Monterey, the setting for John Steinbeck's Cannery Row, and it was close to this part of the town that we parked. While a visit to Cannery Row was of course essential, the real reason for the stop was to visit the Monterey Bay Aquarium, rated as one of the best and biggest in the world. It is a fabulous facility, with a variety of imaginative displays, both models and live, with informative narratives explaining the many aspects of marine life. The centrepiece is a 30ft Kelp Forest Tank, which provides a window on California's marine habitat. We had a great afternoon watching the Sea Otters play, touching sea anemones and stroking the underside of bat rays. Chris particularly enjoyed the brass rubbing area, where you could produce pictures of various sea creatures.

Our next stop was the small resort town of Carmel-by-the-Sea, home of film star (and former mayor) Clint Eastwood. Carmel is a quaint, country village type place, with cottages almost lost in the narrow, tree-lined streets. A collection of expensive shops, art galleries and restaurants are also located within the town and at one end of one street is Carmel Beach, a wide stretch of white sand. We had a short walk around the town, but it wasn't really Chris's 'cup of tea'. Our hotel, the Best Western Mission Inn, was just outside the town and featured rooms with canopy beds, which did impress Chris. The hotel was next to an area called the Barnyard, a collection of shops and restaurants housed in the type of barns that you would see on The Waltons or Little House on the Prairie. One particular place caught our attention, the Sherlock Holmes, a small restaurant filled with the great detectives' memorabilia and meals themed on his tales. As a result Chris was able to enjoy bangers and mash and a cup of tea, while Dad was able to sample beers off a list as long as your arm.

We were up early the next day as we had a long drive south to Los Angeles ahead of us. With breakfast eaten we were soon on the road, Highway 1, or the Pacific Coast Highway passing over Bixby Bridge and through Big Sur. This part of the highway twists and turns along a narrow ledge high above the pounding Pacific surf and provides wonderful, breathtaking views around each corner. To the accompaniment of the Moody Blues on the cassette it was a memorable drive. For a long time after whenever we played the Moodies Chris would recall the sights and experience of that drive. Because of the nature of the road progress is quite slow, so after about an hour and a half driving we stopped for coffee at Café Lucia, perched high above the sea it afforded wonderful views up and down the coast. Suitably refreshed we continued our journey, the road still twisting and turning along the coastal route, through State Parks, and providing further breathtaking views. Gradually the road becomes less twisty and the speed of progress increases, we passed the entrance to Hearst Castle, built on a hilltop by the newspaper magnate William Randolph Hearst, near San Simeon. Time did not permit us a visit (and, if the truth be told, neither was Chris interested) so we pressed on the short distance to Cambria, where we stopped for lunch, but not before we had a brief stop to admire the basking seals which line the beach like dead bodies.

From Cambria the highway widens out and we were able to make speedier progress motoring past pretty places such as Morro Bay, San Luis Obispo (the nearest town to where film star James Dean was killed), Pismo Beach and Lompoc. We took a short detour off the main highway to Solvang for a rest halt. Solvang (including its windmill) was established by Danish settlers and was built to resemble their homeland, much of their culture and cuisine survives so we were able to enjoy coffee and pastries. Suitably refreshed we resumed the final part of the journey which took us past Santa Barbara and Ventura and on to the Ventura Highway and thence the Hollywood Freeway. We arrived on the outskirts of LA just as everyone was going home and the Freeway was packed, five lanes of solid, slow moving traffic, a nightmare. As Chris's eyesight was always good, he was set the task of looking for the exit onto Highland Avenue while I concentrated on the traffic. One good thing about American drivers is when you signal to move lane they drop back to provide a gap, so as we moved along at a steady 30 - 35 mph the prospect of missing the exit was eased. Chris was well on top of the task, calling the names of the exits and relating these to the map. Suddenly up he piped, "Highland Avenue, right in half a mile." Sure enough there it was, a flash of the indicators and we were off the Freeway and heading south past the Hollywood Bowl to our destination, the Holiday Inn Hollywood, a total drive from Carmel of 330 miles. In retrospect it would have been better to split the journey and stop en-route overnight, allowing Chris time to rest.

Our room in the Holiday Inn was on the 14th floor and afforded us a great view out across Hollywood Boulevard towards downtown LA, which was particularly good at night when all the lights were on. The hotel was a short walk to Mann's Chinese Theatre and something that I was quite keen to see. We had seen a replica at Disney MGM in Orlando, which was a good job, as the real one was shrouded in scaffolding and safety netting. As Chris said, with a hint of sarcasm, "you've brought me all this way to look at some scaffolding!" We had to make do then with admiring the various hand and foot prints outside the theatre, Chris's favourites being Donald Duck, C3PO and R2D2. After the disappointment of the Chinese Theatre we walked down Hollywood Boulevard along the Walk of Fame, while it was quite interesting to read off the stars, the whole ambience of the area is very off putting with many run down buildings and cheap shops. After a short time we decided a return to the hotel was called for.

In the afternoon we took the Santa Monica Boulevard to the eponymous beach resort followed by a walk along the beach path to Venice Beach, a fascinating place to visit. Venice Beach is a wacky area - we looked at the stunning sand sculptures and watched the human statues (Chris particularly enjoyed when they moved and frightened people passing by). We enjoyed the Hendrix music played by a guy, on roller blades, dressed in Arabian clothes who is enough of a fixture to make most of the tourist guides. There were escapologists and jugglers and a few eccentrics who seemed to be collecting all manner of materials which they then used to attach to their pedal cycles. There were a few shops selling tacky souvenirs and ice cream and to Annette's delight and Chris's disgust a hairdressers, where she could get her hair done. At least we were able to keep ourselves entertained while the hairdresser worked his magic. We were also able to witness our second film 'set', this time on the beach where several tanned boys and girls were filming an advert for the Mountain Dew drink. As with the film 'set' in San Francisco Chris was not overly impressed. On the way back to the hotel we called in at Century City, one of LA's largest shopping malls, and also the setting for a number of films, which allowed Chris sometime later to point that out to some of his friends.

The following day we paid a visit to Griffith Park, which is just north of Hollywood Boulevard. The road winds through the trees up the side of the Hollywood Hills and leads up to the Observatory. The Observatory and its surrounding area have been used as locations for numerous films including the

James Dean film 'Rebel Without a Cause', which is commemorated by a bronze bust of its star. From the terraces around the Observatory there are excellent views over Los Angeles to the Pacific Ocean and in the other direction of the famous Hollywood sign. After refreshments we continued our drive through the park, although some roads were closed due to the risk of fire. We passed by Forest Lawn Memorial Park, one of LA's largest cemeteries and the final resting-place of many stars. When I suggested that this was the *dead centre* of Los Angeles Chris was not impressed and let out a big groan! From Forest Lawn we drove through part of Beverley Hills down Mulholland Drive and Laurel Canyon Boulevard, the location of some of the mansions belonging to the stars. Unfortunately, it is only possible to get passing glimpses of these homes, although Chris felt that this was most boring as "what do you want to look at some house or the other for?" That evening we located one of Chris's favourite restaurants, a Sizzler, on nearby Highland Avenue where he could enjoy his favourite hot dogs.

The following morning we located on Sunset Boulevard another of Chris's favourites, Denny's, for breakfast. After a leisurely breakfast we checked out of the hotel and headed for Anaheim, albeit via the coastal highway. This route takes you from Marina del Ray through the beach areas of Manhattan, Hermosa, and Redondo (all small attractive resorts), past Palos Verdes and great views of the ocean crashing against the rocks and onto Long Beach. From there we headed for Disneyland. Everything had gone well until we got onto the Garden Grove Freeway, when Dad took the wrong turning and got lost. Now this was not a good move, as in the front was the world's best navigator and in the back the world's best back seat driver! As I tried to rectify the situation I realised we were going round in circles.

"Why don't you stop and ask for directions?" asked the back seat driver.

"Yes, Dad, Mum's right," added the navigator, "this is boring. Are we going to get there by tonight?"

Eventually, I took the advice and pulled into a gas station. Now you would think that somewhere as famous as Disneyland would be well know in the local area, not so. It took four or five people in the gas station to eventually decide on the route that we needed to take. Once back on the road it was only a short time before we found the Disneyland Hotel and pulled into the car park.

The Disneyland Hotel is actually a number of buildings built around a small boating lake and across the road from the theme park. We parked the van and entered the huge lobby that was decorated with all things Disney, including large bronze statues of Mickey Mouse and Donald Duck. I left Annette and Chris looking around the lobby and went to check in. As one would expect of Disney that was undertaken with efficiency and it wasn't long before I rejoined the others.

"We've just had a guy with a guitar singing Disney songs to us and asking where we're from," Chris told me excitedly, "He was really good."

Our room was in the Bonita Tower, so we decided to walk through the grounds and find the room before I moved the car and brought up the luggage. As we headed for the door, at the rear of the lobby, Chris pointed out the singer and his guitar. The guy was 'serenading' two girls, but as we walked past he broke off and sang a song about Chris visiting from Chester and on his way to the hotel room. As you can imagine Chris was quite impressed by this and clearly felt a bit of celebrity!

Once ensconced in the room, and having freshened up, we took a walk around the extensive grounds and then had dinner in the Monorail Café, a 50's themed restaurant, which provided Disney themed kids' meals. We ended the evening with a small piece of Disney magic, Fantasy Waters, a short, but enjoyable show of dancing water, lights and music that of course featured many of the characters formed by coloured light bulbs.

The following morning we were up early, had breakfast and boarded the monorail for the short journey to Disneyland. The monorail track loops through the park and allows the traveller a preview of the delights below. Even though it was still quite early the park was already filling up, it was only later that we realised that the following day was Mothering Sunday in the USA and therefore many people were giving mom an early surprise. Being the original, Disneyland is much smaller than Florida's Disney World, and is a mixture of Magic Kingdom, EPCOT and MGM, but in many ways has a better feel to it, perhaps due to it being smaller and more intimate. Many of the rides are similar to those found in Florida, but some, such as the Matterhorn, are only found in Disneyland. We enjoyed walking around the park, meeting (and being photographed) with Mickey Mouse, Pooh Bear and of course Chris's favourite Tigger. The big disappointment, as far as we were concerned, was the lack of rides on which we could get Chris. Unlike Florida, many of the rides do not accommodate wheelchairs, due I guess to the age of many of them (Disneyland was opened in 1955). Even so Chris enjoyed himself although the highlight came later that evening. Having returned to the hotel for something to eat Chris and I made a second visit to see Fantasmic, a brilliant show featuring water, lights, fireworks (the reason Annette didn't come), and most of the characters on a tableaux on the Rivers of America. The star of the show is of course Mickey Mouse (in the magicians' costume from Fantasia) who takes on and defeats a huge dragon, complete with fire breathing. We had an excellent vantage spot, in one of the wheelchair reserved areas, almost right opposite where Mickey stood. We really enjoyed the show and as we queued to get out Chris was really pumped up and chatting away about the various bits of the show. Needless to say when we got back to the hotel room Mum got a blow by blow re-enactment. It had been a long day and no sooner was Chris in bed than he had gone to sleep. So, with Annette's approval I returned to the park for an hour to have rides on the Matterhorn and Splash Mountain, something I was reluctant to do during the day as Chris could get on neither ride.

Some shopping in the various establishments around the hotel followed a late breakfast the next morning, before we checked out and set off for San Diego. The run down the coast was a pleasant drive, with us arriving in the Mission Bay area of San Diego mid afternoon. As we were a bit too early to check in to the hotel, we parked up near to the Boardwalk and found a place to have a coffee. After that we had a wander around and stood and watched for a little while the local kids on their roller blades. Chris used to watch these types of activities without any outward comment, but I suspect that he would loved to have been able to take part. He tended to make comment more about the potential dangers and how the participants should take more care. No doubt if he had been taking part he would then have been saying not to worry, and it was all very safe.

Our home for the next couple of days was the Catamaran Resort, a large hotel with a Hawaiian feel, overlooking Mission Bay - a large inland lake. Our room was an *efficiency* (a room with a kitchen area) which also had a balcony giving views over the lake. The building the room was located in was separated from the lobby by a garden, laid out with trees, bushes and small streams. However, crossing the garden was a bit of an adventure. Two birds, like crows, had built a nest in one of the trees by the path and everytime a guest walked past they would fly out and attack. This did not impress Chris, nor his Mum, and so they would take a longish detour to avoid the area and the risk of beak or claw injuries. A number of other guests complained to the management and during the next day the nest was removed and the birds 'moved on'. Chris wanted to know if there was a Denny's or Sizzler we could go to for dinner, so I set to looking through the Yellow Pages, eventually finding to an excited "Yes!" a Sizzler. This was located in a nearby area, Tierrasanta, and so with map in hand we set off. After a couple of attempts we eventually located the restaurant, only to be greeted by a long queue. We'd forgotten it was Mothering Sunday. A surprisingly short wait, accompanied by regular moans, followed before we were shown a table and enjoyed the usual Sizzler fare, Chris agreeing that the wait was worth while. By now it was dark and I carefully retraced our route, finally ending up at the junction of Mission Boulevard. I positioned the van to turn left, indicator on and waited for the lights to change. On the green I moved forward, and completed the turn and headed off towards the hotel. Suddenly, a police car with its lights and siren on appeared behind us. It took me a little while to realise it was me he was following and, as I was in the left hand lane, longer still to pull over to the side of the road. Chris was hugely indignant at this affront. "What does the stupid copper think he's doing. I'm going to tell him." A unified "Shut up and don't say anything," came from Mum and Dad. My next mistake was to start to get out of the van. "Get back in and put your hands on the wheel," came a barked order. The policeman didn't have to tell me twice. The next second he appeared at the passenger door, torch in one hand and firearm in the other, looking very similar to Magnum from the TV show.

"Do you know why I've pulled you over?" he snapped.

"Err, no officer, I'm afraid I don't." I replied, glaring at Chris as I could sense he was about to speak, and trying to think if I'd jumped the lights, gone too fast or didn't have the lights on.

"Well, when you turned onto Mission Boulevard you were in the lane for proceeding straight across," he explained, adding "but I guess being English you may not have realised that."

"I'm terribly sorry," I said, still glaring at Chris, who was definitely itching to say something, "but I thought I was in the correct lane."

"That's OK, it's an easy mistake, especially when its dark. Where are you folks from?" With that the atmosphere changed and we had a pleasant conversation about the UK and USA, with Chris now joining in. The conversation lasted for 15 or 20 minutes, before the officer took his leave, apologising for his brusqueness when I'd gone to get out of the van, but explaining that a fellow officer had been stabbed in similar circumstances a few weeks before.

"If you are ever stopped by the police remain in the car and put your hands where they can be seen" was his parting advice. God was I glad to get back to the hotel that night!

We only had one full day in San Diego and there was so much to choose from; the world famous zoo, Balboa Park with its museums including the Aerospace Historical Centre and the Automotive Museum, and Sea World to name a few. We had decided to give Chris the choice of what to do, confidently expecting a trip to the aerospace museum to be the choice. Wrong. "I'd like to go to Sea World, we can go and see Shamu," came the response. Asked if he was sure that was what he wanted, he said it was without any sound of indecision. I always wondered why he didn't choose the aerospace museum, he knew that Annette wasn't that interested in flying things and he was always keenly attuned to what his Mum liked and didn't like. I can only assume that he knew she would enjoy Sea World (Annette had often said that Sea World in Orlando was one of her favourite places), and he did like the whales, dolphins, sea lions and otters. We got the following morning off to a good start by having breakfast in Chris's other favourite eating place - Denny's, before setting off for Sea World which was located just across Mission Bay. It was a great day; Shamu was spectacular, the whales and dolphins playful, the sea lions and otter show (different to the Florida version) greatly amusing helped by a water spitting walrus and the other side-shows, particularly about the ocean, educational. As Chris said as we left at the end of the day "that was great, Sea World is always great." Clearly, his choice had been right.

From Sea World we made our way towards downtown, Annette wanted to visit Horton Plaza which according to one of the tourist guides "is one of the best modern shopping malls in the US, with five floors of shops and restaurants, open-air terraces and quirky directions". Finding the right exit off the Freeway proved a bit of a problem and we ended up nearly at the Mexican border, however it did give us the opportunity to see a large part of the American Pacific Fleet which is based in San Diego. Still with Chris's navigation and a bit of luck we managed to find the Horton Plaza car park just before it went dark. Horton Plaza was almost as good as the guide suggested, one of those places with a good mix of large department stores and smaller speciality shops. Access, as in most places in the US, was excellent and we had a good walk around. We found a nice place to eat as well, Marie Callendar's, a traditional bakery, serving soups, breads, roasts and other inviting meals. Accommodating the wheelchair was no problem, a bit of furniture moving and voila. The waiter was a really nice guy, very pleasant, and when he talked to Chris he got down to his level. It turned out he was a big fan of English football, he and his friends would watch the games on satellite TV every weekend, and he was quite interested in hearing about Manchester United from Chris. Chris thought he was a bit sad, as the waiter supported Aston Villa (apparently his maternal grandmother came from the area), and in the best traditions Chris tried to convert him. Chris explained that we were going to Las Vegas the next day, and by coincidence so was the waiter. "The best place in the world," was his opinion and then he gave us a number of tips on what to do while there. One of the other diners in the restaurant overheard the conversation and wanted to know if he could get a Man Utd. shirt, so Chris suggested that he tried the web site, for which he just happened to have the details.

After an early start, breakfast in the hotel, we set off for the airport. I dropped Annette and Chris off and then took the van to the hire location, returning on the shuttle bus. Our experience of airports in the US has always been good, but this was tested at San Diego. At the security checks Annette and I went one way and by necessity to avoid the metal detectors Chris went the other. It took me a little while to get through the checks and pick up my hand baggage, by the time I reached Chris he was looking somewhat upset.
"What's the matter mate?" I asked him.
"This bloke," nodding his head in the direction of one of the Security men, "got cross with me," he said.
"Why?"
"He told me to get out of my chair and I told him I couldn't. Then he told me I had to, but I can't can I Dad?" continued Chris very indignantly. At this point the Security Man approached.
"Is this your son, Sir?" he enquired. I replied it was.
"I need him to get out of his wheelchair, so that I can search it."
"I'm sorry," I said, "but he is unable to do that as he can't stand up. However, if you wish to search my son or his chair, please do so."
"I'm sorry, he must vacate the chair."
"As I said, that is not possible. But please be aware I'm not stopping you searching him."
"I insist," came the reply.
"But I can't stand," whimpered Chris.
"It's OK, you won't have to," I said, trying to calm him down.
By now a Supervisor had joined us, I explained the situation. "That's OK," he said, "if we can just search the chair, under the cushion and your son that will be fine. Sorry to have caused a problem." With that Chris was searched and we were on our way to the Gate. "Stupid prat!" was the verdict.

The flight, with American West, to Las Vegas is quite short, about an hour, during which Chris engaged the chap sitting next to him in conversation. It turned out this guy owned his own car dealership just outside Salt Lake City and flew to San Diego, via Las Vegas, twice a week. He told us that before the low cost airlines he used to drive there and back, a round trip of 500 to 600 miles! The approach to Las Vegas airport is across the desert and as a result is quite bumpy owing to the thermals. Chris thought the whole thing was tremendous "a bit like being on a roller coaster", although Annette disagreed, sitting as she did with her eyes shut and gripping the seat arms, much to Chris's quiet amusement. Our new friend told us that the turbulence on this trip was quite mild, during the summer it could be 3 or 4 times worse.

The cabin crew on the plane were very pleasant and helpful, allowing us to stow the wheelchair in a locker in the cabin. That meant that as soon as we disembarked Chris could get into his own chair and was therefore much more comfortable. The first thing that we noticed as we entered the terminal building in Las Vegas was that there were one-armed bandits everywhere. Not only could you see them, but you could hear them as well, a noise which became very familiar over the next few days.

Once through the terminal and having picked up our luggage I caught the shuttle bus to the car rental depot, which was a short drive away, returning to pick up Chris and Annette. Chris was made up, the vehicle was a Ford Windstar, just like we had to start with in San Francisco. "We'll just have to hope that there are no mad women drivers here in Vegas," was his other comment. In keeping with the theme of the holiday we had reservations for the MGM Grand hotel, the world's biggest with 5,005 rooms. From the airport it was a short drive to the hotel, which is approached up a drive between multi-storey garages, to the Port Cochere, a multi-laned covered area where you unload the car and leave it and your luggage with valets. A short walk took us into the lobby and as Chris said, "Wow!" It was just enormous, the biggest check-in desk we've ever seen, staffed by more staff than you can imagine with a huge (and I mean huge) video wall behind showing exerts from the EFX show. To the other side of the lobby was a large shop mainly selling MGM Grand branded gifts. Having checked in we set off for our room on the 4th floor of the Emerald Tower (one of four). We left the elevator and walked down the corridor, and walked and walked, it seemed to go on forever before we eventually located our room. One good thing though was a phone call to the Reception and your luggage was delivered to your room.

There is nothing to compare to Las Vegas, it was big, bright, loud, hot, crowded, and just amazing. The front of the hotel, the famous Lion Head, opens out onto Las Vegas Boulevard, the even more famous Strip. Right opposite was New York, New York (with its third scale New York skyline) and next to that the Excalibur (a mediaeval castle). We turned right and walked down the Strip, nearly every step leading to more eye opening sights. We had not gone far when Chris saw a really important sign, yes, the yellow, green and red of Denny's. Hot dogs for tea then. Despite being crowded we were accommodated, "Would you mind the young man sitting at the end of one of the tables in the booths?" we were asked, this meant the wheelchair being partly in the walkway. "Will that be a problem?" I asked. "No problem to us," came the reply. As I said to Annette and Chris, I couldn't see that happening in the UK.

After eating we carried on down the Strip, admiring as we went the large hotels and the building sites. New hotels and attractions are springing up all the time apparently. Having walked quite a way we noticed a large crowd gathering across the road outside the Mirage hotel. Inquisitiveness got the better of us, so we crossed over and on asking the reason for the crowd we were told "the Volcano's going to erupt on the hour." Yes, there in the middle of this small lake was a small mountain. It looked just like you would expect a South Pacific island to look. As the hour approached the crowd got bigger and more expectant, the lights of the hotel dimmed. All eyes were on the mountain, at first there was just a wisp of smoke and then it got thicker, then there was a burst of flame which gradually built up. Then the lava began to flow, slowly at first and then quicker and quicker down the side of the mountain. By now the mountain was into a full eruption with flame and lava shooting into the dark sky. The lava had now reached the water, which began to boil, before it too erupted with fire. From where we were standing, some distance away, the heat from the flames was incredible. The whole spectacle lasted for about 10 minutes before the eruption died down and the peaceful island scene returned. Incredible free entertainment.

Just past the Mirage was Treasure Island, another hotel, but this one based around a pirate theme. Outside on another lake were two almost full size galleons, which at set times, along with their respective crews do battle. We'd missed the first showing and the next was sometime later and Chris didn't want to wait. So we strolled back down the Strip towards our hotel, still enjoying the sights and lights, as well as the warmth (80° to 90° F at 10.00 p.m.). Every fourth car seemed to be a stretch limo and there was a constant buzz of helicopters overhead. There were people everywhere, we'd never seen so many people walking about before in the USA. I asked Chris if he'd like a trip in a helicopter, at first he said that he would, but a little later he said it would be too expensive. I told him that was no problem, if he wanted to go it would be fine. There was a pause before he said he didn't really want to go. In reality he did, but he was worried about getting into and out of the helicopter, as it would have meant lifting. I tried for a short while to convince him to go, but there was to be no moving him. Once he'd rationalised the pros and cons and made his mind up there was no changing it. I admired him for that. He would have loved to have flown in a chopper and I wish I'd arranged it for him before it became difficult. I'm sure we could physically have got him into one, but it was no good arguing, it was doing that which got him upset, rather than him not being able to do things.

Back in the hotel we had a wander round, of course there was the casino with its bandits, roulette and craps tables, as well as various other games to lose money. Besides this there were indoor streets with shops of all types and a food court. Time for coffee and ice cream. While sitting enjoying the refreshments several of the stewardesses off the America West plane saw us and came over to say hello and ask Chris how he was enjoying Vegas. He was always chuffed when people took time to converse with him, he particularly enjoyed asking those folk what they were doing.

Having been late to bed we were up latish the following morning and after breakfast headed for the MGM Grand Adventure Theme Park, yes, the hotel had its own park at the rear. While not on the same scale, either in size or entertainment, as Disney or Universal it was nonetheless quite good fun. We took in a number of the attractions although Chris did not want to go on any of the thrill rides. We did enjoy the Duelling Pirates show and sat and watched the lunatics on the Sky Screamer – a huge arch 250 feet high on which riders lie in a harness, get hoisted up high and then drop and swing, reaching speeds of up to 70 mph. It was an extremely hot day, temperatures where over 105° F and after a couple of hours Chris wanted to move on and do something else, especially in the shade or air-conditioned buildings.

From the MGM we crossed the road to New York, New York and walked through the casino, laid out like Manhattan streets and visited the Coney Island funfair, complete with roller-coaster, on the third floor of the hotel. The fair was made up mainly of side-shows; ball throwing, hook-a-duck, darts, target shooting, that sort of thing. Film of the moment was '101 Dalmatians' and one of the side-shows, get a ball in a jar, offered a toy Dalmatian puppy as a prize. Chris set his eye on one. After several attempts he had failed to score, Dad and Mum did no better. One last go and with the disguised help of the attendant (who by now must have felt sorry for Chris) he got a ball in the bowl and was triumphantly awarded Dipstick the Dalmatian. As Annette said after, it would have been cheaper to just buy one, but it probably wouldn't have meant as much or been as much fun!. From New York we went back in time to a mediaeval castle, Excalibur, complete with wandering minstrels and ladies in period dress. Even the drinks were served in replica pewter or earthenware vessels. Of course, the main attraction, and hardly mediaeval, was the casino. No matter what the time of day (or night) the casinos in all the hotels seemed to be really busy. Moving on from the Excalibur through a covered, air-conditioned walkway, we left behind old England and moved on to ancient Egypt and the Luxor hotel. The Luxor is a giant pyramid, guarded by enormous Sphinx and has numerous Egyptian artefacts on display. I never did satisfy myself whether they were genuine or not, but even so it did prove quite an educational visit. Chris was fascinated by the diagrams showing the interior of the great pyramids in the Valley of the Kings and suggested that we should go there on holiday. Not, I have to say, well received by Mum or Dad, imagine pushing the chair across all that sand!

We had an earlyish night as the next day we had a long drive ahead of us, and what for me, promised to be one of the highlights. Having left Las Vegas we headed south for Boulder City and then the Hoover Dam. The Dam itself is approached down a windy road and provides the way to cross the Colorado River. It is an incredible sight and having crossed over it and passed out of Nevada and into Arizona we stopped at a viewing spot to gaze at this amazing man made structure. From the dam it was a 70 mile drive across desert to Kingman, where we stopped at a small diner for lunch. It was then onto the Interstate and due east for Williams, a mere 120 miles, and following much of the famous Route 66. From Williams it was due north, about 60 miles, through the Kaibab Forest to Tusayan, where our hotel, the Squire Inn, was located.

Once we checked in we took the short drive to the location of one of the seven natural wonders of the world, the Grand Canyon. The approach is through thick forest that suddenly opens out close to one of the viewing points. This being America there is a large car park so I pulled in and parked. As there were no signs it was unclear how far from the Canyon we actually were, so I jumped out saying I'd go and check. It didn't take me long, I walked no more than 20 yards through the trees surrounding the car park. If I'd walked 21 yards I would have fallen in. The view was absolutely stunning, breathtaking. No words can adequately describe what you see and that first visual impact remains with you forever. I ran back to the car, desperate to share what I'd seen with Annette and Chris. I got the wheelchair out of the back of the car and opened the passenger door.

"Come on mate, come and see this," I said excitedly.

"No, its OK, I can see it from here," came the less than enthusiastic reply.

This was just not true, all you could see were trees. Frustration over came me. I grabbed Chris by the lapels of his shirt and through clenched teeth said, "You've not come all this way to sit in a bloody car and not see one of the world's most wonderful sights."

The look of astonishment on his face said it all.

"That'll do," intervened the voice of reason, "of course he wants to see it, don't you love?" And with that I lifted him out and into his chair. Chris being Chris once he felt hard done to would set an expression on his face and it wouldn't change, no matter what. So, with Chris wearing a stern look, we broke through the tree line and there before us was this awesome view. There was no way at this point in time he was going to admit that he was impressed, but you could tell by the way his eyes danced and sparkled that he was looking at a wondrous sight, underlined by a little smile on his face.

Having taken the photos and gazed at the view from several different points along the rim we returned to the car and moved on to Yavapai Point to admire another view. A short drive around the Grand Canyon village enabled us to see one of the giant steam engines of the Grand Canyon Railroad. We had been advised to watch the sun set over the Canyon so we returned to Mather Point, our first stop, and took up position on one of the outcrops. As sunset approached the crowds grew, it soon became obvious why. As the sun sinks in the West it highlights the rocks of the canyon sides which seem to change colour as the sun settles lower, a magical moment, and yes, even Chris was impressed! Perhaps coming all the way had been worth it after all.

We had decided to eat in the hotel and chose the Coronado Room, as the other restaurant served Mexican influenced meals "I'm not eating that muck," said the hot dog king. The Coronado Room turned out to be a good choice, the food was very good, a reasonable number of diners and added to that there was live entertainment by a guy called Mac MacDonald. Mac was a guitar and keyboard playing, singing comic who was very entertaining. He started off performing a number of Cat Stevens and James Taylor songs, moving on to a number of pop standards before asking for audience participation to help him perform 'YMCA' by Village People. Sitting behind us was a family group from Canada and the younger members of the family were persuaded to take part. Taking part meant not only singing, but also wearing silly hats and dancing. Chris was very amused and made a number of amusing asides about the quality of the dancing and singing which had everyone laughing. Following this, ladies in the audience were invited to perform the Macarina. Annette, who is not keen on showing off, threatened death on Chris if he mentioned her name. You could see him mulling over the risks of this, but retaining his head on his shoulders won over watching Mum's embarrassment. Chris was really getting into the swing of things and providing vocal *encouragement* to those on the stage.

Mac moved on to singing comedy songs, using themes provided by the audience. The first *victims* of this were the Canadians (who were also well into the swing of the evening). Mac then asked for a boy's name. "Chris," came the shout from the Canadians, pointing to our table.

"I know a boy who's name is Chris; Eye de eye de eye de O!" sang Mac, "He's got a chair that's really a wiz; Eye de eye de eye de O!"

"Right, now I need a girl's name."

"Melanie," I shouted.

"Shut up, Dad, shut up!"

Mac was in full swing referring to girlfriends, holding hands and kissing. The oohs, aahs and laughs flowed from the table behind us. The cheeks flushed, the eyes blazed, "Shut up, shut up. She's not my girlfriend," protested Chris, "she's just a friend". But it was no good, it was drowned out by the music and laughter.

"Right, I want to go!"

After a bit of persuasion from Mum the 'victim' did eventually calm down, but the face was set again.

Mind you revenge, they say, is sweet. "I need the two best dancers in the room," announced Mac. "DAD," came the loud and clear shout from next to me, Mum's glare sufficient to save her. With the verbal encouragement of our Canadian friends I had no alternative but to head for the stage. A girl from near the bar was pushed forward by her friends. "Right," said Mac, "we need the right costume." Pulling out a Viking helmet for my partner and a foam chicken head for me. Oh yes, revenge is sweet.

"Now, the two best dancers in the Squire Inn will perform .... the world famous ..... Chicken Dance." Great howls of laughter, through which Chris's laugh, could be very clearly heard. Oh yes, revenge is very sweet. With that we were into the dance and total prat status was assured. Of course, Chris ensured that this was captured for posterity by encouraging Annette to take a number of photos. The other thing is you don't realise that the area around the Grand Canyon is 5-6,000 feet above sea level and any physical exercise is quite tiring, especially Chicken Dances. Oh yes, revenge is very, very sweet.

Chris was very adept at identifying the various facilities offered by hotels and soon after we had arrived at the Squire Inn he had announced to us that the "hotel has a Family Recreation Area with video games". As there was no time for a visit when we arrived, as soon as breakfast was out of the way it could be put off no longer. The Family Recreation Area was located in the basement and was almost a little street, featuring as it did a few shops as well as various electronic and table based games. The shops turned out to be of interest to Annette, especially as one was a 'Full Service Salon'. So while Chris and Dad sampled the electronic fantasy world Annette settled on having her hair done, much to Chris's disbelief. Now game playing takes less time than hair doing and so we finished before Mum. Chris was ready to go and was frustrated that Annette was only halfway through. We passed the time away, with some huffing and puffing, by looking at the Grand Canyon Mural in the hotels rear lobby and the various gift shops. Eventually, Annette re-appeared looking less than pleased and sporting a Tammy Whynette like hairstyle, which was heavily lacquered. Chris looked at me, I looked at him. I could sense a comment coming on from Chris, but aware that this might not be well received or prudent quickly whispered, "Don't say a word. Just don't". How we managed not to laugh I'm not sure and we beat a hasty retreat down the passage to compose ourselves.

It was then time to set off on the long return drive to Las Vegas, while the round trip was very long, it was well worth it, even Chris said he'd like to see the Canyon again. With a couple of stops along the way the trip took us a 5 hours before we returned to the MGM Grand. This time we had a room on the 13th floor of the Emerald Tower which gave good views down the Strip. Our visit this time to Vegas was just a stop over as we were flying out the following morning, so we revisited some of the places we had seen before, which included Denny's and the MGM's food court for ice cream.

We needed to be up early the following morning to get to the airport, drop off Annette and Chris, drop the car off at the car rental depot, hop on the shuttle bus, and then get checked in. Once that was out of the way we got breakfast in a coffee shop and watched the aeroplanes coming and going. Eventually, we were on our way to Chicago, and as we took off we got some great views over Las Vegas; the Strip and all those fabulous hotels.

"What a great place," said Chris, "I wouldn't mind coming here again."

The three-hour flight to Chicago was uneventful, but did provide us with contrasting sights of America, desert, high mountains, hills, prairie and farmland. Once landed we called the wheelchair accessible transport we had arranged. In a short time we were loaded up and on our way into the Windy City. Well not so much windy, as misty, although that didn't stop us getting our first glimpse of the John Hancock Tower (the world's 12th tallest building) and the Sears Tower (the world's tallest building[2]) actually appearing above the mist. Our hotel for the next couple of nights was the Hilton and Towers on Michigan Avenue. Now when we'd left Las Vegas the temperature was pushing up towards 100° F and we were dressed accordingly, Chicago was a little cooler. As we pulled up in front of the hotel a doorman wearing an overcoat, cape and top hat greeted us. We unloaded from the van and headed towards the hotel door in our casual holiday gear, in the company of other guests, the men attired in military dress uniform and the ladies in evening dress. As we entered the lobby a string quartet, located on a stage halfway up the stairs, played. "Well," said Chris, "nice of them to put on a bit of a show for me."

Our room was not only huge, but afforded us good views across Chicago, of the 'El' (Chicago's elevated train system), and to the Sears Tower in one direction and to Soldier Field, the Shedd Aquarium and Meigs Field in the other.

"Meigs what?" asked Mum.

"Meigs Field," puffed Chris, "you fly out of it on Microsoft's Flight Sim."

"Oh, great!" responded Mum. Well, I guess to Chris it was, for here was his computer brought to life. He spent quite a lot of time watching the light aircraft taking off and flying out across the lake, complete with running commentary on plane type and pilot actions.

The next day, after breakfast in the hotel, we set off up Michigan Avenue to admire the sights and architecture of the American city which has more of the tallest buildings than anywhere else, or to go shopping. For the first time in nearly three weeks we also sampled rain, although it was only a brief shower. Having taken in the shops, including a number of computer shops were we bought some of the latest PC games, and sampled a number of Chicago coffee shops we headed back down Michigan Avenue. We then turned and followed the Chicago River along Wacker Drive, past the Marina Towers, scene of one of the famous stunts in the movie Bullit, and into Franklin and onto to the Sears Tower.

We had started the holiday by going to the top of a tall building and we brought the holiday to a close by going to the top of the World's Tallest Building - Chris had achieved another of his ambitions. The Skydeck viewing area is 1,353 feet above the ground and is reached in just over a minute in the express elevator, the views are stunning. With the aid of a map we were able to pick out most of the important Chicago buildings, watch planes come and go into O'Hare Airport and watch the cars on the Expressway. Most amazing was watching small planes and helicopters go by below you. It was starting to go dark now and Annette was keen to get back to the hotel before the light went. We had been warned about the beggars in New York, but had not seen any, but a guy *selling* postcards caught us unaware as we left the Sears Tower. Offering up the loose change in my pocket under the instructions of a nervous Annette, we took the card and beat a hasty retreat all the way to the hotel. As Chris was to observe,

[2] The Sears Tower was still the world's tallest building at the time of our visit, it has since been overtaken by the Petronas Towers in Kuala Lumpa.

"I've never seen Mum move so fast."
In the hotel we had dinner in the Pavillion Café where a very pleasant middle-aged Italian waiter served us. He took quite a shine to Chris, chatting to him about the sights of Chicago and was fascinated by Chris's tales of the previous three weeks. "Hey, you'v-a seen more of this country in-a three weeks than I've-a seen in 30 years," he said in his soft accent, "Your-a very lucky boy." After we finished the main course, the waiter returned and asked if we wanted dessert. Chris asked if he could have ice cream. The waiter asked what flavour he would like, listing a whole raft of different tastes. Chris couldn't make his mind up, was it vanilla, should it be chocolate, what about mint? Eventually, he settled on vanilla, with chocolate sauce. When the waiter returned he brought with him the biggest bowl of ice cream you've ever seen, of vanilla, chocolate and mint, with chocolate sauce. Chris's eyes nearly popped out if his face. "A special bowl of-a ice cream-a for a special boy," said Chris's new friend. "Thank you very, very much," beamed Chris. At the end of the meal the waiter leant over to me and said the ice cream was not on the bill, it was his treat - what a lovely gesture. Chris was delighted and before we went he insisted on being taken over to the waiter so he could shake his hand. What a great way to end the holiday.

With the bags packed for the last time, we checked out and put the cases into store. We had time for some last minute shopping in the small arcade of shops in the hotel and to take a walk through Grant Park, opposite the hotel, and down to the shore of Lake Michigan. We'd booked the wheelchair accessible transport to pick us up at 2.00 p.m., in plenty of time to check in for the 6.00 p.m. flight and last minute shopping. In advance of 2.00 p.m. we were assembled in the hotel lobby waiting for the transport, and we waited and waited. As 3.00 p.m. approached I called the transport company, they insisted that the vehicle was booked for 4.00 p.m., but would endeavour to get it to us as soon as possible. As I'd used up all my small change I couldn't get any refreshments, but the hotel's security man took pity on us and arranged for drinks from the bar. I knew that it would be touch and go for checking in, so I called the airline to tell them of the problem. They were quite understanding and said that there would be no problem checking in later. Eventually, the vehicle arrived and with the help of our friend the security man we were loaded up and away. The driver was a tall, athletic black guy, who on being told our dilemma set about getting us to the airport in double quick time. As the Freeway was very busy this involved him taking exits and then rushing up the entrance slip roads, it was just like a scene from a movie and Chris loved it. The driver was actually a student doing work to supplement his income and he was keen to hear about the UK and Europe as he was saving up to come over on holiday. Chris did a good job of selling Chester and was also able to give his new friend a good briefing on York and London.

We arrived at the airport at about 5.00 p.m., said good-bye to the driver, who Chris insisted was given a good tip, even if it meant using his money and rushed to the check in. With the formalities completed we had to run through the Terminal to the Gate, with Chris shouting "Excuse me!", in a scene reminiscent of 'Home Alone 2'. Indeed, whenever we watched the video later, Chris would always recall our mad dash. We just made the Gate, as it was about to close, I realised that Chris hadn't been to the loo. With a little bit of negotiation I managed to persuade the airline staff to give me 5 minutes, I think it was the quickest wee Chris had ever had! When we got on the plane it was packed, apparently a lot of the passengers had been held over from the previous evening when the airport had been closed due to an impending tornado, which had then not materialised. Because we had checked in late our three seats were in different parts of the aircraft, but with the help of the stewardesses and two very helpful passengers (who got our window seats) we managed to sit together. No sooner had we sat down and strapped in than the plane pushed back and we were off.

Chicago is a very busy airport (the busiest airport in the world) and as Chris informed everybody sitting around him that it has the more aircraft movements than any other airport in the world. The queue of planes to get to the runway was like commuter roads at rush hour. As we took off on one runway there were planes on two others taking off at the same time. It was as Chris pointed out 'fantastic'. We settled into the flight heading Eastwards and home. As normal Chris did not sleep and showed no signs of doing so. Fortunately, the film was one he quite liked - '101 Dalmatians'. By now he knew nearly all the words, particularly those from the amusing sketches and despite 'encouragement' from Mum to "not be so noisy, as people wanted to sleep" he insisted on speaking the parts, including all the vocal intonation, much to the amusement of the lady sitting across the aisle from us.

The remainder of the flight passed uneventfully and we landed in Manchester just after 8.00 a.m. Once at the air jetty we had to wait, as is usual, for all the other passengers to disembark before we could. At check-in at Chicago I had confirmed that we would require the aisle wheelchair to disembark and Chris's chair at the door of the plane. So after the last passenger got off we expected to follow. We had got on or off an aeroplane a total of eleven times during the previous three weeks, the service we and particularly Chris had received had been excellent from Heathrow onwards and yet here we were again in Manchester. The stewardesses made a phone call, and then another. Eventually, about fifteen minutes after we had pulled up to the jetty a member of the ground crew arrived and called Chris's name. We signalled our location. "The wheelchair is available," she said.

"Where?" I enquired.

"Just there," she replied, pointing to a normal wheelchair by the galley.

"But, we expected an aisle chair," I pointed out.

Taking a piece of paper from her pocket which she examined, she announced "It doesn't request one here." Well that's OK then.

"How is my son expected to get from here," I said, nodding at his seat, "to there? Unfortunately, he is unable to walk."

"I couldn't half do with a wee," added Chris, who had become quite adept at not going to the loo on a plane.

With that she was gone, reappearing over five minutes later with the correct wheelchair and an operator. Chris was soon off the plane, but not into his own chair, no that was to be collected in the Baggage Hall, but into an airport wheelchair. The stewardesses said good-bye, Chris thanked them for all their help and with that we were off to the nearest loo.

We collected our cases, switched chairs and moved through to the Arrivals Hall

where we'd arranged to meet big Chris. Unlike previous years there was no sign of him.
"Don't worry," said Chris, "he'll be here soon, he's probably just been held up on the Motorway."
"It'll give us time to get a cup of tea," said Annette.
A pot of tea later and there was still no sign of big Chris.
"He won't have gone to the wrong terminal will he?" I asked.
"Of course not!" snorted Chris, "he's much too clever for that."
Another half-hour passed by and still he didn't appear. Now I'd been fully organised for various eventualities with contact numbers etc., but not for this.
"Give Chris a call," said Annette. Ha, if only we could remember the Bolton's number, and much to the annoyance of my family, I (not them) didn't have it written down.
"Phone Nana or Auntie Ju," suggested Chris, "they can look it up in the phone book."
With the Bolton number in our possession I made the call.
"Hello, Anne," I said, as the phone was answered.
"Oh, hello," she replied, "where are you?"
"Manchester Airport......"
"Oh, my god!" Anne cried.
"I told Chris it was today you were back, but he said it was tomorrow. Don't panic one of us will come and get you now."
I returned to Annette and Chris to explain.
"Well, Palion," offered Chris, "you must have written it down wrong."
Despite the clear evidence that **I** hadn't made a mistake it was no use arguing.

Mum, Dad, Tigger and Chris, Disneyland. 10th May 1997

The presentation by Emma Cunliffe of Helsby Golf Clubs powered wheelchair. 12th June 1997

The gang at the Heswall Boys Camp. August 1998

The end of holiday photo with the van and what would turn out to be Chris's last day in Florida. 6th October 1998

Cooking With Lorraine, preparing the ill-fated Chocolate Cake. June 1999

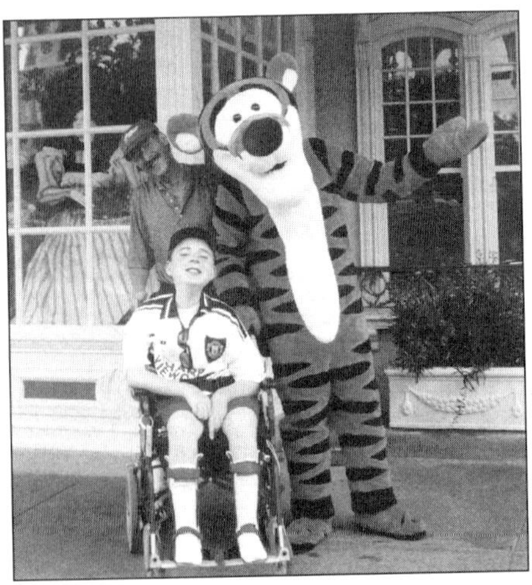

Sure enough Tigger was 'receiving' guests, Chris couldn't miss an opportunity to shake paws and Tigger duly obliged. Dad had to get in the act as well! 1st October 1998

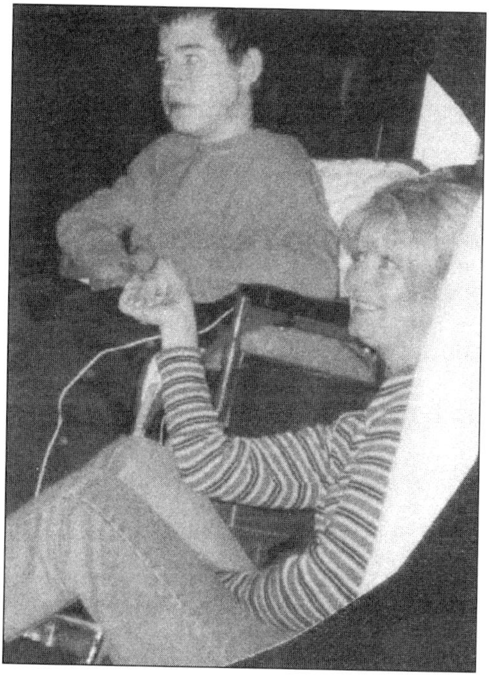

Chris and Pauline,
Hope House

David and Chris –
Mates Always.
20th May 2000

CHAPTER TWELVE
(Hurricanes and 'Killer' Wheelchairs)

The rainy days a man saves for
usually seem to arrive during his vacation.

Anon

For 1998 it was back to Florida for our holiday, the prospect of renewing old friendships with the characters cheered Chris up and he was really looking forward to going. Rather than spend two weeks in Orlando we had decided on a week on the coast, giving us an opportunity to 'see the sights'. We had therefore booked a Fly-Drive through Travel City Direct and after fairly extensive research selected a hotel in St. Petersburg and a Disney Hotel that provided suitable accommodation bearing in mind Chris's special needs. Unfortunately, much to everyone's disappointment there was no room at Disney's Dixie Landings or indeed other Disney hotels in the week we wanted. So after more research we selected the Hyatt in Kissimmee.

Big Chris provided the traditional transport to the airport, albeit in our Galaxy. We checked in for the scheduled depart of 12.00 p.m. on an Airtours flight. However, due to technical problems we did not leave until 2.30 p.m. For a change, we did not have any problems boarding the aircraft, as the aisle wheelchair was available. We had seats close to the front of the plane, with Chris and I in the window seats and Annette just across the aisle. Keeping Chris occupied was key to a successful flight and we were again well prepared with music cassettes, games and books, including his collection of aircraft and I-Spy books. During the flight Chris had noticed a chap sitting in front of Annette listening to a short wave radio and questioned what he was doing. I suggested that he was listening to the radio transmissions between planes, but was not really sure. Soon after this the chap turned around and began chatting to Chris about aircraft. To make conversation easier he swapped places with Annette, and this also gave me a chance to snatch a rest. However, I kept one ear open to the chat, which at times was getting quite 'heavy' regarding aircraft type and engines. When arguing Chris would become quite forceful and would stand his ground firmly, but generally politely. I had learnt to my cost that generally if he took this position it was because he was right (or thought that he was!). The discussion revolved around a particular aircraft, the Israeli Kfir, and whether it was the same as the South African Atlas Cheetah. Chris's new friend was adamant that there was no connection, Chris however was (strongly) of the opinion that the Cheetah was based on the Kfir, the main difference being the Kfir used General Electric afterburning turbojets and the Cheetah used SNECMAs. When he started quoting engine thrust and then the armaments I started to think he must be right. The discussion continued, Chris gradually raising his voice to make his point, despite admonishment from Annette. At this point I stealthily picked up the book on combat aircraft and found the entries for the planes in question. In many ways it was pointless, of course he was right, right down to the thrust figures he'd quoted. I wish I had a memory like that. When we eventually landed at Sandford airport as usual we had to wait for the other passengers to disembark. A gentleman, who had been sitting behind us, paused as he walked past to say, "Well done, young man, it's a pleasure to hear someone so knowledgeable about their chosen subject".

"Thanks," said Chris, with a little smile of satisfaction..

Sandford is much easier to navigate than Orlando International as it is much smaller, serving mainly charter flights, so once through Immigration and Baggage Collection you cross the road and your in the Rental Car depot. So much easier with the wheelchair. As part of the Fly Drive we had upgraded to an MPV, and it wasn't long before we had the keys to a white Plymouth Voyager and were loading up. Owing to the delay at Manchester we were late arriving and by the time we left the Rental Car depot it was dark. It was a good job that we had reservations at the Holiday Inn Nikki Bird in Kissimmee otherwise we would have been very late arriving in St. Petes Beach. Sandford is about a 45-minute drive north of the tourist area of Orlando and can be reached via Interstate 4 or the much quieter Central Florida Greeneway 417. As it was dark and I needed to get use to the car and driving on the right again we chose the latter and set off. We were making good progress, when just as we were approaching a junction this black shape shot up from the side of the road and made us all jump. I braked and swerved and ended up going down the slip road (not what I planned) with both Annette and Chris asking, "what the hell was that?" As I got my pounding heart back in control I replied, "I think, it was a bloody big bird, perhaps an owl".

"Well, it's a bloody good job you didn't hit it or we'd have no windscreen," pointed out Chris, with a fair degree of relief in his voice.

"Anyway where are we?" asked Annette.

After quickly weighing up the road signs I worked out that we were on the John Young Parkway and by following that we would eventually join the Irlo Bronson Highway on which the Holiday Inn Nikki Bird was located. We drove on passing across several roads and still looking for Irlo Bronson. Eventually the line of streetlights ceased and I knew I had gone too far, so remembering the safety tips I pulled into a well-lit garage to check the map.

"Ah, I know what the problem is," I said after a few moments.

"Well, what?" said a voice in the back.

"Irlo Bronson becomes Vine Street and we passed that two or three miles back. So we need to go back and along that," I explained.

"Plonker," came the supportive response from Chris.

We retraced our route and this time reached our objective successfully, checking in around 10.00 p.m. local time (3.00 a.m. UK time). A long, long day.

After such a long day we were up late the following morning, checked out and headed just down the road to the Sizzler for breakfast. Just as we were finishing and about to leave who should walk in but Ray Hall (a colleague from work), his wife Sue, and daughters Jennifer and Rachel. We knew they were in Florida, as we had planned to meet up during our second week, but this was a pleasant surprise. Chris was keen to hear what they had been up to during their first week. Having caught up with their news we set off for the coast. Our room at the Howard Johnson was on the fourth floor and provided a great view across the beach and out across the Gulf. Chris was not interested in the view, he was keener to check out the facilities on the TV. While flipping through the channels, he came across the Weather Channel that was just in the process of providing an update on the progress of Hurricane Georges as it headed towards the Florida Keys. There then followed an interrogation of a less than fully informed father and whether he thought we would be in danger. Being not much wiser on the subject than the interrogator I was unable to answer the questions, but managed to convince him that we were not about to get blown away.

Dinner that evening at a nearby Denny's (Chris's choice) was followed by drinks at the Hotel's Beach Bar. After a short time Chris insisted that we move in doors as there was the odd rumble of thunder and he was convinced the hurricane was about to descend on us. So while Annette and I sat on the balcony, Chris studied form on the Weather Channel.

The next morning once we got Chris up and we'd had breakfast, on the suggestion of Chris we were down to the pool for a swim and a bit of a sun bathe. As the water in the pool was warm Chris really enjoyed the time. By this stage he had lost a lot of his confidence in the water, as we no longer went swimming regularly, but we had perfected a way whereby I half held and half carried him and this enabled me to pull him around the pool. It was great fun if a bit tiring, but with a bit of imagination we could be a powerboat or a supertanker or even a Grand Prix car! Chris made friends with a young girl, Jasmine ("like Princess Jasmine in Aladdin," said Chris) who amazed us all with her ability despite having only one leg. The sun was very hot and to make sure that we didn't over do it on our first day we retired to the room to get dressed. Annette suggested we went for a drive, so after a quick reference of the maps we pointed the car south towards Sarasota. This suited Chris as it meant we had to go over the Sunshine Skyway, a highly impressive four-mile long bridge that soars 183 feet above Tampa Bay, and carries I275. "That's a lovely bridge," was how Chris summed it up.

Our plan was to have a brief drive around and return later in the week to see the sights properly. We idled through Bradenton, and drove past the Ringling Museum and Bellm's Car Museum before reaching Sarasota. We stopped for a drink at the Square Mall, before returning to the car to head back to the hotel. By now the bright blue sky had been replaced by ugly black clouds, which as we drove along got darker and darker, before depositing their contents in a huge torrent. This was the cue for Chris to enter panic mode, as again he was convinced that we were about to be engulfed by the hurricane. The rain eventually eased off and we made good progress up I75, along the I275 and back over the Sunshine Skyway with its huge sail like structures, "This really is a lovely bridge," said a now relaxed Chris. Into St. Pete's Beach, past the pink coloured Don Cesar Hotel, a short drive and into the car park of the HoJo. As we drove up the car park I thought it strange how few cars there were. Maybe they'd all gone out for the evening, as it was now about 6.30 p.m. We got out of the car and headed for the door, "Its very quiet," remarked Annette. The reason then became clear, for there on the door was a notice.

'HURRICANE WARNING. MANDATORY EVACUATION ORDER. St. PETERSBURG BEACH EMERGENCY COUNCIL'.

"I told you, I told you," shouted Chris, "you wouldn't believe me. Hurricane Georges is coming this way. Oh God, what'll happen to us?"

"Look, just calm down, you go up to the room with Mum and start packing and I'll

go down to the Reception and see what we can do," I said calmly, although my heart was beating quite quickly as I tried to rationalise what the options were. The Receptionist told me that a mandatory evacuation order meant just that and apart from one other family we were the only visitors left. As we were travelling independently, I was told that making alternative arrangements was our responsibility, although there would be no cancellation charge for the remaining nights! In the Reception there was a Howard Johnson hotel directory, so with that tucked under my arm I returned to our room. Annette was into the swing of packing and Chris was watching the Weather Channel. We agreed that the best thing was to move in land and the easiest place was Orlando or its adjacent areas. The first option was to see if the Hyatt had vacancies, but if not Annette and I quickly made a short list of hotels from the Howard Johnson brochure. I called the Hyatt, but it was full, so the back up plan was put into action.
"What will we do if we can't get a room?" asked the increasingly pessimistic Chris.
"We'll drive towards Orlando and stop at a few places until we get a room," I said, hoping it wouldn't come to that. I called the Howard Johnson central reservations, the first hotel was full, the second choice was full, I could feel my heart starting to beat faster, and maybe Chris would be right after all! Our third choice, the Howard Johnson Maingate, in Kissimmee West, had room. "Are there are handicapped accessible rooms available?" I enquired. After a short pause, "No Sir, this looks like the last available room. Orlando's very busy tonight."
"I'll take it," I said quickly. It suddenly occurred to me that everybody else had the same idea as us, and if Chris was right from watching the TV the best part of the Florida Keys and the Gulf Coast had been evacuated.

By now Annette had repacked the cases and we bid farewell to our 'home' of one night. We loaded up the Voyager and set off for Orlando at about 7.40 p.m. We wound our way back through a near deserted St. Pete's Beach and joined the I75 and headed towards Orlando. Just beyond Tampa the I75 heads north to Gainesville, the I4 branches off and heads towards the home of Mickey Mouse. The Interstate was absolutely packed, on previous trips along it traffic had been quite sparse, especially once clear of the Tampa area, but on this night both lanes were nose to tail and making progress at a steady 50 mph. Quite scary.

We were making good progress and had covered about three-quarters of the journey when Chris pointed out that the fuel tank seemed to be getting empty. In my rush to get away I had forgotten about petrol. Now American Interstates are not like our Motorways as they don't have Services, but generally signs indicating Gas Stations, Motels and food outlets on normal roads that cross the Interstate. However, this being America the distances between junctions can be quite long, so on top of hurricanes and evacuation Chris had something else to worry about. I could sense him watching the fuel gauge and gradually stiffening up as it fell lower and lower. He knew, as he'd undertaken his usual practice of reading the Owners Handbook on the first night, that there was a low fuel light and as soon as this blinked on he pointed out, with just an edge of concern in his voice that, "The light means the fuel tanks nearly empty, you need to fill up as there is only about fuel for 10 miles". Fortunately, just a few miles later a junction with a Gas Station very nearby appeared in view. The eagle eyes had picked this up through the dark and so with a degree of relief he said, "There's a petrol station, you'd better stop." Well as if I was going to drive past.

Having filled up we completed the journey to the HoJo arriving about 9.30 p.m. Kissimmee was absolutely teeming with cars and people, we'd never seen it so busy. We headed for Reception and while checking in another family who had been staying in the same hotel as us in St. Pete's came in and asked about vacancies, only to be told that the 'inn was full'. "Good job you phoned up, Palion".

Although it was getting late we realised that we had not eaten for a while and so under Chris's instruction we set off for .... Denny's. Although there was a bit of a queue it wasn't long before we were shown to a table and a late dinner was under way. The waitress was very pleasant and made a fuss of Chris. He was keen to share the excitement of the day and explained in an almost heroic manner that we had been evacuated from the coast because of the Hurricane, the waitress getting a bit more of the story on each visit to the table. Chris oblivious to the fact that many other people in the restaurant were probably in the same boat as us.

After a long and tiring day and a late night we were understandably up late the following morning. This in its self was no problem, but getting breakfast was, as every place seemed to have big queues. Anyway, Denny's (again) came to the rescue, but various combinations of cereal, bacon, sausage, pancakes, maple syrup ("Ugh, I don't know how you eat that stuff Dad!"), eggs, coffee and hot tea saw us all well sorted. Chris was disappointed that his friend from the previous evening wasn't there, so he passed some of the time by retelling the story to our new waitress. As it was almost mid day we decided that we would spend the rest of the day taking in the various sights and stopping here and there. The weather was also a bit changeable, sun and cloud, cloud and sun, although it was pretty warm. After brunch, as I guess that's what we had had, we set off in the car for a drive round the Disney World roads before arriving at Disney Village Market Place. We always enjoyed a visit, as although it is a shopping and eating place, it does have that Disney *feel* about it and is quite enjoyable. After walking around for awhile we stopped at the Gourmet Pantry for a drink. Located just by are the 'dancing waters', a set of 30 or 40 water jets that are set in the floor that burst out and form patterns. This feature attracts kids like honey attracts bees. After a short time of watching this Chris decided that he wanted to join in. Now having the wheelchair this is not very practical, but we could still have some fun. So with Annette's warning of "Don't you dare get him wet" ringing in our ears we walked up to the fountains. By watching carefully you can eventually work out the sequence of the water jets, so that then allowed me to push Chris in to the wet zone and back out again without him actually getting wet. This satisfied Chris for a while, but then he began insisting that he got wet. Caught between the Chris 'I want to get wet' and Annette 'don't you dare get him wet" opposing schools of thought I took the only course of action and said, "no, chance!". A bit of moaning later and a few risky moves, which got Chris's legs a bit wet I retreated to where Annette was sitting. "Look at his legs and splints, they're soaking."

"Oh, it's only a little damp, they'll dry out in no time."

"Anyway it was really good fun and I don't mind," said Chris, laughing.
"Well I do! And your father should know better." Cue a fit of the giggles from Chris and I.

From the Market Place we walked through a generally deserted Pleasure Island Disney West Side where we had a walk around the shops, one in particular catching Chris eye. The Guitar Gallery was full, as its name suggested, of guitars - Fenders, Les Paul and Rickenbacher, with costs ranging from a few hundred dollars to a lot of thousands. For some time Chris had had a fascination with guitars, which was rooted in listening to the likes of Mark Knopfler and Chris Rea, as well as using Microsoft Musical Instruments and downloading samples off the Internet. But to see some of these classic guitars up close was quite a thrill.

The effect of the hurricane was becoming obvious with lower temperatures, heavy cloud and frequent rain showers. Not really conducive for walking around theme parks. So the next day after breakfast we drove down I4 to Polk City and the Fantasy of Flight museum. The museum is owned by Kermit Weekes a millionaire with a passion for aircraft. Most of the planes in the museum are airworthy and are flown regularly during the year. The entrance to the museum is a recreation of a 1950's airport complete with a check-in desk and café. To enter the display part of the museum guests have to walk through the fuselage of a B17 and out through the rear door as sounds and lights create the impression that you are a parachutist. The museum is a combination of set tableau depicting particular aspects of aerial warfare and static displays of planes. Chris had built up quite an interest in the Memphis Belle, the famous World War II Boeing B17 Flying Fortress bomber, having watched the film that starred Matthew Modine and Harry Cornick. So he was really excited when one of the tableau included a B17, and while not Memphis Belle, gave him the opportunity to see such a plane up close. Guests where able to walk through the plane and see the bomb bay and flight deck. Of course World War 2 bombers are not wheelchair accessible, so apart from being able to peer in through the door, that was as far as Chris could get. In situations such as this he never showed any disappointment he just accepted that's how things were. But he was keen to know about the inside, so Dad was dispatched through the door to observe the interior and then report back in great detail and answer questions on what had been seen.

The static displays were held in one hangar and included a full size replica of 'The Spirit of St. Louis', as flown by Charles Lindbergh across the Atlantic, a wonderful Shorts Sunderland airboat (absolutely massive) and a Supermarine Spitfire. The latter was one of Chris's favourite planes and he was quite well read on them. While admiring the plane one of the museum guides walked over.
"Good morning folks," he said, "are there any questions you'd like to ask about our exhibits?"
"Does Kermit Weekes fly all of these planes?" asked Chris.
"Yes, he does, certainly those that can fly," said the guide and he proceeded to describe a number of adventures Kermit Weekes had had in various planes.
"Flying the Spitfire must be great," said Chris.
"Yes, he particularly enjoys flying that, I heard him say that it is the best plane he's ever flown. This is a Mark 9," said the guide.

There was a pause, a frown came on Chris's face, a further pause as he weighed up whether to speak or not and then he said, "No, it's not a Mark 9." Oh, God I could feel my self thinking, there's this guy who works here saying one thing and a thirteen year old saying something else.
"Oh, yes it's a Mark 9," came the response.
"No, I'm sorry," said Chris, "but this is a Mark 16."
"I believe it to be a Mark 9," said a now slightly miffed museum guide.
"Well, if it was a Mark 9 it would have a three blade prop, not a four like this. And this has a bubble canopy and clipped wings, neither of which the Mark 9 had and the engine is different " stated Chris. I had no idea if he was right, but if he took this firm a stance you argued with him at your peril[1].
The guide retreated, "Are you sure it's a Mark 16?" I asked. "Definitely," came the unwavering answer. We carried on our visit admiring the other exhibits and were just about to leave when our friend the guide homed in on us. "I've been to check on the Spitfire," he said. Wait for it I thought - a Mark 9. "Your right young fella, it is a Mark 16." A broad grin of triumph spread across Chris's face.
"Thought it was," he said.
From the museum we had a drive around the Florida countryside passing by Cypress Gardens and Bok Tower, before returning to the hotel, where we discovered the delights of the Tikki Bar and Chris struck up a friendship with the barman, Ed. It was while Chris was telling Ed about being evacuated that the heavens opened and it just bucketed down. The paths went from stone dry to like small streams faster than you could say "downpour" and very quickly the straw roof of the Tikki Bar started leaking. Ed found some big sheets of plastic behind the bar and kindly covered Chris over so he wouldn't get wet. It was a good job that Ed provided the cover as it kept raining *stair rods* for 20 - 25 minutes and by staying where he was Chris would have got soaked and if we tried to move him he'd have got soaked as well. As was often the case Chris was quite happy to make a drama out of an event, although there was an element of comedy this time.

The next day the weather was much better, although there was still quite a lot of cloud, so we visited Universal Studios. Since our last visit there had been a number of changes, car parking was now in a huge multi-storey built in preparation for the opening of the new Islands of Adventure. While we were there Islands was just a building site, but we were able to visit a preview show and it promised to be an exciting place to visit.

Our first port of call was the Twister show, based on the movie of the same name. The pre-show entertainment, clips of the film and how it was made, were shown as you queued up through a house that has been supposedly hit by a tornado. You then enter what looks like a small mid-west township and stand on the veranda of a shop looking out across the street and into the prairie beyond. The lights then dim and the wind begins to blow, in the distance (projected against a backcloth) you witness a tornado approaching, the wind gets stronger and then a real twister appears moving down the street. Buildings collapse, telegraph poles get blown over, cows fly through the air, it starts to rain and then the verandas on which you stand shakes, quite violently as the twister passes by. It is a fantastic piece of theatre, and very lifelike. Too lifelike for Annette, who

1 Please note, if these facts are incorrect then this is down to my recollection.

was close to screaming, and Chris who was shouting "Oooh, oooh! I don't think this is very good, oooh, oooh." Funny, when I suggested going to see it again later in the day neither Chris nor Annette were that keen!

There were of course other things to do, including Earthquake. Chris was quite keen to go on Earthquake, a reconstruction of San Francisco's metro, as he recalled the last time we'd visited. It proved to be a bit too rough for Chris and it ended up with Annette having to hold on to him tightly to stop his head flopping around too much. Chris was a bit quiet after that, but soon perked up as we sat at a pavement café and watched the Blues Brothers perform a selection of their numbers. We thought about going on Jaws, Annette thought it would be too rough, but Chris wanted to do it and wouldn't be persuaded differently. The majority of the ride is fine, the boat gets knocked about a little, but right at the end the boat lurches quite considerably as the 'shark' attacks. It was much more severe than we recalled from the last time we went on the ride and Annette again had to grip hold of Chris, although this time she nearly choked him through fear of the 'shark'! Chris and I went to watch the Wild West Stunt Show, which was really funny, especially the warm up which saw 'The Marx Brothers' take part in a water based slap-stick. This caused Chris great amusement until he almost became part of the show and then "it was stupid!"

The next day just for a change we had breakfast at Denny's, during which Chris's favourite waitress got her apron strings caught up in the handles of the wheelchair. As a result she nearly deposited breakfast on the floor, pointing out to her and our amusement "that wheelchairs could be very dangerous". We spent the rest of the morning in the hotel swimming pool and then later took in the shops. Chris didn't mind shopping on this occasion as he had his holiday money and was keen to spend it on computer games. As a result he increased his inventory by two flight sims (Jane's Fighters Anthology and Top Gun: Fire at Will) and the car race Carmageddon 2. The intricacies of the games he was able to share with his friend Ed, at the Tikki Bar, who appeared to be knowledgeable about such things when he could get a word in edge ways.

The danger of the hurricane, for Florida, was now passed (although the Dominican Republic was to suffer immense damage) and the weather was back to what you would expect in September. The day started hot and got hotter, just the weather to visit Disney's new theme park, Animal Kingdom. Our first stop was the 3D show, 'It's a Bug's Life', in the Tree of Life. Disney is usually very good as far as wheelchair access is concerned, but the queue for this show involved guests winding around the roots of the tree and turning sharp corners. It was an absolute nightmare and we were not the only group to voice criticism. At least the show was worth watching.

From there we headed off to see the Lion King show, this was Disney at its best, a mix of actors and larger than life puppets in a production featuring song, dance and acrobatics in the *round*. Disney also redeemed themselves as far as wheelchair access was concerned, special needs guests are allocated specific areas to ensure good views of all the action. All the main Lion King characters were involved; Simba standing proud on Pride Rock, Zazu, and the comical Timon and Pumbaa. Some of the songs were those featured in the film and this gave the audience the chance to sing along, something Chris jumped at. The whole show was uplifting and really great, colourful entertainment, enhanced by juggling and trapeze acts.

Following the show it was necessary to adjourn to the toilets, which were handily placed just across from the theatre exit. Chris and I got sorted quite quickly and were just leaving when walking up the path came Chris's favourite pair, Chip 'n' Dale. Needless to say these guys are being just a little bit naughty, playing the waste bins like drums and knocking the caps off passers by. Chris and I stopped to watch this free show, laughing at the various antics. It wasn't long before they noticed Chris and he soon became their 'target', his cap (which had Tigger on) was 'stolen' and prompted much jollity as they made fun of Tigger, they tickled Chris and ruffled is hair, all with much laughter from their 'target' and the assembled crowd. It was only the intervention from their *minder* that brought the fun to an end, so with 'high fives' from both chipmunks they were off and away, leaving their victim to regain his breath. Unfortunately, Annette who was still in the loo had missed all this, but did get a detailed replay from a breathless Chris.

One of the reasons Annette had been a little while in the toilets was that she wasn't feeling very well, and so after a brief family discussion we decided to return to the hotel so that she could have a rest. Keeping Chris both quiet and occupied at the hotel was going to be quite a challenge so Annette suggested that I took Chris back to Disney, which as we had Hopper passes was no problem. I gave Chris the choice of park and he selected EPCOT as he wanted to visit Innoventions and go on the computers and play the computer games. So, with Annette lying on the bed, I got Chris in the car and off we went to spend the afternoon playing computers. It was always fun to spend one on one time with Chris as conversation ranged from the serious to the funny across every topic, when he was with both of us he had one type of persona, but when alone with either of us he was very different. With me he was always talking about technology, facts and figures or debating the merit of this and that; with Annette his caring side came out chatting about people and what they were doing and when with both of us - well he was just Chris, often playing us off against one another. We had a good afternoon, interspersed with "I wonder if Mum's alright?" and "Its nothing serious is it?" When we returned to the hotel Annette was not in the room, Chris immediately feared the worse (he always was a bit of a pessimist), but I assured him there was nothing to panic about. Annette, who was by now feeling much better, was sitting by the Tikki Bar chatting to some other holidaymakers. Chris was much cheered by this and insisted on a hug from Mum, before explaining what we had been up to. Of course he also had to tell the other people that we had been evacuated from the coast.

The next day was moving day, leaving the HoJo in West Gate to go 5 miles down the road to the Hyatt in East Gate and what would have been our Orlando hotel had it not been for the intervention of the hurricane. Orlando and Kissimmee were still very busy with evacuated visitors and at most meal times finding a seat in a restaurant invariably meant queuing, despite the large number of venues in the surrounding area. This morning was no different and we had visited several before finding one that wasn't overly busy. After breakfast we were back at the hotel to pack, check out and say goodbye to Ed, the bar man. As it was still too early to check in to the Hyatt we drove over to Disney Village Market Place and enjoyed some more retail therapy, coffee at the Gourmet

Pantry, and of course more fun with the Dancing Waters, although this time we avoided getting wet and the resultant ear bashing.

Mid-afternoon we drove over to the Hyatt, located just off US192, across the road from the entrance to Celebration, the Disney township. The Hyatt is a pleasant, but sprawling hotel, with rooms in two storey buildings around swimming pools. Our room, on the ground floor, was very nice with good handicapped facilities including a roll-in shower. The hotel information guide indicated that a shower chair could be requested by calling housekeeping, so after a brief call we waited in anticipation of it being delivered. Sure enough, 10 or 15 minutes later there was a knock on the door, "Housekeeping," said the voice outside. Quick check through the security viewer and open the door. A uniformed worker held out a hand and passed me a small plastic object and said, as they turned and moved away, "Your shower cap, sir". I stood speechless, Annette burst out laughing and Chris simply said, "Prat". Another call to housekeeping, explaining the problem, which caused much amusement at the other end of the phone, resolved the problem.

We had arranged, prior to leaving the UK, to meet up with Ray Hall and his family. So after dinner at the nearby Ponderosa we drove over to their hotel, the Caribbean Beach Resort, in Disney World. Having parked the car we wandered through the shopping and restaurant area of the Resort, eventually locating Ray, Sue, Jennifer and Rachel sitting on the patio area by the swimming pool. They had been in Florida for two weeks and Chris was keen to find out what they had been doing since our chance meeting the previous week, enthusiastically swapping notes about the various theme parks that had been visited by the girls. In turn he enlightened them about the *desperate* evacuation from the coast and how we had nearly been blown away by the hurricane. Jennifer and Rachel were keen to show Chris around the hotel and let him see the various facilities on offer. They showed him the shops and restaurant (and where they got their breakfast) and gave a guided tour of the themed swimming pool, which was still very busy. Following a brief break to get a drink we then had a visit to the beach and to see where you could hire boats. All good stuff which impressed Chris no end. The girls then asked Chris if he would like to watch the EPCOT fireworks, which were visible from the other side of the Resort area. So Ray, Jennifer, Rachel, Chris and I set off across a bridge and island to watch the fireworks, while Sue and Annette sat and enjoyed a drink. With Ray pushing Chris and Jennifer and Rachel on either side holding Chris's hands it was a merry little party. It was quite a walk to the vantage point the girls knew, but it was well worth it, as the fireworks show (part of Illuminations) was very good, the three youngsters providing plenty of oooohs and aaahs. After the show finished and while we were in that part of the Resort Jennifer and Rachel insisted on showing Chris where their room was located and the small, nearby swimming pool. It was a very pleasant evening, which was eventually brought to a close by the lateness and a rain shower.

The next day we were up in good time, visited Denny's in East Gate for breakfast and then on to Magic Kingdom. Chris chose to take the boat across the Seven Seas Lagoon (rather than the monorail). The excitement and anticipation was just as strong as it had been on our first visit seven years before. We stood at the bow of the boat, with the cool wind in our hair, admiring the Grand Floridian hotel as we sailed past and watched as the sights of the Kingdom grew larger. Off the boat once it was docked and across the forecourt made up of bricks with the names of previous visitors to the turnstiles. A Disney cast member walked over and extended a warm greeting to us, presented Chris with a badge and wished us 'a nice day'. We paused under the Main Street Station to put on the sunscreen and then we were there, standing in the Town Square looking up Main Street to Cinderella's Castle. Magic. We had it all planned; rides on Thunder Mountain, the River Boat and, of course, Splash Mountain. First stop though was the loo!

Nature's call sorted out we ambled up Main Street taking in a few of the shops and then headed for Adventure Land. We called in to watch the Zazu and Iago show, an amusing animatronic show featuring the *stars* of The Lion King and Aladdin. From there we walked past the Pirates of the Caribbean ride, "We'll do that later," said Chris and then into Frontier Land. There in front of us was now Splash Mountain. "This is it," I said, "time for a bit of fun." Chris was very quiet as we headed up the path towards the ride. "I can't stay in my chair on this ride can I?"

"No, but I can lift you into the boats, you'll be OK. Come on let's go."

"I'm sorry Dad, but I don't want to go, I don't feel safe." Despite not going on the ride in 1995 I thought he might this time.

"You'll be fine. I won't drop you."

"I know you won't, but I just don't feel safe."

"But you love this ride."

"If he doesn't want to go, then don't make him, he's old enough to make his own mind up," observed Annette. She was right of course. He did know what he wanted and I was trying to almost bribe him into going on the ride for me.

"Look, why don't you go on it, and Chris and I will wait here for you," suggested Annette.

"Yeah, and you can tell me all about it after," added Chris.

I did ride Splash, but it wasn't quite the same, the constant chatter and laughter was missing. We did talk about it after and it was just like Chris was riding it in his mind as I described the ride (and he corrected me when I went wrong!). He didn't want to ride Thunder Mountain either, so we moved on across Frontier Land to Liberty Square. "I'd like to go on the River Boat," said Chris, "I love that."

We boarded the boat and got a place in the bows, casting off for our trip on the Rivers of America. We passed by Splash Mountain and I caught a momentary, wistful look on Chris's face. Later we steamed by the Haunted Mansion, "I'm not going in there, its far to scary," said Chris.

After the River Boat we enjoyed the sights, sounds and smells of Fantasy Land, Mickey's Star Land and Tomorrow Land before stopping at the Tomorrow Land Terrace for a drink. We were just at the right time as we were able to watch the Parade pass-by down Main Street. Mickey Mouse was there resplendent in his Sorcer's Apprentice costume from Fantasia, as was Simba on Pride Rock, and our favourite Tigger, with Winnie the Pooh. Once the Parade had passed by we were able to move up to the Castle forecourt to watch the Disney characters performing a song and dance show of most of the well-known songs from the films. Of course, we were able to join in, Chris singing away and really enjoying himself.

Eventually, as the evening approached we set off down Main Street and headed for the car park. We had just reached the Town Square when Chris shouted, "Look, there's Bouncy Boy (his nick name for Tigger) over there." Sure enough Tigger was 'receiving' guests, Chris couldn't miss an opportunity to shake paws and Tigger duly obliged. As the photos show Dad had to get in on the act as well!

Having said 'Cheerio' to Tigger I needed to pay a visit to the toilets across the other side of the square. While Annette and Chris were waiting for me they were able to round the visit off nicely, as who should appear and put his arm around Chris, but the main mouse himself, Mickey. By the time I returned Mickey had gone, but it left a great big smile on Chris's face. With that we headed out, turned and took one last look up Main Street and locked away the memories of the visit. Little did we know as we walked out under the Main Street Station towards the Monorail that this was to be Chris's last visit to Magic Kingdom, a Kingdom that had provided us all with lots of fun and joy and magic, and provided us with some great memories.

The next day was a 'lazy day', so following breakfast in the hotel, where Chris was able to tell his evacuation story again, we paid a visit to some of the shopping malls along the 192, before visiting Celebration for the Post Office. Celebration is actually within the geographical boundary of Walt Disney World and was set up as a model township, with all the good social values that were once evident in townships through out America. The centrepiece of the town is a large lake surrounded by shops, restaurants, and cinema from which radiate the roads on which the houses are located. It is quite a pleasant place, but very quiet and a little bit staid. However, it does have a nice Coffee Shop, Barnies, at which we could get a drink.

Chris had been itching (not literally!) to get back into the swimming pool, so after coffee we made the short drive back to the hotel. We got Chris into his swimming trunks, got ourselves ready and spent the rest of the afternoon splashing around the pool. Chris would have stayed in the water having fun for as long as possible, but generally it was because he got cold that sessions were brought to a close. So after an hour or so it was time to get out, wrap him in towels to warm him up (even though the air temperature was quite high) and get him dry. Back in the room Annette suggested that Chris had a shower, not his favourite pastime on holiday, so despite his protests in he went. I'm sure that anybody passing the room would have thought, with all the screaming that we were trying to murder him!

The Disney-MGM Studio was to be the venue the next day, so we were up in good time. The studios are a good mix of rides, shows and other attractions, many of which are wheelchair friendly. Our first port of call, after the toilets, was The Great Movie Ride which transports guests back through many well known movies and in some cases involves live action. One part means the cars in which you sit passing through a scene from Alien, Chris was not amused when the Alien appeared and dripped *stuff* all over his legs nor my singing when we passed through Casablanca. After The Great Movie Ride we headed for a ride

through Catastrophe Canyon and to Chris's disappointment he didn't get wet. From the Canyon we headed to see the Voyage of the Little Mermaid, a really good multimedia show featuring film and live action as well as clever use of lasers, bubbles, smells and wind. As we exited the shop we noticed just across the square a line of people queuing to meet Mickey Mouse.
"Do you want to say hello?" I asked.
"Yeah, lets go see Mick," replied Chris, so we joined the back of the queue, which wasn't particularly long, but was moving slowly.
Mickey Mouse, in common with the other characters that appear in the parks, has a 'minder' to ensure that they do not get manhandled (yes it does happen) and that they are reminded when to take their leave and go for a drink. Mickey's minder kept a low profile as he greeted his fans, ushering the next group up and making sure others did not overstay. We gradually moved up the queue, but there were still about four or five families in front of us. The minder walked up the queue saying, "Mickey will be leaving in a few moments to get a drink, but will be back out shortly so please wait."
"Oh damn," said Chris.
"Are you going to wait?" asked Annette.
"Yeah, I think so," replied Chris.
By now the minder had reached our position in the queue. He came over and asked how many were in our party. "Just the three of us," replied Chris. "Come this way, please," he said, undoing the rope that marked the queue. He then proceeded, with us walking along behind, past the other families queuing. Mickey was just saying Good-bye to another family. "Mickey," said the minder, "I've got a very special guest who's come to see you," pointing to Chris. A huge smile formed on Chris's face, Mickey almost bounded over to where we had reached, took Chris's hand and gave it a warm shake. Chris chatted away, Mickey responded with head and hand movements, and we had our photo taken. It was another great moment, then suddenly Chris said, "Thanks Mickey, but you better go and get your drink" Mickey acknowledged Chris's suggestion, he waved, we waved and we parted. Great!

We took in the Muppets 3D film show, which is always good fun, and the Indiana Jones Stunt Spectacular, with Chris particularly enjoying the bit were the guy from the 'audience' gets knocked about by the female stunt co-ordinator. From there we were off over to the Tower of Terror as Chris insisted that I had a go. Unlike a previous year he decided that he would miss out the pre-show, no risk of getting on the ride that way, and with Annette met me in the shop at the exit of the ride. I was greeted by a barrage of questions and insistence on me describing the ride in detail, which allows Chris to tell us he would have been terrified!

We had breakfast in the Hotel the next morning, this gave Chris another opportunity to tell his evacuation story to the waitress, who was completely oblivious to the fact that there had been such an event. This of course gave Chris the chance to explain to the waitress not only how hurricanes are formed, how they are named, but how this one had passed through the Caribbean, across the Keys and then across the Gulf of Mexico. Nothing like educating the locals while you're on holiday. The rest of the day was spent visiting various local sights and shopping malls, including the newly opened Pointe Orlando, on International Drive, which features the giant toy shop FAO Schwarz. This gave Chris the chance to spend the rest of his money (and some of ours).

The end of the holiday was now approaching, but we had more 'Disney Day' to do at EPCOT. Before that though we called in Denny's in West Gate for breakfast. The waitress came over to take the order for drinks, who we recognised as being the one who had got caught up in the wheelchair the week before. "Oh, no," she exclaimed, to the great amusement of Chris, "it's the return of the killer wheelchair!"

The visit to EPCOT was fun, one of the highlights being the visit to 'Honey I Shrank the Audience', a far fetched story in which Professor Zalinski uses his ray to supposedly shrink the audience, which then gets into a number of scrapes and lucky escapes. In one of these a plague of mice rush off the stage and up through the audience. As this happens plastic tails in the seats tickle the backs of your legs, just as mice tails would. Well, it was a close call who jumped out of their seat higher, Annette or Chris.

After a boat trip across the lake, we got to meet Jafar and Aladdin in Morocco and Quasimodo in France, before watching the Chinese musicians playing the enormous drums. Further on we sat and watched Goofy playing with a group of kids in the fountains and generally being, well, goofy. At the end of a good day we returned to the hotel to start packing, although that evening we did have one final treat in store. We had booked a table in the Rain Forest Café in Disney Village Market Place, so after getting ready we drove over in plenty of time. We advised the 'greeter' we had arrived and waited to be called.

After a short wait the announcement said, "Barratt, table of 3. Your safari is about to start". We made ourselves known and were shown to a table right by one of the animatronic elephants. The Rain Forest Café is very good, set out as a jungle, with large tanks of tropical fish, coloured birds (real and otherwise) and numerous different animatronic animals. The ceiling is made like a night sky, which over time changes and is lit up by the odd flash of lightning. Also every now and then the animals stir, making appropriate movements and noises. The staff are all dressed in safari gear to add to the effect. It was a really good evening and a great way to end the holiday.

So to the last day, which after breakfast, meant completing the packing. Annette took the traditional photographs of Chris and I by the car, and then we were loaded, checked out and away. We called in to Florida Mall for last minute shopping and then headed north on I4 towards Sandford airport. We arrived in plenty of time to check in, confirming that we required the aisle wheelchair both to embark and to disembark at Manchester. While Annette spent the last of her money in Duty Free, Chris and I found an outside viewing area and watched the various planes coming and going. Before we knew it, it was time to board the Airtours 767. With the usual American efficiency Chris was transferred to the aisle chair and we quickly got him seated and settled. Forty minutes after we boarded, we taxied out and were off on the flight home after another great holiday. As Chris said, "It wasn't perhaps the best of our visits, but it was different having to be evacuated. Still, I really enjoyed it".

The flight was not without incident as one of the passengers suffered a panic attack mid way through the flight. The crew quickly got things under control, helped by a nurse who was on board. By the time we arrived in Manchester everything was OK and the passenger had recovered, although Chris was most concerned for her well being. As normal on arrival we had to wait until all the other passengers had disembarked, before we could get off. However, despite the request, the usual Manchester Airport malaise struck when the ground crew arrived without the aisle wheelchair. More waiting, before the necessary equipment was located and we could get off.

Oh, yes, big Chris met us this time without mishap!

CHAPTER THIRTEEN (Friends)

Like a star upon life's blue sky
You shone and always will....
Sharon Carrington

The problem with this Chapter is really were to start and how to structure it. Nearly everybody Chris met he regarded as his friend and he treated all his friends in exactly the same way. For sure, there were those people that were that little bit special that he really took to heart, but for him there was nearly always a place for people to be his friend. He could however be quite uncompromising with people who he didn't like, had upset him once too often or woe betide had been unpleasant to his parents or friends. He had an ability to make friends with people of all ages, of all capabilities and of all interests. Perhaps that was because one of his gifts was the ability to talk (and talk a lot) about almost anything and everything. Perhaps it was because he was such a pleasant person, more often or not seeing the good in people than the bad, that attracted people to him. Mostly though he just enjoyed the company of people and especially his friends.

After some thought I decided the best way to write this Chapter was to do it in alphabetic order so no favouritism can be implied, that was how Chris would have seen it, and anyway if I had tried to rank people I would not have got it right. So here goes.

Barlow, Anthony - Chris first became friendly with Anthony during his weekly visits to Dorin Park which started in 1995. They *braved* a first visit to the Heswall Boys Camp together in August 1996 and their friendship increased when Chris started at Dorin full time in September 1996. However, their friendship would occasionally hit a rocky patch, generally caused when Chris was either playing with or talking to other school pals. Anthony wanted his full attention. Over time these disagreements became more frequent, especially as Chris's friendship with Daniel became stronger. Chris would come home upset at the things Anthony had said to him. Annette tried to get Chris to understand how Anthony might feel and that he should try and keep him involved. Chris would try and things would be alright for a period, before another falling out. As time went on, while Chris became more and more exasperated at Anthony's behaviour he would try to remain friendly and help Anthony along. After Chris's passing Anthony remembered him thus, 'When I was sad Chris cheered me up. He was my friend, I miss him'.

Bolton, Chris and Anne - I'd known Chris since early 1974 when he came to work at the County Council. Chris and Anne had been guests at our wedding and so it was no surprise when they were some of the first visitors we had when Christopher was born. According to Annette our Christopher was named after Uncle Chris, as "if he grew up to be like him then he wouldn't be so bad". As Chris grew up he would share many of his interests with big Chris, a common passion being planes and flying. Chris recalls, "If you wanted to know anything about missiles ask Chris. I know 'a bit about aircraft' and could 'hold my own' in a debate with Chris on aircraft. But debate missiles with him if you dare! We went to RAF Cosford for the open day and Mike and I were introduced to 'the missiles'. This is an AMRAM its .... and this is a Sparrow........, this is a Sidewinder like the ones used on the Harrier and so it went on along missile alley. What a knowledge gleaned from many sources!" As Christopher had no grandfathers, male influence within the family was quite limited and big Chris filled this void, acting as a major role model for Chris. Overtime big Chris was a regular visitor to our house, where he would spend much of the time either chatting to Chris or sharing time on the computer (usually flight sims). The flight sims provided great entertainment, the conversations that took place between them was just like you would hear on a flight deck.

When we first went to America big Chris offered to take us to the airport, Chris was quite pleased as he got to go in big Chris's car. However, it was the trip back from the airport in 1995 that Chris remembered the most. Keen to enjoy the ride in big Chris's car to the maximum he convinced Chris to take a detour home. This involved carrying on from the end of the M56 to Queensferry and then down the Sealand Road and then towards Saughall and our house. This means a trip over the Seahill Road Railway Bridge, which is quite steep and taken at speed is a bit like a roller-coaster. Now this is something not enjoyed by Mrs. Barratt, but encouraged by "faster, Chris, faster" we almost took off as we went over the bridge, which was greeted by laughter from the three men and "wow" from the front passenger seat, but resulted in me getting a slap. "What did you hit me for?" I asked. "Because I can reach you and your not driving," came the reply. More laughter from the front.

Anne was a much calmer influence and would share with Chris aspects of family life, how the girls, Nicola, Sarah and Amy were and what they were up to and later how Anthony (Nicola's husband was). She was also very understanding, came and sat with him when he was in hospital and would help by listening to him. Since we lost Chris, Anne and Chris have been wonderfully supportive to Annette and I, despite their own sense of loss. As they wrote, "In loving memory our beloved 'Mate', Chris, who was brave, thoughtful and gave and brought so much love and happiness to everyone he met. We will love you always our brave little fighter pilot".

Bridge, Kirsty - Chris first met Kirsty when he began his one-day a week at Dorin Park and would come home describing this freckled faced, always smiling, little doll. From then on Chris had a soft spot for Kirsty. When he started full time at Dorin Kirsty was on the same bus as Chris and he was pleased when he sat close to her so he could chat on the journey. Kirsty has a very quiet voice and some words can get 'lost', but not to Chris. As with all his other friends he was on the right wavelength and instinctively knew what was being said. One school sports day Kirsty was captain of the Red team, while Chris was a member of the Blue team. Despite the fact that his team didn't win, he was over the moon that Kirsty's team had won and as team captain she got to be presented with the Team Award. In all the time Chris was at Dorin I don't think he ever had a cross or negative word to say about Kirsty. During 2000 it became known that they regarded themselves as an 'item'. Trips to the cinema (chaperoned by Norma!), and the social events at the Croft, as well as shared evenings at Choices. They could be seen at school sitting next to one another, little fingers hooked together. When Chris passed over Kirsty was overcome, and many months later is still broken hearted. It was very fitting that Kirsty was the first recipient of the memorial trophy at Choices and while she was clearly moved at having won, her first thought was to share the trophy with her and Chris's friend Katie Gerrard.

Carrington, Melanie - started at Dee Point School on the same day as Chris and from that day on they became good friends. During the time at Dee Point they were not always in the same class, but they would always be looking out for one another. As the years went by and Birthday Parties came around Melanie would be at the top of Chris's guest list and he would go to Mel's party, sometimes other than Mel's brothers being the only boy present. When Chris wanted his birthday celebration as a day out at Blackpool it was Mel he invited, for the Christmas Party during his first year at Dorin Park it was Mel who he asked along. After they started their secondary schools they did not see each other quite so much, but whenever Chris was unwell Mel would call to see him and that cheered him no end. I remember one day when we were at Mel's home and Sharon (Mel's mum) announced, much to Mel's embarrassment, that she had a boyfriend. Chris asked who it was, did he know him? Mel replied with a name to which Chris said, "If he doesn't look after you Mel, you tell me and I'll sort him out". At the end Mel was very upset and struggled to understand the loss of her friend, as she wrote, "I've so many beautiful memories of times spent with you. I will miss you forever and will never forget my special friend, I was so proud to be your friend".

Carrington, Sharon and Billy - Mel's mum and dad had also known Chris since the early days at Dee Point. As time went by they ensured that Chris was included in any activities and he was grateful of that. He quite enjoyed Sharon's company, especially when she told the odd risqué joke and made use of the odd colourful word for which he would reproach her with a loud "Arhh, Shaz swore". The Christmas he was very poorly he hadn't laughed much for several weeks, but by the time Sharon and family left after their visit he had livened up a lot. In our book of memories Sharon and Billy wrote, 'Your smile, your face, the way you laughed will stay with us all until we can all get together again and party'. Sharon and Billy's sons, Jordan (Jo) and Anthony were also friendly with Chris and he particularly liked playing with Jo. Through Sharon Chris met her mum and dad, Celia and Les. As with many names Chris shortened the name to Ceels. She summed up the thoughts of many people when she wrote, "Only 15 years to make an impression on so many people's hearts, only 15 years to cram so much fun into a short time. Yet! After 15 years so many broken hearts you left behind".

Chard, Vicky - Like Melanie Carrington, became a friend of Chris on the first day of school at Dee Point. Throughout the time at school they were nearly always in the same class, attended the same events organised by the school and generally performed on the same night in the school productions. Vicky took it upon herself to look after Chris once he started to use the push wheelchair at school and was happy to fetch and carry for him. At the age of eleven Vicky and Chris went their separate ways to Secondary School, but Vicky was one of the few people from Dee Point who kept in touch. Sometimes she would telephone and some times she would call around (accompanied on occasions by her parents, Di and Dennis, and sister Lucy). There was one occasion when she called round with another friend and they all spent time chatting in the garden. A little while later Chris reappeared and stated to Annette with great indigence, "Do you know what Mum? That Vicky smokes! Disgusting habit, phone Di and tell her". Every time he saw her after that he would ask was she still smoking and tut loudly when she said she was.

Churchman, Lorraine - Lorraine was the class room assistant in Chris's first year in the Senior Department at Dorin and they soon established a mutual respect. Lorraine was like having a mum at school and provided Chris with a great deal of support, both physical and emotional. It was always reassuring to know that Chris was being so well looked after. During term time there were constant reports about what had been going on and what Lorraine had said and what Lorraine had done. Much later when Lorraine gave Chris some news in confidence, he kept it to himself, not even telling Annette or I. In subsequent years when Lorraine was undertaking her role in other classes, Chris would still search out Lorraine for advice and support, or a friendly chat, her counsel was very important. As with a number of his friends, their families simply became an extension to Chris's. So Lorraine would be prevailed upon to provide updates on Laura and James, her daughter and son, which would be duly relayed to Annette and I with suitable observations on matters by Chris.

Cooper, Paul - Along with Anthony Barlow, Paul was one of Chris's first friends at Dorin Park. He also *braved* that first visit to the Heswall Boys Camp in 1996. Paul is a great fan of Everton (like Ian Shingler) for which Chris would tease him mercilessly. Chris also had a great ability to start Paul giggling. Chris often chose lessons in which to do this. Paul would start giggling and the classroom assistant (Ian) would try to get Paul to stop and concentrate on his work. Chris would get Paul going again, Ian would try to dampen it down only for the class teacher to have words with Paul, and tell Ian to keep control. Chris by now was nowhere to be seen.

Evans, Pauline - Pauline entered Chris's life when he first went to Hope House as one of his prime 'contacts'. Like many people who came into contact with Chris she was mortified that such a dreadful thing as MD could affect such a nice lad. But also like many other people she was able to see through the disability. She was a great ally to Annette in ensuring that he behaved properly while at Hope House and that he took showers regularly. For Chris she was a great friend and provided much love and support, both while at Hope House and through telephone conversations. She was someone he could completely trust. Pauline was very protective of Chris, but when there was a need she could put him back on the straight and narrow. If they had cross words (a rare occasion) they would do their own thing for ten or fifteen minutes and then it would all be forgotten.

In the February following the loss of Chris, Annette and I had an appointment to see Dr. Quinlivan at Oswestry, by coincidence Pauline telephoned a few days before and asked if she could meet us. Over coffee the three of us chatted about Chris and what he had got up to at Hope House, how he had dealt with his disability, how he had managed to transcend people's ages and how she really loved him. Pauline that day was radiant, dressed in blue and looking very happy. Two weeks later Pauline was killed in a car accident. It was such a dreadful loss of a great friend and a truly caring person. At least we can be sure that wherever Chris and Pauline are, there is someone ensuring showers are being taken regularly!

Ford, Matty – Chris met Matty at Hope House and soon became friendly with him. Due to his disability Matty was unable to speak, but Chris was able to understand and 'converse' with Matty. They shared a similar sense of humour and would giggle away at many different things. Chris also established a friendship with Matty's brother Richard and sister Emma. When Matty passed over it affected Chris deeply, he would often reflect on his time at Hope House in Matty's company. Matty's mum, Jackie, summed it up nicely, 'We will miss your friendship Chris....still you and Matthew will be having all sorts of fun – free of all your problems. My memories of shared times at Hope House are some of the best".

Gerrard, Katie – It was inevitable given that I was acquainted through work with Katie's dad, Bob, that Chris would seek her out and make himself known on his first day at Dorin Park in September 1995. While Katie's initial reaction was 'who is this mad man', they soon established a close relationship, Chris often referring to Katie as 'my special friend'. To start with Chris would trap her in the corner so that he could talk to her, but after a while she was quite happy to do so, as Chris didn't talk about football to her like the other lads. For those who don't know her, Katie converses through eye-pointing, facial expression and head movement which sometimes provides a challenge even for her parents, Sandra and Bob. Shamefully I have to admit that I find it very difficult to understand, which undoubtedly frustrates Katie and prompted Chris to justifiably call me a 'plonker' and a 'dipstick'. He would remonstrate with Annette and tell her "to talk normally to Katie". For Chris, talk normally was no problem, he was quite simply 'switched' on to Katie's wavelength. I have witnessed Katie and Chris in conversation, Chris talking at twenty to the dozen and Katie's eyes darting here and there, face changing from smile to grimace and back to smile, head turning here and there and them both clearly understanding the other. On one occasion Chris came home from school to tell us that Katie was having her Wish granted and was going on a plane, to Disney World, with Bob, Sandra and sister Emma.

"How do you know that?" I asked, not for a moment believing he had been able to find out so much information.

"Katie told me," he replied, in a voice that said 'How else?'.

"Are you sure?"

"YES!"

Right I thought! So the next day I spoke to Bob at work, asking if Katie and the

family were off to Florida, as a Wish. Bob said they were, but how did I know as they hadn't told anybody yet. I repeated my conversation of the night before.
"I know," said Bob, "it would have been in her book (that's used for message passing between home and school), I'll check".
The following day he called me.
"Mike, there was nothing in Katie's book about Florida". I didn't have the courage to tell Chris I'd checked up on him.

Katie enjoyed Chris's company as he always made her laugh, whenever she was upset at school Chris would be found and quickly and gently calm her down and cheered up. They shared many special times, an afternoon drinking coffee at Madison's, social evenings with pizza, chips, videos, music and other friends at the Croft (courtesy of Norma), weekends at Hope House. Katie looked on Chris for help and support and was deeply upset at his passing. Right up to the present she tells Sandra that she talks to Chris and that Chris talks to her and makes her laugh. She also has a small Tigger, which mysteriously moves about her room and gets put in odd places, make of that what you will.

Katie has an older sister, Emma, and it was regular occurrence for Chris to come home with stories about her and what she'd done to Katie or what she'd had of Katie's. You can imagine the criticism that poor Emma got for upsetting Katie in such a way!

Green, Mollie & Bernard - Mollie and Bernard live next door but one and were always very kind to Chris. On some summer days he would drive down their driveway and have a chat. When Tim and Jo from next door moved, Chris was very impressed that Mollie and Bernard became the new carers for Meg the cat who stayed behind. Mollie and Bernard always remembered Chris at Easter and Christmas and after Easter 2000 he produced a 'Best Neighbour' certificate to say thank you.

Harpley, Josie - Josie came into our lives soon after Crossroads began to provide us with some respite hours. She is very much a no nonsense type of person, but also one who is able to understand other peoples needs and provide suggestions and guidance without making the decision for that person. Over the time that Josie knew Chris she helped Chris to understand his own feelings as well as taking into account those of Annette and I, for that he was very grateful. He also knew that he could not get away with anything with Josie, he did try, but Josie's implacable approach soon stopped this. When Chris was out of sorts or ill Josie would often call in, either at home or hospital, to cheer him up or help us out. Chris was very protective of Jos (as he called her), and any attempt by me to take the mickey of her was quickly (and sometimes painfully) stopped. In Jos Chris had a dependable and trusted friend, always looking forward to her visits on Thursdays. Josie was one of the few people that made it into Chris's inner sanctum, to whom he would entrust some of his personal thoughts and worries. With Jos, he was in very good hands.

Hellon, Norma - when Trena Salmon left Barnardo's in late 1998. Norma took over as Chris's project worker. They immediately hit it off and quickly established a strong friendship and a mutual respect. In many ways Chris looked on Norma as a 'big sister' and over time she became his confidant, telling her a number of his innermost thoughts, thoughts he didn't or couldn't share with Annette and I, knowing she would keep them to herself. Looking back there were times when Chris asked me what appeared to be odd, out of the blue questions. I suspect that he was testing to see if Norma had spoken to us. He would be satisfied that she had not.

Norma was one of the few people outside of Annette and I that he trusted, not only with his inner most thoughts, but to look after his physical well being. It was to Norma that he turned when he realised one of his friends at school was deeply unhappy and needed help, and in 2000 when our holiday to Florida was on the horizon, it was Norma he told first that he didn't want to go. Norma's listening and advice must have helped him enormously when faced with telling Mum and Dad. Norma volunteered to speak at Chris's funeral as "it's the least I can do for my friend". Twenty four carat gold.

Hellon, Abigail - Through Norma Chris met Abigail, Norma's nine-year-old daughter, when Abi started going to the cinema with Chris and Norma. They quickly became friends as they had the same quirky sense of humour and this was cemented when Abi started going to Choices to help out. Norma told us of how they would chat away to each other about all sorts of things during the taxi ride to and from Choices, often just giggling away. On one occasion as the taxi was passing the Countess of Chester Hospital Chris pointed out that he had spent a week there being *decoked*. Abi was enthralled as Chris described the procedure and concluded, "that there was a rumbling from below and then my a**e exploded". Abi just collapsed laughing, Norma tried to stifle any reaction and the taxi driver just looked amazed. For one so young Abi shows a wonderful sense of understanding and caring, clearly attributes that she has inherited from her mum. Not only did Abi and Chris enjoy each others company, but Abi was happy to help Chris and on many occasions became his hands and arms.

Norma has another daughter 4 year old Katie and Chris also regarded her as his friend. Unable to say his name properly it was Katie that christened him 'Christobear', which became a popular reference. It was lovely to see her holding Chris's hand while trotting alongside the wheelchair. He loved nothing better than Katie sitting on his knee while he drove around. While mentioning the Hellon family it would be unfair not to mention husband Dave who on a number of occasions shared visits to the cinema and was firmly in the category - friend.

Holmes, Laura - Another of Chris's friends from Dee Point day one. Chris always had a soft spot for Laura and would 'look out' for her. Laura repaid that by helping Chris by pushing him about in the wheelchair and getting his coat at break and after school. They spent most of their schooling in the same class. Laura was one of the people in the school he felt safe with. When they went their separate ways at the end of Junior School Laura stayed in touch, rarely forgetting birthdays and Christmas. During mid 2000, Laura called in to see Chris a couple of times and they happily recalled their time at Dee Point and talked about what the future might bring. Since Chris's passing Laura has regularly remembered her friend by placing flowers by his nameplate at the Crematorium. More recently, having passed her GCSEs she is to undertake a course to become a Nursery Nurse - Chris would have been very proud of that.

Jarvis, Paul - one of Chris's first friends at Dee Point and probably his best friend during that period. With Richard Brookes the trio could be quite a handful. Paul often visited Chris at home and after they went their separate ways to Secondary school Paul still came to visit, usually bearing gifts that were well received.

Johnson, Michael - One of Chris's inner circle of friends at Dorin Park, one of the 'gang', as Chris would put it. Big Mike shared an interest in football and motor racing and so they were more often than not the topics of chat in the playground. They also formed a bond as Mike suffers from a form of Muscular Dystrophy. If Mike had a fall Chris was often on hand, to check he was OK and carefully place his wheelchair so Mike could pull himself up.

McCoy, Lyndsey - another of Chris's friends at Dorin Park, albeit their friendship had its ups and downs. Some weeks Chris would come home from school and it was all positive stuff, how they had done this, that or the other. On other weeks it was Lyndsey this and Lyndsey that, and "Do you know what Lyndsey did/said?". Overall there were more positives than negatives and Lyndsey did like Chris's jokes!

Riffel, David - Like Pauline Evans, David became Chris's friend from the first time they met at Hope House. Chris had been impressed that he received a Christmas card from David and Pauline, in advance of his first stay. He got on very well with David and they shared a similar humour, which on more than one occasion Pauline was the victim of. Chris enjoyed hearing about David's life in the Navy, before he became a nurse, and the ins and outs of David's family life. He was very impressed with David's golfing and music playing abilities. In return Chris was happy to provide David 'training' on computers and planes, they also shared many other interests. On one day David, who was off duty, rode over to Hope House on his motor bike to show it off to Chris, something which they had often talked about. They went outside, "What's this?", "What's that?", "How does that work?", "We'll go back in now!", leaving David open mouthed and thinking, "Well thanks very much!" The irony of it all was the bike broke down on the way home and David had to push it!

Whenever arrangements were made for Chris to stay at Hope House he insisted that it was at a time David was on duty. For one he very much enjoyed David's company and what they got up to and for two he trusted David to look after him as much as he trusted Annette and I.

On Chris's birthday David made the effort to come over to Chester to wish Chris a Happy Birthday and share a piece of cake. On the first visit Pauline was also able to come, but in subsequent years Pauline was working so David came alone. Chris was delighted with David's visits and said how much it had made his day. In June 2000, David phoned, explained the situation to Annette, and then asked to speak to Chris. He apologised and said he wouldn't be able to come that day. Chris passed the message to Annette, clearly disappointed, when there was a knock at the door. "Go and answer the door Chris, while I chat to David," said Annette. "What?" asked Chris. "Go and answer the door!" Loud tut, but off he went, opened the door and "Dayveed". David was standing in the doorway big smile on his face, talking to Annette on his mobile phone.

David was a major influence on Chris and a great friend. David says that Chris inspired him. It was fitting that when the time came for Chris to go he was in David's company listening to his jokes. Mates Always.

Salmon, Trena – Trena was one of the first project workers from Barnardo's to establish a long-term relationship with Chris. Initially this involved visits to see him at home, sitting with him while Annette and I went out and then taking Chris out to the cinema or town. He thoroughly enjoyed his outings with Trena (occasionally accompanied by her husband Steve – good conversations on cars included), although Trena did make him cry! Well actually the video of Titanic they sat and watched one evening was the real cause. One of Chris's high points was when Trena and Steve brought their new daughter, Rhiannon, round to meet Chris and she sat on his knee. Trena wrote of their outings, 'I will remember a fun loving cheeky popcorn eating kid. I will cherish our special trips out and will remember you always'.

Shingler, Ian – Chris first met Ian during 1999 when he started at Dorin Park undertaking NVQ training. From all accounts they hit it off immediately, helped no doubt by their mutual love of 'Only Fools and Horses'. As Chris pointed out on one occasion, "The only sad thing about him is that he supports Everton". After the Statementing in early 2000 it was recommended that Chris was allocated a one-to-one to help him physically. He was really pleased when Ian was appointed. Mr. Owen told of their first encounter after the appointment was announced Ian strolled up to Chris and simply said, "From now on, I'm your minder". Chris just radiated at the thought. Chris would come home from school full of stories of what they had been up to during the day, the tricks they had played on each other and other pupils. Arriving home one afternoon he proudly told his Mum that Ian had been teaching him to swear in German, and proceeded to demonstrate his prowess at this new skill. "Well I hope you don't go around saying that all the time". "(Tut). Of course not". Mind you it did come in useful when shouting at Michael Schumacher when watching Grand Prix. Ian brought a *male* perspective on life, not only for Chris, but the other boys at Dorin, giving him a person to whom he could talk about those things boys want and need to. There is no doubt that in the short time they shared they became very good friends, and by all accounts enriched each other's lives. "Lovely jubbly".

Stevenson, Laura - Laura was another of Chris's friends who enjoyed his joking and humour, but also found that he was a good listener and was capable of providing good advice. When she was down or upset she would often seek Chris out and he would do his best, usually successfully, to cheer her up. For a period, while Chris was still shopping with us, we would bump into Laura and her Grandma in the coffee shop of the supermarket and it was always nice to see her face light up when she saw Chris.

Stretton, Kurt - Chris had known Kurt from his days at Dee Point and was quite friendly with him at Dorin Park. Kurt was a bit older that Chris, but they were often seen sharing a joke or two, the content of which is probably not the sort we could share! They also had a nice double act during the JC2000 performance.

Sweetman, Charmaine - Chris and Charmaine got on well, apart from a taste in music that was poles apart. It was this that caused considerable friction, with Chris constantly sniping at Charmaine's choice and regularly taking the mickey out of Adam Ricketts, an absolute favourite of Charmaine's. The corridors of Dorin Park would, apparently, often reverberate to the pair arguing about music. Charmaine was another friend who enjoyed Chris's jokes. She also found that he was dependable, "I could trust him with anything. I told him a secret and he didn't tell anybody".

Tench, Kylie - When Chris transferred from the Parker's bus to a taxi in early 1999 he shared the journey with six year old Kylie and her mum Sue, who acted as escort. His journeys to and from Dorin were nearly always filled with chatter, fun and joy. Chris had a real soft spot for Kylie, more often or not referring to her as 'sweet heart' or 'Bab'. Every morning almost the first thing he would ask would be how Kylie was, and whenever she was ill he would be most concerned. He would want to know all the details and would quiz Sue until he was satisfied. Kylie for her part would be first out of the taxi at night and come and alert Annette that Chris was home and help put down the ramp so he could get in the house.

Tyldesley-Wain, Daniel - a list of Chris's friends would not be complete without Daniel. From the moment that Dan started at Dorin Park Chris took him under his wing, showing him round the school and telling how the school worked. They became inseparable at school, Chris and Dan, Dan and Chris. Those people who saw them together talked of book-ends, of the greatest of mates. Daniel suffered from Cerebal Palsy[1], was fed through a gastronomy tube (of which Chris knew everything there was to know), and although unable to talk he could communicate through arm, eye and head movements. That didn't stop Chris knowing what Dan wanted to say or do, he became his unofficial translator in school. To watch Daniel and Chris together was almost magical, their capability to have a conversation was incredible, and their relationship was very close.

They shared a passion for Manchester United, loved motor racing and aeroplanes. If Dan was ill, Chris would pester Angela (Dan's one to one at Dorin) for

[1] During October 2000 Daniel was diagnosed as having Pelizaeus-Merzbacher disease (PMD).

information and this would be relayed back to us on his return home. When Dan was admitted to hospital at Alder Hey Chris insisted that we visit him, making sure that we went bearing gifts "to cheer my mate up". One such visit in June 2000 was made despite the fact that Chris himself was uncomfortable, Dan was worth the effort and more. We arrived one afternoon to find Dan in a small side ward lying in bed, clearly unwell. Chris glided into the room, smiled and said, "Hi ya, Mate". The smile on Dan's face couldn't have been wider or brighter. "If you have that effect on him you can come everyday," said the nurse in attendance. Needless to say this completely passed Chris by, he was already deep in conversation with Dan, telling him about the events going on at school. They were the closest of friends and with Dan passing over, just four months after Chris, they are probably reunited and causing havoc somewhere. Just before Dan left us he told his mum that he could see Chris sitting at the end of his bed. Their friendship is probably summed up in a poem Chris wrote in 1999.

FRIENDSHIP

In school I have a friend
Called Daniel.
Daniel is my best friend.
Daniel and I like aeroplanes and cars.
We both support Manchester United football club.
I hope Daniel can come to my house
When he is better.
I like the way
He laughs and giggles,
He is always happy,
He makes me smile

Chris Barratt (14)

Waite, Lizzie – Lizzie was another friend he made at Dorin Park, a couple of years older than Chris, tall and attractive. Over the months they had a bit of a love/hate relationship, one moment being good friends, the next not talking. Often the bust up would be over some pop group or the other or an argument about the best football team. Perhaps a short note that Lizzie wrote to us sums it up best, 'I am very upset about Chris. I didn't realise that when I saw him at my 18th birthday party it would be one of the last times I saw him. I've sent you a copy of the photograph that was taken of Chris and me at the Party and as usual on it he is being cheeky to me. I remember sometimes at school we used to wind Charmaine up about Adam Ricketts. Sometimes he used to be a bit grumpy over the football score, especially if Man U. had lost and Liverpool had won. He was my boyfriend for a time, but we soon split up when I found out that he was two timing me. Still we were good mates even after this and I'll miss him an awful lot.'

While many of those that have gone before in this chapter became part of Chris's extended family, there are those in the family that were not only 'friends', but had a great deal of influence on Chris, and it is only right that they are included in this piece.

Barratt, Nana – as with many grandparents my mum was to spend a lot of time with Chris. Once at school he would visit on a Saturday or Sunday and usually stay for lunch. During the school holidays he would spend at least one day a week with Nana and as he got a bit older they would walk to the river, visit the local village were my Grandfather and Great Grandmother had lived or go on day outings to the seaside or zoo. Chris would also accompany Nana on the day trips she organised for King's Lea House (where Grandma lived). Once into the wheelchair trips out were a bit more difficult and over time ceased. Chris still went to Nana's, either at the weekend or in the school holidays and the days were filled by games, videos, games console or books. In the latter few years, both as Chris got older and heavier and Nana got, well, more mature in years, it became much more difficult for her to manage Chris. While still happy to visit, the visits were shorter and he insisted on me staying so that he could be moved or lifted.

Tilston, Nanny – Annette's mum lived quite close to us. To start with Nanny would collect Chris from Dee Point and later it was at her house that Chris would be dropped off and from where we would pick him up on our way home from work. He quite liked going to Nanny's, "because Nanny makes nice dinners" and more often than not he could get away with all sorts of things. During the winter, in his younger days and during the time he went to Dee Point, he would wear a bobble-hat, most of these creations having been knitted by Nanny. There was the seasonal Father Christmas one, the Reindeer one, the Aeroplane one and more. In late 1994 and early 1995 Annette's mum started to become absent minded and would repeat items of conversation. A blood problem was diagnosed, but in April she was admitted to hospital in a very confused state. There was a period where Nanny did not recognise people and Chris could not really understand this. He hated the idea of Nanny being in hospital. In mid June 1995 Nanny passed away. Clearly Chris was very upset, but he was just as concerned for his Mum and how she felt and for several days he fussed around her, insisting that I did this and that to help. He was left with some very happy memories of a lovely person.

Tilston, Paul – Although Chris and Paul had spent time together before, it was during the time that Nanny was in hospital that Paul started to come to our house on a regular basis. Initially, it was so I could look after both boys while Annette, John and Julie went to the hospital. Later, Saturday evenings visits became a weekly happening. Paul and Chris would usually hide away in the dining room, either playing the computer or Nintendo, or both (sometimes with one of the computer and the other on the Nintendo). On other nights they would watch videos in Chris's room, sharing a passion for 007. In summer months they would rush round the garden, Chris in his chair and Paul on a bike. The one thing that was common throughout was the laughter. While they did argue it was over trivial things like the best football team or best racing driver. They seldom fell out, but if they did it was the proverbial storm in a teacup. Chris loved to hear about Paul's exploits at Tae Kwon Do, going to watch lessons on a couple of occasions, and he positively glowed as Paul gained his various grades[2]. When the adapted Galaxy was due to be delivered it was Paul that Chris invited to share the moment and was the first person to be invited to go for a ride.

Generally they were well behaved, but they could have their moments, usually egging one another on. One evening they were at Paul's playing on his Playstation, everything appeared to have been fine. Later, after Chris had returned home it transpired that they had eaten a pile of Vitamin E tablets, that they thought were sweets, with Paul popping them happily into Chris's mouth. Fortunately, no harm was to come of this rashness!

They may have been cousins, but they were also great friends.

Tilston, John and Julie – Julie was there right at the start, she was there right the way through and was there at the end. Auntie Ju, supported by Uncle John, provided stability for Chris and great support to Annette and I. When Chris was still mobile under his own steam there were days out, one of the most notable being a 'fun' day to the Sun Centre at Rhyl when between Chris and Paul they caused havoc! During the summer holidays Julie would come to our house, accompanied by Paul to look after Chris while Annette went to town. On other days Annette would look after the boys while Julie was in bed following her night shift at the hospital. When John and Julie got a dog, Mollie, a lovely natured collie, Chris adopted her as the family dog. While he loved to see Mollie, he would not entertain her jumping up at him. Somehow Mollie sensed that and was always very reserved when Chris was about.

Smith, Doris (Grandma) – Chris was Doris' Great Grandson, of which she was very proud, but to all of us she was Grandma. She was 78 when Chris was born and living at Kings Lea House, a sheltered housing community for older people. Chris was a regular visitor, calling in either with me on the way to Nana's or with Nana herself. He would go to the Christmas Fair at the House, often returning with more money than he went, as well as various prizes, given to him by "the old ladies". Grandma was very independent and Chris would often say to her, "It'll be nice when you're 100, you'll get a card from the Queen" and "I'll be, what Dad, oh yes 22". Laughter from both. "I'm not sure I want to be around that long," said Grandma. "Course you do Grandma". However, it was not to be, as at Christmas 1996 Grandma was taken ill and had to have a pacemaker fitted, being in hospital over Christmas. It was Chris that chivvied us along to visit her and take her presents, "You can't have Christmas without presents Grandma". Sadly, Grandma wasn't fit enough to return to Kings Lea House and moved to Orchard Manor Nursing Home. My weekly visits continued and the first thing he did when I came in was to ask how Grandma was. Chris would still visit her, but less frequently than before, although when he did he brightened her day. After one visit as we were pulling out of the car park he started crying, just softly. After I managed to placate him he explained that he didn't like to see Grandma looking so sad, "that's just not how Grandma should be, I feel so sad for her".

[2] In May 2001 Paul became a Tae Kwon Do Black Belt, First Dan. Chris would have been very pleased and very proud.

At Easter 1999, just a week after Chris's last visit, Grandma passed quietly away at the age of 92.
"Well," said Chris through his tears, "she didn't want to be 100, did she?".

CHAPTER FOURTEEN (Millennium)

Men are like the stars;
some generate their own light
while others reflect the brilliance they receive.

Jose Marti

We had not celebrated the turning of the year for some time, Annette and I knew that it was taking us one more step along a road on which there would be no happy ending. While Chris always made noises about staying up to see the New Year in he invariably asked to go to bed at some point in the evening and then fell asleep before 12 o'clock. He was extra keen to see the beginning of the new Millennium and on and off watched on the TV the various celebrations around the world. As Julie was working John and Paul came round and Paul's presence gave Chris the impetus to stay up and keep going until midnight.

As midnight in the UK arrived the moment was celebrated by the odd tincture by the adults and a macho attempt at drinking beer - failed - by the boys. This was followed by a great fireworks display, as the local neighbourhood (and the rest of Chester) lit up the sky, which was watched with great enthusiasm by the boys and with fingers in ears by Annette! For Chris it was to be the start of a full and eventful year.

The year was not very old when the first key event occurred. Early evening of Monday 10th January the phone rang. It was Anne Bolton, I could tell from the tone of her voice that all was not well, she'd called to say that Chris had had an accident while flying his glider and was in hospital, with a suspected fracture of his back. His other injuries where limited to a gashed leg and bruising, but it would be a few days before the doctors would be able to determine the full extent of his injuries. Anne assured us that there was nothing we could do, and that she would keep us informed. During the conversation our Chris had come into the room, he'd overheard what had been said and was very upset, tears streaming down his face. He was very concerned, he wanted to know just how bad Uncle Chris was and could we go and see him. Throughout the evening he kept asking this question and that question, I knew there was something on his mind, but he was reluctant to ask. Eventually, while lying in bed that evening he asked, "Will it mean that Uncle Chris will be in a wheelchair?"
"I don't know," I said "we'll have to wait and see. But I really hope not."
"So do I," said Chris tears welling in his eyes "that would be really bad for him."
With that the conversation changed tack, but it was very clear that this was weighing heavily on his mind.

Around this time travelling any distance was becoming a problem, as Chris was uncomfortable in being transferred to and travelling in the Galaxy we then had. However, he was quite keen to visit Uncle Chris and we were getting ready for a visit when Anne called to say that Chris was home. He'd been seen by a specialist and had compressed a number of discs in his spine, bruised some muscles and lost a few inches in height, but he was otherwise OK. He would however have to wear a *corset* for a while to support his back. Our Chris was very relieved when told of this news, it was like a veil being lifted and he became much more relaxed. The following week Uncle Chris came down to see us and was able to compare notes with Chris on the difficulties and discomforts of wearing a support jacket. As Uncle Chris said, he could now empathise with Chris in what such a jacket meant[1]. Chris remembers the time thus, "By January 2000 Chris was in a great amount of discomfort from his 'back brace'. About this time I had had a gliding accident which resulted in me having to temporarily wear a surgical corset. I visited to show all at 193 that I was still in 'one piece' and I will always remember the compassion shown by Chris. "Are you OK Uncle Chris?". "Does it hurt?" and all this from a teenager who was in far greater pain than I was."

A short while before Christmas Norma had asked us if we had any objections to Chris attending a conference being organised by Ellesmere Port and Neston NHS Primary Care Group and Barnardo's on 'Care and Health Needs of Disabled Children in Recreational and Informal Settings'. The organisers were looking for a number of special needs children to attend to give their views. Annette and I had no objections, but we were not sure if Chris would go, suggesting that Norma asked him. To our surprise he said he would, probably as he was to get a day off school! Actually, he would do anything for Norma.

The conference was held in late January and as the date approached I asked Chris on several occasions if he wanted to prepare anything. His reply was that he was only required to help discussions in small workgroups and he would just answer the questions put to him, thanks. Norma had arranged to pick Chris up in a taxi for the short journey to the Civic Hall in Ellesmere Port, where he met up with his friend Kirsty Bridge and another young delegate, Tom Shannon. By all accounts the day went well and when Chris came home Annette asked him how it had gone, he said fine and disappeared in the direction of his computer. When I came in from work I enquired how the day had gone, to be told it had been OK; did he enjoy it? "Yea, it was alright" "Did you say anything?" "A little bit, sorry I'm trying to concentrate on this game" in other words you're dismissed.

The Conference, which was attended by health and social care professionals of all types, was opened by Andrew Miller, MP for Ellesmere Port and Neston, who explained the purpose of the day and the current government initiatives. The young delegates were then asked to address the audience, not exactly what Chris was expecting. Kirsty went first and had her speech read out on her behalf, to be followed by Chris. Norma takes up the story. She asked Chris if he wanted her to come to the front with him. "No thanks," came the reply and with that he drove off, positioning himself before the audience. "Good morning, my name is Christopher Barratt, I'm 14 years old and I have Duchenne Muscular Dystrophy. I've not always been in a wheelchair, when I was young I could walk, I've been in a wheelchair since I was 8 years old." Chris then proceeded to explain to the audience the problems with transport and access in this country, he related how the Americans tackled these problems, describing the buses in New York and informing the audience that 85% of buses there are wheelchair accessible. He told how on all his travels in America he hadn't been anywhere that he hadn't been able to get into and how places and people in America made every effort to accommodate wheelchairs. He talked about how he felt when people looked at him in his chair and how he was no different to others. At no

[1] Chris made a full recovery from his injuries, although he still has some treatment and he is in the process of regaining his normal height. He has however given up gliding, but still flies powered aircraft.

time did he show that he felt sorry for himself. Norma told us how proud she was of him and that, when he had finished, he got a wonderful reception from the audience. Yvonne Bohdanowicz, who was also present, added later, that her sense of pride, having known Chris for so long, was immense and having looked around the audience the impact he had had was amazing with a number of the delegates wiping away tears.

Yvonne and a few other delegates sat with Norma, Kirsty and Chris over lunch. As was normal he didn't eat much, he had an audience and he wanted to talk and tell jokes ("Don't tell Mum") which by all accounts had the group in fits of laughter. Following lunch there were a number of smaller workgroups and Chris took an active part answering questions put to him and volunteering information.

"So Chris," I asked a few days after the Conference and now being aware of what happened, "did you say anything?"
"No, not much."
"Well, did you enjoy it?"
"Oh, yes."
"Would you go again?"
"Guess so."
End of discussion.

During 1999 one of the performances of 'Don't Worry' Dorin Park's JC2000 entry to the competition was videoed and submitted. In total there were 18,300 entries throughout the country, and some schools were selected to perform in one of 12 regional finals. In early 2000, to the school's great credit and enormous pride Dorin Park was one of ten schools selected in the North West to perform at the prestigious Bridgewater Hall in Manchester, on the evening of March 21st 2000.

Having seen Chris perform in the "Don't Worry" production for the parents at Christmas we were well aware of the role he had and we were so proud that he (along with the other pupils) were to be afforded the opportunity to *tread the boards* in such a marvellous venue. Chris was a little less impressed.
"You'll go down as a great Thespian," I told him. "You can be a real luvvy."
"I've done it enough already, and I don't want to do it again."
"But, it's the chance of a lifetime. I wish I could do it."
"Well, you do it then!"
"Thespian's can be so temperamental," I quipped.
"If you don't stop going on about it I won't be going." He snapped back. "Tell him, Mum."
"Well, if you don't want to do it, you'll have to tell Mrs. Sallis," said Annette, "and you (looking at me) can leave him alone."

The logistics of getting 32 cast members, plus teachers and helpers, props and wheelchairs to Manchester was itself an enormous undertaking, the school hiring two specially adapted coaches. It was necessary for the school party to arrive at the Bridgewater Hall early afternoon for rehearsals etc. while the performances did not start until 7.30 p.m. This was during the time that Chris was getting uncomfortable in his wheelchair and having to take rests. He was not overly impressed with the prospect of a long day. Annette arranged for Chris to arrive at school late morning in time to get the coach, thus having a shorter day. The school staff were very understanding and as always incredibly helpful.

As this was such a special and for us, momentous, occasion we had assembled a good-sized party of family and friends to travel to Manchester to support the school, along with the families of other pupils. We had to travel up in a number of cars and our party consisted of Nana, Auntie Julie, Auntie Anne, Uncle Chris, Norma and Abigail, Pat Skelton, Annette and I. Having entered the theatre Annette was keen to find the Dorin Park party to ensure Chris was OK. The Bridgewater Hall is huge and we eventually found a number of the Dorin group on their way to watch the early acts, as Dorin Park was scheduled to perform as the first act after the interval. We were told that Chris was elsewhere with Ian Shingler and Mr. Kidman, and that he was fine and enjoying himself.

We had seats to the left side of the auditorium, up above the stage, so that the view we had was very good. Having looked all around we still could not see Chris, but eventually located him – right below us. The first five performances were generally quite good, with Manchester's Trinity C of E High School 'St. Patrick's Breastplate' being excellent and setting a high standard. Having enjoyed the ubiquitous interval drinks we returned to our seats full of anticipation. Compere Steve Fortune came out onto the stage, which was filled in the shadows by the performers from Dorin Park. Steve Fortune explained to the audience that the JC2000 competition was open to all schools, regardless of colour or creed, and included special needs schools. He explained what Dorin's production was about and then said, "Ladies and Gentlemen, Dorin Park School present 'Don't Worry'."

The spotlight came on and picked out Chris, smartly dressed in his new silky green shirt ("you can't wear any old thing," Annette had said), glided forward a few feet, did a complete 360° turn, and moved towards the front of the stage. God, even before he spoke I nearly burst with pride. Chris stopped and started to speak – Oh no we couldn't hear him. He stopped speaking, switched on the chair and moved forward three feet, stopped again and began, his voice big and clear, "Do not worry about your life. Look at the birds in the air. They do not sow or reap or store away in barns and yet heavenly father feeds them." He finished the piece, smiled briefly and returned to his place besides Kurt Stretton. The performance continued, the kids were clearly enjoying themselves and giving it their all. Chris had several more pieces during the play, including being one of the 'cool dudes'. The performance went very well, as good as they had ever performed it, the songs were all sung with great enjoyment and for us it was easy to pick out Chris's voice. The performance was soon over, too soon really, and as the last notes of the final song drifted away the audience led by the Dorin Park supporters exploded with applause. All the other schools had got good responses, but Dorin Park were the only school that night that got a standing ovation. It was a truly marvellous moment and one that everybody connected with the performance could be justifiably proud of. The evening ended with all the performers back on the stage to sing the JC2000 Theme Song 'A Legend in my Time', led by Steve Fortune. We have a video of the night to remind us of a wonderful and moving occasion.

Unfortunately there was no opportunity to see the kids at the end of the night, that would have to wait until we were able to pick Chris up back at school. First off the bus was Kirsty Bridge, she had clearly enjoyed herself as she almost bounced off the bus in her wheelchair. Chris followed a little later, a broad smile on a tired face. Annette and I greeted him with congratulations for a great performance. "It wasn't just me you know," he said "everyone was great, they were as good as me."

In September 2000, during a visit Annette and I made to the school I was talking to Mrs Sallis, the drama teacher who had directed 'Don't Worry', and saying how proud we had all been of not only Chris, but the whole cast. Mrs. Sallis told of how the production had been put together, adding that it was constructed around Chris as they had identified that they needed someone to carry it. Mrs. Sallis went on that Chris had thrown himself into the development process, contributing ideas, providing words for the songs and lines to be spoken, he encouraged the other pupils to contribute and learn their parts. She concluded by saying that in all the time she had been teaching she had never been so moved by anything quite so much, "Chris", she said, "had changed her life." As Mrs. Sallis wrote a little later, "My other memories of Chris that have had a great deal of affect on me are those associated with JC2000. Nobody will know how proud I was of Chris. He was obviously in discomfort, but doing the part well, not letting himself, his parents or his mates down was so important to him. An organiser of the event, after the performance, spoke to me about Chris. She commented how powerfully he had communicated the words. Chris was a living example of someone who lived for the day and gave everything to the word "NOW". Working with him, was for me, a moving spiritual experience, and I am not a religious person." Mrs. Roberts, who wrote the music for 'Don't Worry', noted, "My own abiding memory of him will always be his part in the JC2000 production and of his being a happy, intelligent, kind and caring young person. How proud you must be of him."

A couple of days after the performance at the Bridgewater Hall Chris's new wheelchair was delivered. In August 1999, Uncle Bert had sadly passed away after a short illness and we had been left a legacy in his will. Over time Chris had become more and more uncomfortable and was taking rests on his bed. We felt that a new chair, tailored to his requirements would ease matters. After taking advice from Jenny Whitall (from the NMC) and Eric Malkin (of Five Towns, a mobility specialist) we had settled on a Quickie F55, with 'tilt in space' ability. My mum had also benefited in Uncle Bert's will and she kindly provided some of the £5,500 funding for the chair. Chris was almost speechless on the day it arrived and couldn't wait to try it out. The F55 is an imposing sight, with large chunky rear tyres, big front casters and heavy weight tubing, Chris had chosen a dark green colour. Eric quickly adjusted the chair to fit Chris and then he was away. From his first powered chair he had been a very competent and skilled driver and he was soon demonstrating the capability of the chair (which incidentally had a top speed of 10 mph). The *piece de resistance* as far as Chris was concerned though was the front and rear lights, the indicators and the hazard lights. Whenever we had visitors out would come the F55 and a full demonstration of its capabilities would be provided. I have to say it was an impressive piece of kit. One problem that we found with the chair though was that when Chris was driving quickly his hands would bounce off the centre mounted control box. With Eric and Jenny's help we were in the process of sorting this and a few other minor problems out when August came. However, in the short time that he had the F55 Chris got enormous pleasure from it and was immensely proud of his "fabulous chair".

We had not gone away in 1999 as with Chris being unwell and taking time to recover we had been reluctant to book anything, so as 1999 moved towards its conclusion we planned the summer 2000 vacation. After some discussion we decided on Florida, realising that this would most likely be the last time Chris would be able to travel the distance. I set about planning the trip, settling on an early May trip with flights on Virgin from Manchester, a week in Clearwater Beach and a week at Disney's Dixie Landings, both with wheelchair accessible rooms and a ramped van to get us around. This would be the first time we would be staying in a Disney hotel and the prospect of flying on a 747 added to the excitement. As always the build up started early, watching various promotional videos and clips of Florida from holiday programmes. Looking back there wasn't quite the same enthusiasm this time, but I guess that in my excitement I failed to see it. Not only did I love Disney, but I also loved watching Chris and how he enjoyed the whole Disney experience and sharing that with him. Then one evening, March 24th, about five weeks before we were due to go, while lying in bed Chris suddenly said, "Dad, I need to talk to you."
"Yeah, what can I do you for?"
"You're going to hate me," came a subdued response.
"I shouldn't think so, I love you too much for that," I said, a sense of unease rising within me. A long pause followed.
"What is it that you want?" I asked.
"Dad, I don't want to go on holiday," the last word almost being lost in a sob.
I was quite shocked really, but none the less took him in my arms and gave him a big squeeze.
"That's OK, don't worry. But why don't you want to go? I thought you liked America and Disney?" I asked.
Eventually, through the tears came, "I do, I do, but I can't face the journey. I'll just be too uncomfortable".
"But you'll be fine with the RoHo cushion and the chair support Mum and I have bought."
"I'm sorry Dad, but I just don't want to go. Will you tell Mum?"
Annette was in the kitchen when I told her. She was not, I don't think, that surprised with Chris's decision and was off to his room to comfort him. The following Wednesday we had all been invited to the 10th Birthday Party of the Neuromuscular Centre at Winsford, as we had raised funds for them in previous years. Chris decided at the last minute that he didn't want to go, he didn't want to travel the distance in the Galaxy as he would not be comfortable, so Annette and I went. It was a very pleasant and well attended event, hosted by the centre's president, Matthew Kelly, who kindly wrote a message for Chris. During conversations with Jenny Whitall and Kate Fox the subject of Chris not

wanting to go on holiday came up. Both Kate and Jenny expressed the view that it was very mature of Chris to make such a decision, something they both admired. They also expressed the view that Annette and I should still go, as we would benefit from the rest.

Chris was very pleased with his note from Matthew and wanted to know what had taken place. Annette told him what Kate and Jenny had said about us going to Florida.

"That's a good idea, I could go to Hope House," he said. I wasn't sure that this was such a good idea, much as I wanted a holiday I was not that keen on going without Chris. Anyway, I thought the chances of Hope House being able to accommodate Chris for two weeks at short notice was probably impossible. Well, cutting a long story short, Kath at Hope House worked miracles and was able to find room for Chris – he was delighted, Annette relieved and me unsure. I have to say that if Hope House had not been able to accommodate Chris there is no way we would have gone, we simply would not have trusted anybody else with his care for that length of time.

Before we went on holiday there was the School 'Camp'. This was the annual sleep over at the school when a small number of pupils spent Friday and Saturday on special events, spending the night in the school. They are always popular events, but with the care and support that Chris needed through the night, let alone his Tempur mattress and so on it was not possible for Chris to 'sleep over'. Instead, we would pick him up late evening and return him to the school early morning for breakfast so that he didn't miss anything. Attending this camp along with Chris were Daniel, Laura, Alicia, Celyn and Katie Mercer – a really happy group. Chris was really happy as his mate Daniel was there and when Annette and I arrived to pick Chris up we couldn't go until Daniel was safely in bed and we could say goodnight.

The following morning we were up promptly – "I need to get to school to see if Dan's alright and help to get him up." So by 8.45 we were knocking on the door at Dorin Park school. Some of the group were up already (and some of the staff looked like they had had better nights!), but Chris was more interested in finding his mate. They were all soon ensconced in the kitchen having breakfast and preparing for the trip to the Candle Factory at Burwardsley. It was from here, under the guidance of Lorraine Churchman that Chris bought a wooden pendant and key ring, inscribed 'Chris' on one side and our names on the other, which have become treasured possessions. When picking him up later that afternoon we couldn't leave until he had made sure that Dan was safely seated in his mum's car and was on his way home.

The next couple of weeks passed very quickly as the holiday beckoned, but just before we went Chris spent the day at The Croft, accompanied by Norma and other young people, participating in a study being organised by Dr. Wendy Mitchell and Dr. Tricia Sloper of the University of York. The project, 'Sharing Value', was to find out about good and helpful services (such as people, places and clubs) for young people with an illness or disability. Having participated in the Social Services seminar earlier in the year, Chris was very keen to join in and give as much help as possible and express his views. On his return home he was full of news, he particularly liked Dr. Mitchell, "who knew what was what".

It was arranged that the group would meet again in the Autumn half-term to review progress and exchange further ideas. Sadly, for Chris, that was not to be. Dr. Mitchell wrote at that time "Although we only met Chris once he was a fun, enthusiastic and vibrant member of the young people's group and contributed some really interesting and important ideas towards the 'Sharing Value' project. In fact, I have drawn extensively on Chris's ideas and comments in order to write a recent journal article expanding how disabled young people and their families' view 'quality' in services".

The day after The Croft it was time to take Chris to Hope House for his 'holiday'. He was adamant that he was not going in the Galaxy, he would he said be too uncomfortable, so we arranged for a taxi with Frank, who regularly took Chris to school and often to the Youth Club. Norma offered to travel with Chris and as often Abi accompanied her. We were just about to leave when we had a phone call from my cousin Pat, who was now living in Ireland. She was on a visit to the UK and wanted us to meet her partner, John Ryan. We explained the situation, but agreed to briefly meet at a hotel on our route to Oswestry. This was the first time that we had met John, but as usual Chris was very welcoming, chatting happily to John. The meeting was relatively short, as we had to be on our way, although it was agreed that Pat and John would call to see us next time they were over.

Chris settled into to Hope House as quickly as normal; down to his room, quick look around and then off to the games/computer room, leaving us to sort out his clothes and care notes. He took time out to show Norma and Abi around and offered them a cup of tea. The evening went quite quickly and we had to set off for Chester. We said good-bye to Chris and he came to the door with Annie to wave us off. He was quite cheerful, but as we drew away out of the drive I felt quite upset and bereft as he was not coming with us.

A lot of people that knew Chris were full of admiration that he had opted not to travel to the States, and to allow Annette and I to go. Some of these friends made a great effort and went to visit Chris at Hope House during the two weeks we were away.

Chris and Anne Bolton made one of the first visits and Chris was happy to show them his room, the lounge, the games room and the dining room where they took tea. He sat and chatted for quite some time and seemed to be enjoying himself. On a subsequent visit in the second week Chris and Anne could see that he was not as bright and was beginning to miss us, telling them that "perhaps 10 days would have been long enough". Josie also paid a visit and was given the guided tour and got to meet a number of his friends at Hope House. Norma, Abigail and Katie also went to see him and by all accounts he had a great afternoon of fun with Abi. Katie meanwhile was entertaining some of the other children with an impromptu puppet show in the Play Room with Sandie. Accompanied by Mrs Karling and Lorraine Churchman a number of his friends from school drove over to Oswestry on one afternoon, which was a great and pleasant surprise for Chris. And of course, Katie Gerrard and her mum and dad also visited him. This visit was just after Bob had picked up his new adapted Citroen Berlingo. Once Chris realised this everyone had to adjourn to the car park so, as Bob said later, Chris could give it the official inspection. He insisted on driving up and down the ramp several times to try it out, conferring with Katie on how good it was. He wanted to know the engine details (1800cc, Petrol, not as big as the Galaxy he was getting!), who'd done the conversion (Brotherwood's) and how fast does it go (fast enough). More conferring with Katie, who thought the whole thing was hilarious.

While we were away we phoned Chris every other day. Generally, the phone calls were fairly brief - "Hello, how are you?" "What have you been doing?" "Are you eating OK?" "Are you going to the loo OK?" a short general chat and then "Sorry, I've got to go now as I'm busy on the computer/got to help with Ashley/helping David with any number of names/about to test the fire-bells with Eric/or a number of other reasons." But, on the last two calls he wanted to chat a bit longer and during our final call from the hotel he said to Annette, "Don't go yet Mum I want to talk to you a bit longer." By now it was the longest we'd ever been apart from him and it was clear he was missing us. Mind you, that was true of us as well, while we had enjoyed the rest, Disney was not quite the same without Chris (we only spent one day in the parks). If someone had said the holiday was over midway through the second week we'd have been happy to go home.

We arrived back early morning from Florida and we were collected from the airport by big Chris, had a quick cup of tea at home before setting off for Hope House. We'd arranged for Frank to come to Oswestry later that morning to bring Chris home. When we got to Hope House Annette and I ran across the car park to be greeted in the hall (where he'd been hovering apparently since early morning) by a relieved looking Chris. There were hugs and kisses all round and "Ooh, I've missed you so much." from Chris. It was good to be back in his company and I resolved there and then that I would not spend that length of time away again. An ironic thought in relation to what was to unfold only a few months later.

It wasn't long before the materialistic side took over and he wanted to know what we had brought back off holiday for him. Amongst the numerous computer games was the latest version of Microsoft's Flight Sim that allows budding pilots to fly Concorde, which just happened to be Chris's favourite plane. Some of the other things we brought back included a couple of bottles of A1 Steak Sauce, sand and shells from Clearwater Beach ("if you can't go to the beach, the beach can come to you"), a NASCAR baseball cap and numerous other Disney things. No wonder the case was so heavy - or was that the kitchen sink?

Within days of Chris receiving the Achievement Award at Dorin Park, probably Chris's most exciting moment of the year arrived. On 31st May the wheelchair accessible Galaxy arrived. I was fortunate that I benefited from a company car and the company had generously allowed me to have the car adapted, although it had taken some time to reach agreement. The car had been on order for a few weeks and, as it was half term, Chris was at home. He'd invited Paul to come and witness this great moment. He'd been busy telling everybody about the new car, what the engine size was, what colour it was, how the ramp worked. As mid afternoon approached there was still no sign of the car when the phone rang. It was a chap from Brotherwood's asking for directions to the house, these duly given there was a rush to get outside. Five minutes later a lorry, pulling a

trailer, approached the house ..... and went straight past.
"I'm sure that's it," said a slightly annoyed Chris, "it definitely said Brotherwood on the side. Didn't it Paul?"
"Yes, it did," came the reply, which disappeared into a howl of laughter. This did nothing to ease Chris's annoyance.
"This is stupid!"
However, within minutes we were back to large smiles as the lorry and trailer reappeared and this time pulled up by the house. The driver quickly unhitched the trailer and opened the back of the lorry, pulled out the ramps and reversed out a magnificent blue Galaxy to gasps (and not only from Chris and Paul). "Isn't she beautiful," chirped Chris. This was truly *his* car.
The car was duly parked in the drive and the guy from Brotherwood's took us through the procedure for loading and securing the wheelchair. Chris having already seen the Gerrard's car was already an expert, but patiently watched and listened as the process was explained. To ensure that the lesson had been understood it was necessary for me to load the chair and secure it in place, needless to say I got a full set of verbal instructions to follow. Having successfully demonstrated that we knew what we were doing, the guy from Brotherwood's left us to it.
"Right Dad, come on lets go for a drive. You can come to Paul. Are you coming Mum? And Auntie Ju?"
"OK, just me and Paul." So with that we loaded up the chair, secured it in place and set off for a drive around the local roads. The position of the chair in the rear of the car provided its occupant an excellent view, of not only where we were going, but also of the driving controls and gauges. The return of the back seat driver.
The arrival of the Galaxy meant that we could again get around like a family, Chris was very comfortable, securely strapped in his chair.

The first longer journey we took in the Galaxy was to visit Chris's best friend Daniel who unfortunately was again in Alder Hey Hospital in Liverpool. Whenever Daniel was unwell Chris's concern for him was almost painful to watch, he would fret about him every day, asking Angela (Dan's one-to-one at school) if she knew how he was, had she heard from his mum, had she been to see him. The trip to Liverpool also gave Chris the opportunity to view two of his favourite buildings, the Metropolitan and Anglican Cathedrals. As they came into sight Annette and I would be bombarded by various facts and a raft of questions (most we couldn't answer). Once we'd arrived at the hospital Chris was bursting to get going and was up and away before I'd managed to close up the Galaxy. We located Dan's ward and gained entrance. Chris was off up the ward with his head turning left and right as he tried to find his mate. Suddenly he came to a halt, "Alright, mate. How are you?"

This was not the first time that we'd visited Daniel in hospital and the effect of the cheery greeting was always the same, no matter how poorly Dan was at the time. The figure in the bed would stir, the arms would lift, the face would break into a huge smile and the eyes would twinkle. Chris would manoeuvre his way alongside the bed and would then be able to hold Dan's hand, see his face and be able to 'talk' to his mate. On this visit Dan's mum, Jane, was able to get

Dan out of bed and into his chair so the conversation could now continue face to face. The topics covered included the latest news from school (who was doing what and to whom), football news especially about Manchester United, motor racing and how Mika Hakkinen was doing in the World Championship (neither of them liked Michael Schumacher) and a lengthy discussion on planes. Chris would enquire about Daniel's family, his little sister Rebekah, his dad Dave and Dan's nan. Chris would give an update on what he'd been up to which of course on this occasion included a detailed description of the Galaxy.

In June we took a trip out to Hope House to visit Chris's special friend Katie, who was having a break there while her mum and dad had a well earned rest in sunny climes. As chance would have it I was a little late in from work that night, to be greeted by a slightly irked Christopher, "Where have you been? You know we're going to see Katie tonight." "I know, I know, there's plenty of time" was my only defence. Talk about being nagged! Hope House is a 45 minute drive from Chester so we were soon there, as was the norm Chris was in a hurry to get out of the car and was off across the car-park before you could say 'Katie Gerrard'. Alison was looking after Katie and we found them in the Dining Room. Katie was so excited at seeing Chris that she nearly came out of her chair. As it was a lovely summer evening we took a walk around the gardens and walked down to the pond to watch the ducks. Chris chatted away busily with Katie, their empathy was wonderful to behold. In his way Chris cared greatly for Katie, he was always checking that she was OK, making sure that people around her knew what she wanted and when. But most of all he made Katie laugh and when Katie laughs you can't but help joining in, she has the most wonderful happiness in her voice.

We returned to the Dining Room for a drink and Katie was able to show us her photographs from the family holiday in Florida which they had taken courtesy of the Round Table Children's Wish. They had clearly had a great week and had met all the important characters. For Katie, Donald Duck was the favourite and there were some good shots featuring the small webbed guy with Katie, who was now proudly displaying her Donald Duck badge. Chris, of course, wanted to have a day by day report, much to Katie's amusement.

As the evening wore on Chris took me aside, "What are we going to do when we go?", he asked, "Katie's bound to get upset."

"Well, we can't go without saying good-bye. I'm sure that she'll be alright and Alison will look after her."

"Yes, but Katie will cry a lot."

"I know, but she'll be fine with Alison and she'll calm down after a little while."

Eventually, it came time for us to leave and we all walked out to the car park, where we bumped into another family who were just arriving. Chris slipped into his role of adapted Galaxy salesman enthusiastically describing the benefits of the design and how it worked. He encouraged Katie to sit inside and sample the delights. After a while we managed to get Chris in, he was excellent at avoiding certain things by creating diversions. We eased out of the car park and waved good-bye to Katie and Alison, and just as Chris had predicted Katie was starting to cry. All the way home it was "She'll still be upset, you know. " , "I wonder if Katie's OK now?"

Saturday 17th June was an important day for Chris as he had been invited to present the Young Carers awards at the Barnardo's Open Day. He'd already helped Hope House and Crossroads with publicity and now he had the opportunity to help another important organisation. Barnardo's had wanted a celebrity to hand over the awards, but it was suggested by Norma that they look no further than their own celebrity – Chris. Wonderful.

During May Chris entered a competition in the local Chronicle newspaper to win tickets to the Cosford Air Show. He was delighted when he found that he had won a family ticket for four. The obvious person to accompany us was big Chris, who was now fully recovered from his glider accident and an expert in aviation (unlike Dad who was only good at listening about aircraft). Sunday 18th June dawned very bright and soon warmed up into a lovely day. Cosford is over an hour's drive from our house and as soon as big Chris arrived we set off. Chris had decided to take his new Quickie wheelchair, this would be the first time that he had spent an extended time in it. On the journey we had to stop a couple of times to adjust his sitting position, but by and large he was OK. As we turned off the M54 we were directed the opposite way to which we had expected to go, before being directed down a series of country lanes. After a little time we came up behind a queue of traffic, which was not what Chris wanted to see, he was never the most patient of travellers. Fortunately, the lane was under a canopy of trees and so we were out of the direct sunlight as the day was now scorching hot. After queuing for about 30 minutes we reached the entrance to the air base – the crowds were incredible. We were pointed to the disabled parking area and unloaded. It was by now very, very hot, "Hotter than Florida," said Chris, as we headed for the attractions. There were already a lot of aircraft movements so our progress was very staccato as we stopped every now and then to watch a plane or helicopter fly past. The commentary from the wheelchair was coming thick and fast, with questions and observations to big Chris. The discussion was wide ranging, the history of the plane, the type of engines, the role of the aircraft and so on. By now we had made it to some of the static displays and so we viewed these with an expert eye, the technical discussion continuing at a pace. I just listened.

Initially, Chris was doing alright, but as the day wore on it became more difficult and the heat was making him more and more uncomfortable, especially due to his support jacket. Repositioning Chris in the chair increased in frequency, so we headed for the exhibits in the hangars, watching films on various aspects of RAF activities and both static and physical displays. Every now and then we would pop outside, staying in the shadows, and watch the flying displays. Some of the stunts were incredible and we were treated to the sight of some wonderful planes, including to Chris's delight a number of Spitfires.

In one of the hangars there was a display of photographs and equipment belonging to Air Reconnaissance. We were studying an aerial photo of London when a Sergeant manning the display approached Chris. He introduced himself as Giles Penfound and asked Chris if he was interested in photography. When Chris replied in the affirmative, the Sergeant proceeded to explain and demonstrate the camera he was carrying. It looked just like a normal 35mm SLR camera, but was in fact a digital camera. He explained how front line troops now use this technology and then by using cell phones can transmit the pictures immediately back to their HQ. Sergeant Penfound having asked if he could take his photo took a couple of shots, one with big Chris and I spoiling it! He then showed how the photo could be downloaded to a PC and using a software package change aspects of the shot by 'brushing' out details. To conclude Sergeant Penfound asked if Chris would like a copy of the pictures. Chris said he would so we wrote down our postal and e-mail address. When Sergeant Penfound saw the e-mail address he said he would forward the photos over the Internet when he got home that night. Chris thanked the Sergeant and shook his hand (with a little help).

By now Chris had had enough, even though the show had not finished, and wanted to go home, but not before a detour through one of the museum halls to show big Chris the display of missiles. As we proceeded past the exhibits Chris rattled off, with a nod of the head in the direction of the subject, "That's a HARM, that's a Sidewinder, that's an AMRAM." and so on leaving several people standing open-mouthed.

The journey home was not the most enjoyable of experiences for Chris, as by now he was really very uncomfortable. It was partly alleviated by big Chris sitting in the rear passenger seat and letting Chris lean on him. I think that big Chris's experience of wearing a support jacket after his glider accident had helped make him more aware of the issues associated with wearing such a jacket. Fortunately the road and traffic conditions were good as we made our way home so we made good progress. By the time we did get back to the house Chris was close to tears and as soon as we got in he wanted to go and have a lie down on his "lovely" bed and rest his back. He was really grateful to 'big' Chris for helping him out and making the journey easier. Even so, shining through the discomfort came his enjoyment of the day, he even talked about going the following year "....and perhaps it won't be so hot."

As Chris wrote later in his book at school.

The RAF Cosford Airshow

The airshow was very, very loud. One of the planes went from 0 to 65,000 feet in 20 seconds. There were lots of people there. There were some amazing helicopter stunts. They were flying backwards, turning upside down and going up and down very quickly. One of the planes flew 200 miles in ten minutes. It really was a great day out.

After a couple of hours rest Chris was ready to get up and get on with things. Of course this meant booting up the computer and immersing himself in the latest game or games. On this occasion that meant Microsoft Flight Sim and he was soon taking to the skies over Chicago having taken off from Meigs Field. A little while later there came a shout, "I've just looked on the Internet and I've got a message from Giles Penfound." A few clicks later, a download and an unzip and we were looking at the pictures taken that afternoon. Chris was very impressed, as well as delighted, and immediately sent back an e-mail expressing his thanks. The photograph of the Chris, big Chris and me is a great memory of a super enjoyable day.

Friday June 30th marked Christopher's 15th birthday. He had not had a birthday party as such for a few years as he was not that bothered feeling he was too old for all that, although we had usually marked the event with a tea or cake and some friends or relatives dropping by. During the year Chris had been at a few celebrations held at the Youth Club, but when Annette asked him if that's what he wanted to do he was very firm that it wasn't, "too much fuss!". That would probably have been it if it hadn't been for Norma. She told Annette that Chris secretly did quite like the idea, but didn't want loads of people. From that small acorn. Annette asked Norma if the party could be held at The Croft, the house in Mannings Lane owned by Barnardo's. After checking with her manager Tonia, the go ahead was given. Bearing in mind that Chris didn't appear to want a huge attendance only his close friends like Daniel, Katie, Kirsty, Abigail and Liz were invited, along with cousin Paul and Amy, as well as *older* friends like Chris and Anne, Josie, Ian, Dave, Pat and Yvonne.

Keeping it secret from Chris was not easy, there were mums to tell, arrangements to be made and preparations for the evening. Annette had planned that all the guests would arrive in advance and would be able to surprise Chris when he arrived. Norma was a wonderful help as not only did she help Annette with the shopping, but stored most of the food and took it to The Croft, where she set it out. The next problem was getting Chris to The Croft without him realising what was really happening. The day of the party was also the day on which we had tickets for the Broughton Airshow at Hawarden (also won by Chris through a competition), but the weather on that Saturday was quite dreadful, cold, heavy rain and low cloud, not conducive at all for flying. As the day wore on there was no improvement and after a phone call to big Chris (who knows about these things) it was concluded that it was no point in going. This of course caused a good deal of misery in certain quarters as Chris had been looking forward to going. As was now necessary Chris had a rest on the bed in the late afternoon and his mood was not helped when Annette announced that he needed to get up and get changed as we were going out.
"Where are we going?" asked Chris, in that bored teenager voice.
"I need to take some things to a friend's house," came Mum's reply.
"Can't you go some other time?"
"No"
"Well, do I have to get changed?"
"Yes"
"Ooh, ... flip."

Not long after, he was up, washed and changed, but still moaning as he was now waiting for Annette to get ready. Chris passed his time on the computer and was even less impressed when it was announced it was time to leave, just as he was halfway through a game. By now the rain had stopped and it had warmed up a little, so into the Galaxy, careful and clandestine loading of several bags of provi-

sions, and away. As we drove along Saxon Way John and Paul were coming the other way (on their way to pick up Pat).
"There's Paul and John, what are they doing here?" queried Eagle Eyes in the back.
"I don't know, perhaps Uncle John or Paul has a friend around here," I ventured.
"Well, Paul doesn't," came the terse reply, "perhaps they're going to our house. Quick! Turn round!"
"I shouldn't think they're going there," I said, with *knowing* confidence.
"Anyway, we're going out," Annette added.
"Yes, where is it we're going?"
"You'll know when we get there," said Annette.
Big sigh of resignation from behind.

We carried on the journey, with the conversation covering numerous subjects, until as we were going up Kingsway Chris interjected,
"This is the way to The Croft."
"Oh yes, so it is," I said.
"Is that where we're going?"
"I don't think so, Dad's just going this way."
By now we were turning into Mannings Lane.
"We are going to The Croft. What for?"
"Well we might be just going past it," I said. But by then we were there and turned into the drive.
"We are going to The Croft," came the an excited shout from Chris. "Look, there's the Bellingo, ... and Dan's van, ... and Norma's car, ... and Josie's car, ... and Ian's car. What are they all doing here?" In his excitement he'd missed the outdoor candles and the banner in the window.
"Happy Birthday, Chris – it's a surprise party," said an equally excited Annette. With that Chris turned to Annette and said with a big smile on his face, "You're a bugger," and then turning to me, "and you're a bugger."
I couldn't get him out of the car quick enough, as soon as the belts were off, he was gone, with Annette and I running along behind. Chris drove up the ramp to the front door, paused, Annette pushed it open and in he went to be greeted by a big cheer, party poppers, and streamers with "Sex Bomb" by Tom Jones playing, followed by a rendition of 'Happy Birthday'. The smile on his face said it all. Chris was in his element, there he was with his best mate, Dan, dear friends Katie and Abigail, and as we found out later, girlfriend Kirsty, as well as many other of the people that were important to him. It was a wonderful evening Chris scuttling around chatting to everyone, Katie laughing, Dan chuckling and smiling, Kirsty driving round chasing everyone, Lizzie telling us about her forthcoming move to college, Abi fussing around Chris. Paul was being macho drinking beer, Katie (Hellon) and Rebekah were happily playing with one another and pinching the little cakes to eat the icing. Norma had arranged a special birthday cake made in the shape of **007**, along with a Golden Gun, for a special agent. Chris was most impressed and helped by Annette cut into it. "We'll keep the gun for later," he said. Unfortunately, he didn't get his gun, as by the end of the evening the barrel on it had been eaten! Step forward Katie Hellon. When it was

Chris, Norma, Kirsty, Nicola and Tom; Social Services Conference.
28th January 2000

Paul and Chris 'celebrate' the arrival of the adapted Galaxy. 31st May 2000

Determination Award

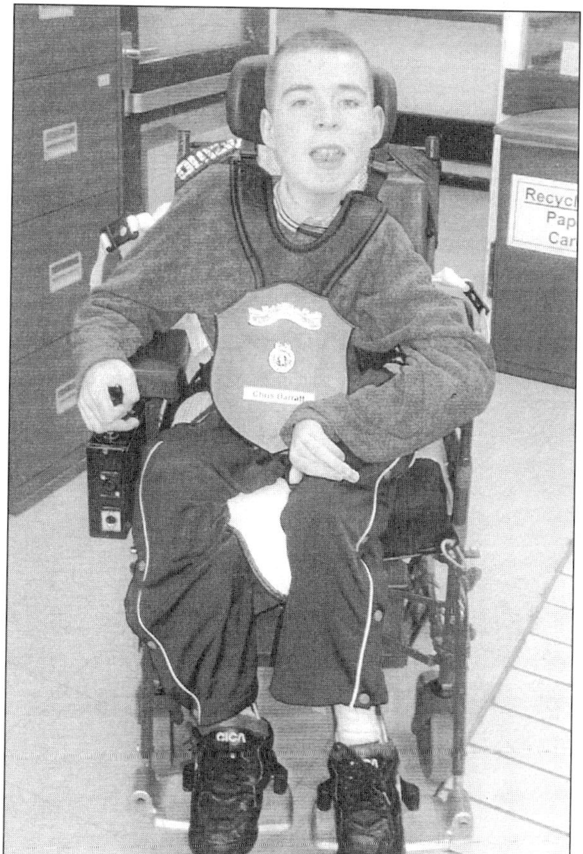

May 2000

In May 2000 to his great pleasure Chris was awarded Dorin Park's Determination Award. 26th May 2000

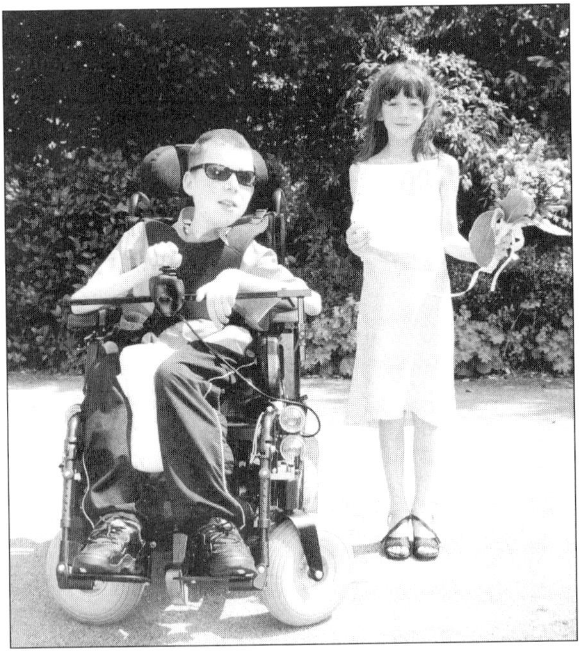

Barnardo's Open Day. Chris's friend Abi with her Young Carer's Award. 17th June 2000

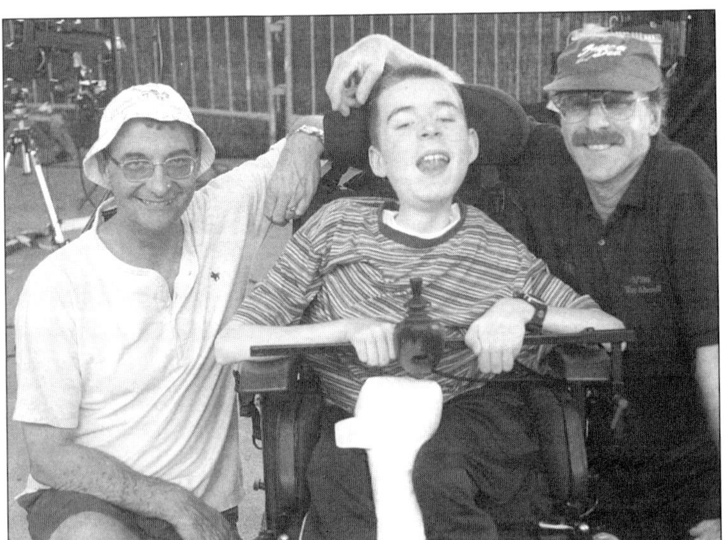

Chris, Chris, Dad RAF Cosford Airshow, 18th June 2000
(Photo: Giles Penfound)

Daniel, Katie and Chris - The Three Musketeers.
Chris's 15th Birthday Party, The Croft, July 1st 2000.

The joy of victory after years of trying shines through. Christopher and Quickie F55. Dorin Park Sports Day 19th July 2000

eventually time to go Chris saw everybody off, seeing each of his friends into their respective vehicles, making sure that they were belted and strapped in. Amy Hughes wrote to us later saying, "I wanted to tell you both how glad I am to have known Chris, he was so funny and he made me laugh! His birthday party was lovely, seeing him with all his friends who he cared about, he was a great person with a wonderful personality and I will never forget him".

Two weeks after Chris's party it was Kirsty's birthday and she held her party at home on a lovely Saturday afternoon. A number of her friends from school and Barnardo's joined her family to celebrate. As Chris had had a rest on the bed and we then needed to get him sorted we were a little late arriving. When he did make his appearance Kirsty came bouncing over to greet him, a big beautiful smile on her face. She took him off to show him around and meet other people. The welcome that Chris got was only equalled by the welcome Kirsty gave Norma, when she arrived with Abi. Kirsty nearly came out of her chair with excitement!

August was now upon us and at the start of the month my cousin Pat, accompanied by John, came to visit as we had arranged in April. John had spoken to and e-mailed Chris about a particular computer flying game that he had, but was having trouble getting to grips with. Chris had told him to bring it with him and he would show him how to play it, even though Chris did not have this particular game. Within a short time of Pat and John arriving the game was loaded onto the PC and Chris and John were huddled around the keyboard.

"Do you want the instruction book?" enquired John.

"Nah," came the reply, "we'll just try it out."

And with that Chris launched the game. After a few abortive attempts at getting the 'plane' to fly, it was up and away. The guns and missiles were mastered (a particular problem of John's) and missions flown. John sat amazed, mouth open.

"Jeez, I've been trying to do this for months."

"Well, you know how to do it now."

The rest of the afternoon was spent demonstrating and playing various computer games, talking about aircraft and particularly the Beluga which flew over the house almost on cue, watching in-bound Atlantic flights and racing each other in wheelchairs - Chris of course winning most of the races.

CHAPTER FIFTEEN (Last Goodbyes)

When I'm away please take good care of my heart
And when I'm gone say a prayer for love

C.Macdonald/R.Macdonald - Run Rig

Daniel's 15th birthday was on Tuesday 22nd August and we had all been invited to his party that afternoon. Chris was very excited at this, we had been intending to visit Daniel's home for sometime, but for one reason or another we had not got it organised, and at last we would be.

The day was bright, sunny and warm, a contrast to the preceeding days. We set off in plenty of time to reach Daniel's house in Leeswood by 2.00 pm. Unfortunately, Daniel's dad had given us misleading directions and so we ended up going the wrong way, not once, but twice. This was not going down well with Chris. The mutterings from the back of the Galaxy made this very clear. Eventually, 45 - 55 minutes late we arrived in the small Welsh village and quickly found Dan's house. The birthday boy was in the garden looking out for his guest. The frown on his face quickly changed to a bright smile as reversing down the ramp of the Galaxy came his mate. Chris's whole mood changed as he launched into the story of why he was late and that it was my fault and that he thought we would never get to the party and .... and .....

The afternoon was going well, but Daniel was feeling uncomfortable and despite it being his birthday he had to go for a lie down on his bed. That was no problem for Chris who immediately positioned himself at the bedside and continued the conversation, interspersed with watching Dan's birthday video on Formula 1, a shared passion of them both.

Dan did manage to get up later, enjoyed the traditional singing of 'Happy Birthday', the blowing of the candles and the lovely birthday tea, put on by mum Jane. Gradually, people made their way home. I kept suggesting it was our turn to leave, but some how there was always an excuse or reason to delay. "Dan just wants this", "Dan wants me to.....", "I'm not ready to go yet", "Can't we stay a bit longer" and then Jane added that Daniel wanted to share something special with Chris, Annette and I. Through the charity, "Make a Wish" Daniel had been the guest the previous week of the Jaguar Formula 1 racing team at Silverstone. He met the drivers, met Jackie Stewart, had been driven around the track by Luciano Burti in a Jaguar XK8 and been presented a bottle of champagne. It was the champagne he wanted to share with his friend, to top off his day. So there we were Daniel, Chris, Jane and Dave, Annette and I enjoying a chilled glass of France's best as the evening cooled and the sun set. We eventually persuaded Chris it was time to go and with Chris shouting farewell to his mate we set off for home at about 8.30 pm having had a wonderful and memorable afternoon. In many ways he was as happy that day as we'd ever seen him, it was the last time the mates would see each other.

The following morning Chris was up at his normal time, despite the previous late night (for even though he was 15, he generally went to bed by 9.30/10.00 p.m. as he would be feeling physically tired or needed to rest his back). Off I went to work and he spent the day on his computer or watching videos. As usual when I came in from work I would spend time chatting to Chris (usually at the computer) and then, after getting changed, give him his tea. He'd decided that for this night's tea he would have Oxtail soup and bread, and that he'd have it in his bedroom watching his current favourite video, 'The Royle Family'. He was his normal cheery self, but half way through tea he suddenly said he had wind in his tummy. We had got used to this happening occasionally, since his constipation trouble, and had found that a good cure was a drink of Andrew's Liver Salts. He happily took the drink and following a loud belch, followed by a big laugh, said he felt much better. However, little more than an hour later he informed us that the pain was back and he wanted to go to bed. We knew from experience that it was pointless arguing, so we got him ready for bed.

Initially, Chris seemed to be better, although he said he still felt sick. However, as the night wore on he became more and more restless. Annette and I were up throughout the night as we tried to get Chris comfortable and relieve his discomfort. First thing the next morning Annette phoned the doctor and requested a home visit. Chris remained in bed and throughout the morning we encouraged him to sip water and to eat biscuits and bread sticks to try to overcome the wind. The feeling of sickness had worn off, but the tummy pain remained and he was belching regularly. Our initial concern was that he was constipated, but our by now well practised checks suggested that this was not the case. Just prior to lunchtime the doctor arrived and following a potted history from Annette, proceeded to examine Chris. The doctor discounted constipation, and thought an appendicitis unlikely, before suggesting that Chris may have some inflammation of the stomach or intestine. She prescribed Gaviscon Extra, writing out the prescription and advising that if we were worried to call again. The medicine was duly obtained from the local chemist and Chris took it without fuss.

After a little while Chris said he felt a bit better, our natural reaction being "Oh, good". However, he was still in bed and reluctant to get up. Chris's cousin Paul came around during the afternoon and they both watched various videos and TV programmes. Chris appeared to be slightly better and certainly enjoyed his time with Paul, as the laughter from the bedroom testified. Thursday evening was our night for shopping and as usual Josie from Crossroads arrived at 6.00 pm. Annette and I weren't sure we should go, but Josie insisted we should go and that she would look after Chris. We did not take as long as normal returning to find that Josie had persuaded Chris to have not only his medicine, but also a small amount to eat and drink. To further enquiries Chris said he felt better and "No thanks, I've had enough to eat".

Despite further medicine Chris had another disturbed night, unable to get into a comfortable position long enough to go to sleep. Annette and I spent another sleepless night as we tried to eleviate Chris's discomfort, although rubbing his tummy did seem to provide some relief. The following morning Annette called the doctor again, speaking to another practice partner. He reassured us that the action being taken was satisfactory. Some time previously we had arranged a trip to Hope House for Chris on the forthcoming weekend. During the day both Annette and I asked him if he still wanted to go. He replied that he did, adding on a few occasions that "David (Riffel) will be there, and I want to see him". We asked again, right up to the time that we needed to get Chris up, get dressed and set off. He was adamant that he was going and "Yes he did feel better, thank you!"

Having got his kit together, although worryingly he was not too concerned as he normally was about which videos, CD and computer games he wanted to take, we loaded up the car and set off. Having got up and into his chair he seemed much brighter and altogether much chattier. We drove across the town and out onto the A483 towards Oswestry. The Chris Rea tape, *God's Great Banana Skin*, a favourite of Chris's was playing and he was singing along to the various tracks, instructing Annette and I to sing (if that's how you describe the noise we make) at various points.
"How's your tum now?" I asked.
"Oh, it's OK now. I feel much better," replied Chris, returning to his singing.

The rest of the journey was a delight, the singing continued interspersed by Chris's jovial chatter on, as usual, many different subjects. We arrived at Hope House at about 6.30 p.m. and parked in the car park, unloaded the car and were greeted by Jan Langley and a trainee nurse, Hannah. Rather than have a cup of tea we decided to take all Chris's kit down to his room and *check-in*. Chris had remained cheerful, but after about 15-20 minutes he told us he wasn't feeling well again and he wanted to get into bed. We asked if he wanted to go home, but he was adamant that he wanted to stay, so we got him into his pyjamas and into bed. Soon after Lesley, one of Hope House's Nurses came into to see Chris. She greeted Chris in her usual way by taking his hand and kissing him on the forehead. Having chatted to Chris, she turned to Annette and asked if we would mind if she sent for the doctor, as she was concerned about the way Chris looked. Of course, Annette said we didn't mind, as always we just wanted what was best for Chris.

The evening of Friday, 25th August was lovely, quite mild with a slight breeze. The view from Chris's room over the rolling Shropshire fields to the distant hills was very reassuring. Having called the doctor Lesley returned and took Chris's temperature, oxygen saturation level and a 'wee' sample. She than asked if she could speak to Annette in the garden. Lesley proceeded to explain to Annette that she was worried that Chris may have an appendicitis, but warned that if he had to have surgery he may not survive either the operation or post-operative care owing to his poor lung capacity (brought on by the scoleosis of the spine). Adding that ".. the heart is a muscle". In many ways we didn't want to hear this, it was something we had dreaded for a long time. Annette called me into the garden, but telling me what Lesley had said was very difficult as Chris, who was now feeling more uncomfortable, kept shouting for me to rub his tummy and move his position to try to get him more comfortable. However, no sooner did I get him in one place than he wanted moving again. I had not seen him like this before, even the previous two nights had not been this bad. It was very distressing and must have been absolutely awful for Chris. Even though he was uncomfortable he still did not moan about his predicament. Both Annette and I felt so helpless, so useless, whatever we tried to do did not seen to help.

About 7.30 pm the doctor arrived, it was not the normal Hope House doctor (who had been called away), but a locum from the ShropDoc service. He reviewed the observations, taken earlier by Lesley. The urine sample that showed higher levels of ketones and white blood cells. He examined Chris and after a little while he said that he thought that Chris had a urinary tract infection, but that it was possibly an appendicitis. He prescribed some antibiotics and advised that Chris could have some pain relief, but that he was unwilling to give anything too strong as it would mask the pain, which was a key indicator of the appendicitis. Chris took the antibiotics and soluble Panadol, as usual, without complaint, but remained uncomfortable and constantly moving.

Annette and I had originally not planned to stay, Chris enjoyed his weekends at Hope House without Mum and Dad interfering! However, the staff made a room available for us if we wished. The evening wore on with little improvement in Chris's condition, but also without it getting worse. The doctor called in again about 11.00 pm and examined Chris again. He was still of the opinion that it was probably a water infection, but couldn't rule out the appendicitis. He suggested that Chris was admitted to the hospital in Shrewsbury where they would be able to observe him better and perhaps improve his pain relief. Our initial reaction was to agree. However, when we sat down and thought it through more clearly it was clear to us that this was not necessarily a good move. The hospital was in completely the opposite direction to where we lived and therefore away from our family and friends who would be able to help us with Chris if a longer stay in hospital was necessary and they would not have the special Talley air mattress that Chris used. We discussed the options with Gwyn, the night shift team leader, and concluded that it would be better for Chris to remain at Hope House and review the situation in the morning.

The staff of Gwyn, Ruth and Hilary were wonderful, both to Chris and to us. They insisted that we get some sleep, telling us that they would call us if anything changed. The night passed quite quickly, interspersed by an almighty thunderstorm, although perhaps not so for Chris who continued to be uncomfortable and require constant position changes. Annette and I got a call at 7.30 am, the Hope House doctor, Simon Robinson, had called in and had examined Chris. He thought that he might have an appendicitis, but couldn't rule out the water infection, but felt that he should be admitted to hospital. We asked if Chris could go to the Countess of Chester Hospital, as he was known to the doctors and staff there, we could get his Talley air mattress from home for his comfort and we would be able to get help from family and friends. Dr. Robinson went off to arrange the admission, returning 5 - 10 minutes later to say that it was OK and he would arrange an ambulance. As this was likely to take some time I asked if we could take Chris to Chester in his wheelchair in our car, as we could go immediately and so get there quicker. The doctor thought that this was a good idea, adding, "There is an urgency, but it is not an emergency." By this time Chris had started to be sick, which he found quite distressing.

I explained to Chris what we had to do and while he was not overly pleased with the prospect of going to hospital (he asked if he could stay at Hope House with David looking after him) he eventually did agree to go. Between Annette, David, Jan and myself we proceeded to get Chris ready, getting him into his support jacket and sitting him in his chair. Once in his chair, and very much unlike him, Chris got very agitated and had a panic attack. He wanted to get back into bed. David and Annette tried to reassure him and with the words "I'm a fighter pilot, I'm OK now," he calmed down. David suggested that we take off his jacket, as it wouldn't harm him not wearing it for the relatively short time while we made our way to Chester and if he sat in the back of the car with Chris he could provide some support. Once the jacket was off Chris was much more comfortable and settled down a bit, although he was still being sick. All I could think of at this time was getting Chris to hospital and getting him sorted out. I found the discomfort he was suffering and the sickness very distressing, I hated seeing my son suffer so and not for the first time felt so helpless. I knew, from Annette's demeanour that she was frantic with worry too. I was just focused on getting Chris to hospital.

We got Chris's belongings together, carried them to the top of the house and I moved the car to the front door, returning to get Chris. He was now quite calm and set off, passing Hannah, the trainee nurse in the corridor. "Goodbye, Hannah," said Chris, "its been nice meeting you." continuing up the passageway towards the front door. A voice came from one of the other bedrooms, it was Alison, one of the care team. "Where are you going, Chris?" she asked.
"I'm off to hospital," came the reply.
"I'll see you when you come back." Short pause. "Maybe."
With that Chris was off up the passageway. About halfway up we met Lesley coming the opposite way. She took Chris's hand and kissed his forehead. "Are you off to hospital now?" she enquired.
"Yes, I have to go," responded Chris (in what in retrospect was an almost wearisome voice).
"We'll keep your room ready, in case you want to come back or need to recuperate." Short Pause. "Yes, maybe."
And with a click and whirr of the chair motors he was off.

At the top of the passage are two double doors at right angles to each other, forming a sort of chicane, with Chris's driving skills the doors were simply taken flat out. To the left of the doors is the Computer Room (a favourite haunt of Chris) and to the right the Dining Room (which was busy with breakfast). Without a pause and without a look either way Chris sped across the entrance hall to the front door, which was already open. I'm not usually affected by such things, but as Chris and I went through the door I shivered, a sudden feeling that **we** were leaving for the last time swept over me.

Chris hardly paused, he seemed quite resolute now as he drove up the ramp and into the car, I strapped in both the wheelchair and Chris himself, piling in his belongings behind him, keen to get off. David, Annette and Jan had followed us up to the top and were organising who was doing what. David had brought up a small bottle of oxygen just in case Chris had another panic attack on the journey and placed it in the front of the Galaxy. Annette got in the front, David in the back alongside Chris and Jan fetched her car, as she was to follow us to Chester so that she could bring David back to Hope House. It was just after 9.00 am when we set off, Chris looking back at Hope House, then down the hill and through Morda and turned towards Oswestry. The Chris Rea tape, from the previous evening, was still on in the car and Chris picked up singing. Through Oswestry and down to the A5/A483, turning left and heading towards Chester. As it was Bank Holiday Saturday there was quite a lot of traffic on the road, despite it being fairly early. All I could think of was getting Chris to hospital and getting him sorted, so I was concentrating on the driving, overtaking where safe, but keeping up a reasonable speed, while making sure that Jan was keeping up with us. Chris continued to sing along to the tape and chatted to David, he seemed quite relaxed now although I'm sure he was feeling below par.

David asked if he could tell a few risqué jokes, and encouraged by Chris started to do so. We passed the junction for Chirk, the B5070, and headed down a dip which takes the road over a tributary of the River Dee. Chris Rea was singing "I'm Ready". Having told the first joke (which I have to say was not that good!) David proceeded onto a second. ("Made my decision; Gonna see this one through" sang Chris Rea)

Having crossed the river the road rises up towards the junction where the A5 parts from the A483, about 6 miles from Hope House, and heads for Llangollen. David finished the joke. ("'Cos I'm ready").
"Didn't you find that funny?" I heard David ask.
"Chris, are you alright mate?" said David.
"Chris," David said, with more concern in his voice, "Chris talk to me."
"Oh, no. Something's gone wrong!" As David said this, Annette turned round and gasped, as she realised what had happened, and I looked in the rear-view mirror. Where I would normally see Chris's smiling face, all I could see was a gaunt look with his eyes staring upwards. My heart raced and sank at the same time. I felt sick.
"You'd better pull over quick," ordered David. As fate would have it there is a lay-by just before the A5 turning and I swung in and stopped. ("Star of hope, shine on me").

I'm not totally sure what happened next, but I ended up sitting in the other rear passenger seat, and having undone the seat belts and Chris's wheelchair harness tried with David to revive Chris by massaging his chest and giving him oxygen. I knew from almost the moment I got in the car that it was pointless, for as I got in I had put my cheek against Chris's and felt how cold it was. Annette mean time had run back to Jan, who had pulled in behind us, and asked her to phone an ambulance on her mobile phone. David by now had realised the futility of our efforts and got out of the car and gently suggested that Annette should get in and hold Chris with me. We held him tight, we told him that we loved him and told him we didn't want him to go, it was too soon for that. We kept holding him, talking to him, until the ambulance arrived and the paramedic wanted to see if he could help. The expression on his face said it all; he asked what Chris's name was and then gently lifted him out of the car and placed him on the stretcher. The paramedics asked if we wanted them to try to revive Chris, grasping at a final straw we said we did, the paramedics did all they could and got Chris into the ambulance. Annette and I followed and with the siren blaring we set off to what turned out to be the Maelor Hospital at Wrexham. David, driving the Galaxy, and Jan followed on.

Throughout the journey to the Maelor the paramedic kept Chris's airway open, but we knew that we were just looking at a shell of what used to be our lively, lovely and intelligent son. His journey was almost over. We were met at the Maelor by a very nice Staff Nurse, who showed us into a small room with four or five chairs and a small table and asked if we'd like some tea. As we arrived a number of doctors had appeared and examined Chris, before he was carefully taken into the A&E reception ward. Very soon after a gentle looking man with glasses, white hair and beard entered the room. He was he said in a soft gentle, Welsh accent Dr. Owen. He told us that he had examined Chris and that as we had already acknowledged he was beyond resuscitating; he expressed his deep sympathy. He further explained that as the circumstances were unusual it would be necessary to advise the Coroner's Officer, but he assured us that he would do everything he could to help matters along. By this time David (now sporting the start of a black eye having walked into the door of the Galaxy) and Jan had arrived, and they were shown in to the room in which Annette and I sat. They were understandably both terribly upset and deeply affected by the events that had unfolded just 30 minutes before. Throughout the period all I could think of was what I had done by subjecting Chris to the journey only for him to end his life in some grotty lay-by.

In the room was a phone, which we asked if we could use. Annette first called her brother, John, and our sister-in-law Julie, who immediately said they would come to the Maelor. The next call was to our friends, Chris and Anne Bolton, who dropped everything and arrived at the hospital 20 minutes later. They like John and Julie provided us wonderful support through the rest of the day while no doubt suffering from the huge loss of Chris themselves. Over the next couple of hours there was much coming and going as Dr. Owen and the Coroner's Officer, PC Gareth Williams, helped to sort out the situation regarding a post-mortem. The paramedic that had attended to Chris at the roadside came in to express his condolences and apologise for not being able to do more. Chris would have approved of that. We had every opportunity to see Chris, the Staff Nurse could not have been more caring. Chris looked very comfortable, like he was sleeping, with a familiar little smile on his face. It was ironic, and not a little poignant, that one of the first people to see Chris, after Annette and I, was Julie - it was like the clock had rolled back 15 years and 2 months to that very first day.

Eventually, PC Williams returned to say that the Coroner had, after discussion with Dr. Owen, agreed that no post-mortem was necessary and the cause of death could be recorded as Duchenne Muscular Dystrophy. Chris Bolton kindly undertook to phone Clarke's the undertakers and arranged for Chris to be picked up and taken home to Chester. It just remained for us to say thank you to the staff and bid a tearful goodbye to David and Jan. Annette and I returned home sitting either side of Chris's empty wheelchair in Chris's Galaxy, driven now by Chris Bolton, and accompanied by Julie. John and Anne Bolton followed on in their respective cars.

When we arrived home it was already mid afternoon and Annette started the painful task of phoning around our friends to tell them the sad news. I had one more difficult task, and that was to tell my mother. I knew she would be terribly upset and it was for that reason that we had not phoned her from the hospital. Chris and Anne volunteered to take me. When she came to the door she must have realised something was wrong, seeing me with Chris and Anne. I sat her down and quietly explained what had happened, the anguish in her face was clear to see, but she did not react as badly as I thought she might. We had prewarned her neighbour, Hildred, of the situation and she came around with her granddaughter, which helped to lighten things.

John and Julie and Chris and Anne stayed quite late with us, we also had the first of many visitors, but once everybody went it was a very strange feeling. We were so used to the tick tick tick of the computer keyboard, or the occasional outburst because something had gone wrong, or the whirr of the chair motors as Chris came in for a chat or to watch the TV. It was a long restless night, during which we got up a number of times and called on the soothing properties of the teapot. We were up quite early the next morning, Sunday, but it wasn't long before there was a knock at the door and John, Julie and Paul came in. They were just the first of many visitors throughout the day and indeed the next couple of weeks. It was testimony to how popular Chris was that people wanted to share their memories of him with us.

Later that morning while standing in the kitchen with Josie, our friend from Crossroads, Julie asked whether we had started to consider what arrangements would need to be made. We said we hadn't, but agreed that we would need to, and a number of suggestions were made with regard to where the funeral might take place and what we may do afterwards. I said I assumed that we would simply come back to our house, but Julie thought that this would be impractical, as there would be too many people to accommodate. I said that I couldn't believe that to be the case, we were after all only talking about a 15-year-old lad. Josie and Annette agreed however with Julie and after some further discussion it was suggested that The Croft would be a good place, Chris had always enjoyed going there. Josie volunteered to ring Norma to see if she could arrange it.

During the afternoon I accompanied my mother to the Chapel of Rest to see Chris. He was just as we'd left him the day before at the Maelor, he still looked to be asleep and peaceful and the familiar little smile remained on his lips. While

I felt a kind of relief that he was free from his wheelchair and the dreadful ravages of MD, I also felt an immense grief and huge sense of loss. Annette and I had lost an enormous part of our life.

The following day, Bank Holiday Monday, it had been arranged for us to go to Hope House to collect the Death Certificate. Chris Bolton offered to take us, I was very glad he did, as I did not fancy driving the Galaxy there without Chris. The journey took place with minimal conversation and as we passed the lay-by in which we'd stopped the car went very quiet. Returning to Hope House was in many ways quite difficult (although in retrospect I'm glad we did go). As always happened we were met at the door, fittingly by David (sporting a black eye from his argument with the door of the Galaxy the previous day, as he said, "that would have made Chris laugh"), and shown into the lounge. Over tea we were joined by Pauline and Mary and later by Alex the 'resident' physiotherapist. We chatted about the previous weeks events and of peoples recollections of Chris, of how he'd disregarded his disability and got on with his life and how he brought much joy to those who'd come into contact with him. Hearing these things we began to understand just what a remarkable son Chris had been, and this was to be brought home to us more so over the next few weeks.

CHAPTER SIXTEEN
(Strange Events and Coincidences)

When it is dark enough,
you can see the stars.
Charles A. Beard

Looking back over the twelve months prior to August it was like Chris had been putting things in his life in order. Over the period Chris would ask Annette and I to find and put on videos that had been made of the Christmas productions at Dee Point, he would talk about his friends that we watched and reminisce about the activities connected with the production. Safely filed.

He also asked us to watch the video on which we had recorded various pieces taken from the TV holiday programmes about Disney, some going back to 1990. We had to get out the diary and photo albums that we had of each holiday and recall the events, recalling in detail our goes on the rides and the many other things we had done. We got out the video on which there was a recording of the ITV programme 'Highway', in which Harry Seacombe had taken a group of underprivileged children to Disney World. One of the boys, Danny, had Muscular Dystrophy and Chris took a special interest in him. The video features many people who work for Disney and perform charitable work, it includes the choir from Orlando Cathedral singing a number of hymns and Harry also sings, including a wonderful version of 'When You Wish Upon a Star'. Chris made Annette and I watch this video several times, on one occasion asking what we thought might have happened to Danny and comparing his progress to himself, not in a self pitying sort of way, but more of concern for the young lad in the film. Sorted and filed away under 'Happy Memories and Disney'.

During his time at Dee Point Chris had been very friendly with Laura Holmes and they exchanged birthday and Christmas cards, although they hadn't seen one another for a couple of years. Then one day in early July 2000 there was a knock on the door and it was Laura. She explained that she cycled past our house on her way to and from her Saturday job and had often thought about looking in on Chris, but on this occasion she said she had felt a *pull* to do so. Chris was genuinely happy to see Laura, a big smile appearing on his face. They sat and chatted for quite some time, reminiscing about their time at Dee Point, recalling happy times and laughing about certain pupils and members of staff, as well as catching up on what had happened to them since moving on. Laura was to call one more time, recalling more from their past and as always Chris wanted an update on Laura's family. Dee Point nicely tied up.

One afternoon, soon after the adapted Galaxy had been delivered, we had dropped Annette off in town and Chris wanted to go for a drive. "I know," he said, "let's go through Handbridge."
"Handbridge?" I queried.
"Yes, I'd like to see 'The Magic Secret' again, not to get out 'cos the wheelchair

wouldn't get up, but just to see it again. I've not seen it for ages. And we could see the swings."
We drove through Chester and down Bridge Street and then over the Old Dee Bridge, slowing down as we went past Edgar's Park.
"There it is," he said excitedly, " 'The Magic Secret', it really is magic you know."
There was a long pause and then he added, as if his mind was somewhere else, "I used to go there when I was small with Nana ..... and with you. It was mag.... OK, we can go now." I could almost see his mind replaying those happy times, just like a film, a time when he could walk.
"Are you sure you don't want to get out?"
"Yea, let's go." Subject: Parks/Days with Nana - filed.

From Handbridge Chris insisted that we head for Broughton, where his friend Katie lived. I told him that we weren't calling unannounced, so he accepted just seeing where Katie lived. As we reached Broughton I pointed out the pub in which Katie's sister worked and immediately spotted Katie and her mum standing outside.
"Quick, quick, STOP," shouted Chris, "No! turn round."
A rapid trip around the roundabout and we pulled up by Katie and Sandra. Arrangements were quickly made and we adjourned across the road to Madision's coffee shop. The rest of the afternoon was spent drinking coffee/tea, eating cakes, chatting and laughing - oh yes, lots and lots of laughter. Wonderful, Special Friend locked into memory.

Later that month we were visiting the local Greyhound Shopping area one afternoon, making good use of the new adapted Galaxy, Chris was also giving his new chair an outing when we bumped into Carol Cartwright and her husband. Coincidence? Chris had not seen 'Auntie' Carol (from Playschool) for many years, although Carol had kept in touch through friends as to Chris's progress. In his usual way he made a big fuss of Carol, wanted to know how her son Colin was, and wanted to show her and her husband the car. Of course he recalled his time at Let's Pretend and how much he had enjoyed it. Playschool sorted.

Anne Bolton told us how on the last day before Chris was taken from us he spoke to Anne on the 'phone. Normally he would 'sign off' by asking Anne "How's everyone?" But this time he closed by asking "How's Uncle Chris, How's Sarah, How's Antony and Nicola and How's Amy!" Strange? At the time she had put it to the back of her mind. It was only later, after hearing the news that the significance of it came back to her.

Returning from Hope House, with Chris Bolton, having collected the Certificate, on the Bank Holiday Monday we passed the lay-by in which we'd stopped the previous dreadful Saturday. Big Chris sees it thus, "Chris's last journey in the ambulance was to the Wrexham Mealor where Anne and I came to comfort Mike and Netty. Mike was distraught and what was making it all the worse was in Mike's words "that Chris had died in a grubby little lay-by on the Wrexham to Oswestry road". I know that road quite well and there are few lay-bys and the very one Chris passed away in was next to the Chirk microlighting airfield. Mike took comfort from the vision of Chris's spirit saying "Right I've had enough of this! I'm off" and climbing into his favourite plane, speeding off, climbing ever higher through the valleys between mountainous white clouds to the stars. Nice one mate! **Per Ardua ad Astra**."

During July we had had the bungalow repainted and it was now resplendent in cream with blue window surrounds. The windowsills are made of concrete and Ray, the painter, had used thick primer to form a base, before the undercoat and final gloss coat. On the Tuesday after Chris's passing Annette called me to Chris's bedroom. There she pointed out the paint on the windowsill. It was lifting in three or four places, just like it had been picked by little fingers. Nothing strange there perhaps except that the paint on the other eleven windowsills was perfect (and remains so).

I had been in Chris's bedroom most days since his passing, closing the curtains and putting on the night-light he insisted on having. Some of his clothes were hanging on the back of the bedroom door and behind those was a Year 2000 calendar featuring his favourite Formula 1 racing driver, Mika Hakkinen. It occurred to me that the calendar had not been changed, so took it down and turned in over from July to August. The calendar was a mix of action and personal shots, but the one for August caught my eye. That months picture was a side shot of the top half of Hakkinen, in a pensive pose, with his hands together as if he was praying. Strange? Coincidence?

For a few days after Chris's passing his computer had not been switched on, but letters and other documents had to be written. Everything went well until I came to print - and nothing. I tried everything I could think of, but to no avail. After a couple of days during which the computer worked fine apart from the printing I was getting very frustrated. Annette mentioned the problem to Sharon Carrington, "Ah well," she said, "you know what the problem is? As it was Chrissy's computer you'll have to ask him to let you use it."
So later that day Annette did just that, "Come on sweetheart, your Dad needs to use the computer, let him use it."
On Annette's insistence I tried to print again - the printer burst into life and out came my letter. Strange?

A short while after Chris's funeral we were told this story by an emotional Nikki Barrett. On the morning of Chris's funeral Nikki and her husband Lee had arranged to take their daughters to Nikki's mum's. Isabelle was very concerned about Chris; was he safe? and had his Guardian Angel taken care of him? Now I understand that a departed soul is met by their Guardian Angel and when they're safe they send a message back to earth, usually in the form of a white feather, to show all is OK. To try and calm Isabelle down, Lee and Nikki searched everywhere in the house for a feather, but to no avail. After the service they picked up their daughters and returned home, to be greeted in the doorway of Isabelle's bedroom by a white feather, a feather that Nikki and Lee swears was not there when they went out and with no indication of where it had come from. Isabelle now keeps the feather in her jewellery box. Strange? Coincidence?

Later Lee told of us another story about Isabelle who was putting on a 'show' one day in late October 2000 for her mum, dad and sister and sang, "Chris we know you will look after us two. When we see a rainbow Chris we know its you". And later she said, "Look a rainbow, Chris has got his arms around the world". What a lovely thought, from now on I shall always think of Chris when I see a rainbow.

Katie Gerrard has on a shelf in her room a small soft Tigger, a favourite Disney character of both Katie and Chris. Over many months this Tigger keeps moving, not just falling off the shelf, but getting into various places around the room. Initially, Bob and Sandra thought nothing of it and Katie thought it all very amusing. It is not possible for Katie to move it, sister Emma denies it is anything to do with her and when asked about it Katie is adamant that Chris is moving it. Twelve months on and Tigger's still moving. Strange?

In June, Annette and I, along with other parents were invited by Hope House to their 'Summer Snowflakes' Day. A day on which those children that have passed away during the year are remembered, through words and music. Annette had decided that she wanted to deliver the tribute to Chris herself, a tribute which she had asked Mrs. Sallis to write. The event takes place next to the lake in the Hope House garden, the day was windy, dull and overcast, with a threat of rain. Jon Mills introduced Annette, she stepped forward, mounted the podium and stood in front of the lectern. Just as she started to speak, like a huge spotlight, the sun illuminated her. She read the tribute and as the last words floated away on the wind the sun went in. Coincidence?

CHAPTER SEVENTEEN
(A Celebration of Chris's Life)

Some people come into our lives and quickly go,
Some stay for a while and leave footprints on our hearts,
And we are never the same.

Anon

From the first day of Chris's passing and throughout the next couple of weeks we had a stream of visitors; relatives, friends, neighbours and staff from Dorin Park, who wished to express their condolences and wanted to talk about Chris. One of the things that struck me was just how upset everybody was, I don't think there was anybody who came through the door in the first few days that wasn't in tears. In a strange way it was comforting to know that so many people cared so deeply about Chris. In amongst the visitors the phone was constantly ringing and it was all we could do to keep up. We were inundated with flowers, cards and letters, all saying the most wonderful things about our son, for which we were very, very grateful. Through all of this we were helped enormously by John and Julie and Chris and Anne who turned up, and not only provided love, care and support, but ensured that the many visitors were also catered for.

One of the first visitors was Ceris Owen, Deputy Head at Dorin Park, who told us of what the loss of Chris would mean to the school. He had acted as a translator for the children who found communication difficult, a good listener to many who were perhaps having difficult times and a friend and motivator to many in the school, including some members of staff. Ceris added how much he personally would miss the jolly chats he had with Chris.

Ian Shingler, who was Chris's *one to one* at Dorin Park, was terribly upset by the passing of Chris, but shared with us his stories of Chris's girlfriends and activities at the Youth Club. We laughed at these stories and at the way in which he and Chris would replay scenes from Only Fools and Horses, and at how Chris would get Paul Cooper giggling in class before sliding away and leaving Paul and Ian to get a scolding from Mrs Karling. They had only known each other a short time, but their relationship was first class.

Dr. John Gibbs, Chris's Paediatric Consultant, told us one evening how surprised he was that Chris had gone so early, although he was concerned about how the winter would have affected him. He recalled how ill he'd been at Christmas 1998, but how his fighting spirit saw him through, and he recalled his determination to see through the ghastly treatment for severe constipation, meaning an extended stay in the hospital. He also painted a picture of how Chris may have deteriorated in the coming months, perhaps losing his ability to use his arms, and therefore the computer and wheelchair, and then the ability to speak. He told us he would not have wanted that for Chris, as the one thing he respected was Chris's love of life.

Mrs Karling and Mrs Brown, teachers at Dorin Park, told how they admired Chris for his contribution to lessons, even though in the latter months he was very uncomfortable. He was in many ways the heart of the class. He was regarded as the school expert on computers, frequently sorting out the problems the other pupils (and some of the staff) had.

As the time approached for the final trip we made a final tearful visit to the Chapel of Rest to say goodbye to Chris, now dressed in a new Manchester United shirt, with his name on it, that Sharon and Billy had bought for him. The smile was still there, but he looked much older, more mature, it was if he'd become a young man. Annette had written a beautiful letter to Chris telling him all the things that you should say while you can, but somehow never get around to. This letter was placed in Chris's hand, along with a tribute written by cousin Paul, a touching letter from his long time friend Melanie, a colourful tribute where the capital letters of each line spelt out Christopher which was produced by his friend Abigail. And so it was we saw our precious son for the last time.

With the help of family and friends we sorted out the necessary arrangements. Annette didn't want the funeral to be a sad affair, but a celebration of Chris's life. We decided that it would be nice to have someone who knew Chris well to speak a few words. There were a few people we thought of immediately, but guessed that faced with the task they may not be able to hold their emotions in check. The issue was quickly resolved when Norma volunteered, to be followed by Mr. Owen, who in turn suggested that Mr. Kidman, Dorin Park's Headmaster, would also be honoured to speak. So, with the help of Rev. Peris Williams the service was formed around three speakers.

The funeral, on 5th September, was arranged for 9.45 am at Holy Trinity church, a short distance from our house. Family and close friends started to assemble at our house from about 9 o'clock. Sharp at half past nine, as arranged, Mark from J.C. Clarke's knocked on the door. At the top of the drive stood the hearse in which our son lay. On the coffin a display of blue and white flowers spelling 'CHRIS' from Annette and I; and a heart shaped cushion of multi-coloured flowers from Nana; a red and white football, from Julie, John, Clair and Paul. We had asked for no other flowers reflecting something Chris had said to me a few months before. On seeing a funeral pass by with the hearse packed with flowers he had said he thought it a terrible waste of money, money that could be given to charity.

For the very last time Chris left our home as the cortege moved slowly away from the house and proceeded on its short journey to Holy Trinity Church. As we approached the church the nearby roads were full of parked cars and the cortege slowly followed a walking Mark to the gates of the church. The Reverend Williams met us, he asked how we were and then added that the church was almost completely full, as full as he had ever seen it. After a short pause we followed the Reverend and the bearers into the church. The church was absolutely packed and a sea of faces greeted us with most people dressed, as we had asked, not in black, but in colours. Strangely though it was Pauline

Evans, in a bright red suit ("in honour of Man Utd."), that stood out towards the front of the church.

We sat down, Annette and I close together to give each other support, surrounded by so many people, many of whom Chris had touched with his love, or friendship, or humour, or care, or who had simply met him, but some who just wanted to express sympathy. There were his friends and staff from his schools, from Crossroads and Barnardo's and of course Hope House. We sang "He's got the whole world in his hands", a favourite song at Dorin Park and one that had been suggested by the staff there, and "Morning Has Broken" which Chris had always loved listening to.

Mr. Owen came forward and told the congregation about the school's triumph at JC2000 and how Chris had been asked to recite an extract, Don't Worry, from Matthew, Chapter 6, verse 26 before a large audience.

> *Do not worry about your life. Look at the birds in the air. They do not sow or reap or store away in barns and yet heavenly father feeds them.*
> *See the lilies of the field grow. They do not labour or spin. Yet not even Solomon in all his splendour was dressed like one of these.*
> *Seek first his kingdom and righteousness.*
> *Do not worry about tomorrow, for tomorrow will worry about itself. Each day has enough trouble of it's own.*

Mr. Kidman told the congregation of Chris's special gifts, his desire to win, his love of the school, the pupils and the staff, his keenness to organise, in an at times, amusing, but deeply moving address. Several people, including our niece Clair and our friend David Riffel said to us afterwards that they felt they wanted to applaud at the end, but had refrained as we were in church. I'm sorry they didn't clap, that would really have amused Chris! Rev. Williams added at the end of the address that the Lord and his angels had better watch out or that they would be in danger of being organised once Chris arrived. Norma, in a short, but emotional address told the congregation of the type of friend that Christopher was, how he was great fun to be with and how protective he was to all his friends and family, reminding us how for one so young how 'old' he could be.

With the church service over we travelled the short distance to the Crematorium, to conclude the Celebration of Chris's life. As we entered, the Cat Stevens' song "Oh Very Young" was played, the words being very poignant.

Oh very young
What will you leave us this time
There'll never be a better chance to change your mind
And if you want this world to see a better day
Will you carry the words of love with you
Will you ride the great white bird into heaven
And though you want to last forever
You know you never will
You know you never will
And the goodbye makes the journey harder still

When planning the service we had asked if the song could be played all the way through as it is only 2½ minutes long. Mrs Clarke had said she would do what she could, but the Crematorium may not be able to do so. As it turned out there were so many people queuing to get in that they played the song through twice. Just before the service started David Riffel stepped forward and placed a small Origami flower on Chris's coffin beside the other floral tributes. He told us later that he'd made three out of the same pieces of paper, he had kept one, Pauline had the second and Chris the third. The committal service was quite short, the Reverend Williams handing the care of Chris over from Annette and I to a greater force. The moment I guess most people dread arrived and so through tear stained eyes we saw the curtains close and we said good-bye. Norma had suggested that we should use a record that Chris really liked and would sing loudly along to at the Youth Club, so the service could finish on an upbeat moment with S Club 7's "Reach". The first verse being: -

When the world, leaves you feeling blue
You can count on me,
I will be there for you
When it seems, all your hopes and dreams
Are a million miles away,
I will re-assure you

We've got to all stick together
Good friends, there for each other
Never ever forget that
I've got you and you've got me,

So...
Reach for the stars
Climb every mountain higher
Reach for the stars
Follow your hearts desire
Reach for the stars
And when that rainbow's shining over you
That's when your dreams will all come true

With the service over, we received the mourners which seemed to last forever and then we adjourned to The Croft, a short drive across Chester. As we pulled up outside the gates we could see the garden was full of people, I think it was then that I fully realised how many people had taken the trouble to come and share with Annette, the family, our close friends and I a wonderful tribute to Christopher. He truly had touched many people's lives. Oh yes, Julie was right, our house wouldn't have been big enough.

As Val Moore, a friend of Annette's wrote to us later, "I want to say what a lovely service you had for Chris. It was a change to hear such an honest description of someone who has died. We all knew that Chris wasn't a 'goody goody' all the time - he was human like the rest of us. But he was also very sensitive to everyone else's needs and wants and this came over very well in the service. He was obviously very well loved. I've never been to such a well-packed church. No words can bring him back but the short time he was here he obviously made an impact."

There was just one final act that we had to do for our son and that was to ensure he was placed in a safe place and to scatter his ashes. The choice of location was quite straightforward; Chris would be laid to rest in the care of Annette's mum, Nanny. We chose a spot between four trees that marked the corners of a square that was lit by the afternoon's sunshine. Accompanied by Nana, John, Julie and Paul, Chris and Anne, Sharon, Norma and Dave, Josie, and Bob and Sandra we bid farewell. Annette spread the ashes and we spoke a few words.

Chris - "And how's Lorraine?"
"How's James?"
"How's Laura?"
Chris - "Bathroom Lorraine, sorry to be a nuisance."
Chris - "How's Dan? Is he still in hospital? Dad said we could go and see him. Poor Dan."
Chris - At Playtime "Will you put my hat and scarf on. I'd better have them as you know how Mum worries."
Chris - "Guess what happened to me last night? - I left my chocolate cake on the roof of the taxi!"
Chris - A very special person, and special people are never forgotten."

(Lorraine Churchman)

When you are sorrowful, look again in your heart and you shall see that, in truth, you are weeping for that which has been your delight.
(Kahil Gibran - the prophet)

Do not stand at my grave and weep;
I am not there. I do not sleep.
I am a thousand winds that blow,
I am the diamond glint on snow……
I am the sunlight on ripened grain,
I am the gentle autumn rain.
When you awaken in the mornings hush,
I am the swift uplifting rush
Of quiet birds in circled flight,
I am the soft stars that shine at night,
Do not stand at my grave and cry;
I am not there. I did not die.

(Anon.)

The celebration was over, no more days out, no more airshows, no more Disney days, no more….., the Walk of Life was complete.

One question remains, had Chris had a good Quality of Life?
I hope so, I really hope so.

CHAPTER EIGHTTEEN (So.....)

........who was Christopher? It would be easy to eulogise and I guess to some degree that's what this book has been, a eulogy to a son, a travelling companion, a fellow enthusiast and a friend. Like all kids Chris could be difficult, naughty, and petulant, get cross and angry, but never nasty or dishonest. All parents have aspirations for their children, and Annette and I were no different. Chris could probably have been anything he wanted to be. He chose to be a little boy, a remarkable young man and a friend to many. I have been hugely privileged to call him son and to be called, by him, Palion.

I struggled initially to understand why so many people felt the way they did. After all he was just a teenager. To Annette and I of course he was special, he was our son, our only child, but to everyone else? Over the weeks and months that followed our loss I thought about what people had said and why. I still don't have a satisfactory answer, but I think I understand a bit more - despite his own disability and difficulties he never openly let that affect him. He simply got on with life - he was more interested in events, facts and figures, places, people and trying to help his friends and acquaintances. For someone so young he had astuteness far above his age, he had humour (quirky at times) and a certain sparkle, always at the heart of things, a guiding light - a star. We all miss that.

Despite his own problems, which in the last 12 months had been really awful, he seldom complained about his situation - he was more concerned about others ("is your back alright with lifting Dad?"). There was one occasion that I recall when he did put himself first. It was soon after Grandma had passed away and death was clearly on his mind. We had one of our three way chats. Chris wanted to know who would look after him when Annette and I died. We explained that when that happened, hopefully sometime to come, there would be many people who would want to help, but probably Auntie Ju and Uncle John. Satisfied, a little tear at the thought of losing Mum and Dad, a little hug from Mum and subject closed. Never spoken of again.

People often remarked about Chris's ability to communicate with people, especially those who had no speech. I witnessed it all the time, with Katie, with Dan, with Matty Ford and many others. I have seen him meet such a young person for the first time and almost immediately begin a 'conversation', instinctively knowing what was being 'said'. I have no rational explanation, but have wondered on many occasions if these youngsters have developed a substitute method, a form of telepathy? Stupid, naive, illogical - perhaps.

As I said in the Preface I was inspired to write this book by the things people said and wrote to us and so I think it would only be right and proper to let some of those people have their say now.

Chris, although my cousin, was much more than that to me. He was a real mate, someone you could talk to, someone you could have a laugh with, someone you could compete with, and someone you could trust. He was always game for a laugh, and we often used to talk about people we liked, and we hated, and we had a number of things in common. For example, we both liked computers, although he liked flying games, and I can't stand them, we mainly liked the same sort of games as each other. He was my cousin, but I never really thought of him as that, I thought of him as a real good mate, with a lot of good qualities, including patience, perseverance, indomitable spirit, and normally self-control. Maybe we fell out over a few things, but we always made them up with each other a couple of minutes later, which sort of made me think more of a mate than a cousin. We liked the same sort of films, actors, girls and things like that. One of the best times we used to have was during chat rooms over the Internet, where we probably had the best laughs, and when we used to stay up till 1 o'clock in the morning, when my mum came to look after him, with me. Saturday was probably by far the best day of the week, because nearly always it was guaranteed that I would see him again, and play a few games, watch some videos, and have a good laugh. We used to walk round the road and had a damn good time there, racing, and talking to people we knew. I really admired him, for putting up with what he did with no complaints. Now without him, life will never be the same, because they say there's only one in a million, and he was that one.
Paul Tilston

Once in a lifetime you might be lucky enough to meet someone 'Special'. Chris was very special. He possessed rare gifts that ordinary people just could not hope to achieve if they tried all their lives. Chris only had 15 years, but he touched everybody he knew forever.
He had an amazing zest for life, and a unique sense of humour, most of all an unequalled compassion for others.
I always think of him as Shiny, Sparkly and Splendidly bright.
We are proud to have been part of his life and miss him everyday.
Like a loss of sunlight on a cloudy afternoon. Gone too soon.
Aunty Julie, Uncle John, Clair and Mollie the Collie

Christopher was like a ray of sunshine that has left a warm and permanent impression on the hearts of everyone who met him.
Auntie Tricia and John

I remember being told about Chris Barratt coming up to the Seniors (at Dorin Park). I didn't know much about him, just that he seemed a bit 'mouthy'! – a bit loud. I met Chris and saw a young boy with Muscular Dystrophy looking for a way to find his position with his peers. He wasn't particularly keen on football. He loved computers, and aeroplanes, but the other children weren't interested in the history of planes. He wanted to be liked. Being in a wheelchair changed his normal route:- very confusing! I think I always wanted to reassure him that he

had a friend in me. To have a son with a short life span must have been absolutely unbearable and in helping him to have a few normal years, then my part was to be there for him when you weren't with him, to reassure you. He was competitive, got bored, had sulks and was impatient, and he kept problems to himself. A year or so on he had established himself and his confidence had grown. He liked to be part of things. He didn't brag about anything. He was very positive about right and wrong. He used his voice (his only weapon), not only now to voice his opinion which he had to do when he genuinely believed an injustice had been done, but to show concern and affection for his friends. He loved to make Paul Cooper laugh - usually by saying "Hasselback" (a known footballer to Paul). This was done in lesson. At first Paul would be told off time and time again until we realised what Chris was saying and doing to Paul. We had to tell Chris off!
He became excited about playtimes. Why I thought? Until he came in one day with a long face, not wanting to talk about the problem. I found out later it was girls, relationships and who had ditched who. It made me happy because it was so normal. It was a shock when Chris died, to say the least. We'd all commented on how down hill he'd gone month by month. He cared so much for you and Annette. It touched us all. "You'd better put my coat and scarf on at breaktime - Mum worries". Mum will only worry. We often heard that. When Chris had problems with his bowels he would confide with me in the bathroom. I know he hated hospitals, but one day he was over the moon that he didn't have to go to hospital and told me all the things he'd been taking to stop him being constipated! He wasn't just pleased for himself, but pleased for Mum as well.
Chris always asked about my husband, my daughter Laura and son James. Chris had become very mature and could always be trusted to keep a secret and so I eventually told him that my husband and I had split up. This, and the knowledge that Geoff was a policeman, Chris kept to himself. "And how's Lorraine then, how's Laura, how's James?" - everyday. I visited Chris at Hope House, when Mum and Dad were away. It was there I realised that he had a lie down everyday. He must have been tired out at school. I mentioned this back at school and within an hour Karen (Flynn) had sorted out a bed with appropriate pillows. We just wanted Chris to stay at school as long as possible.
This young confused boy in such a short time became such a mature young man - much older than his years. "Don't tell Mum, she'll worry". "It's alright Lorraine, Dad'll lift me when he gets home".
I was amazed at his knowledge of aeroplanes. Chris never bragged, but his knowledge would come out in history.
He was proud of Dad's karting skills.
In the last few months, there was no impatience, no crossness and no being bored, but he still had his principles. He hated injustice and was still competitive, and what a grown up young man who had become so patient.
I remember the first parents evening at school. Annette's concern was whether Chris had any friends. Just look at all the people at the funeral and Kirsty still gets upset about Chris.
Lorraine Churchman (Dorin Park)

I have been trying to rack my brains about any more stories to be included in your book. It's all memorable, mostly just mates chatting, as you do. We talked about so much and nothing. There was the time when I offered to shave him. He had loads of single hairs all over his chin and sides. After much deliberation, he agreed, and the next day I brought my electric razor in, he flatly refused a wet shave. Just before we did the deed, there was still many questions!!! Will it hurt? Will it cut me? Loads of questions about how the foil worked. Eventually we got started and within 2 minutes it was all over. Chris had a big grin on his face. I think there was an air of 'I am the bravest!' and boy did he look handsome after, he just had to show himself off to everyone and they all made a fuss. Centre of attention again.
The only other one I could think of is the time when I took my camera in to work to take a picture of the two of us. Unknowingly, there was only one picture left on the reel. Pauline took the picture, the motor began to rewind the film, and the rest is history. Lots of memories from one single photograph. Two wonderful people.
David Riffel (Hope House)

It has been a privilege for me to spend the last few months with Chris as his one to one, and I shall always be grateful for all the help he gave to me. Chris was a very caring young man, always helpful, and he had a great sense of humour. He also had this amazing determination to get on with life and he would often spend time telling me what we would be doing in the future together.
His determination and his will to win at all costs would often cause us to argue. I remember a Boccia tournament we attended in Widnes, although we won I seemed to spend most of the time telling him to calm down when things didn't seem to be going in our favour. He was just the same in lessons when we took part in any sort of games. I will never forget all the planning that went into his race on Sports Day, he spent weeks telling me how he was going to 'wipe the floor' with the opposition, and I spent weeks teasing him with threats to 'grass him up' to Mr. Owen.
We also shared a similar sense of humour and would spend ages quoting things from 'Only Fools and Horses', I have lost count of the times he said to me "Oh shut up you tart" or he called me a "plonker" or a "dipstick", and I hasten to add these pleasantries would be returned.
Football and motor racing was another interest we shared and these two topics led to a great deal of debate, and endless teasing. I never did manage to convert him to Everton, and believe me I tried.
One area were he had myself and many others beaten hands down was with his knowledge of aircraft and all things relating to this subject. He would often tell me of the airshows he had been to, and was able to go into such great detail of what he had seen, his memory was quite remarkable.
Chris was a truly remarkable young man and I will always be grateful for the time that I spent with him. He was kind, caring, and an inspiration to everyone that knew him. He was also a good mate, and I will never forget him.
Ian Shingler (Dorin Park)

For Chris. I love science. Ask anyone – "That Mrs Brown, she loves science". I love teaching science (well mostly). The reason I love teaching it is the reaction you get, shock, surprise, sometimes naiveté and sometimes wow! It's great after complete silence for what seems like hours (or days). There through the air, piercing the empty hush is not only the answer but a full explanation – That was Chris.
Whether it was Electricity & Magnetism, Forces and Motion (Chris's speciality), Life Science or Earth and Space. Oh Yes! Earth and Space. He was superb. Well, I do see Chris as a type of comet – I'll explain.
Whenever he appeared you could study him in the distance, but before you knew it he was right there at speed with a tail, usually of younger pupils or his gang! He came in like a messenger, full of power, sounds and light and then after impact he was gone.
Chris though will never 'leave' our space, he's made his mark upon the earth and as comets do Chris's 'crater' will remain. He has made an impact on many lives, his friends, family, staff and especially his science teacher. I really miss the Christopher Barratt comet.
I hope to see it again some day.
Di Brown (Dorin Park)

Chris, I've so many beautiful memories of times spent with you, Blackpool, Christmas parties and the fun we shared in your garden. I will miss you forever and will never forget my special friend. I was so proud to be your friend. I know we shall see each other again, but it hurts a lot till then!
Melanie Carrington

Chris had so many friends and people who loved him and cared about him. It's hard to say good-bye to a very special boy. Chris leaves us all with very precious memories. Full of fun and mischief his strength of character. He will always have a very special place in our hearts. He was a caring thoughtful boy. He was Katie's special friend. They had lots of fun and laughs together, we will miss our chats. Chris always enjoyed his friends. He liked his music, his wicked sense of humour. His jokes, his videos, computers, cars and planes. He was so proud of his new car. We will all sadly miss him, but never, ever will he be forgotten.
Sandra, Rob, Emma Gerrard

Chris was a very special young man. Always chatting, very caring towards his classmates and the rest of the pupils and staff in school. Especially interested in planes and fast cars. He asked me umpteen questions about my father who used to be an aircraft electrician who worked for the Ministry of Defence. Needless to say I couldn't answer any of his questions. He was especially caring after my fathers death and constantly asked after myself, Ben and Sam. He also told me umpteen jokes to cheer me up. I shall miss him.
Karen Flynn (Dorin Park)

When Chris first came to Dorin Park he was very, very competitive! In one PE lesson he was lined up to race against 3 other pupils in wheelchairs. Just as I said, "Ready, steady ....." his hand reached out and he switched off the wheelchair alongside him! I really had to control my immediate reaction, which was to laugh of course, and I had to pretend to be amazed that he could do such a thing! From then onwards he still wanted to win, but not at all costs - he cheered other pupils and wanted them to win - as long as it wasn't his race!
Chris's presence in a group always added a vitality and interest that I shall miss greatly. His contributions to Dorin Park School will remain with us - a super lad.
Jill Smith (Dorin Park)

I always think of Chris with Daniel. He could not have been a better or finer friend. "Alright mate?" he would constantly ask, and Daniel would positively glow in the warmth of the friendship.
In English, Chris was Daniel's interpreter. He knew what Daniel wanted to say. When we were looking at different scenes from "Romeo and Juliet", and expressing the ideas, using modern language, Daniel and Chris had a great time reconstructing the scene between Tybault and Romeo.
The tenderness and care Chris felt for Daniel is probably something which has altered my own outlook, and something I will treasure most in my memories of Chris. He gave such happiness to Daniel, and Daniel gave such happiness to Chris. It is indeed friendship on a Shakespearean level.
Pauline Sallis (Dorin Park)

Chris and I go back to the Juniors, when as a volunteer, I used to look after Chris in the swimming pool. I used to croon 'Trust in Me' (from the Jungle Book) as he was very nervous on his back in the water. I think it must have worked, because later looking after Daniel, Chris used to tell him that everything would be OK while he was with me.
Dan and I will greatly miss Chris - he would always join in with us if we had to get in groups, and always knew what Daniel wanted to say - when I had gone through everything that I could think of - he used to amaze me. Chris was such a good friend to us both, always caring about us and always helpful in so many ways.
Chris will be greatly missed and will always be remembered as a very caring and compassionate friend.
Angela Quick (Dorin Park)

Chris used to call into the school office quite often - more so over the last couple of years. He was always polite and well mannered; he collected the registers for the Senior Department, and occasionally delivered messages for them. Chris would happily run an errand for me. We often had a chat and shared the odd joke together (as you know Chris had a wicked sense of humour!!!) Chris would never linger long as he was always keen to get back to his class to see what was going on.

Chris was very caring towards other pupils in school, and he would readily help one of the little ones if their wheelchair was in a jam, or if they found themselves lost around the corridor by my office.
I think Chris had matured these last few years and grown into a very pleasant young man, I will miss him around the school, and I will always remember him.
Julia Wynn (Dorin Park)

He was an exceptional young man, and I am proud and honoured to have known him. We shared many times together when he stayed at Hope House, and I have many precious memories that will remain with me forever. I feel that my life is better for having met Chris, and he taught me many things. The words Chris said in that video (of JC2000) was a reflection of him. He taught me to value what I have.
You must have been so very proud of him. He may have died in body, but he will live on in the hearts of all those that were lucky enough to have known him.
Thank you so much for allowing me to share in a small part of Chris's life. He is and always will be a star.
Mary (Hope House)

I felt I wanted to write to you to let you know how much I thought about Chris and how much I will miss him. I've been listening to "True Colours" by Phil Collins and couldn't help thinking that that was Chris – a unique and special human being who was never afraid to be himself, never unsure about what he needed to say. Which is one of the many reasons he captured my heart.
One of the greatest gifts your son ever gave me was to believe in myself – to accept and enjoy who and what I was no matter what. Something he carried off naturally everyday.
He was a young man who was able to help those around him to look beyond the frailties and disabilities of MD – to take time to see the wonderful and unique person inside – someone with great personality and fun. Thank you for allowing me to be one of many who shared your son's life.

PS I just had to silently dedicate Sunday's (2000 Belgian) Grand Prix to Chris – what a fabulous manoeuvre by Mika Hakkinen over Michael Schumacher. Chris would have loved that!!
Kim (Hope House)

Nothing I can say will ease your pain, but I know you take comfort from the fact that Chris was so liked and loved, not least by myself. He always had a cheery word and a smile that touched my heart. He was a brave young man who I shall always remember with a sense of privilege to have been part of his life.
Lesley (Hope House)

I was quite close to him and looked after him quite a few times. He was a great lad and I was hoping that my friend from Norfolk who has a Lotus Elise would get up to give him a ride in it, but unfortunately it didn't happen in time. However Chris did get to see some photographs of it that I brought in for him. Chris had a lovely caring side to his nature and he always worried about the other children especially those most vulnerable. I always admired the way in which he often thought about them before himself. He was a very "instant" person and I remember feeling immediately comfortable and at ease with him, and as he got to know you more he became more cheeky and often asked for a kiss. I will miss his cheeky ways and our chats together.
Annie (Hope House)

I will always think of Chris with great affection and admiration. I feel very privileged to have had the honour and pleasure of working with him. He always seemed so happy and cheerful. He was so friendly, generous and helpful. He was great to have a chat with. He was so full of enthusiasm, vitality and good ideas. He will remain an inspiration to us all.
Pauline Sallis (Dorin Park)

We have to say it was a privilege to know Chris, who will always remain the main man in our hearts.
Lee and Nikki Barrett (Friends)

I will always remember Chris as a strong-minded and mentally athletic young man whose abilities far outshone his disabilities. His strength and courage to battle through his illness is testament to the love and devotion of a wonderful family. So glad to have known him.
Trena Salmon (Friend)

I must first of all apologise for the delay in writing this letter, to be honest I know how I felt about Christopher's passing away but putting it down in words for you both has proved very difficult. Although I never got to see Christopher as often as I would have liked I was constantly amazed by his love and enthusiasm for life. We shared our interest in aviation and his depth of knowledge always surprised me. Although his time with us was short I have a special place in my heart for him. I will remember him for his impish humour and cheek.
Dave Park (Friend)

Chris was such a lovely boy, - so courageous and cheerful. It was always a pleasure to talk to him, and we are not the only ones who will miss him. We shall always remember him, his intelligence and his zest for life.
Mollie and Bernard Green (Neighbours)

Despite all his problems and difficulties Christopher was an inspiration to us all.
Carol Cartwright (Play School)

It has been a privilege to have known Christopher. Despite many restrictions, your tremendous love and support for Christopher enabled him to experience a highly enriching and stimulating life.
Dr. John Gibbs (Consultant)

In the short time that I knew him I grew very fond of him. He was an intelligent, questioning, cheerful young man who has coped with the awful problems of dystrophy in his own courageous way.
Carolyn Evans (Oswestry Hospital)

To Chris-A Great Friend

Chris, I first met you in '98
and you soon became a very good mate.
You would whizz around in your chair
and do just about anything for a dare.
Your love of computers was a fascination
and you never ran out of patience
We'd sit and chat about fast cars,
Our dreams you'd think from Planet Mars!
For we both loved the Lotus
and to ride in one was our focus.
You were also "one of the lads"
into Man U and who was "sad"
Shania Twain and pretty girls were your deal.
And it was chips, chips, chips for every meal!
The precious memories of you that we store away,
Help us face another day.
We miss you Chris and will forever
and we will forget you never.
Your photographs smile at us from the wall,
I hope that now your having a ball.
For when I look up at the sky each night.
I know that you're not out of sight.
Because there is another star.
Its big, bright and new.
And guess what Chris,
I'm sure its you.
Lots of Love Annie **(Hope House)**

And then of course there was the view that Mum shouldn't know about - Chris, you were the only person in school who appreciated my taste in music! Who will I sing 'Space' songs with now? To me you'll always be the image of The Rampant Romeo! ♥ Forever
Heather (Physiotherapy)

And So !!!

When Chris died I didn't believe that it was true, I was heartbroken and wanted to die too. Chris understood me and we had a special relationship. He made me laugh and he made me happy. He was NEVER lost for words and ALWAYS had an answer for everything and everyone.

Chris liked a joke and a gossip, especially with the girls. He told us some grotty and rude jokes (some of which cannot be repeated on paper (Ha-Ha!)).

I have so many memories of Chris, they bring a smile to my face when I think about them. I think about Chris often and will never forget him. He was my best friend.

Love always,

Katie.
XXXX

CHAPTER NINETEEN(Mr. Kidman's Tribute)

From the Celebration of Chris's Life, September 5th 2000.

"It is a privilege to represent Dorin Park School in paying tribute to Chris today.

Chris was a very special young man, with special gifts, who was blessed in very many ways; Chris was a very caring individual; who saw it as his right, no, indeed his duty – to look out for others. Chris had a great sense of humour and almost anyone was fair game for his teasing.

Chris was a very competitive young man. Never mind this mamby pamby rubbish about it's taking part that matters.
Chris was there to WIN!!!
Chris was also a very bright young man, and a person of tremendous courage. However, above everything else, Chris saw himself as an organiser.

In fact often it seemed as if Chris assumed the role of Head Boy. An unelected and self-appointed position, that gave Chris the right and duty to ensure all was right with the world and in particular that Dorin Park was running as it should.

Any misdemeanours, infringements of general conduct would be reported by Chris to a member of staff. So and so has done this, that or the other. If appropriate action wasn't taken then poor old Mum and Dad would get an action replay at home.

How we as a school shall cope without his ever-watchful eye I shudder to think.

Talking to staff over the last week, it is Chris's caring attitude, his protection and concern for the well being of others, that is mentioned again and again. Chris was always looking out for his 'mates'. The fact you went to Dorin Park School automatically qualified you for the title 'mate'!

Chris was considerate of all pupils at Dorin Park. In the playground it would often appear that Chris was a modern day Pied Piper, with him being followed by an entourage of younger pupils.

Nevertheless, Chris had some close friends, Katie, Kirsty, Hayley and at times Anthony. However, Chris had a particular soft spot for Daniel.

Feeding Chris was apparently a nightmare if Dan was placed behind him. Chris would give a running commentary saying, "what's Dan doing now? Is he OK? Has he finished his feed yet?" In such circumstances Chris would be threatened with all sorts. But whatever the level of intimidation, his concern was always Daniel!!

On several occasions Dan would be quite animated, attempting to explain something to staff, when Chris would interrupt and say, "I think Daniel is trying to say....." and proceed to suggest what it might be. The sentence would then be concluded with the phrase,
"Is that right Dan?"
Two key things about these interchanges -
The first is that Chris always gave Dan the right of reply, illustrating the respect he had for others. The second, and indeed more annoying point, is that he was invariably right!

However, his caring nature never got in the way of some serious teasing. If you supported a different team from Manchester United, then you were due for some serious stick. Chris's Dad supports Liverpool, and this just confirmed to Chris what we all know. That dads know nothing.

If you were foolish enough to support Everton, it was then that the ribbing was merciless. As Paul, a fellow pupil, Ian, an assistant who recently supported Chris, found out to their cost.

Chris also knew Paul was particularly easy to make giggle, which Chris would successfully do during lessons. When an assistant tried to refocus Paul onto completing his work, occasionally the teacher would intervene, and Paul would blame the assistant. In the meantime Chris had toddled off, complete with smirk on his face!

Chris was a fan of 'Only Fools and Horses', and would often quote phrases from the programme, such as "plonker", "dip stick" and if he thought no one else was litening "Oh shut up you tart".

Chris, as I have already mentioned, had a very competitive streak in him. Actually that sounds rather inadequate. Chris had a very, very, very competitive streak. Chris was seriously competitive. Chris would take no prisoners. For example, (Mum and Dad may wish to hum during this bit) in one PE lesson when pupils were asked to race. The teacher went through the usual bit about trying your best. Then came the standard start to the race. Ready ...... Steady ......, but on steady Chris's hand had reached across to the next wheelchair to switch it off.

Because Chris was such a good and confident wheelchair driver, at sports days race starts would be staggered. And Chris being such a good driver, would have furthest to race. Invariably, Chris could not make up the extra distance in time. That was until this year, and his new high-powered wheelchair. This was a wheelchair with flashing lights, tilting seat. What this wheelchair couldn't do wasn't worth talking about. This was a wheelchair built with steroids. Mr. Owen started the race with Chris positioned somewhere on the other side of Upton. This did not matter. Chris won the race handsomely. I am still unsure which tasted better for Chris; winning the race so convincingly. Or watching Mr. Owen's face drop at the speed of the chair!!

In a recent Boccia Tournament, Chris was very determined to do well and for his team to do well. He was so involved in the game that, in different circumstances, Chris would have been physically restrained in case he took a pot-shot at somebody. He has obviously been watching too much of Roy Keane.

Chris was very definite about his likes and dislikes. At lunch time a select few would eat in a quiet area in school, and be able to listen to their own choice of music. Chris would invariably pick Chris Rea, however if Chris didn't like some one else's choice, he would talk loudly through the whole album.

Chris was a very bright young man. His interests also reflected his interest in speed.

- He enjoyed going fast in his chair.
- He loved cars. All cars.
- He particularly enjoyed motor racing with Hakkinen a favoured driver. Schumacher, Chris had no time for.
- Chris also loved planes. I for one could not hold a conversation with Chris on planes, his knowledge was so extensive. In fact Chris would interview staff members who had been abroad on holiday.
- What was the plane they travelled on.
- Chris would show his usual patience when the reply was "Well I know it had two wings and an engine".

Chris was also brilliant on the computer. It allowed him to explore his areas of interest. It was an area where his physical disability did not greatly restrict him. As usual Chris would be keen to help anyone struggling with IT skills. Many pupils and staff have been grateful for his level of computer expertise.

It is difficult to talk about Chris without mentioning his Mum and Dad. Or as Chris would put it - "Me Mam and me Dad". So much of Chris's successes and interests were because of them.

Chris had a passion for America, and visited there on several occasions. In fact Chris saw himself as a seasoned world traveller. Chris was full of stories and was quite an American expert. It is also to his credit that he insisted his Mum and Dad still continued with the planned visit to the States earlier this year, as Chris was unable to accompany them because of his deteriorating health.

The family's generosity extended to others. One of Chris's friends, Katie, joined the family for one of their days out. Such a good time was had by all that after the weekend Katie insisted on telling everyone about the day in great detail.

Chris's Mum and Dad were very significant for Chris. They themselves could not do enough for Chris, or indeed the school.

As you have already heard Chris was a key figure in the school production "Don't Worry" held at the Bridgewater Hall. The whole event was extremely successful. It is a reflection of Chris's determination and courage that when he

approached the front of the stage to recite the verse from the bible Chris realised that the microphones were not picking his voice up.
Chris stopped.
Moved forward.
And started again.
As cool as a cucumber.
A true professional.
In fact when Chris saw the video, his comment was: "I can't cope with this.
Me Mum will cry all the way through this. Mums always cry".

Chris's courage was also reflected in the manner he managed his deteriorating condition. Chris became increasingly limited in his movements. With each reduction in his physical ability, Chris was reminded,
Week after week,
Month after month
That today was inevitable.
He did not complain.
He accepted his condition.
His only concern was an attempt to remain comfortable.

This was the mark of a very brave young man.
In my view a true hero.

What would Chris think about today. He would have been delighted to see so many people turn up just for him. He would be impressed. Except he would try to keep all that to himself. His comments would be restricted to teenage utterances such as – "Oh, don't make a fuss!"

However I think that Chris may have had some sympathy for some of the words from Dr. Martin Luther King's famous 'I have a dream' speech given at the Lincoln Memorial.

The final words of the speech are inscribed on Dr. King's headstone.

These are very appropriate for today,
For Chris.

Free at last.
Free at last.
Thank God Almighty
I'm Free,

At Last!

Mr. Philip Kidman
Headmaster, Dorin Park Special School, Upton, Chester.

CHAPTER TWENTY (Epilogue)

Come up and feel the sun
A new morning is begun
Another day will make it clear
Why your stars should guide us here

Mark Knopfler

Life of course never really comes to a complete stop, at least not for those left behind. Annette and I knew that we had a special son (I guess most parents think that of their off spring), but just how special had been brought home to us through the weeks following Chris's passing. The number of people that came to see us, the number of cards and letters, the number of people at the Celebration of Chris's Life, and the words that were written or said about him showed that to us quite clearly. But perhaps the most striking tribute were the donations made in Chris's memory. Chris had not wanted flowers, the money should go to charity he had said, well it did. Through the generosity of so many people we were able to donate £1,460 to Hope House, £600 to the Neuromuscular Centre, £167 to Crossroads and £100 to Barnardo's - a grand total of £2,327. Chris would have been very chuffed at that and no doubt amused that he raised as much as my marathon efforts. Our many and sincere thanks to everyone who provided such a fitting tribute.

There isn't a day that goes by that I don't think about Chris (and I know Annette is the same), there isn't a day that goes by without some thought or the other making my eyes fill up. The gap that Chris has left in our lives is too big to describe adequately. We are left in the knowledge that he somehow touched so many people in so many different ways. But five words kept being mentioned when people spoke about him - caring, competitive, laughter, jokes and remarkable. As Annette's mum said on more than one occasion, "He has, you know, been sent for a purpose".

I frequently reflect on that Bank Holiday in August and the events leading up to it. It seems now with hindsight that Chris knew somehow that the dice were to be rolled for the last time that weekend. Watching all the old videos, visiting favourite places and seeing old friends, even his much-wanted triumph at the school sports were steps along a route to some final point of destiny. He was adamant, absolutely, about going to Hope House that weekend. There was no dissuading him, he knew from his previous experiences that the folk at Hope House knew how to deal with the loss of young people and care for their parents. If it hadn't been for my haste in wanting to get him back to Chester, something that he didn't really want, he may have passed away peacefully in bed. I shall always deeply regret forcing him into that last journey. Right at the end I let him down. Annette on the other hand views the situation differently - at least he was with us, with his friend David, in <u>his</u> car, listening to his favourite music by Chris Rea.

But there is no substitute, no substitute for the whirr of the chair motors, the black cap and sun glasses, the little chuckle, the click-click of the computer keyboard and the little smile that we knew so well. "Ooh, I have missed you".

Fast forward to May Bank Holiday 2001 and the first time in the year that Annette and I where in the garden together. Annette saw him first, a little robin, still with his beautiful red breast. Having watched Annette for a little while he flew down the garden to where I was cutting the grass and landed on the fence. He bobbed up and down, turned his head to one side and then flew back to Annette. This went on for quite a bit of the afternoon and was reminiscent of the way someone else zipped back and to in his wheelchair. We both thought it separately, and said it later that evening. Perhaps, just perhaps, this was Christopher Robin?

A million stars shine in the darkest night
From across the universe there comes eternal light
From this blue world to a new world
Somewhere life goes on.

Gerry Rafferty